Ninja Girls

1

Hosana Tanaka

Translated and adapted by
Andria Cheng

Lettered by
North Market Street Graphics

Ballantine Books ★ New York

Ninja Girls, volume 1 is a work of fiction. Names, characters, places, and incidents are the products of the author's imagination or are used fictitiously. Any resemblance to actual events, locales, or persons, living or dead, is entirely coincidental.

A Del Rey Manga/Kodansha Trade Paperback Original

Published in the United States by Del Rey, an imprint of The Random House Publishing Group, a division of Random House, Inc., New York.

Del Rey is a registered trademark and the Del Rey colophon is a trademark of Random House, Inc.

Publication rights arranged through Kodansha Ltd.

First published in Japan in 2006 by Kodansha Ltd., Tokyo, as *Rappi Rangai*, volume 1

ISBN 978-0-345-51242-0

Printed in the United States of America

www.delreymanga.com

9 8 7 6 5 4 3

Translator/Adapter—Andria Cheng
Lettering—North Market Street Graphics

CONTENTS

Honorifics Explained v
Ninja Girls volume 1 1
About the Creator 192
Translation Notes 193

HONORIFICS EXPLAINED

Throughout the Del Rey Manga books, you will find Japanese honorifics left intact in the translations. For those not familiar with how the Japanese use honorifics and, more important, how they differ from American honorifics, we present this brief overview.

Politeness has always been a critical facet of Japanese culture. Ever since the feudal era, when Japan was a highly stratified society, use of honorifics—which can be defined as polite speech that indicates relationship or status—has played an essential role in the Japanese language. When addressing someone in Japanese, an honorific usually takes the form of a suffix attached to one's name (example: "Asuna-san"), is used as a title at the end of one's name, or appears in place of the name itself (example: "Negi-sensei," or simply "Sensei!").

Honorifics can be expressions of respect or endearment. In the context of manga and anime, honorifics give insight into the nature of the relationship between characters. Many English translations leave out these important honorifics and therefore distort the feel of the original Japanese. Because Japanese honorifics contain nuances that English honorifics lack, it is our policy at Del Rey not to translate them. Here, instead, is a guide to some of the honorifics you may encounter in Del Rey Manga.

-san: This is the most common honorific and is equivalent to Mr., Miss, Ms., or Mrs. It is the all-purpose honorific and can be used in any situation where politeness is required.

-sama: This is one level higher than "-san" and is used to confer great respect.

-dono: This comes from the word "tono," which means "lord." It is an even higher level than "-sama" and confers utmost respect.

-kun: This suffix is used at the end of boys' names to express familiarity or endearment. It is also sometimes used by men among friends, or when addressing someone younger or of a lower station.

-chan: This is used to express endearment, mostly toward girls. It is also used for little boys, pets, and even among lovers. It gives a sense of childish cuteness.

Bozu: This is an informal way to refer to a boy, similar to the English terms "kid" and "squirt."

Sempai/
Senpai: This title suggests that the addressee is one's senior in a group or organization. It is most often used in a school setting, where underclassmen refer to their upperclassmen as "sempai." It can also be used in the workplace, such as when a newer employee addresses an employee who has seniority in the company.

Kohai: This is the opposite of "sempai" and is used toward underclassmen in school or newcomers in the workplace. It connotes that the addressee is of a lower station.

Sensei: Literally meaning "one who has come before," this title is used for teachers, doctors, or masters of any profession or art.

-[blank]: This is usually forgotten in these lists, but it is perhaps the most significant difference between Japanese and English. The lack of honorific means that the speaker has permission to address the person in a very intimate way. Usually, only family, spouses, or very close friends have this kind of permission. Known as *yobisute*, it can be gratifying when someone who has earned the intimacy starts to call one by one's name without an honorific. But when that intimacy hasn't been earned, it can be very insulting.

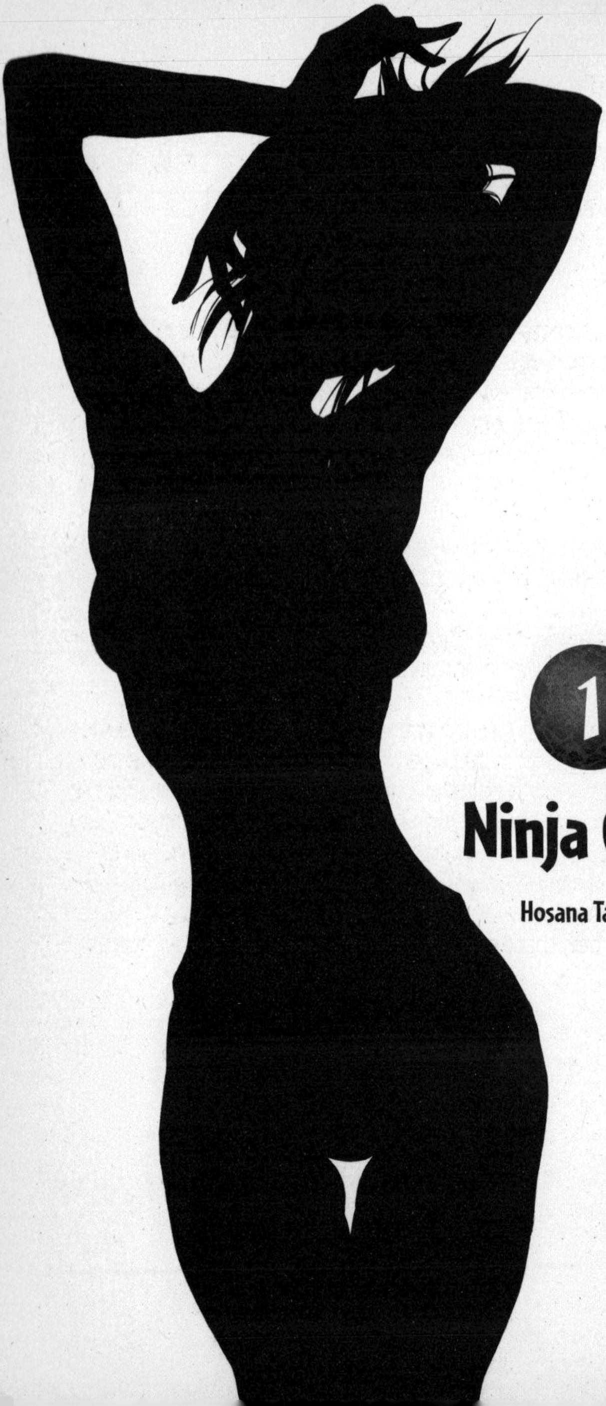

1

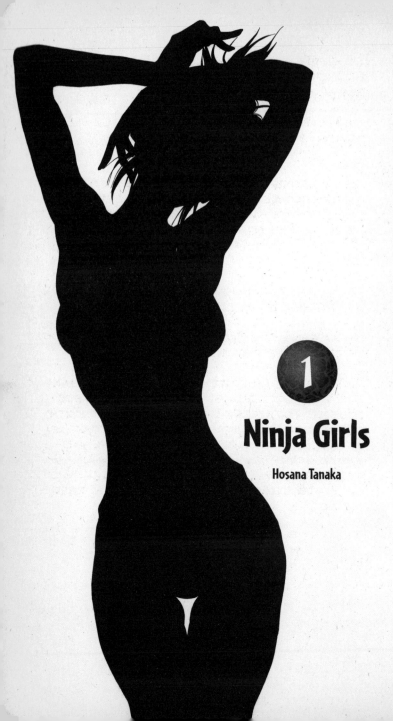

Ninja Girls

Hosana Tanaka

Ninja Girls
Volume 1

Contents

1 Encounter Rebellion 4

2 Departure Rebellion 49

3 Bedding Room Rebellion 86

4 Nursing Rebellion 120

5 Uncertainty Rebellion 158

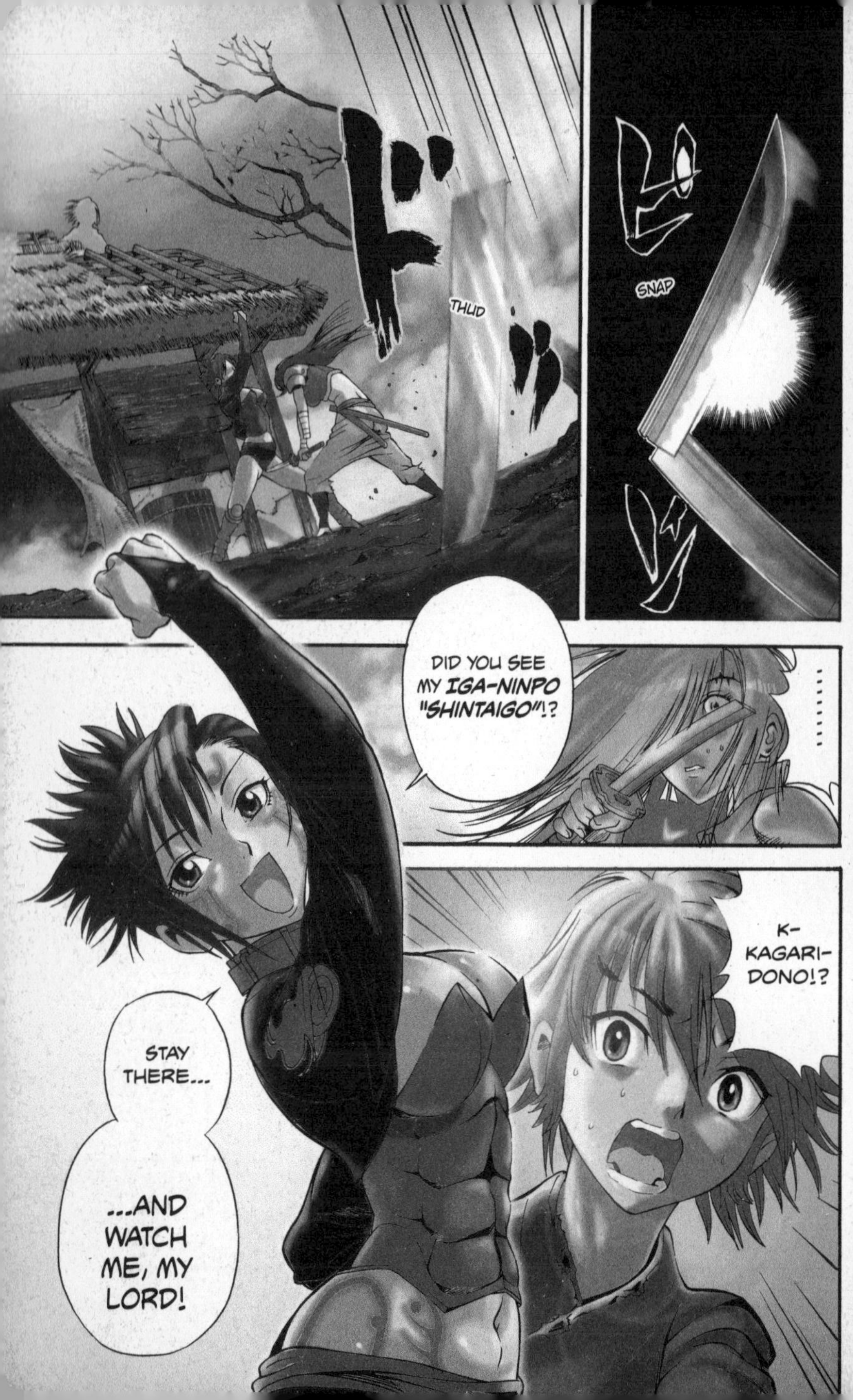
SNAP
THUD
DID YOU SEE MY IGA-NINPO "SHINTAIGO"!?
......
K-KAGARI-DONO!?
STAY THERE...
...AND WATCH ME, MY LORD!

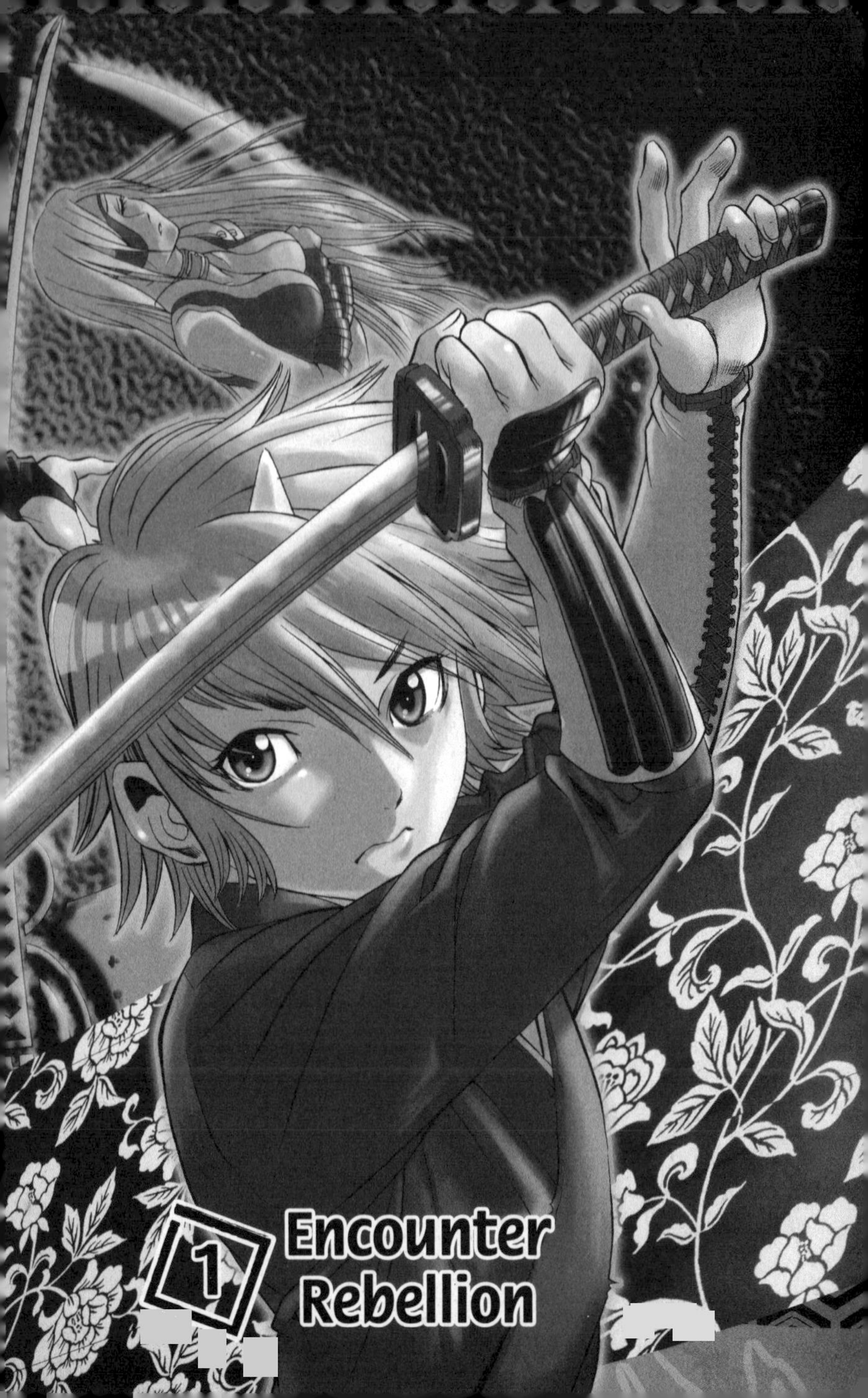
1
Encounter
Rebellion

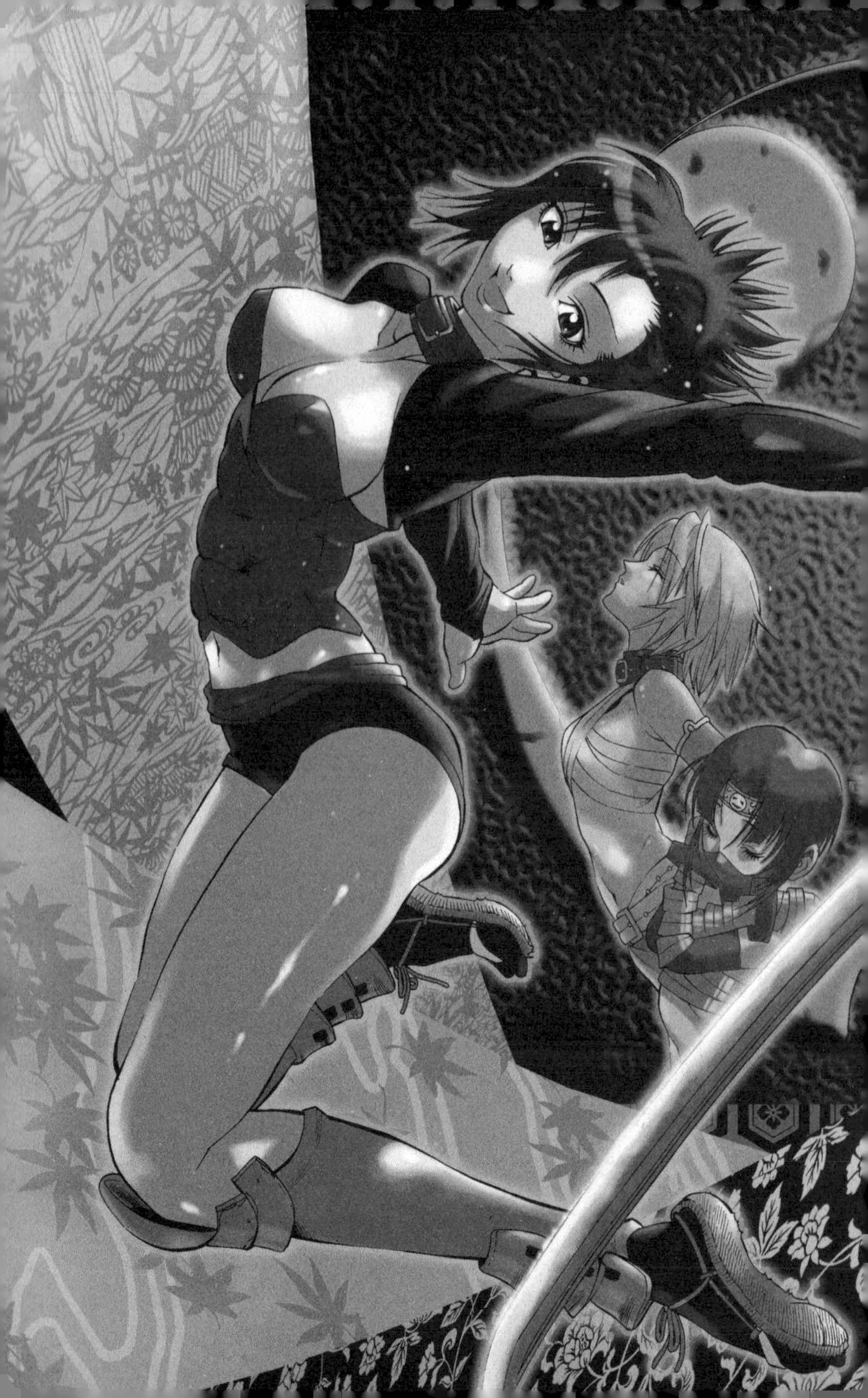

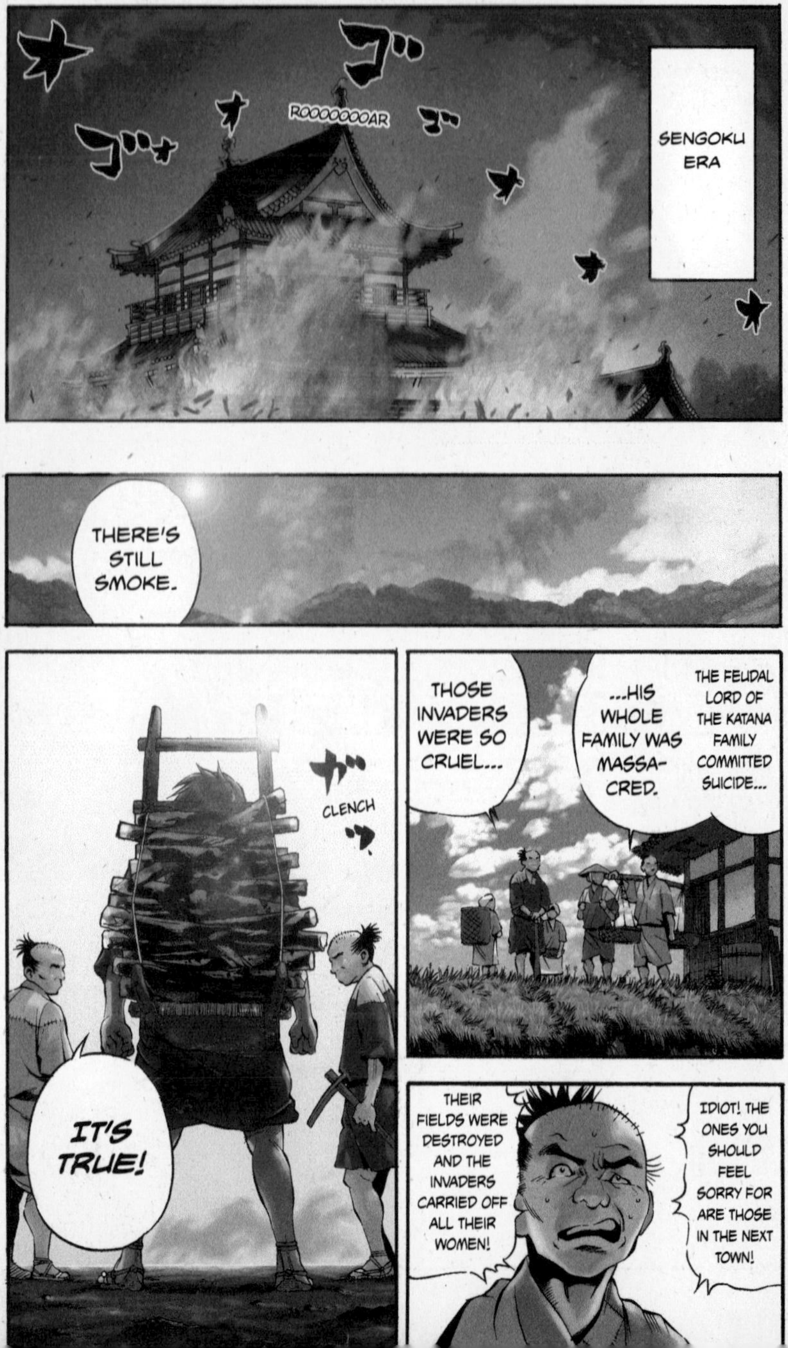
SENGOKU ERA
ゴゴ
ROOOOOOOOAR
オ
ゴォ
オ
THERE'S STILL SMOKE.
THE FEUDAL LORD OF THE KATANA FAMILY COMMITTED SUICIDE...
...HIS WHOLE FAMILY WAS MASSA-CRED.
THOSE INVADERS WERE SO CRUEL...
IDIOT! THE ONES YOU SHOULD FEEL SORRY FOR ARE THOSE IN THE NEXT TOWN!
THEIR FIELDS WERE DESTROYED AND THE INVADERS CARRIED OFF ALL THEIR WOMEN!
ガ
CLENCH
ッ
IT'S TRUE!

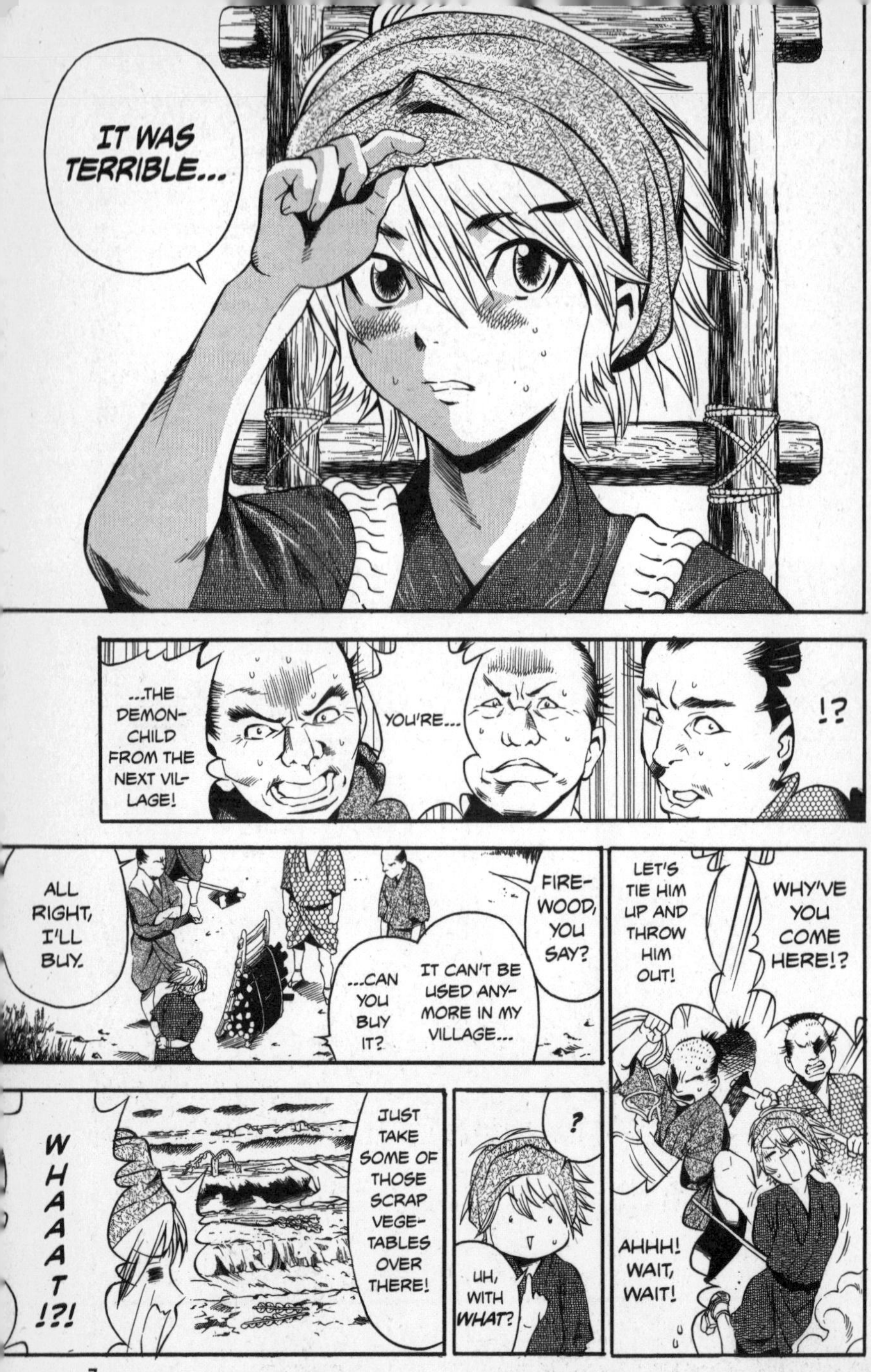
IT WAS TERRIBLE...
!?
YOU'RE...
...THE DEMON-CHILD FROM THE NEXT VILLAGE!
WHY'VE YOU COME HERE!?
LET'S TIE HIM UP AND THROW HIM OUT!
AHHH! WAIT, WAIT!
FIRE-WOOD, YOU SAY?
IT CAN'T BE USED ANYMORE IN MY VILLAGE...
...CAN YOU BUY IT?
ALL RIGHT, I'LL BUY.
?
UH, WITH WHAT?
JUST TAKE SOME OF THOSE SCRAP VEGETABLES OVER THERE!
WHAAAAT!?!

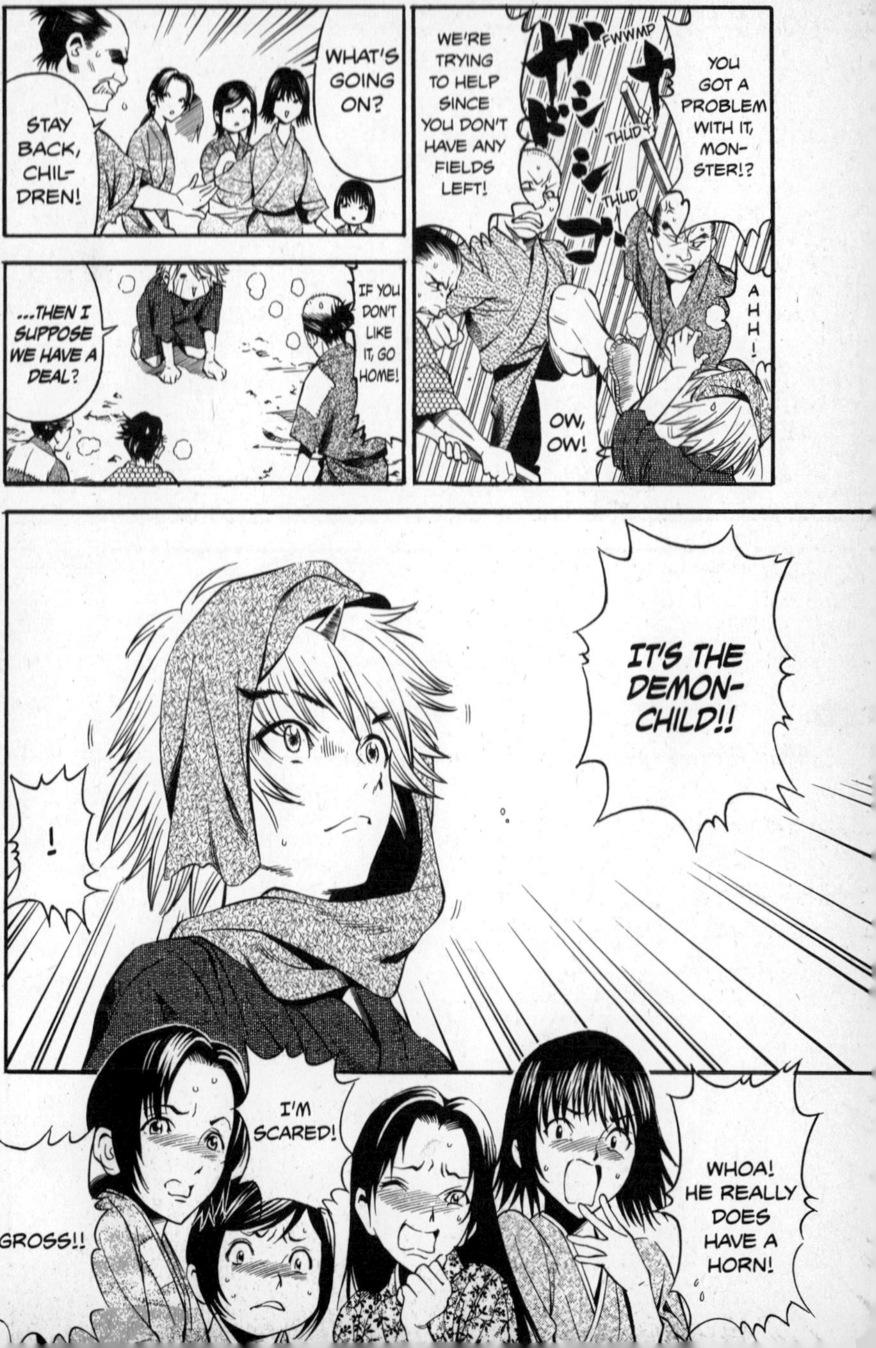
YOU GOT A PROBLEM WITH IT, MON-STER!?
FWWMP
WE'RE TRYING TO HELP SINCE YOU DON'T HAVE ANY FIELDS LEFT!
THUD
THUD
AHH!
OW, OW!
WHAT'S GOING ON?
STAY BACK, CHIL-DREN!
IF YOU DON'T LIKE IT, GO HOME!
...THEN I SUPPOSE WE HAVE A DEAL?
IT'S THE DEMON-CHILD!!
!
WHOA! HE REALLY DOES HAVE A HORN!
I'M SCARED!
GROSS!!

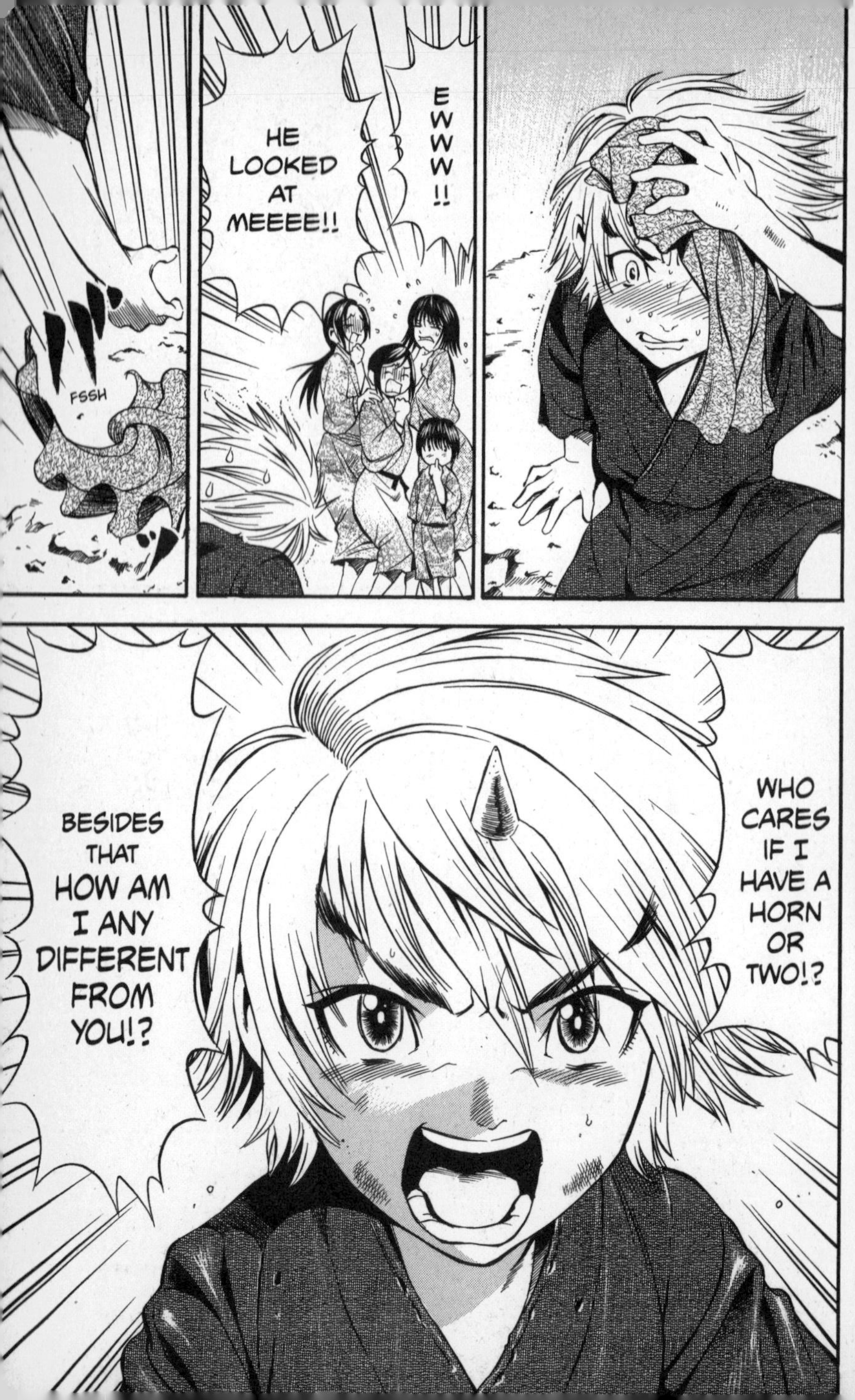
EWWW!!
HE LOOKED AT MEEEE!!
FSSH
WHO CARES IF I HAVE A HORN OR TWO!?
BESIDES THAT HOW AM I ANY DIFFERENT FROM YOU!?

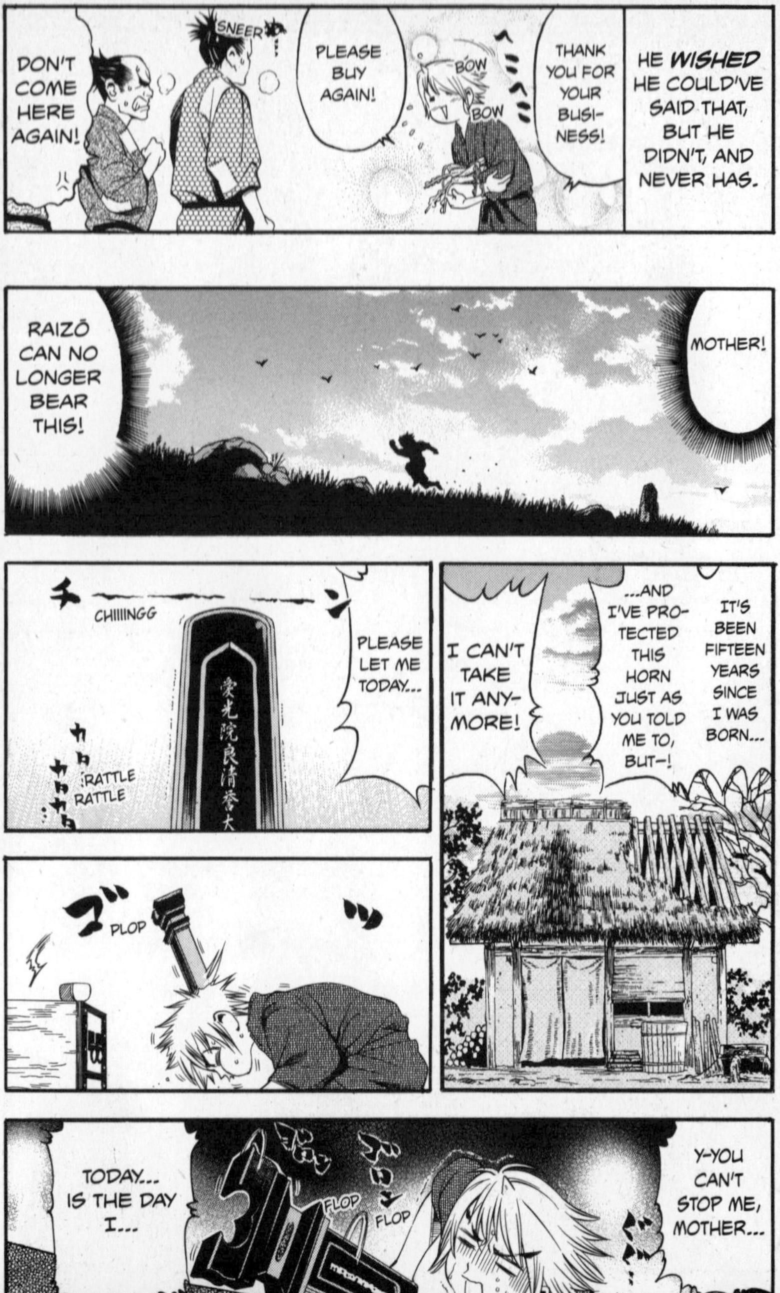
HE *WISHED* HE COULD'VE SAID THAT, BUT HE DIDN'T, AND NEVER HAS.
THANK YOU FOR YOUR BUSI-NESS!
BOW
BOW
PLEASE BUY AGAIN!
SNEER
DON'T COME HERE AGAIN!
MOTHER!
RAIZŌ CAN NO LONGER BEAR THIS!
IT'S BEEN FIFTEEN YEARS SINCE I WAS BORN...
...AND I'VE PRO-TECTED THIS HORN JUST AS YOU TOLD ME TO, BUT—!
I CAN'T TAKE IT ANY-MORE!
CHIIIINGG
PLEASE LET ME TODAY...
RATTLE RATTLE
PLOP
Y-YOU CAN'T STOP ME, MOTHER...
UGHH
FLOP
FLOP
TODAY... IS THE DAY I...

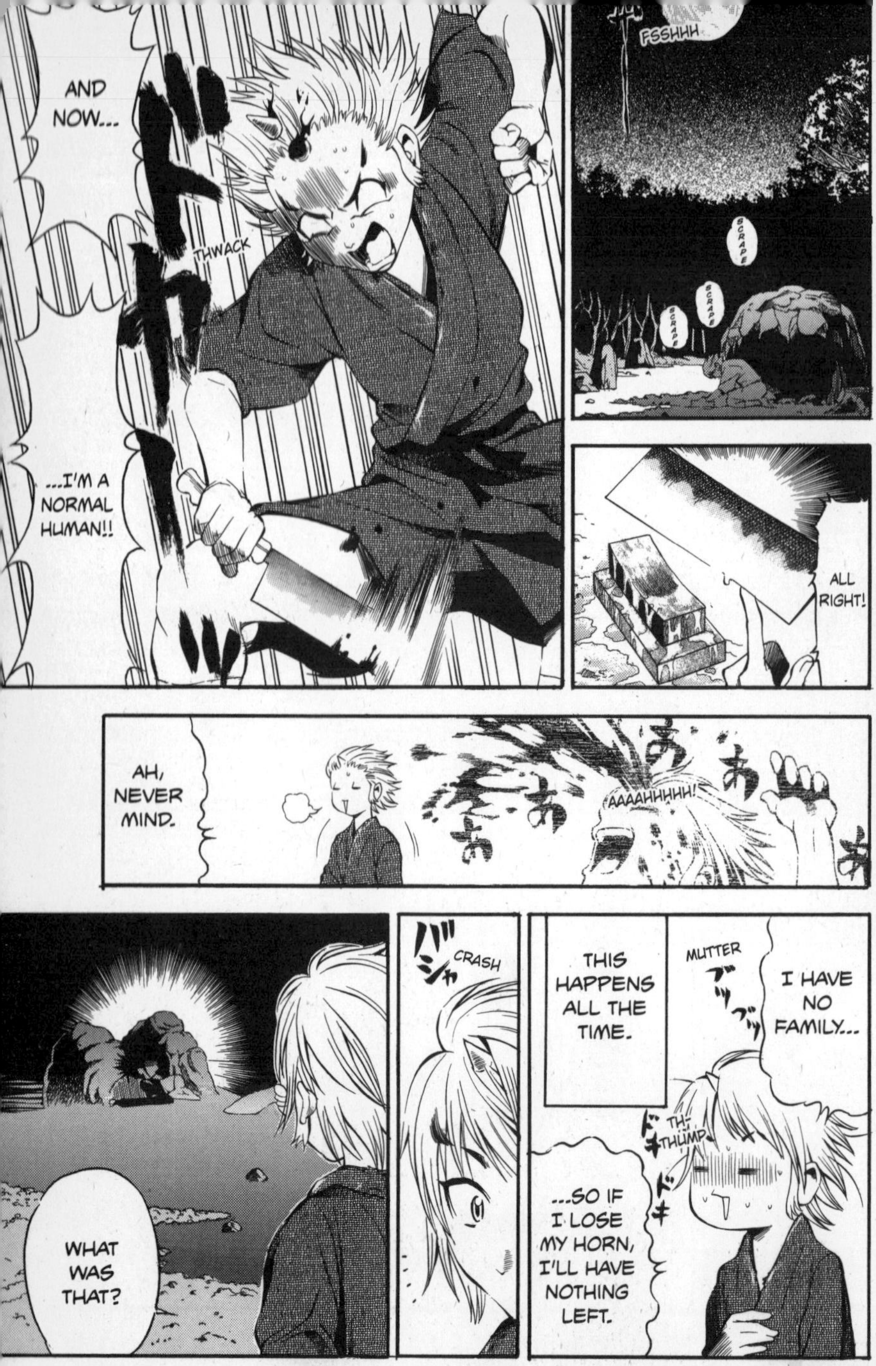
FSSHHH
SCRAPE
SCRAPE
SCRAPE
ALL RIGHT!
AND NOW...
THWACK
...I'M A NORMAL HUMAN!!
AAAAHHHHH!
AH, NEVER MIND.
I HAVE NO FAMILY...
MUTTER
THIS HAPPENS ALL THE TIME.
TH-THUMP
...SO IF I LOSE MY HORN, I'LL HAVE NOTHING LEFT.
CRASH
WHAT WAS THAT?

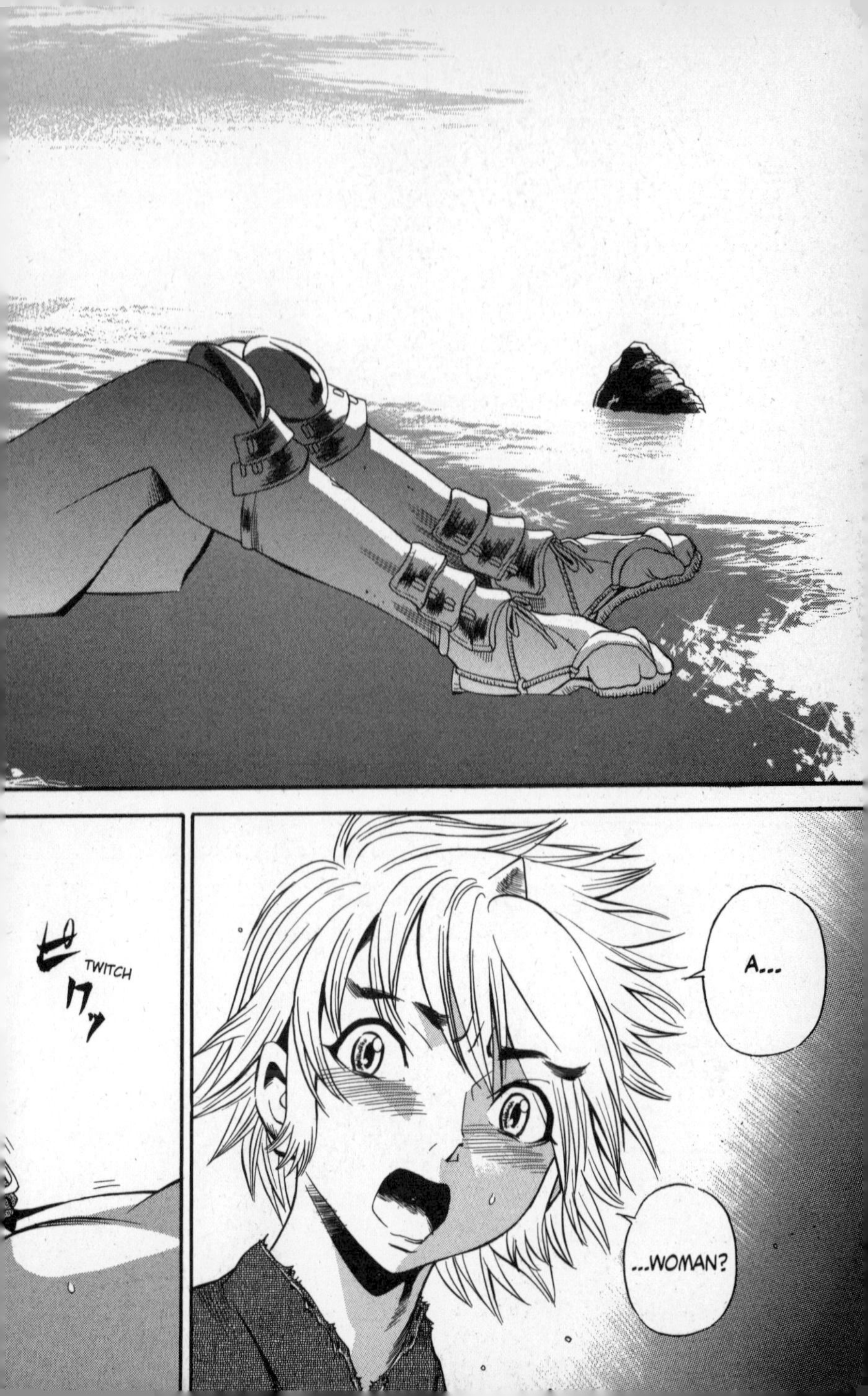
A...
...WOMAN?
ビクッ
TWITCH

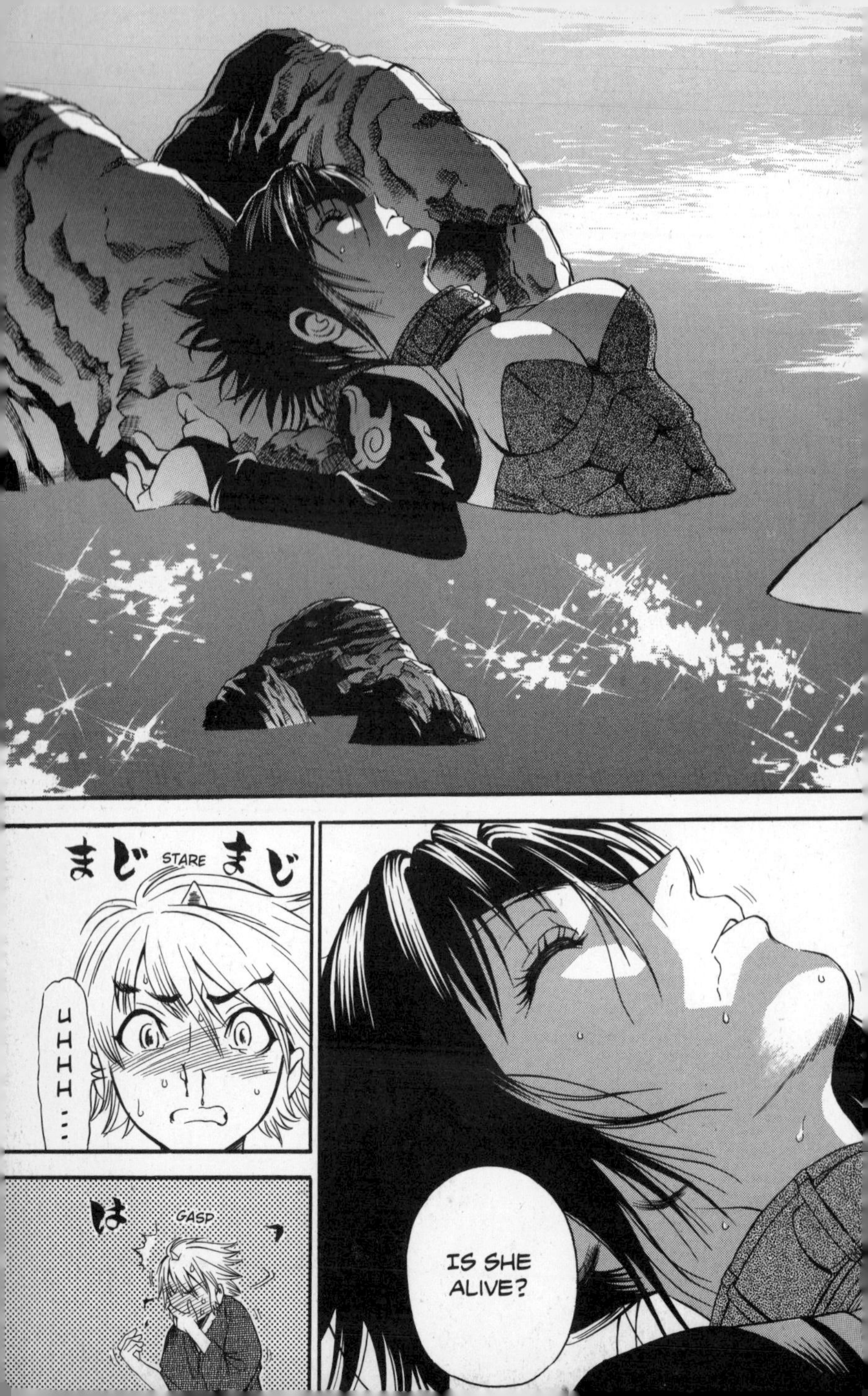
IS SHE ALIVE?
まじ STARE まじ
UHHH...
は GASP

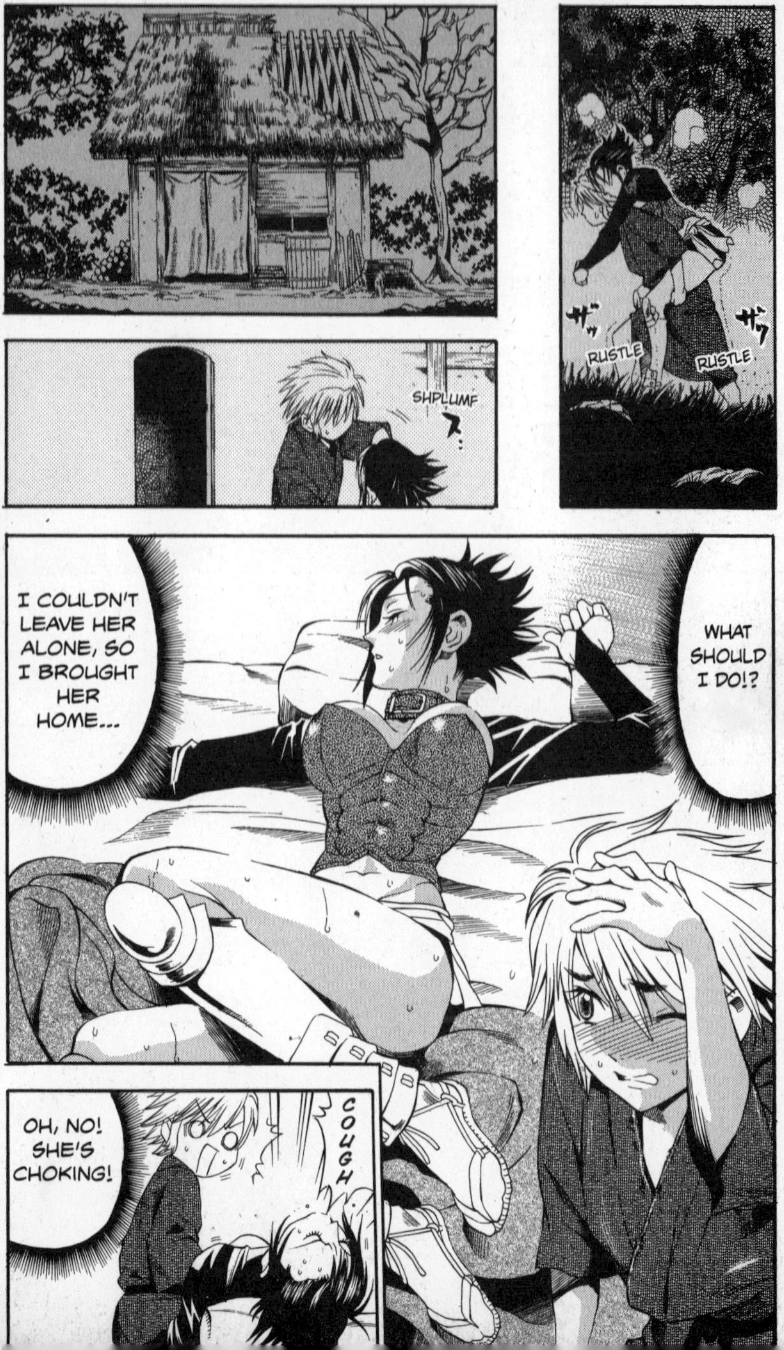
ザッ
RUSTLE
ザッ
RUSTLE
SHPLUMF
WHAT SHOULD I DO!?
I COULDN'T LEAVE HER ALONE, SO I BROUGHT HER HOME...
COUGH
OH, NO! SHE'S CHOKING!

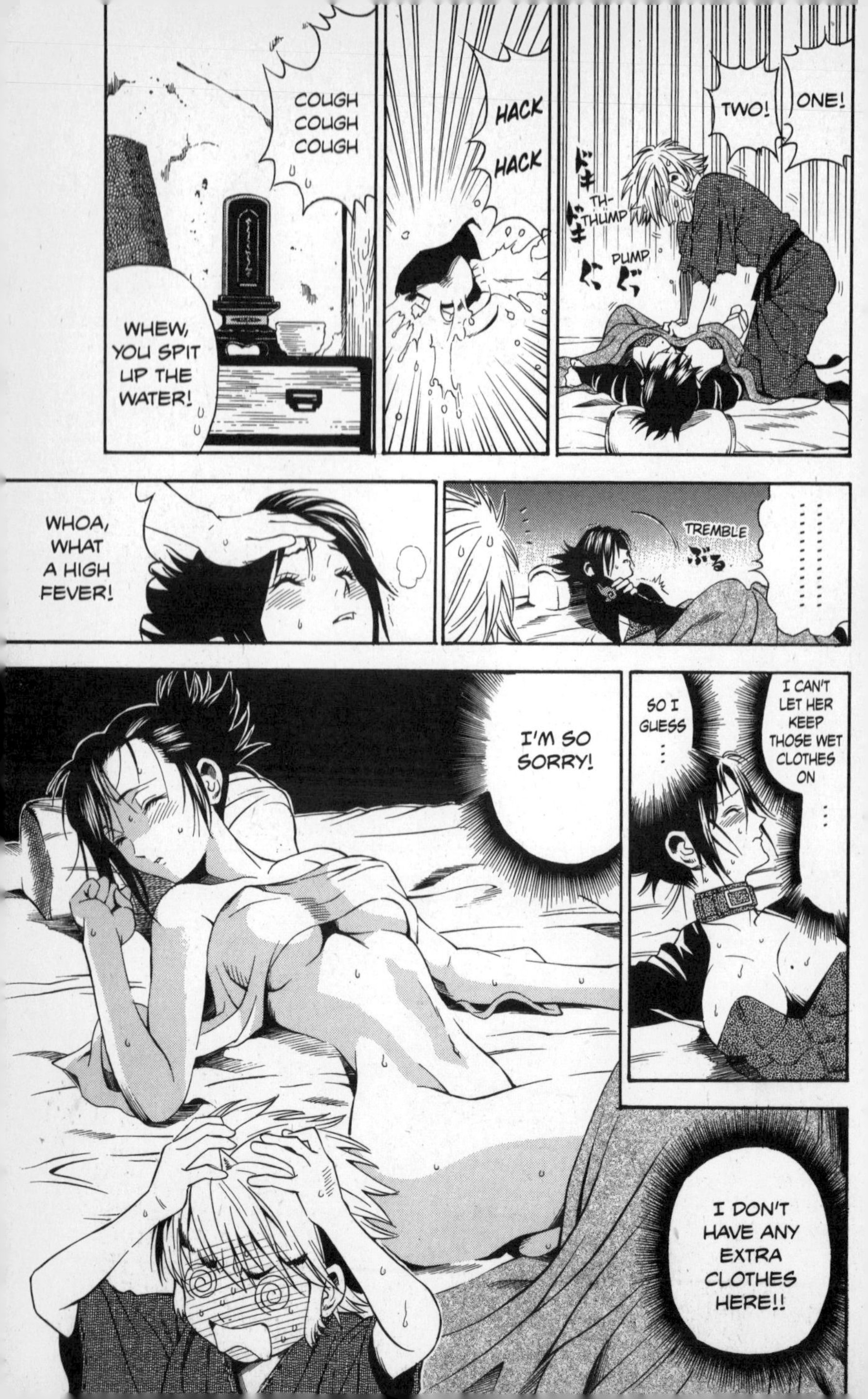
ONE!
TWO!
ドキ ドキ TH-THUMP
ぐ ぐ PUMP
HACK
HACK
COUGH COUGH COUGH
WHEW, YOU SPIT UP THE WATER!
......
TREMBLE ぶる
WHOA, WHAT A HIGH FEVER!
I CAN'T LET HER KEEP THOSE WET CLOTHES ON ...
SO I GUESS ...
I DON'T HAVE ANY EXTRA CLOTHES HERE!!
I'M SO SORRY!

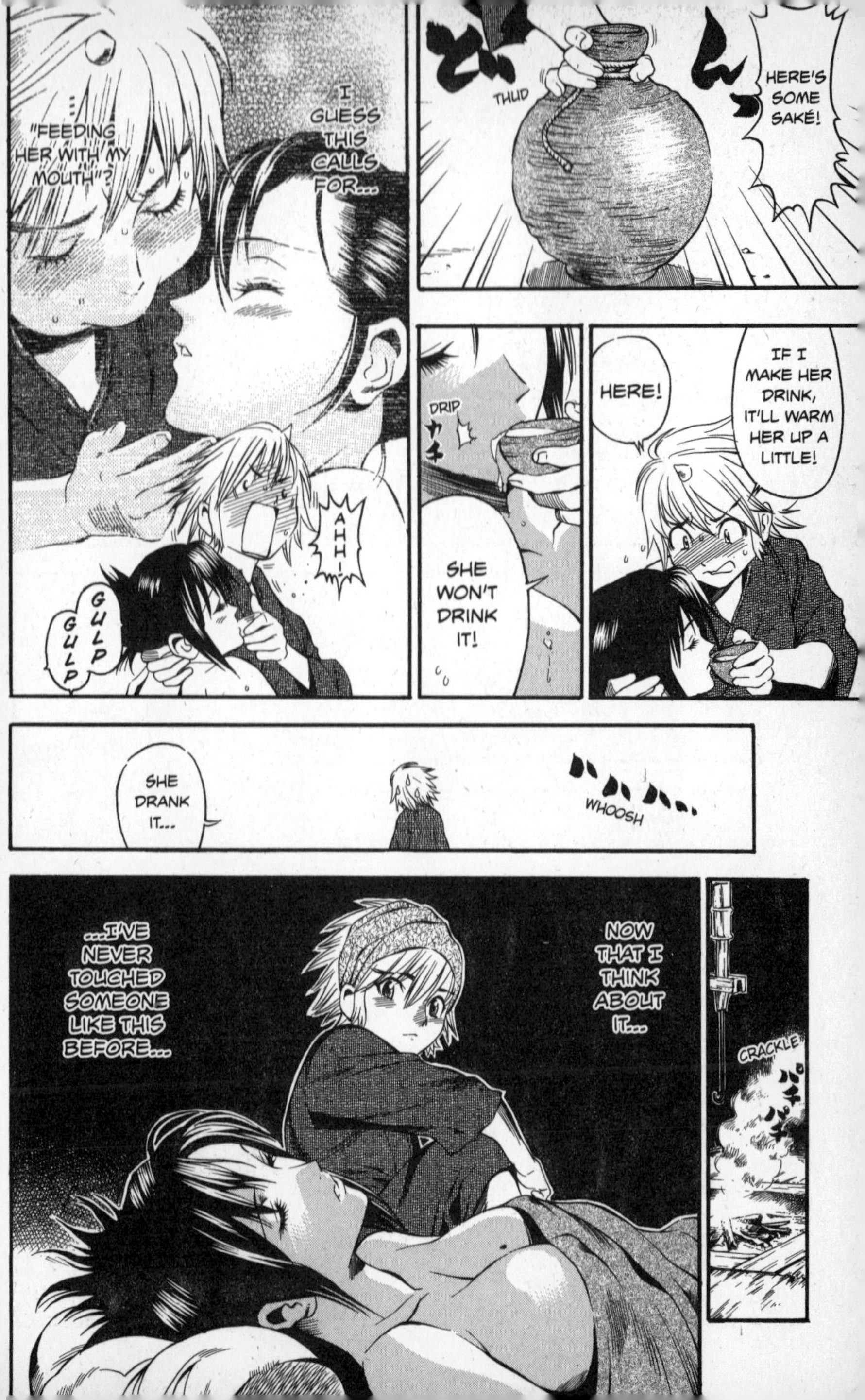
HERE'S SOME SAKÉ!
THUD
IF I MAKE HER DRINK, IT'LL WARM HER UP A LITTLE!
HERE!
DRIP
SHE WON'T DRINK IT!
I GUESS THIS CALLS FOR...
..."FEEDING HER WITH MY MOUTH"?
AHH!
GULP GULP
WHOOSH
SHE DRANK IT...
CRACKLE
NOW THAT I THINK ABOUT IT...
...I'VE NEVER TOUCHED SOMEONE LIKE THIS BEFORE...

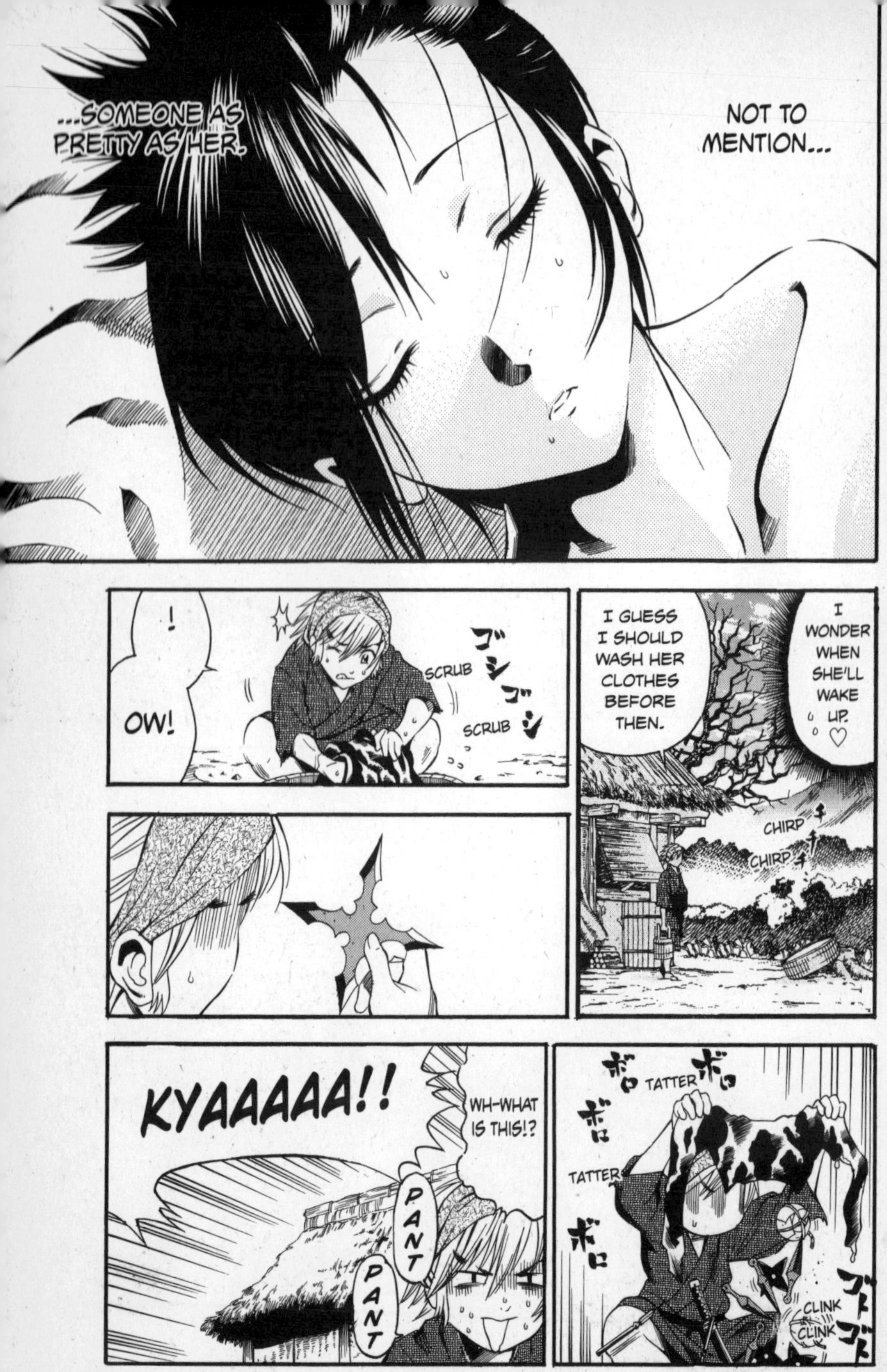
NOT TO MENTION...
...SOMEONE AS PRETTY AS HER.
I WONDER WHEN SHE'LL WAKE UP. ♡
I GUESS I SHOULD WASH HER CLOTHES BEFORE THEN.
CHIRP
CHIRP
!
OW!
ゴシゴシ
SCRUB
SCRUB
ボロボロ
TATTER
ボロボロ
TATTER
ゴトゴト
CLINK
CLINK
WH-WHAT IS THIS!?
KYAAAAA!!
PANT
PANT

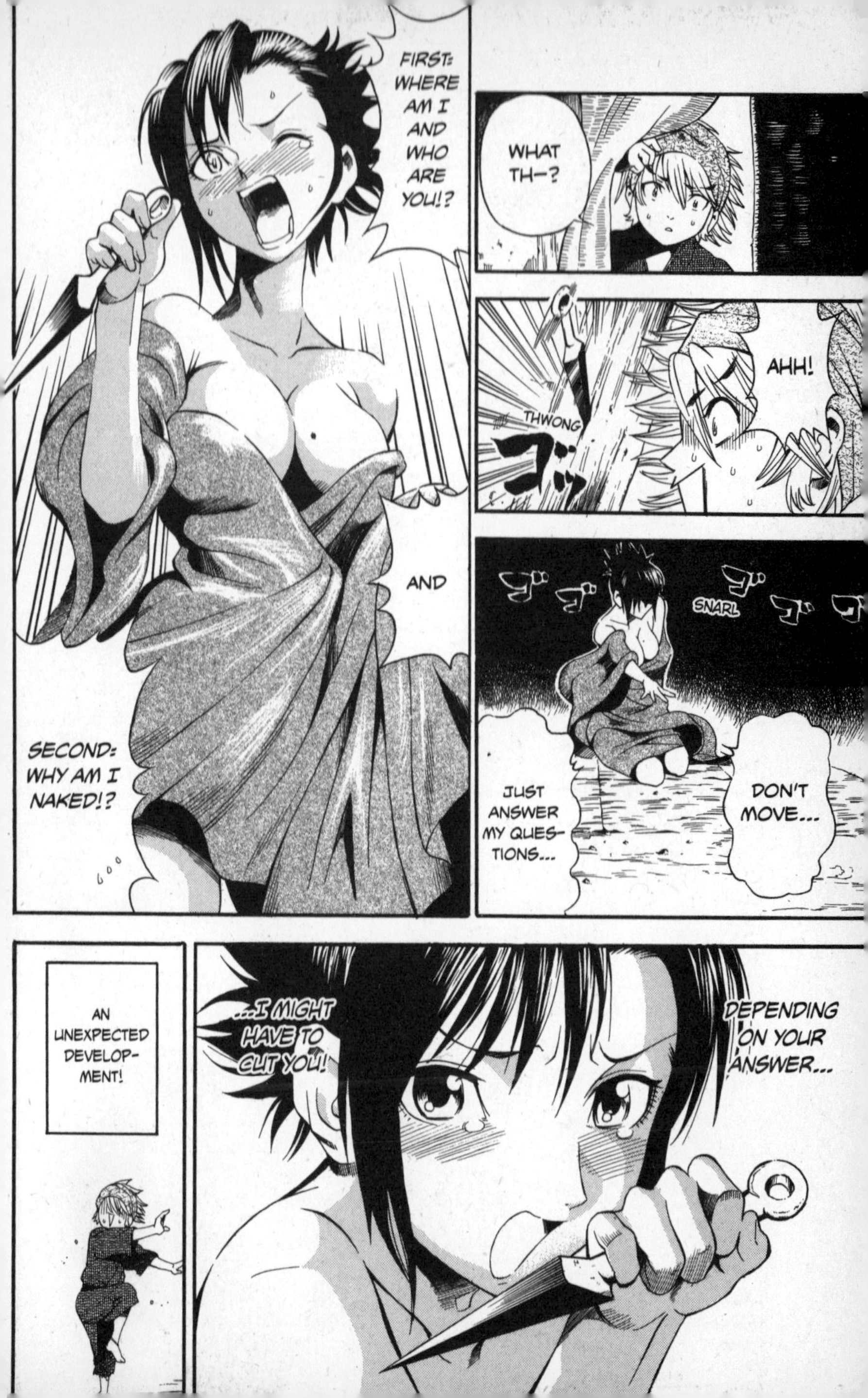
WHAT TH–?
AHH!
THWONG
SNARL
DON'T MOVE...
JUST ANSWER MY QUESTIONS...
FIRST: WHERE AM I AND WHO ARE YOU!?
AND
SECOND: WHY AM I NAKED!?
DEPENDING ON YOUR ANSWER...
...I MIGHT HAVE TO CUT YOU!
AN UNEXPECTED DEVELOPMENT!

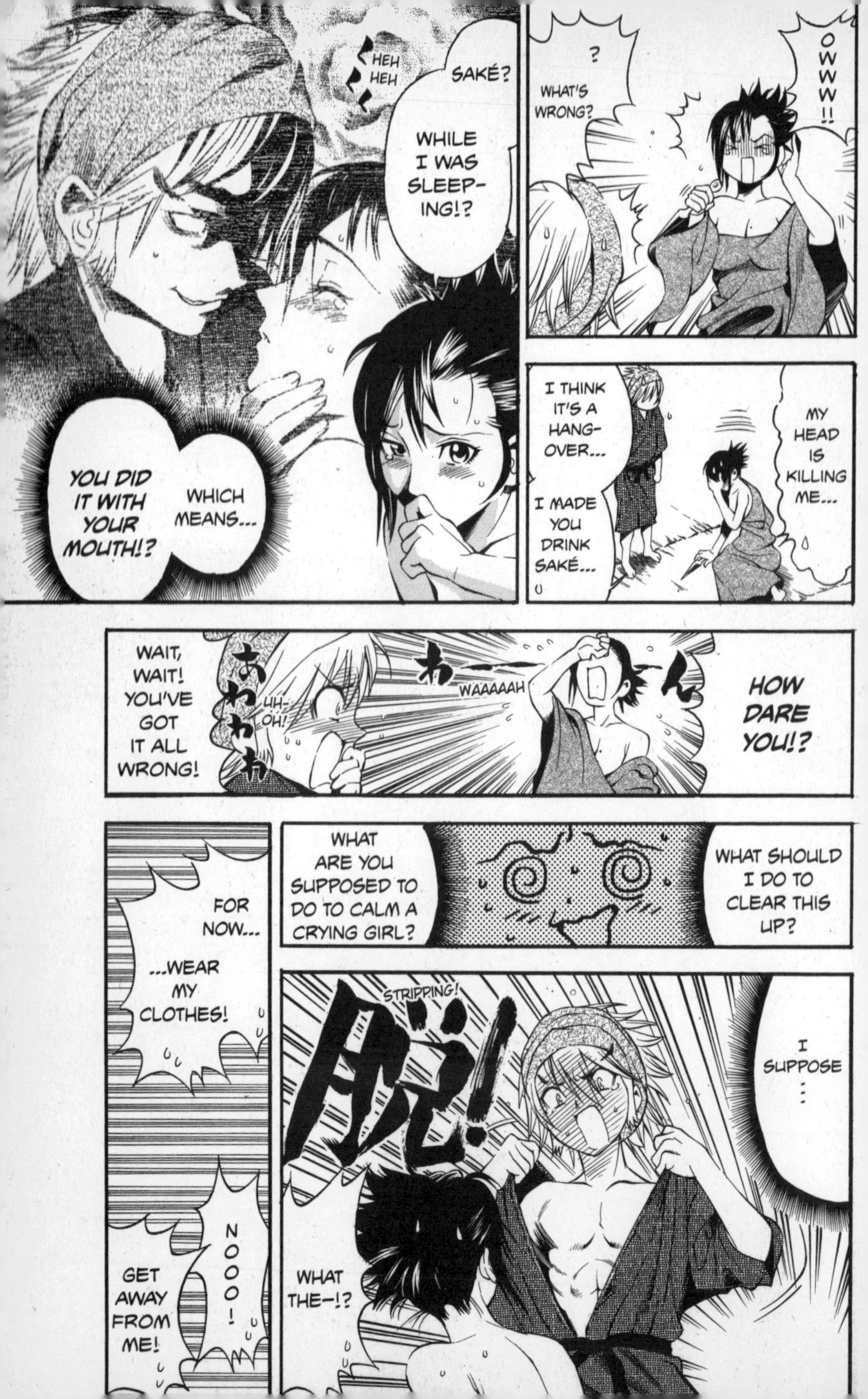
OWWW!!
?
WHAT'S WRONG?
MY HEAD IS KILLING ME...
I THINK IT'S A HANG-OVER...
I MADE YOU DRINK SAKÉ...
SAKÉ?
WHILE I WAS SLEEP-ING!?
HEH HEH
WHICH MEANS...
YOU DID IT WITH YOUR MOUTH!?
HOW DARE YOU!?
WAAAAAH
UH-OH!
WAIT, WAIT! YOU'VE GOT IT ALL WRONG!
WHAT SHOULD I DO TO CLEAR THIS UP?
WHAT ARE YOU SUPPOSED TO DO TO CALM A CRYING GIRL?
I SUPPOSE...
STRIPPING!
WHAT THE-!?
FOR NOW...
...WEAR MY CLOTHES!
NOOOO!
GET AWAY FROM ME!

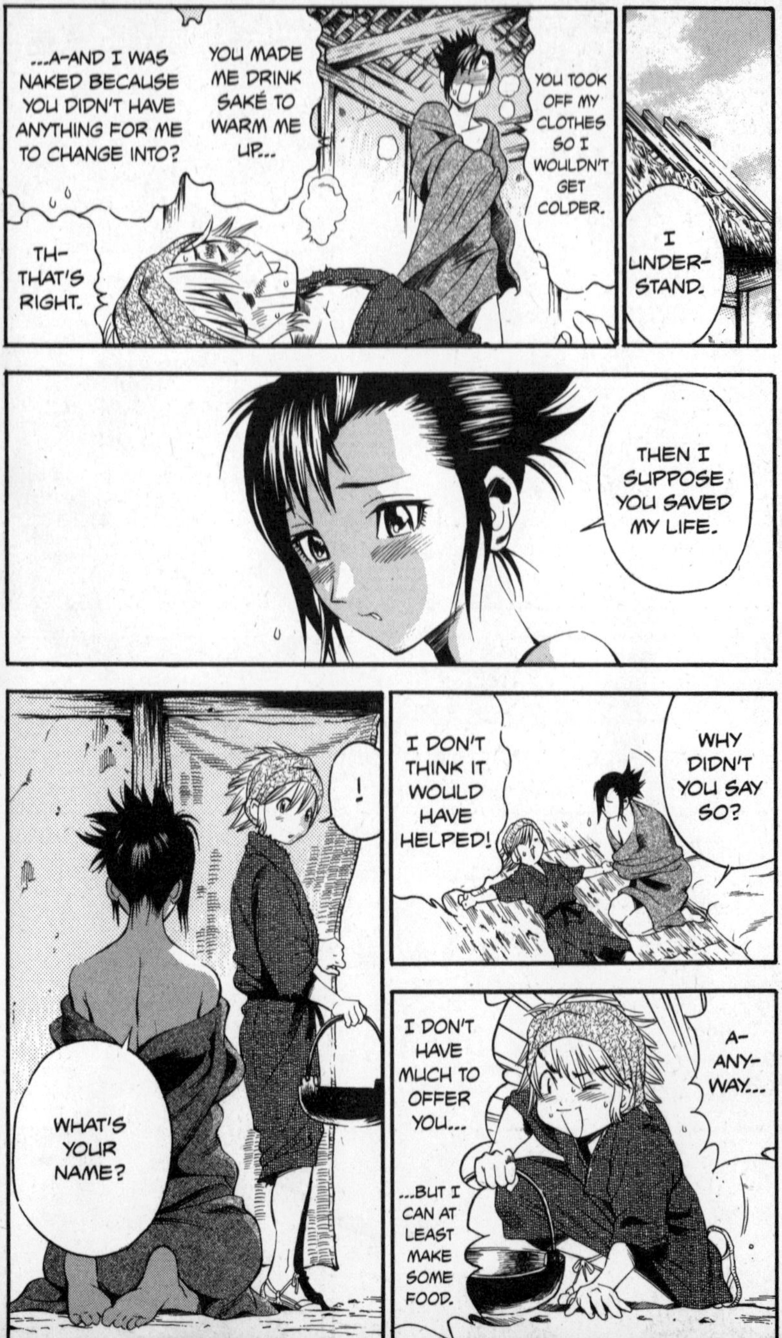
I UNDER-STAND.
YOU TOOK OFF MY CLOTHES SO I WOULDN'T GET COLDER.
YOU MADE ME DRINK SAKÉ TO WARM ME UP...
...A-AND I WAS NAKED BECAUSE YOU DIDN'T HAVE ANYTHING FOR ME TO CHANGE INTO?
TH-THAT'S RIGHT.
THEN I SUPPOSE YOU SAVED MY LIFE.
WHY DIDN'T YOU SAY SO?
I DON'T THINK IT WOULD HAVE HELPED!
A-ANYWAY...
I DON'T HAVE MUCH TO OFFER YOU...
...BUT I CAN AT LEAST MAKE SOME FOOD.
!
WHAT'S YOUR NAME?

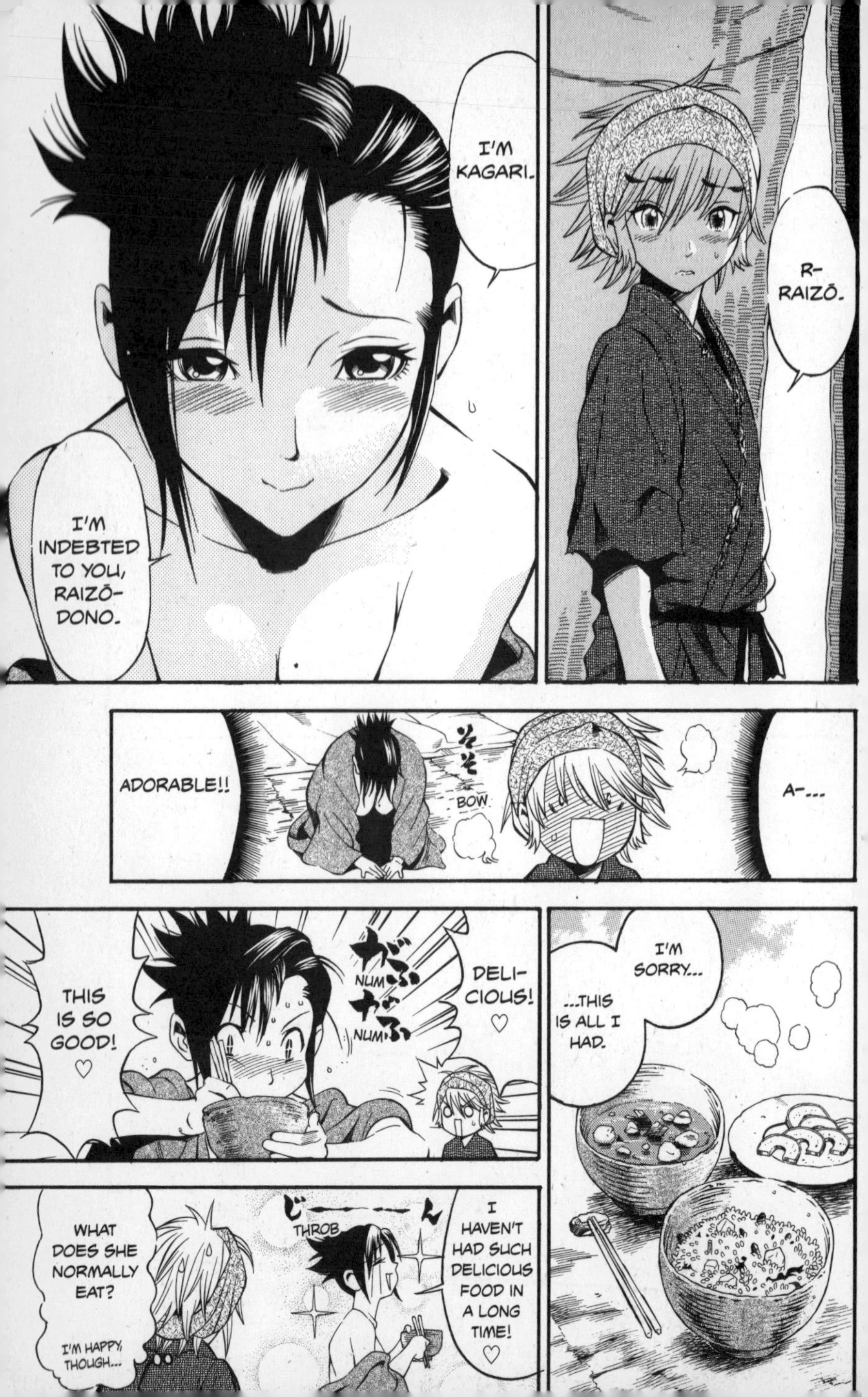
R-RAIZŌ.
I'M KAGARI.
I'M INDEBTED TO YOU, RAIZŌ-DONO.
A-...
BOW
ADORABLE!!
I'M SORRY...
...THIS IS ALL I HAD.
DELI-CIOUS! ♡
NUM
NUM
THIS IS SO GOOD! ♡
I HAVEN'T HAD SUCH DELICIOUS FOOD IN A LONG TIME! ♡
THROB
WHAT DOES SHE NORMALLY EAT?
I'M HAPPY, THOUGH...

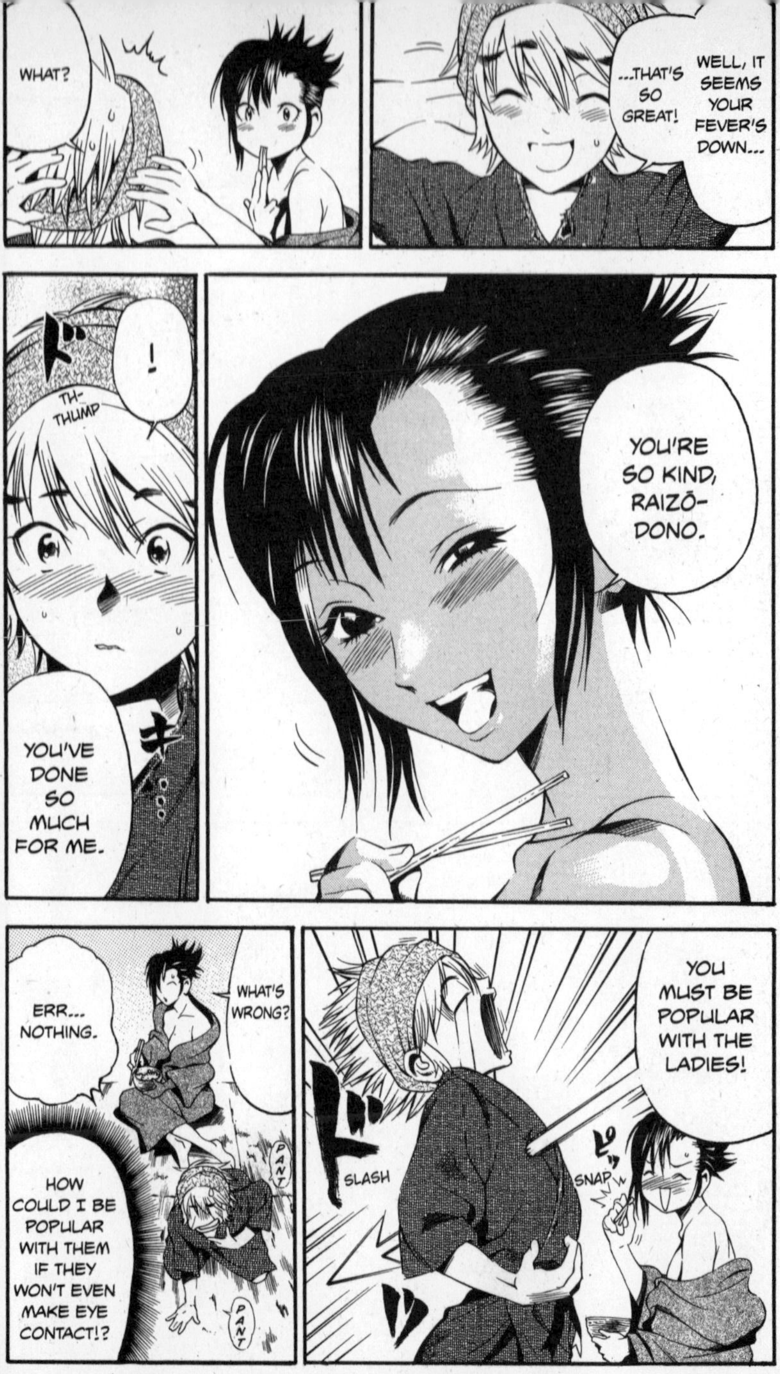
WELL, IT SEEMS YOUR FEVER'S DOWN...
...THAT'S SO GREAT!
WHAT?
YOU'RE SO KIND, RAIZŌ-DONO.
!
TH-THUMP
YOU'VE DONE SO MUCH FOR ME.
YOU MUST BE POPULAR WITH THE LADIES!
SLASH
SNAP
WHAT'S WRONG?
ERR... NOTHING.
HOW COULD I BE POPULAR WITH THEM IF THEY WON'T EVEN MAKE EYE CONTACT!?
PANT
PANT

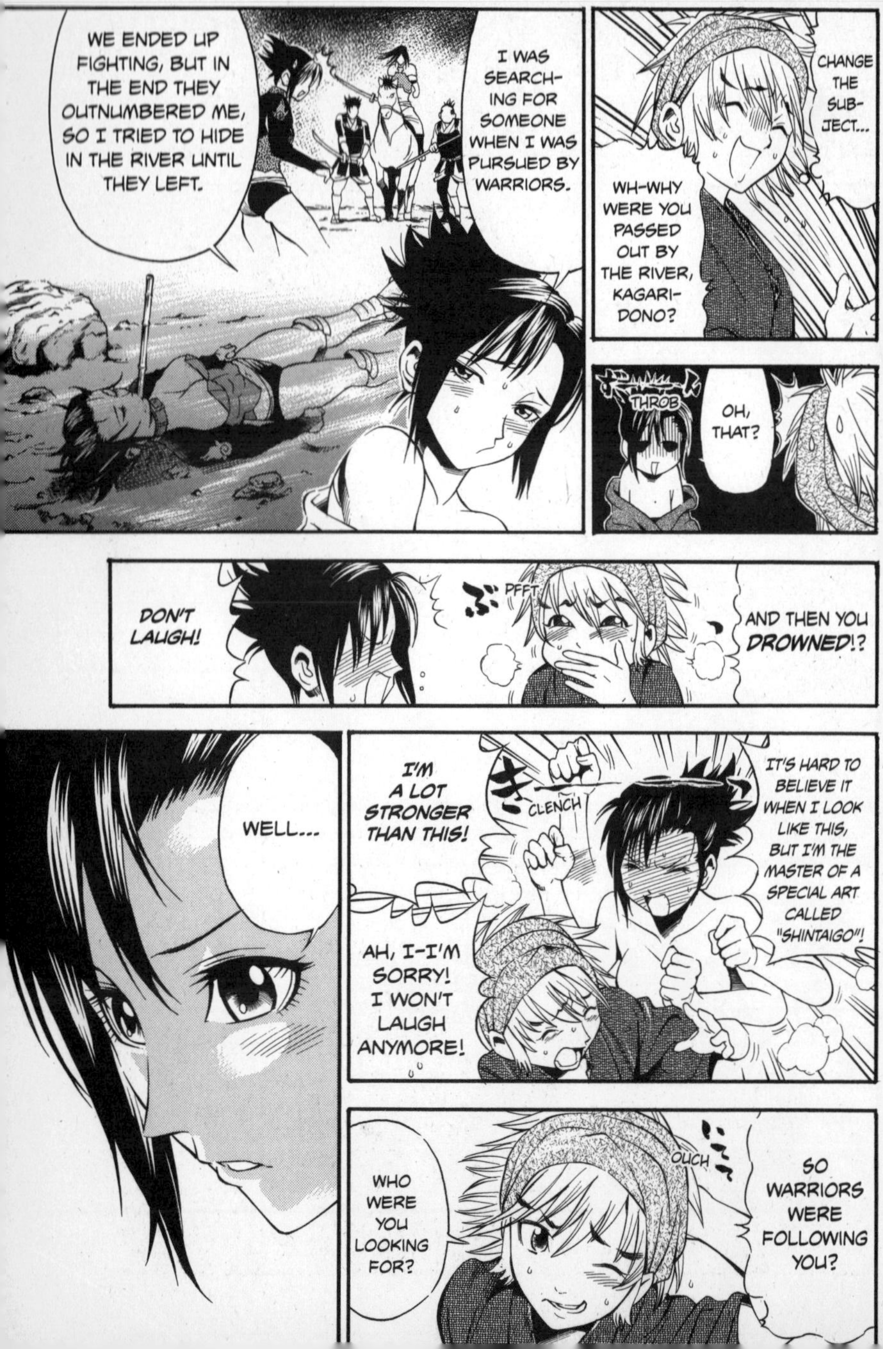
CHANGE THE SUBJECT...
WH-WHY WERE YOU PASSED OUT BY THE RIVER, KAGARI-DONO?
THROB
OH, THAT?
I WAS SEARCHING FOR SOMEONE WHEN I WAS PURSUED BY WARRIORS.
WE ENDED UP FIGHTING, BUT IN THE END THEY OUTNUMBERED ME, SO I TRIED TO HIDE IN THE RIVER UNTIL THEY LEFT.
AND THEN YOU DROWNED!?
PFFT
DON'T LAUGH!
IT'S HARD TO BELIEVE IT WHEN I LOOK LIKE THIS, BUT I'M THE MASTER OF A SPECIAL ART CALLED "SHINTAIGO"!
CLENCH
I'M A LOT STRONGER THAN THIS!
AH, I-I'M SORRY! I WON'T LAUGH ANYMORE!
SO WARRIORS WERE FOLLOWING YOU?
OUCH
WHO WERE YOU LOOKING FOR?
WELL...

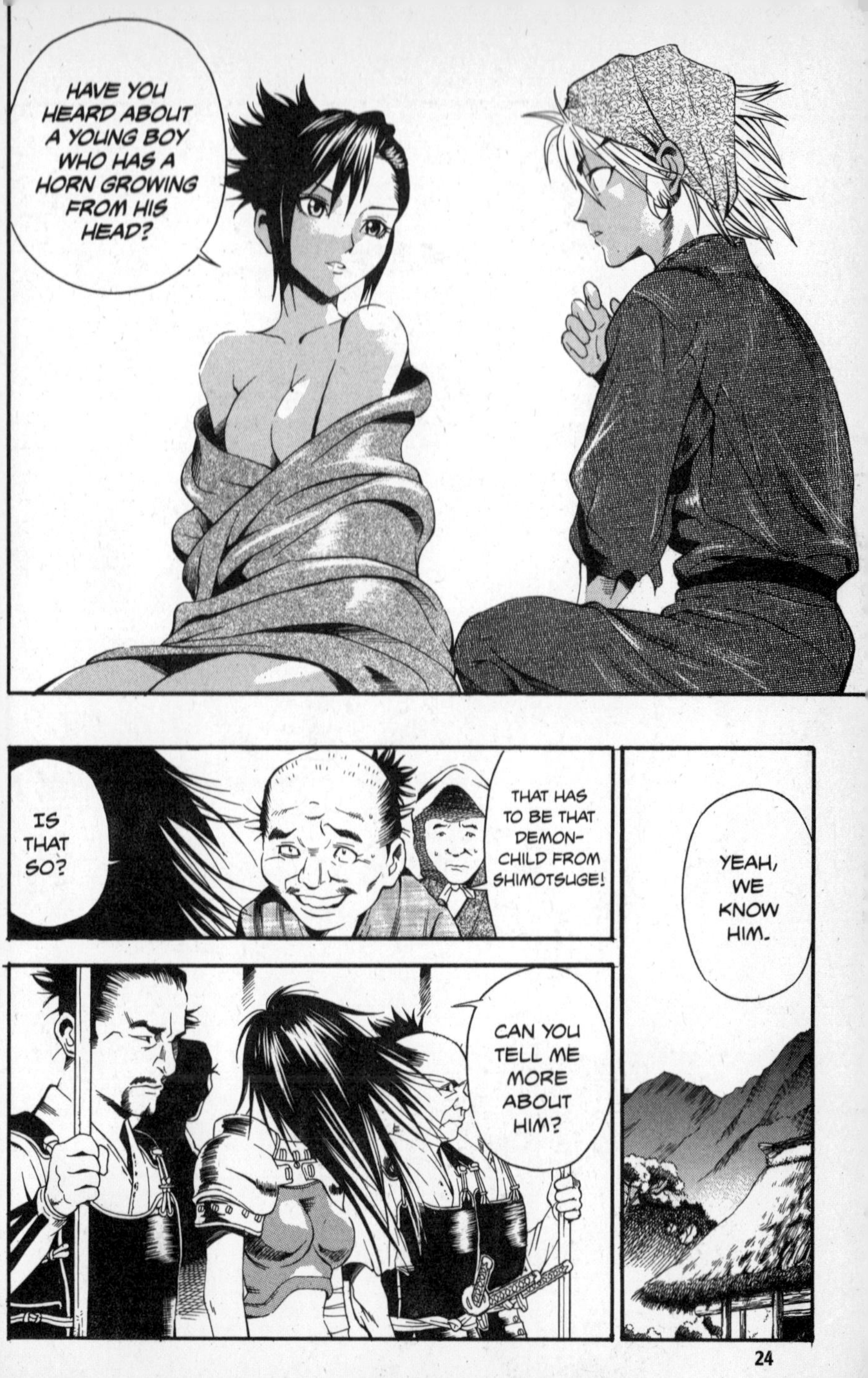
HAVE YOU HEARD ABOUT A YOUNG BOY WHO HAS A HORN GROWING FROM HIS HEAD?
YEAH, WE KNOW HIM.
THAT HAS TO BE THAT DEMON-CHILD FROM SHIMOTSUGE!
IS THAT SO?
CAN YOU TELL ME MORE ABOUT HIM?

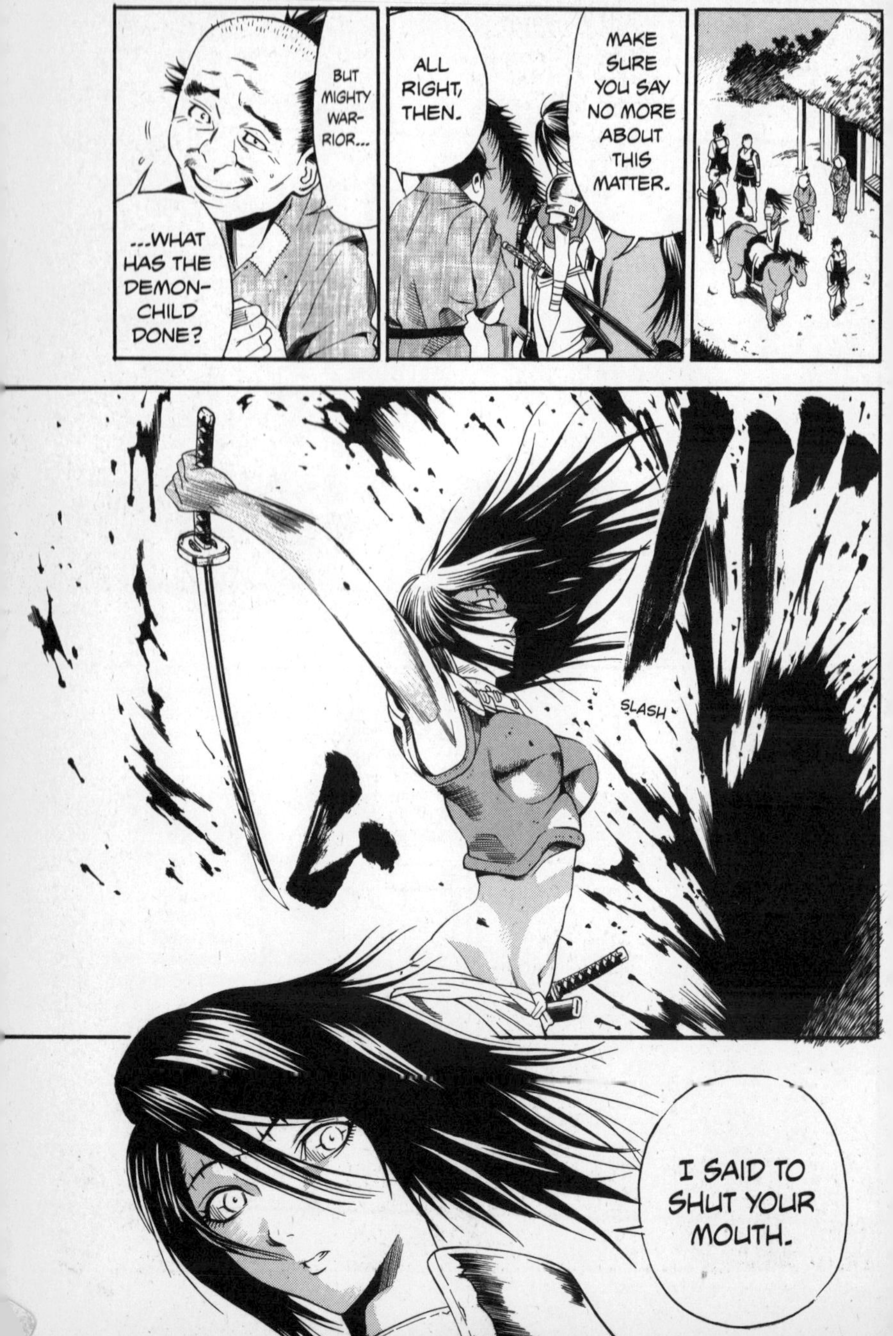
MAKE SURE YOU SAY NO MORE ABOUT THIS MATTER.
ALL RIGHT, THEN.
BUT MIGHTY WAR-RIOR...
...WHAT HAS THE DEMON-CHILD DONE?
SLASH
I SAID TO SHUT YOUR MOUTH.

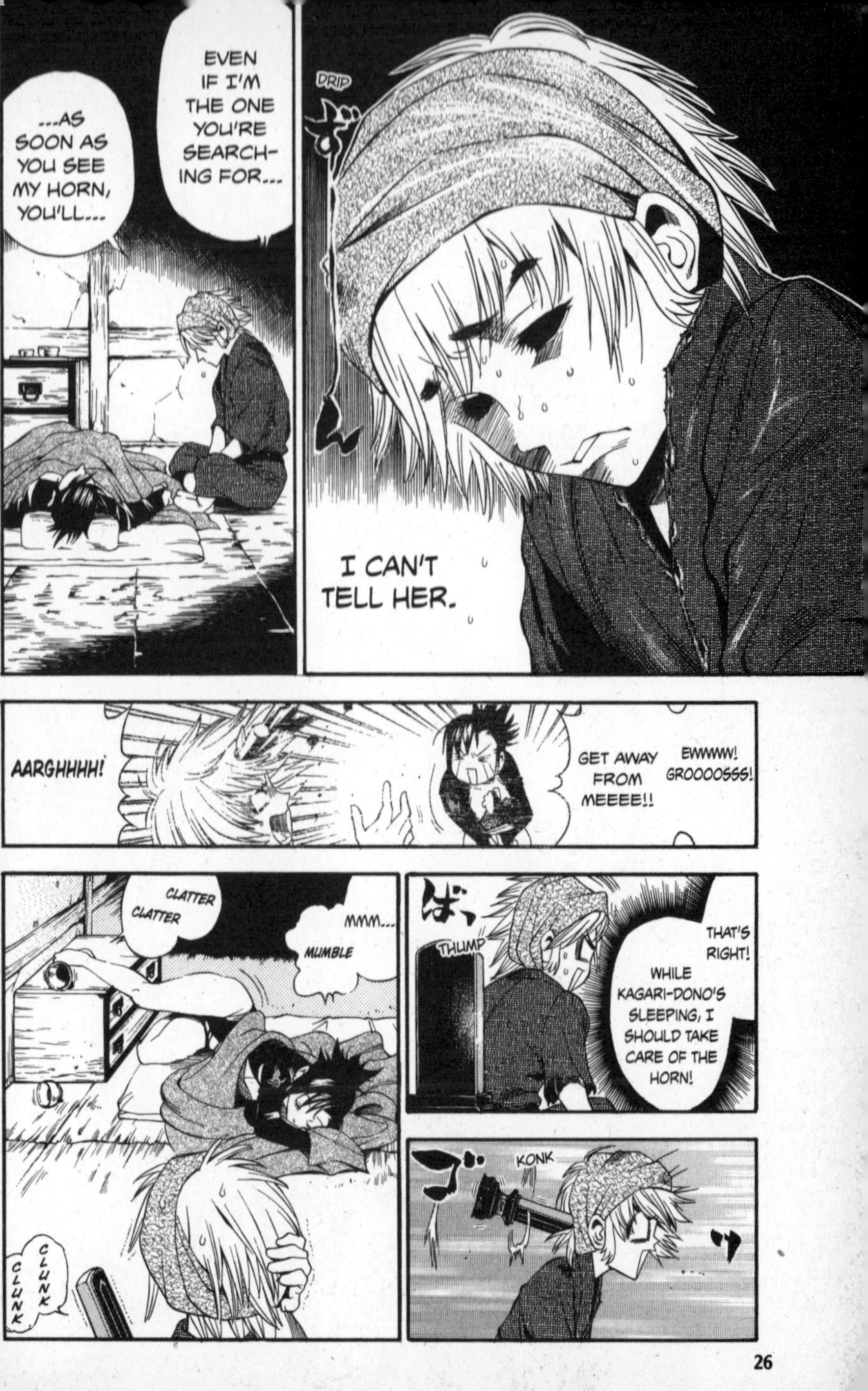
DRIP
I CAN'T TELL HER.
EVEN IF I'M THE ONE YOU'RE SEARCH-ING FOR...
...AS SOON AS YOU SEE MY HORN, YOU'LL...
EWWWW! GROOOOSSS!
GET AWAY FROM MEEEE!!
AARGHHHH!
THUMP
THAT'S RIGHT! WHILE KAGARI-DONO'S SLEEPING, I SHOULD TAKE CARE OF THE HORN!
KONK
...
CLATTER
CLATTER
MMM...
MUMBLE
CLUNK
CLUNK

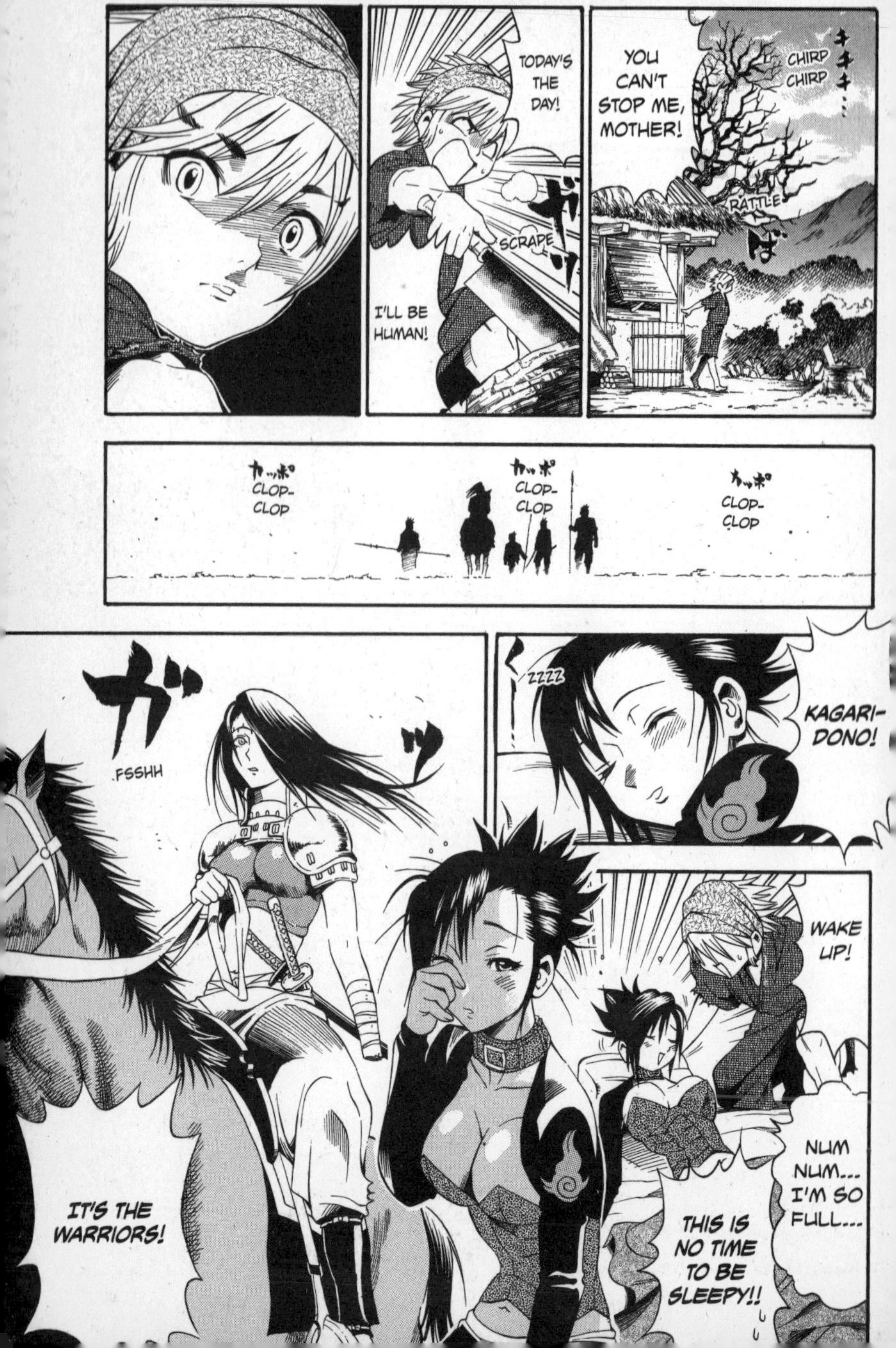
YOU CAN'T STOP ME, MOTHER!
CHIRP CHIRP
RATTLE
TODAY'S THE DAY!
SCRAPE
I'LL BE HUMAN!
カッポ
CLOP-CLOP
カッポ
CLOP-CLOP
カッポ
CLOP-CLOP
KAGARI-DONO!
ZZZZ
WAKE UP!
NUM NUM... I'M SO FULL...
THIS IS NO TIME TO BE SLEEPY!!
FSSHH
IT'S THE WARRIORS!

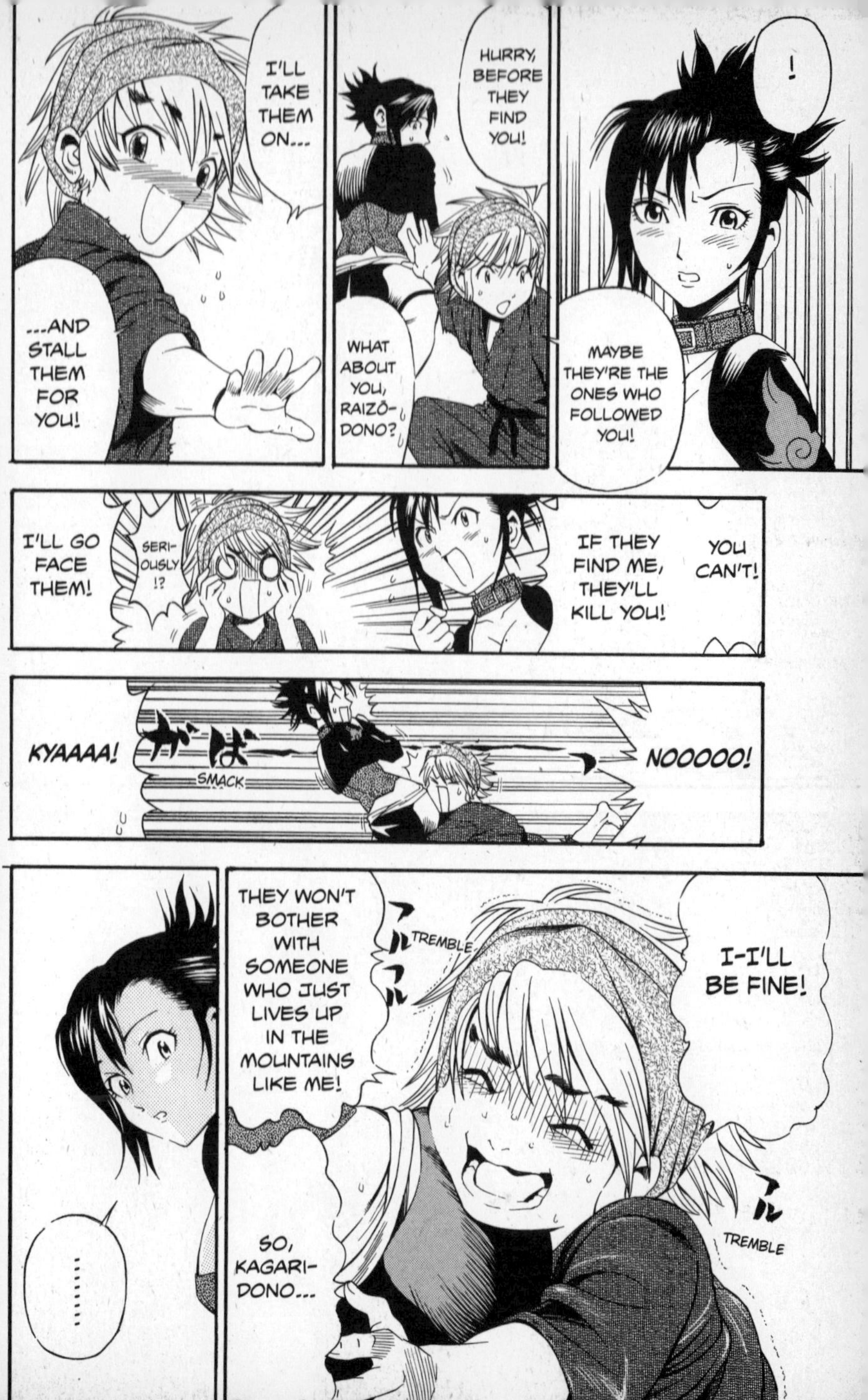
!
MAYBE THEY'RE THE ONES WHO FOLLOWED YOU!
HURRY, BEFORE THEY FIND YOU!
WHAT ABOUT YOU, RAIZŌ-DONO?
I'LL TAKE THEM ON...
...AND STALL THEM FOR YOU!
YOU CAN'T!
IF THEY FIND ME, THEY'LL KILL YOU!
SERI-OUSLY!?
I'LL GO FACE THEM!
NOOOOO!
がば
SMACK
KYAAAA!
I-I'LL BE FINE!
TREMBLE
TREMBLE
THEY WON'T BOTHER WITH SOMEONE WHO JUST LIVES UP IN THE MOUNTAINS LIKE ME!
SO, KAGARI-DONO...
......

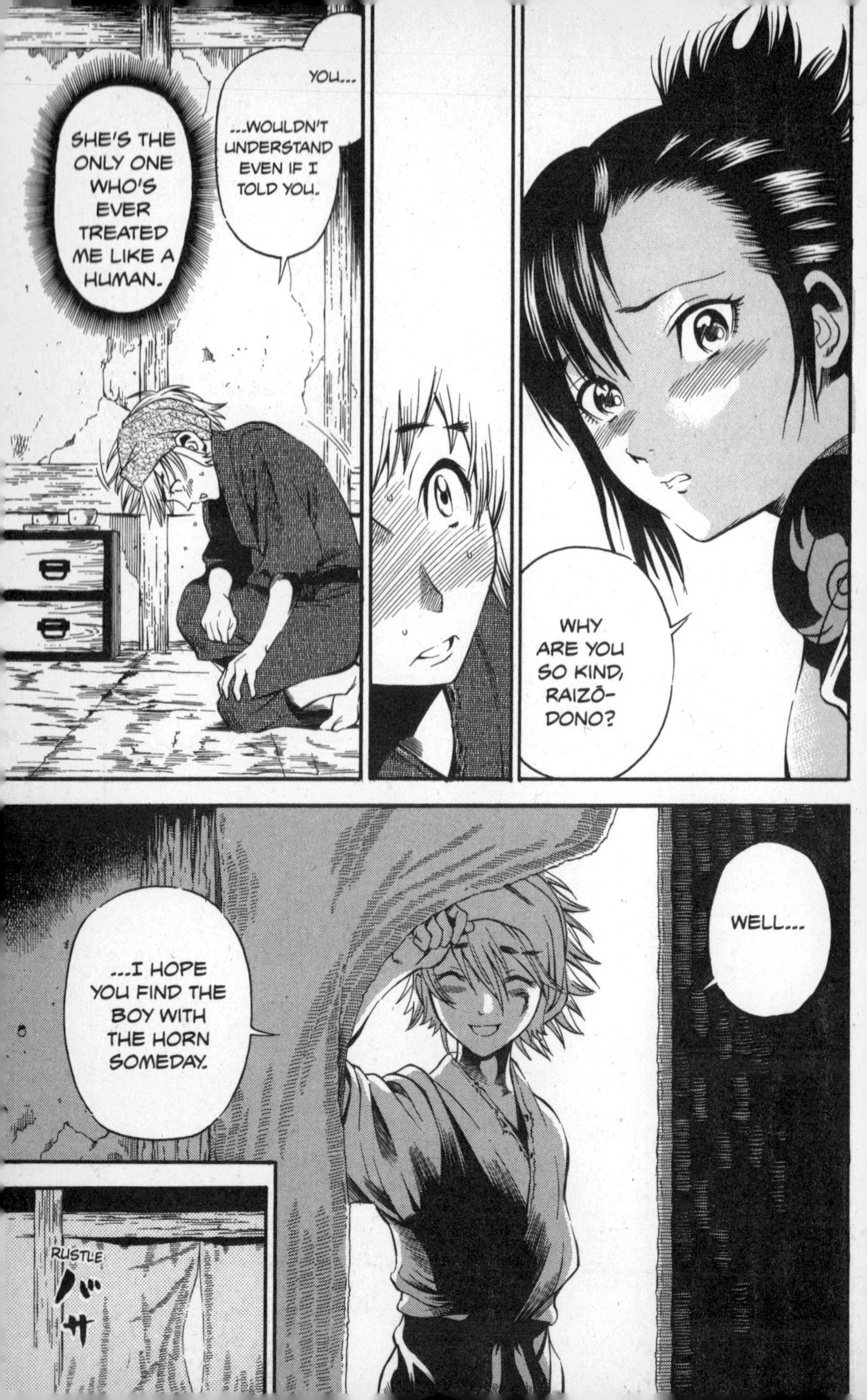
WHY ARE YOU SO KIND, RAIZŌ-DONO?
YOU...
...WOULDN'T UNDERSTAND EVEN IF I TOLD YOU.
SHE'S THE ONLY ONE WHO'S EVER TREATED ME LIKE A HUMAN.
WELL...
...I HOPE YOU FIND THE BOY WITH THE HORN SOMEDAY.
RUSTLE
バサ

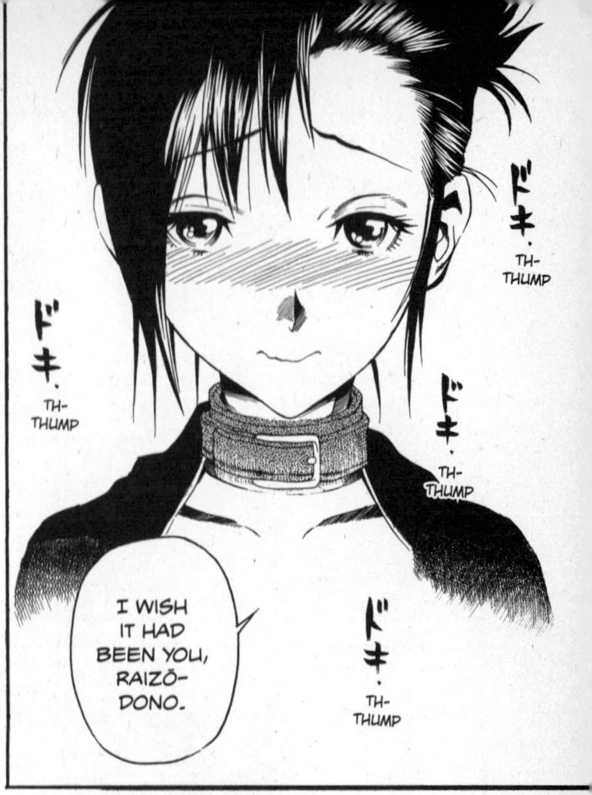
ドキ
TH-THUMP
ドキ
TH-THUMP
ドキ
TH-THUMP
I WISH IT HAD BEEN YOU, RAIZŌ-DONO.
ドキ
TH-THUMP

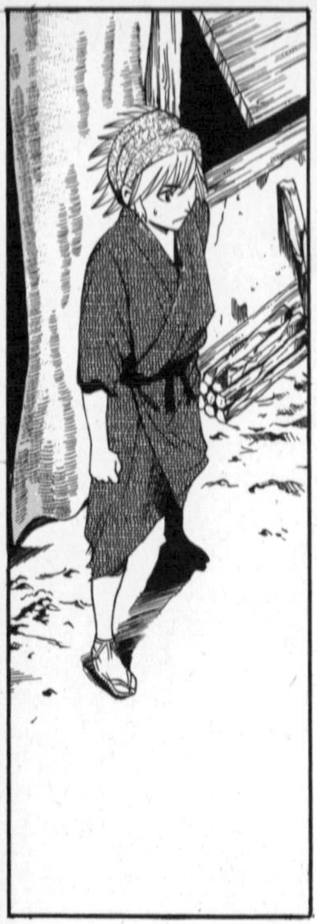

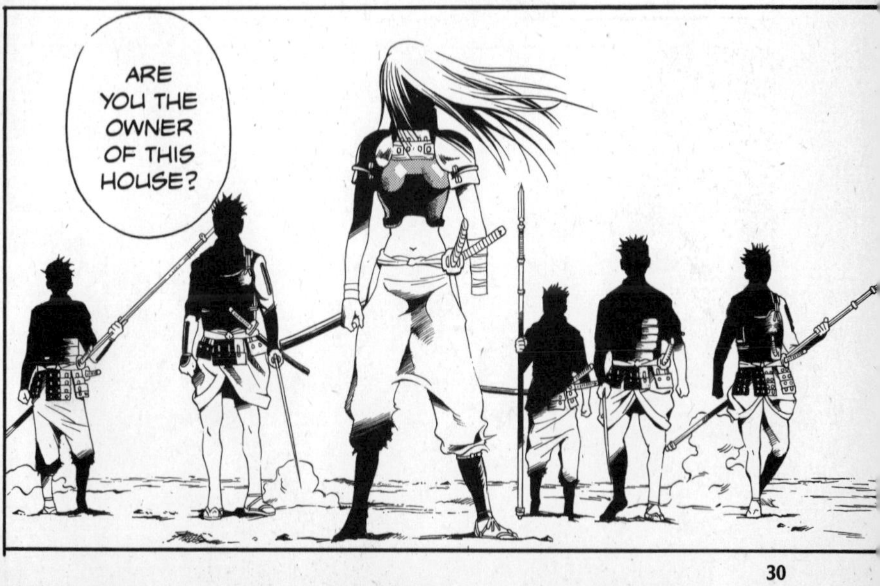
ARE YOU THE OWNER OF THIS HOUSE?

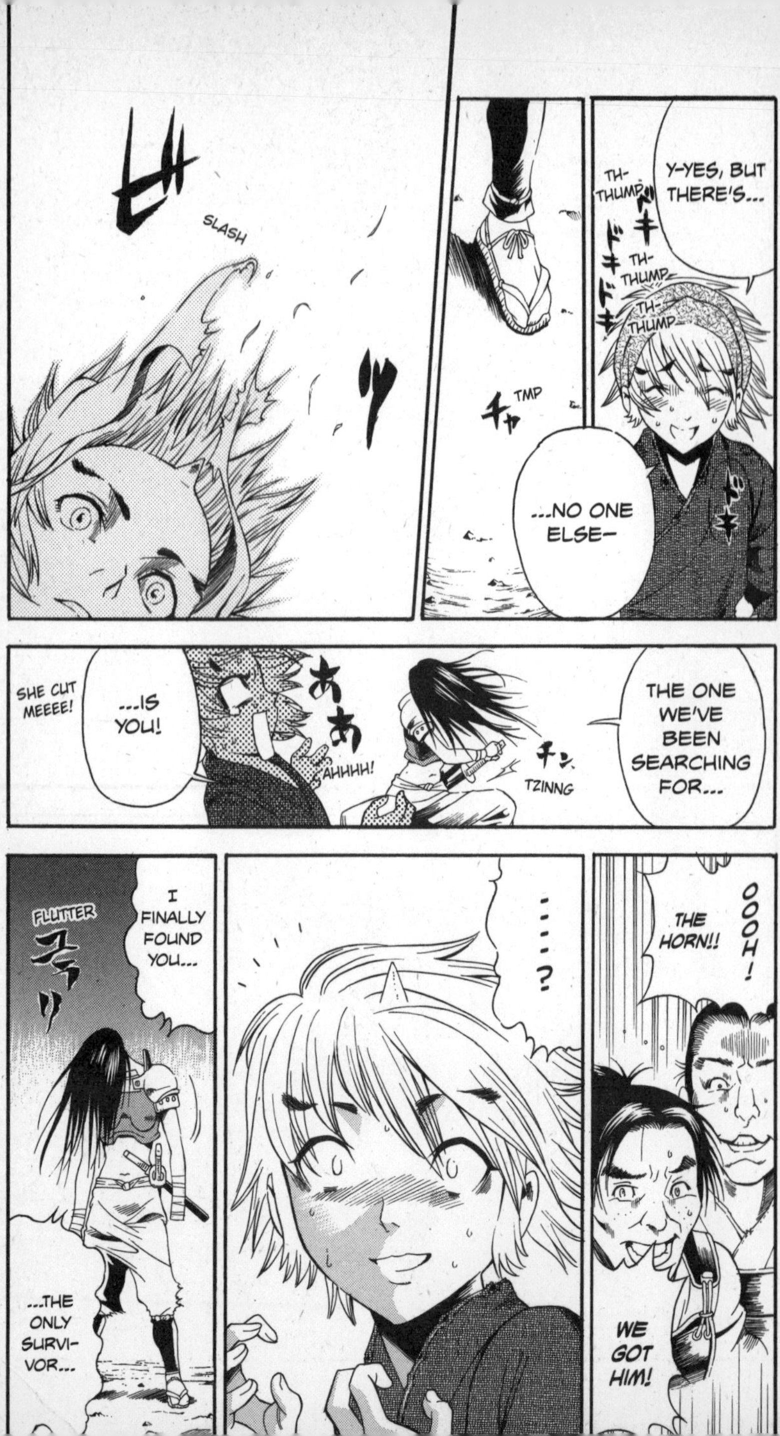
Y-YES, BUT THERE'S...
TH-THUMP
TH-THUMP
TH-THUMP
TMP
...NO ONE ELSE—
SLASH
THE ONE WE'VE BEEN SEARCHING FOR...
TZINNG
AHHHH!
...IS YOU!
SHE CUT MEEEE!
OOOH!
THE HORN!!
WE GOT HIM!
.....?
I FINALLY FOUND YOU...
FLUTTER
...THE ONLY SURVIVOR...

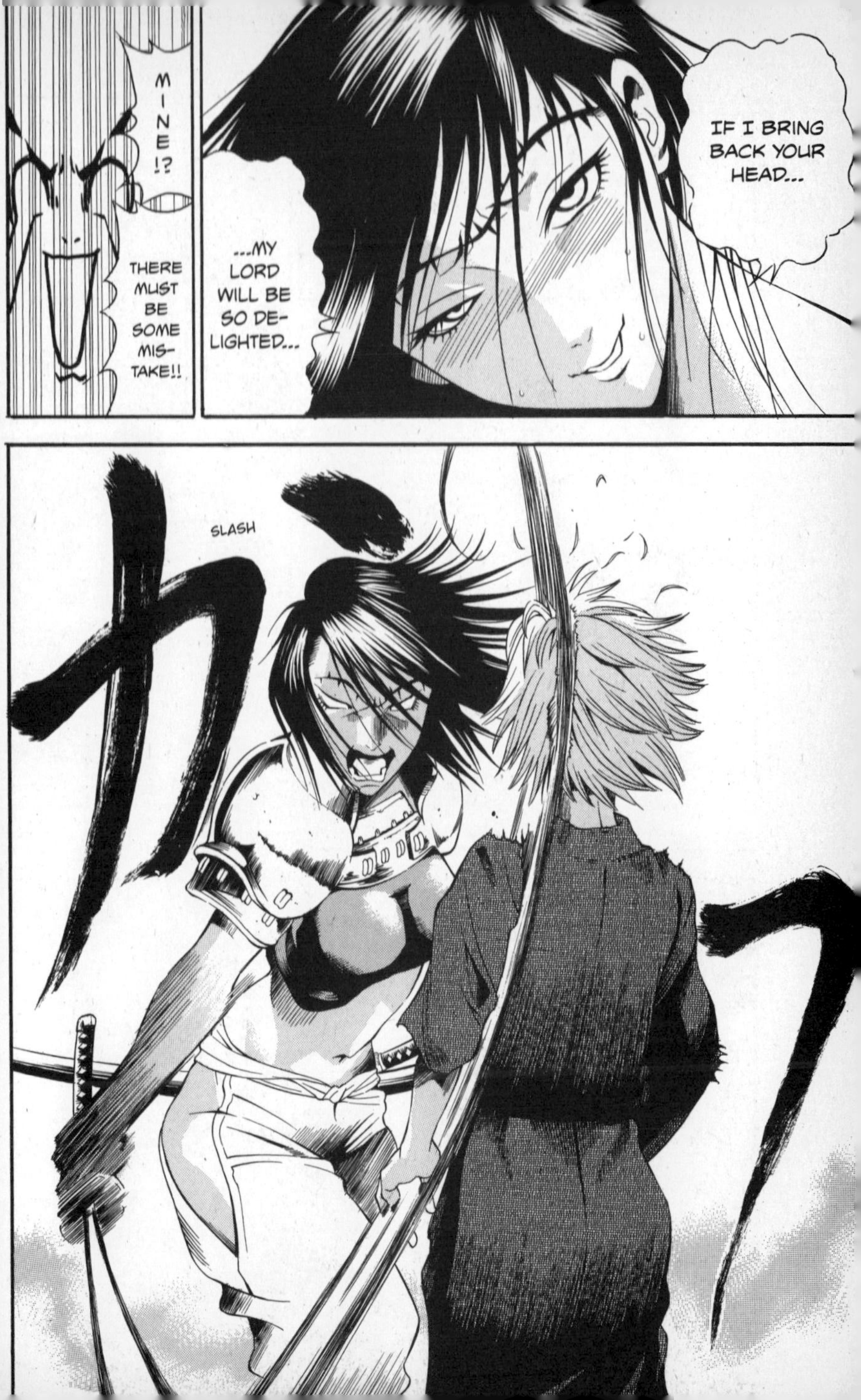
IF I BRING BACK YOUR HEAD...
...MY LORD WILL BE SO DE-LIGHTED...
MINE!?
THERE MUST BE SOME MIS-TAKE!!
SLASH

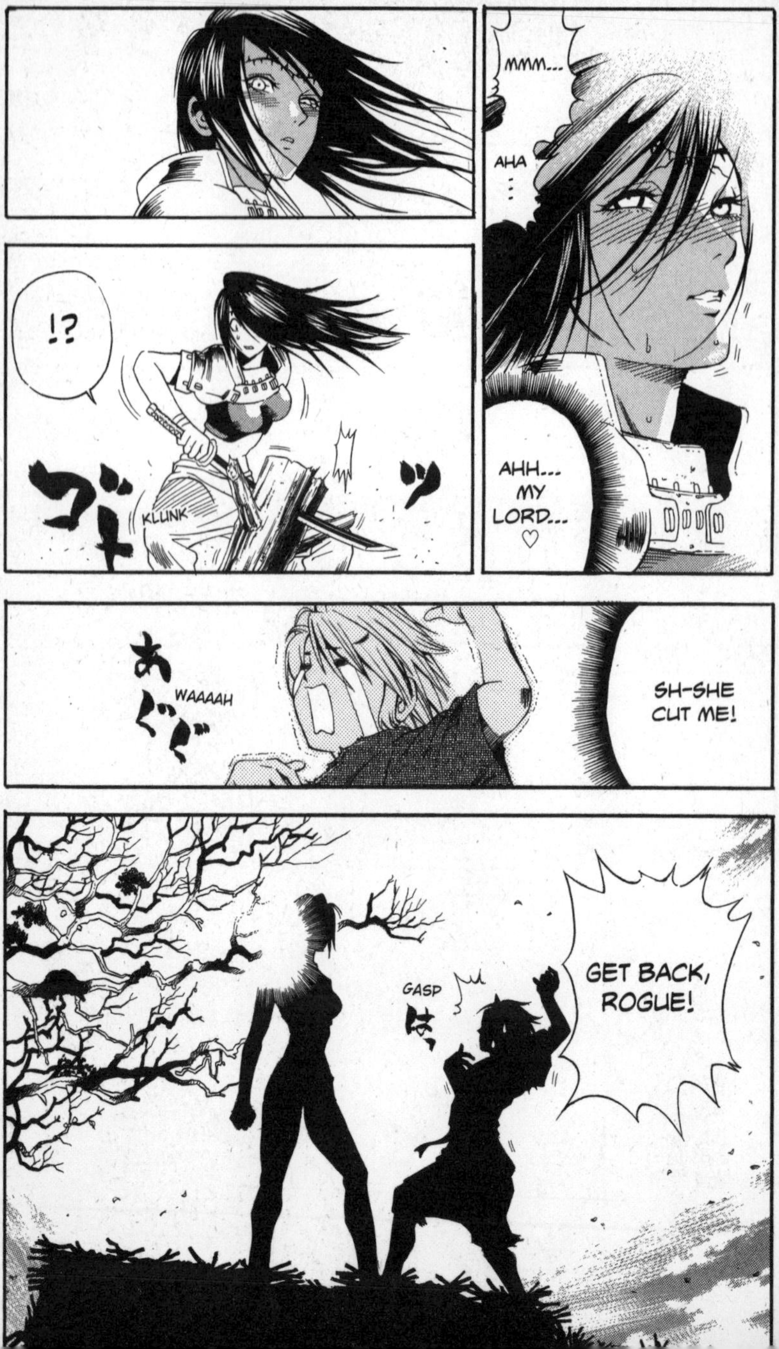
MMM...
AHA...
AHH... MY LORD... ♡
!?
ゴキッ
KLUNK
SH-SHE CUT ME!
あぐぐ
WAAAAH
GET BACK, ROGUE!
GASP
はっ

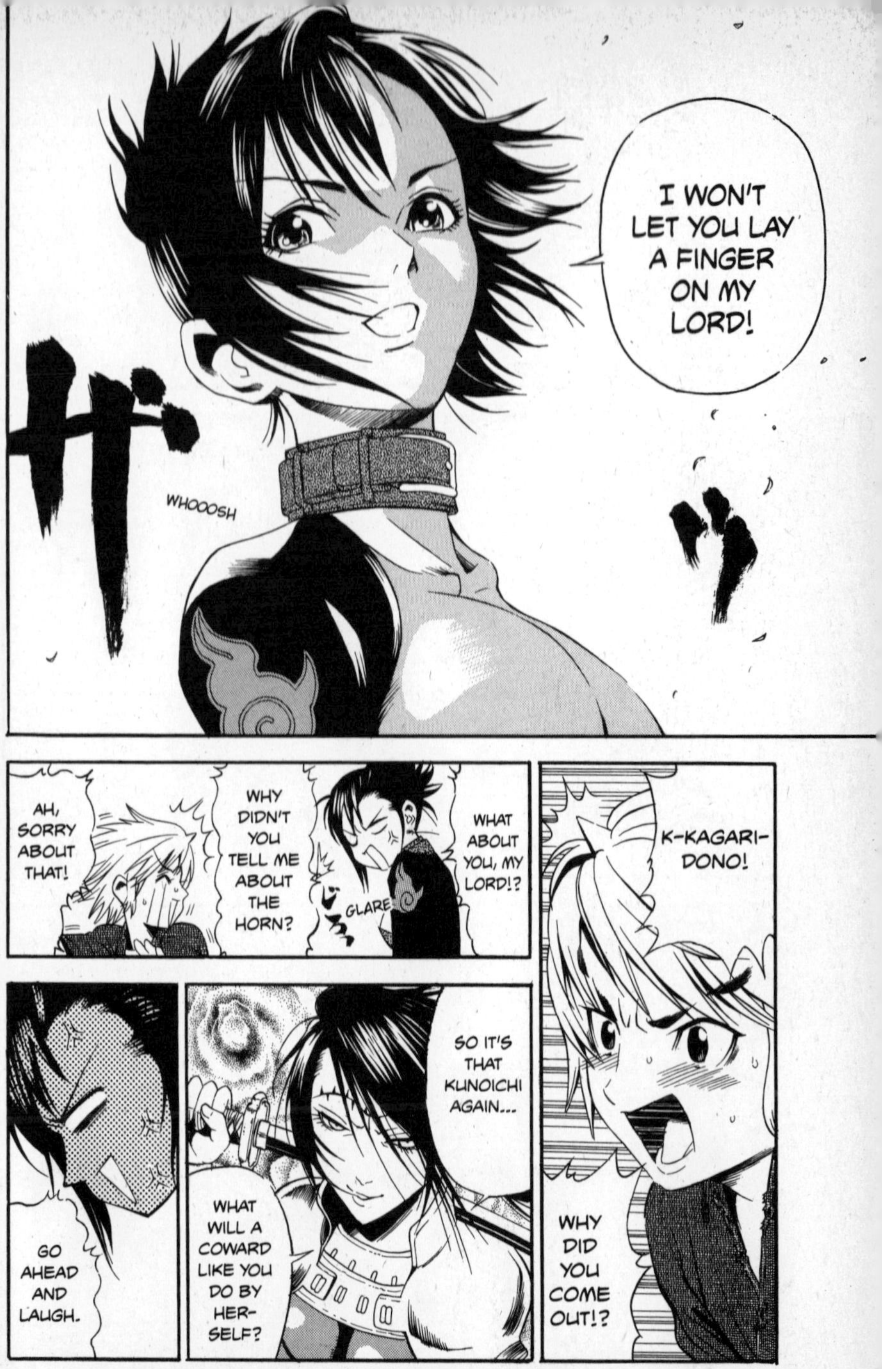
I WON'T LET YOU LAY A FINGER ON MY LORD!
WHOOOSH
K-KAGARI-DONO!
WHY DID YOU COME OUT!?
WHAT ABOUT YOU, MY LORD!?
GLARE
WHY DIDN'T YOU TELL ME ABOUT THE HORN?
AH, SORRY ABOUT THAT!
SO IT'S THAT KUNOICHI AGAIN...
WHAT WILL A COWARD LIKE YOU DO BY HER-SELF?
GO AHEAD AND LAUGH.

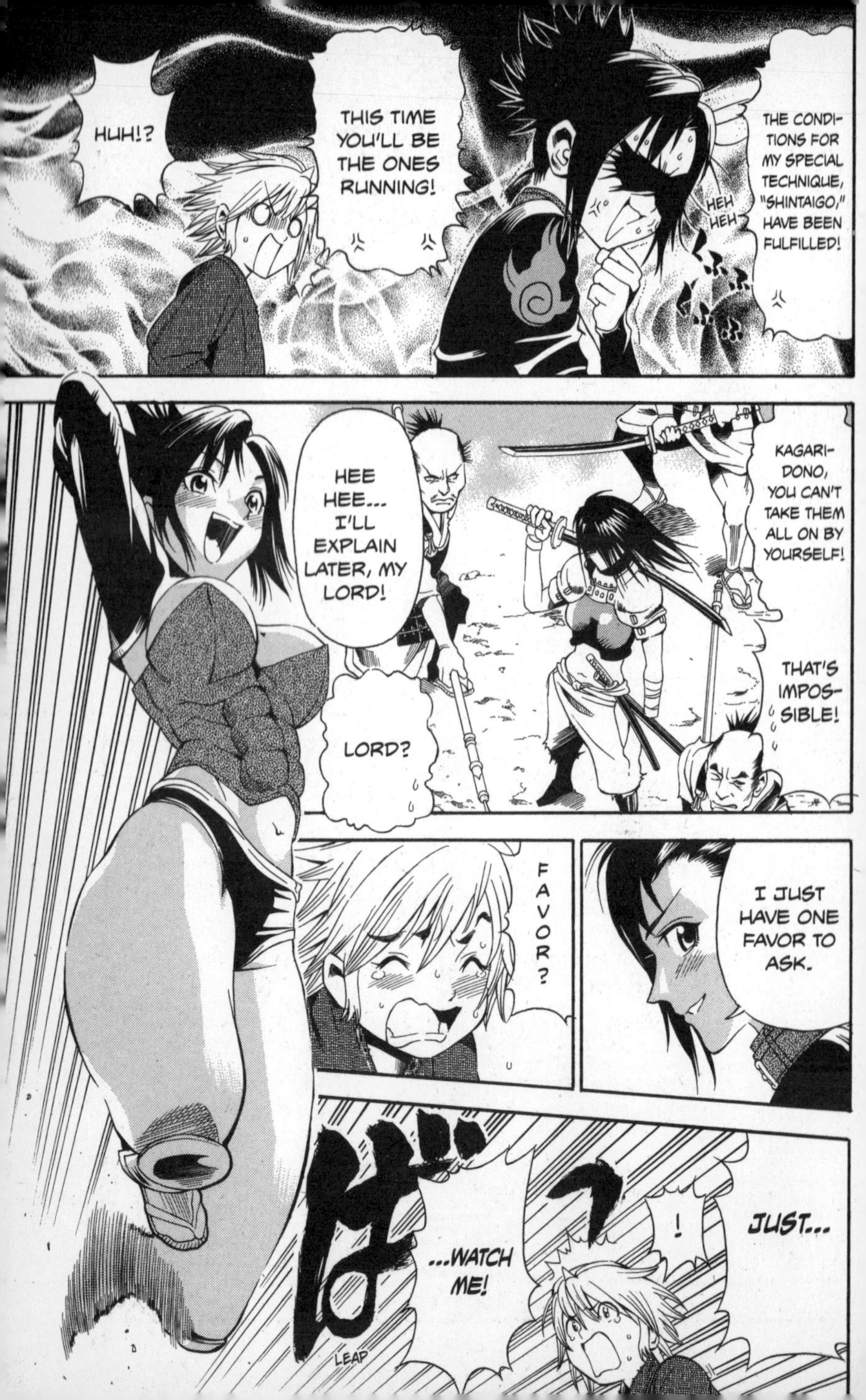
THE CONDITIONS FOR MY SPECIAL TECHNIQUE, "SHINTAIGO," HAVE BEEN FULFILLED!
HEH HEH
THIS TIME YOU'LL BE THE ONES RUNNING!
HUH!?
KAGARI-DONO, YOU CAN'T TAKE THEM ALL ON BY YOURSELF!
THAT'S IMPOSSIBLE!
HEE HEE... I'LL EXPLAIN LATER, MY LORD!
LORD?
I JUST HAVE ONE FAVOR TO ASK.
FAVOR?
JUST...
!
...WATCH ME!
LEAP

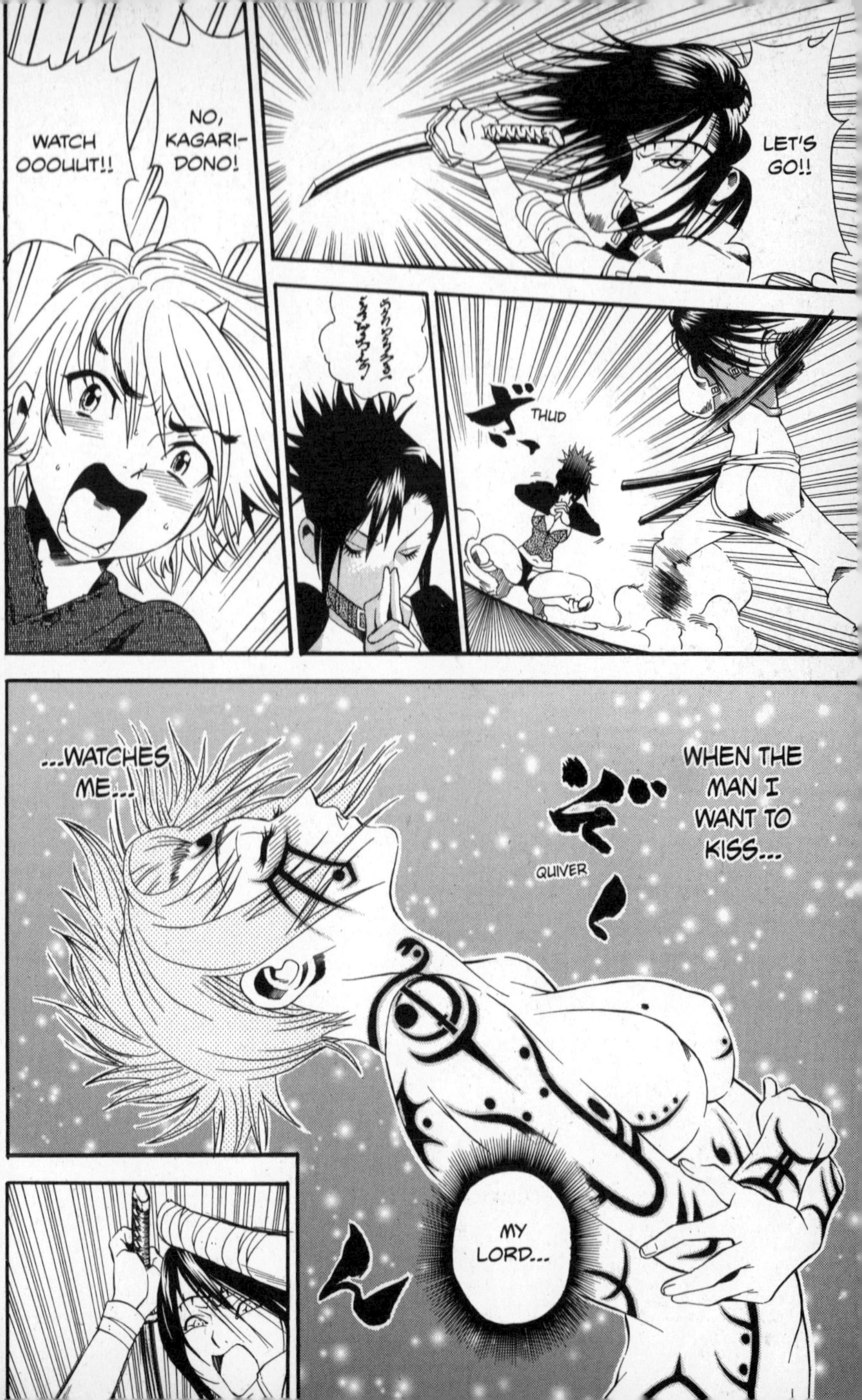
LET'S GO!!
THUD
NO, KAGARI-DONO!
WATCH OOOUUT!!
WHEN THE MAN I WANT TO KISS...
QUIVER
...WATCHES ME...
MY LORD...

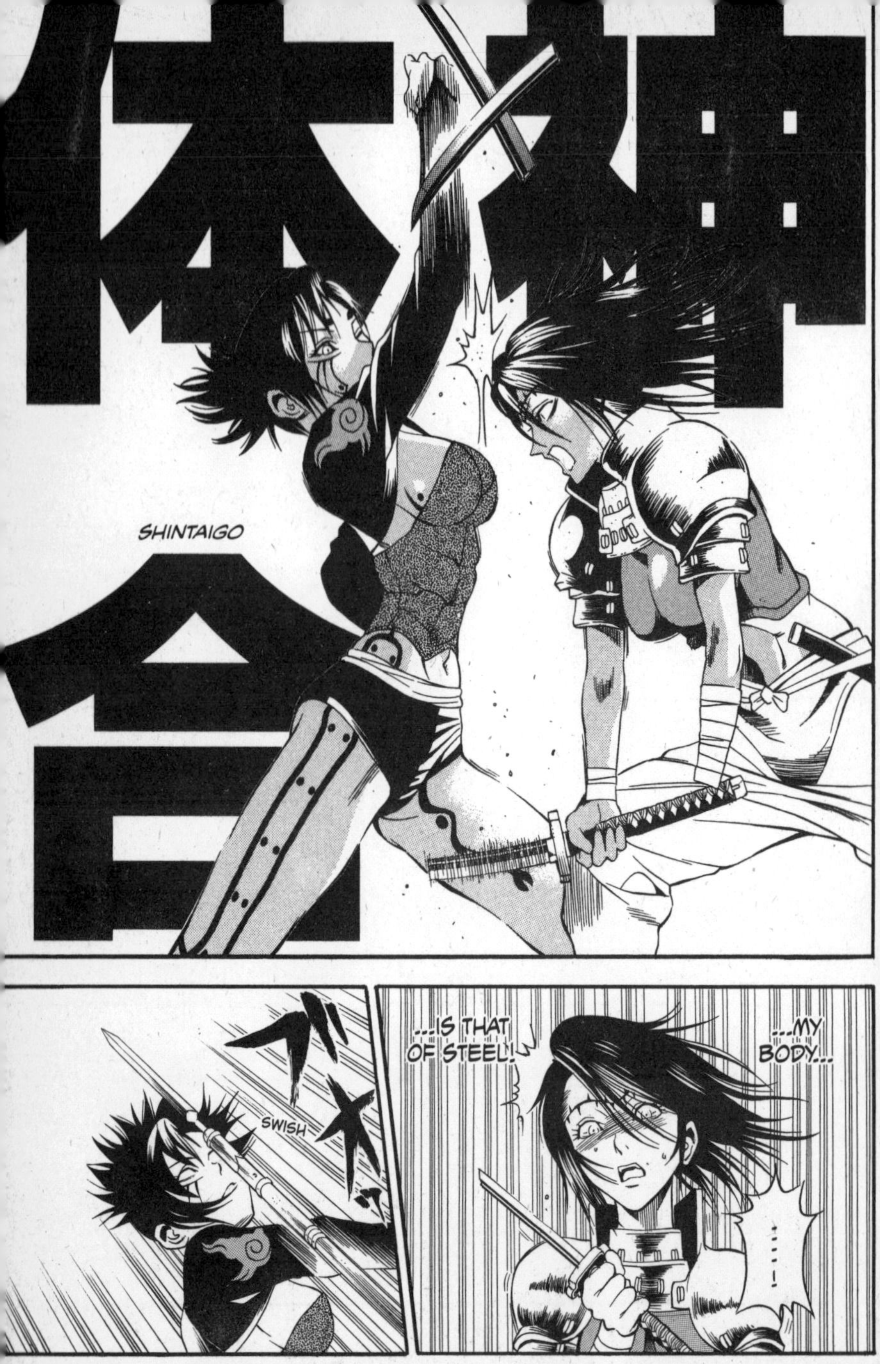
神体合
SHINTAIGO
...MY BODY...
...IS THAT OF STEEL!
...!
SWISH

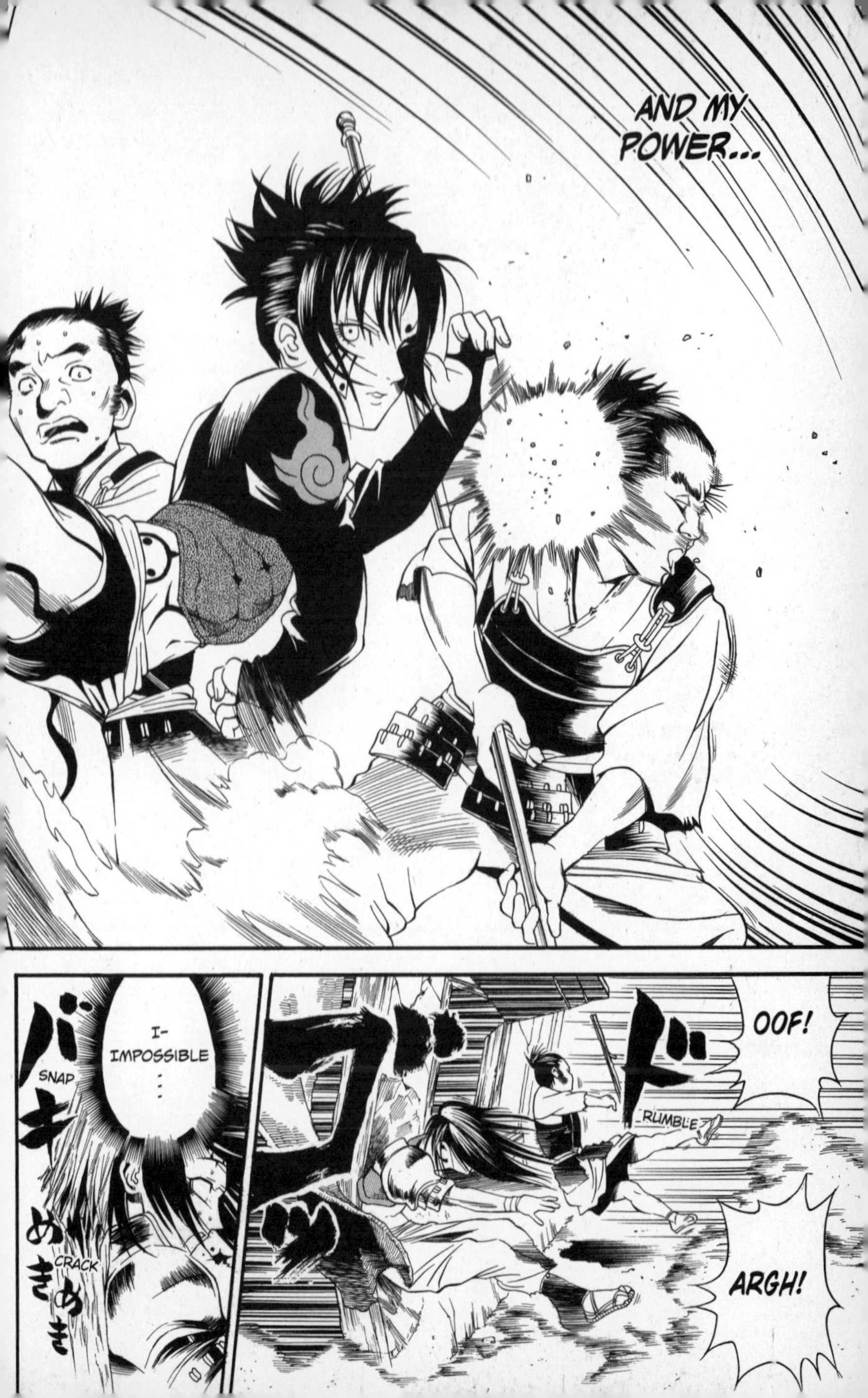
AND MY POWER...
ド
OOF!
RUMBLE
ARGH!
I- IMPOSSIBLE ...
バキ
SNAP
めきめき
CRACK

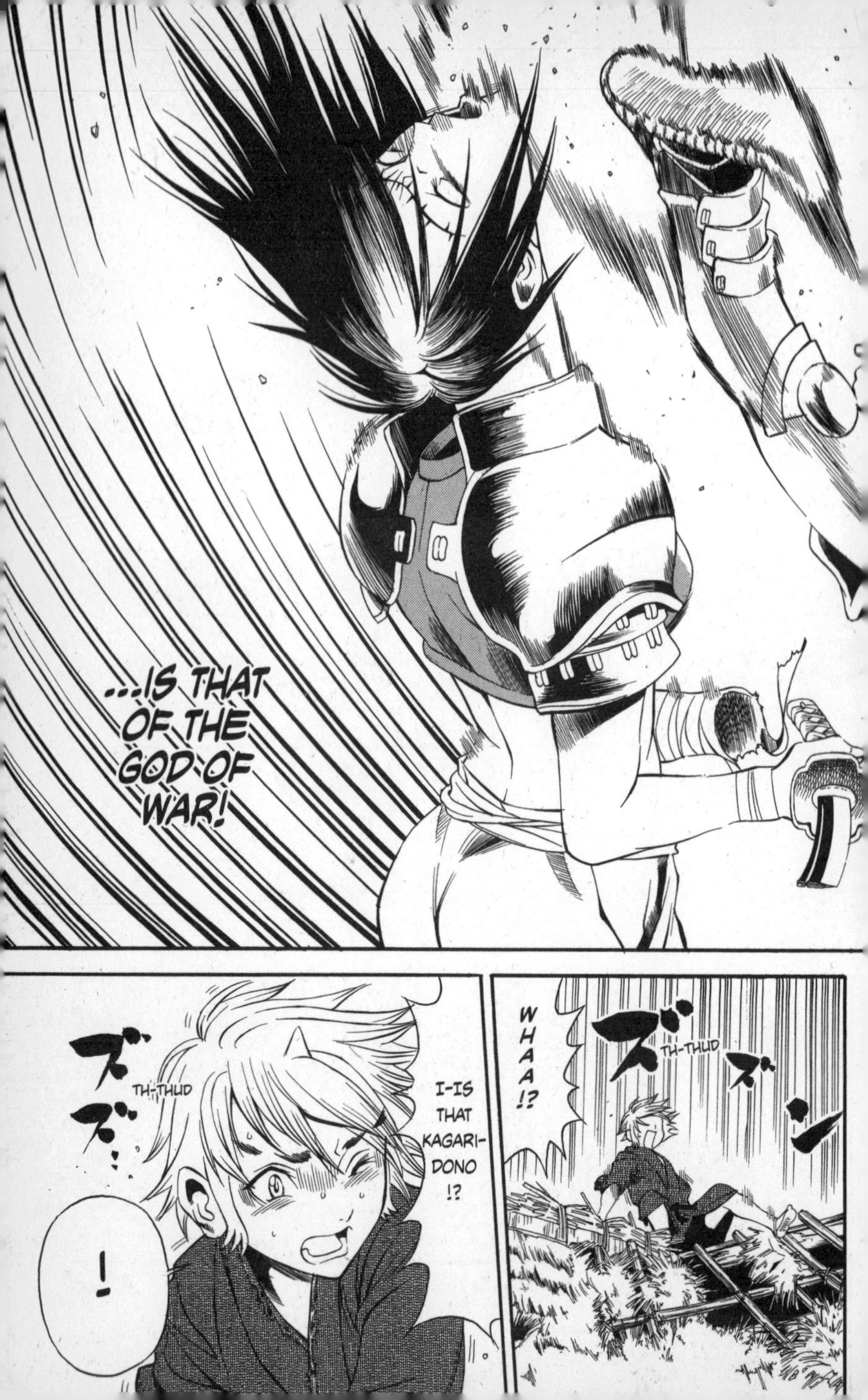
...IS THAT OF THE GOD OF WAR!
WHAAA!?
TH-THUD
I-IS THAT KAGARI-DONO !?
TH-THUD
!

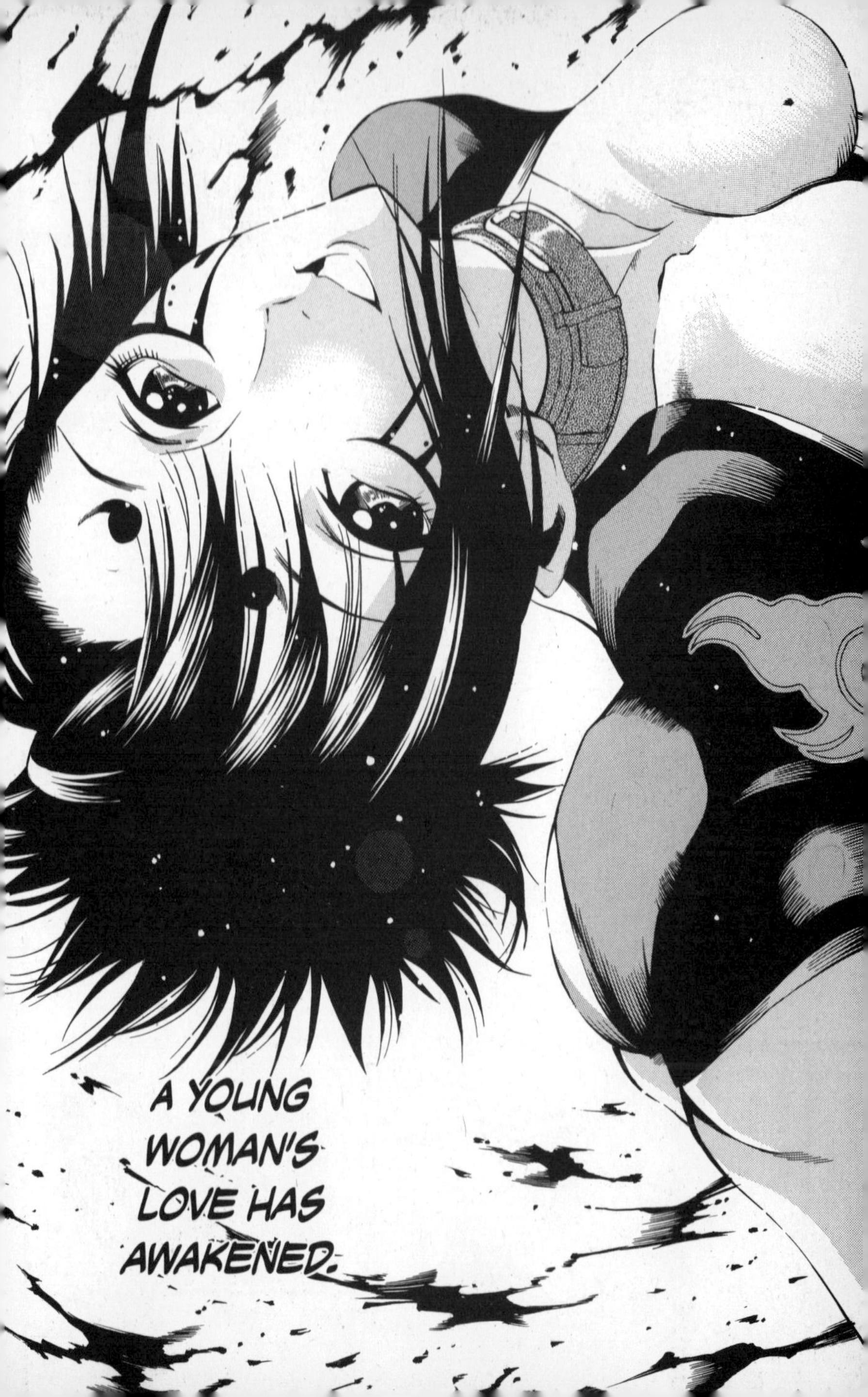
A YOUNG WOMAN'S LOVE HAS AWAKENED.

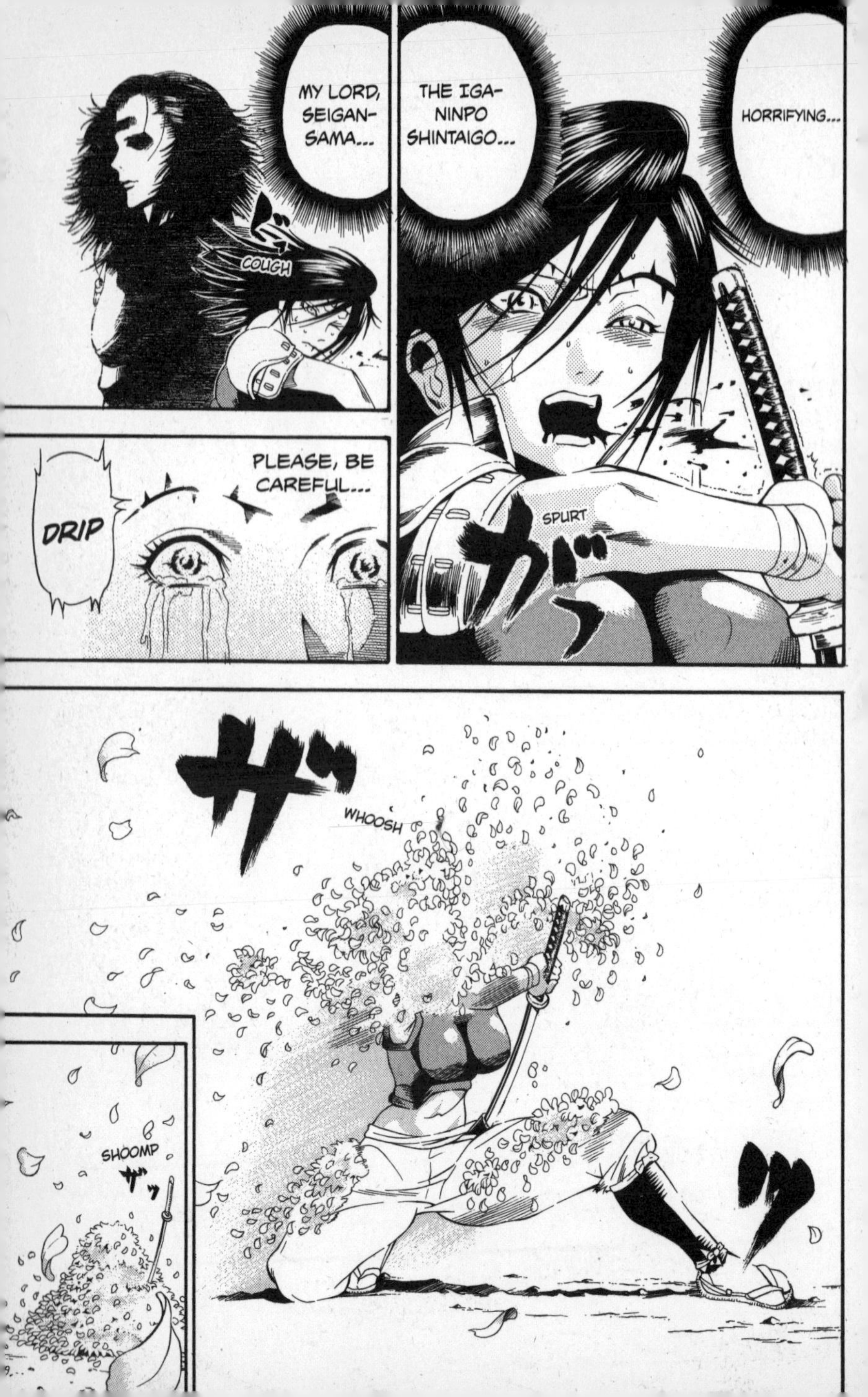
HORRIFYING...
THE IGA-NINPO SHINTAIGO...
SPURT
MY LORD, SEIGAN-SAMA...
COUGH
PLEASE, BE CAREFUL...
DRIP
WHOOSH
SHOOMP

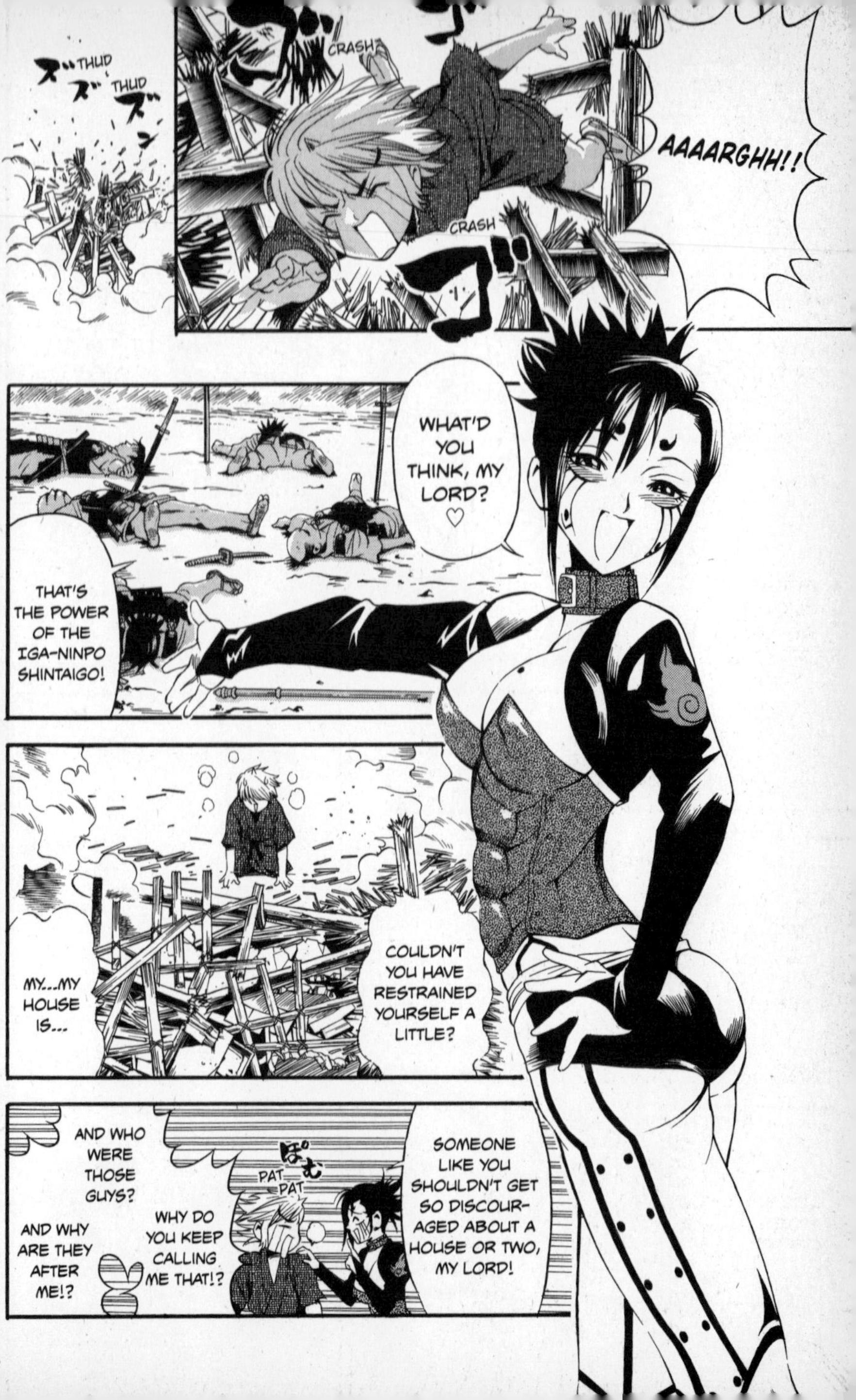
AAAARGHH!!
CRASH
CRASH
THUD
THUD
WHAT'D YOU THINK, MY LORD? ♡
THAT'S THE POWER OF THE IGA-NINPO SHINTAIGO!
COULDN'T YOU HAVE RESTRAINED YOURSELF A LITTLE?
MY...MY HOUSE IS...
SOMEONE LIKE YOU SHOULDN'T GET SO DISCOURAGED ABOUT A HOUSE OR TWO, MY LORD!
PAT PAT
AND WHO WERE THOSE GUYS?
WHY DO YOU KEEP CALLING ME THAT!?
AND WHY ARE THEY AFTER ME!?

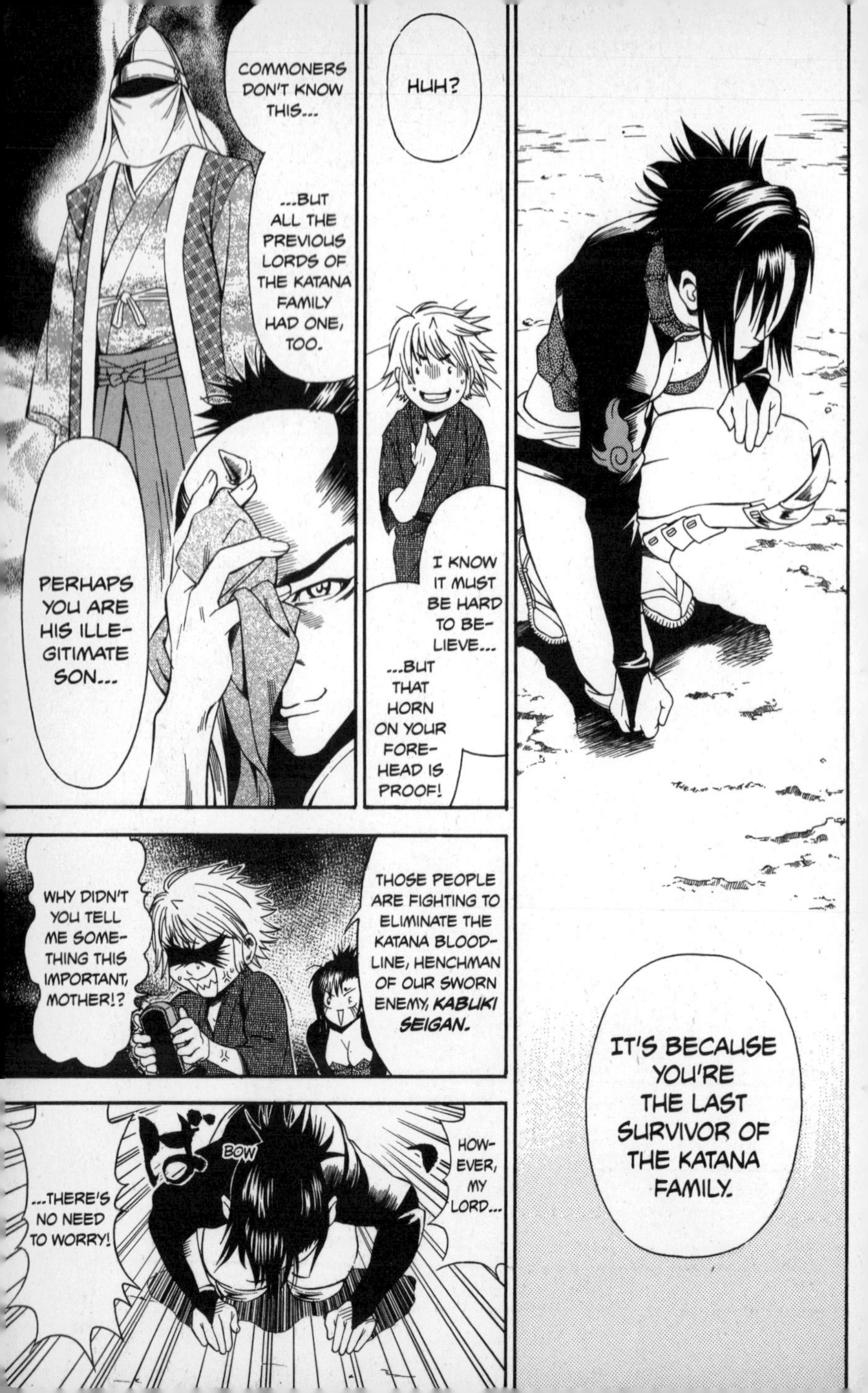
IT'S BECAUSE YOU'RE THE LAST SURVIVOR OF THE KATANA FAMILY.
HUH?
I KNOW IT MUST BE HARD TO BE-LIEVE...
...BUT THAT HORN ON YOUR FORE-HEAD IS PROOF!
COMMONERS DON'T KNOW THIS...
...BUT ALL THE PREVIOUS LORDS OF THE KATANA FAMILY HAD ONE, TOO.
PERHAPS YOU ARE HIS ILLE-GITIMATE SON...
THOSE PEOPLE ARE FIGHTING TO ELIMINATE THE KATANA BLOOD-LINE, HENCHMAN OF OUR SWORN ENEMY, ***KABUKI SEIGAN.***
WHY DIDN'T YOU TELL ME SOME-THING THIS IMPORTANT, MOTHER!?
HOW-EVER, MY LORD...
BOW
...THERE'S NO NEED TO WORRY!

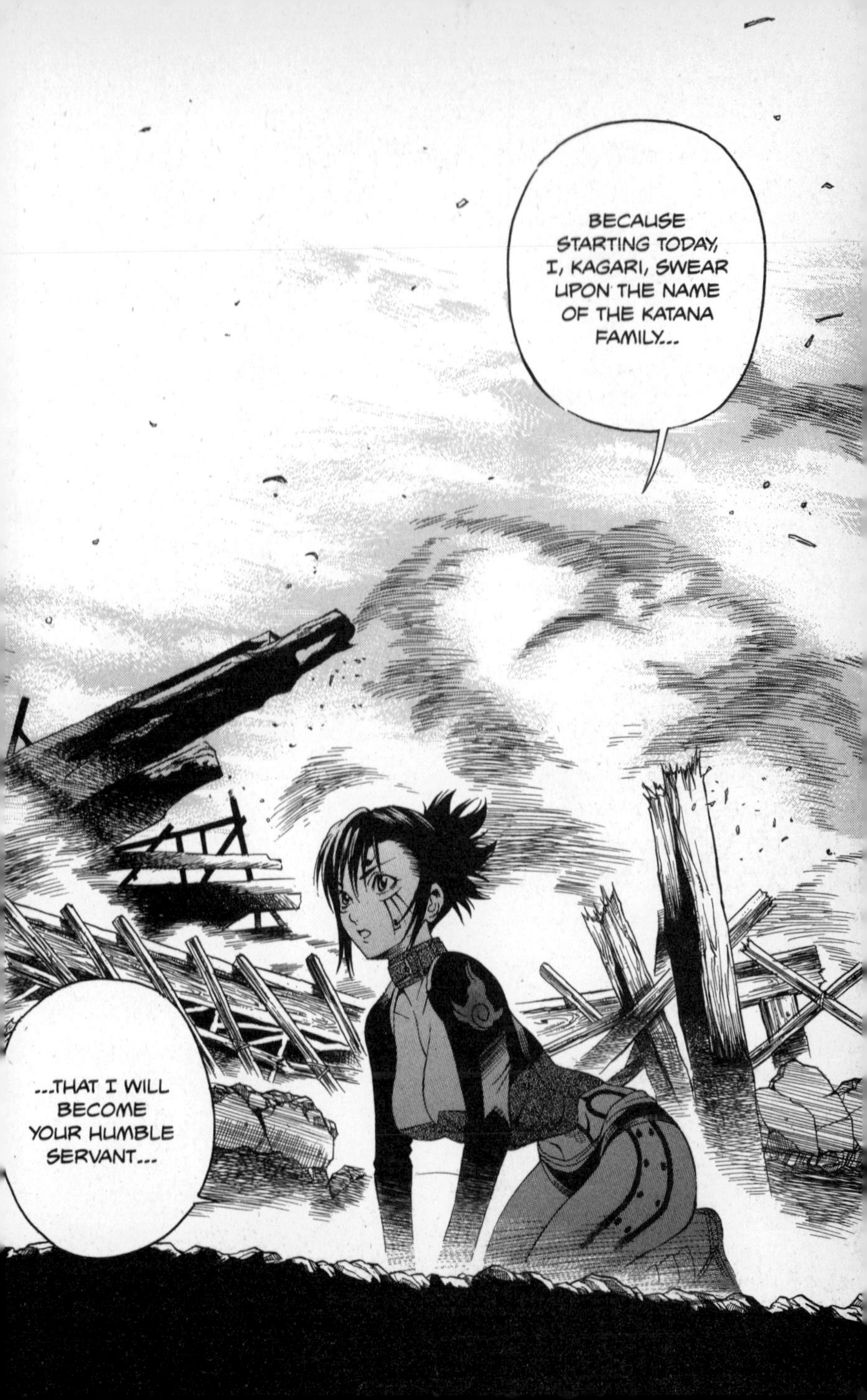
BECAUSE STARTING TODAY, I, KAGARI, SWEAR UPON THE NAME OF THE KATANA FAMILY...
...THAT I WILL BECOME YOUR HUMBLE SERVANT...

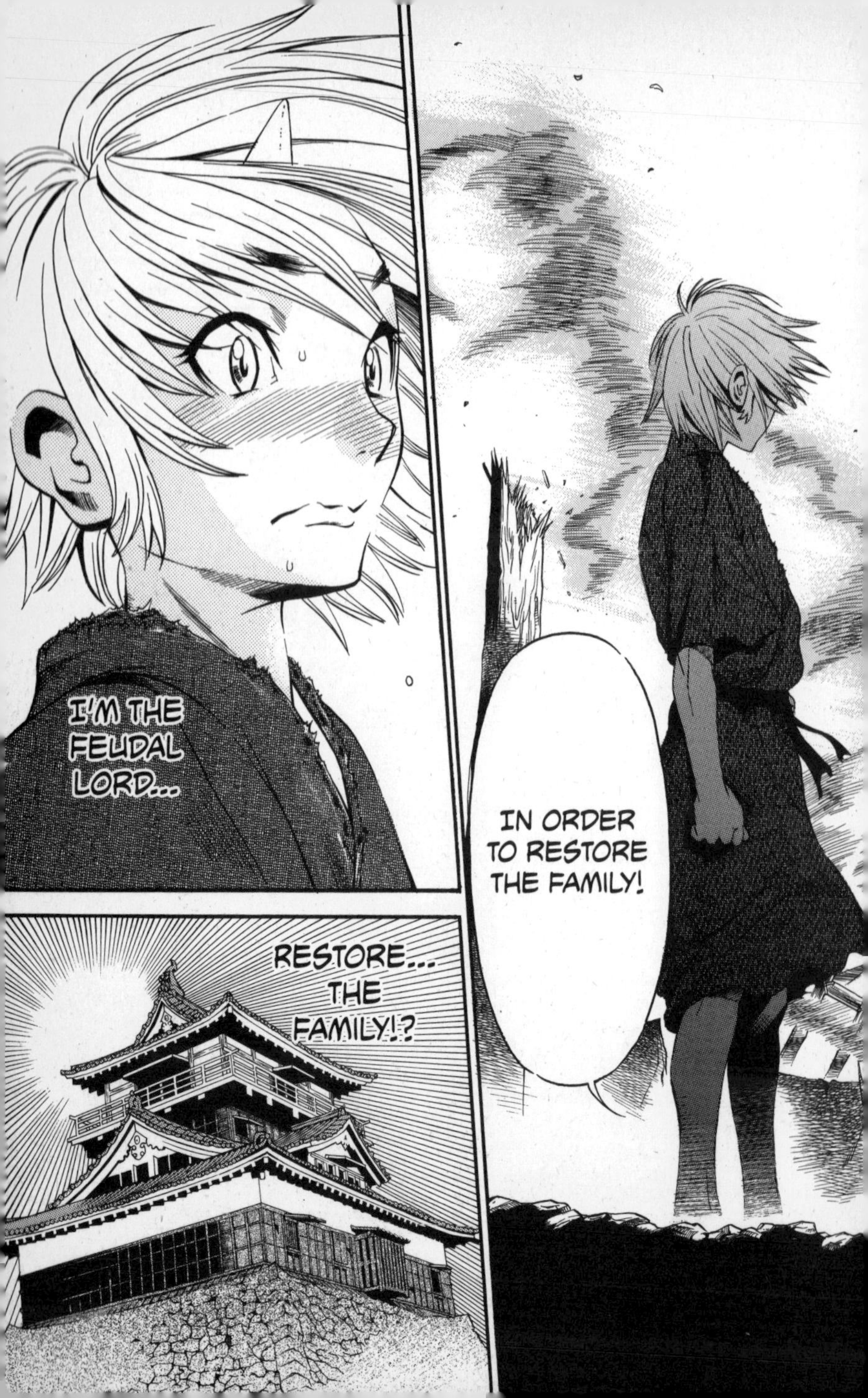
IN ORDER TO RESTORE THE FAMILY!
I'M THE FEUDAL LORD...
RESTORE... THE FAMILY!?

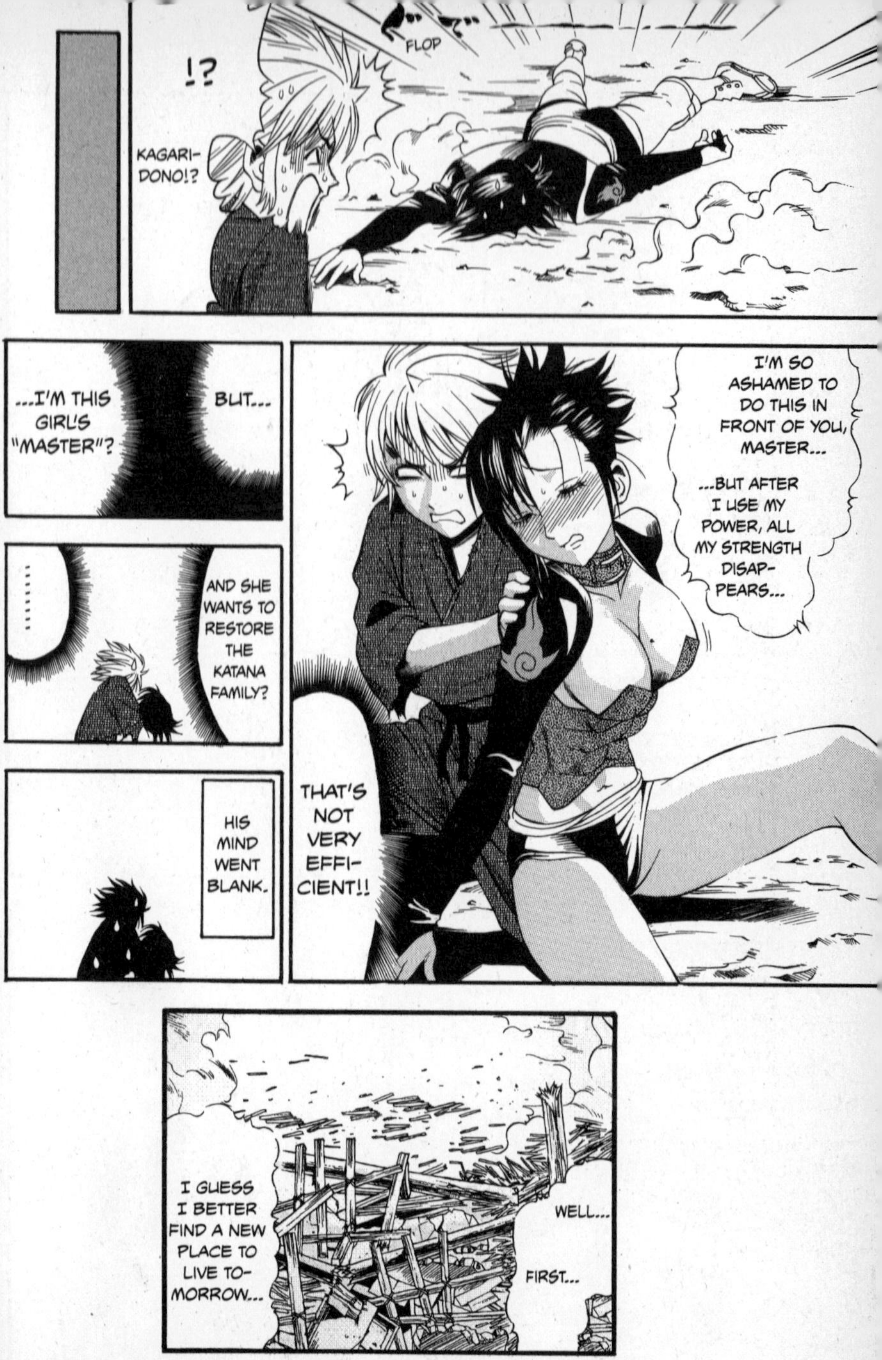
FLOP
!?
KAGARI-DONO!?
I'M SO ASHAMED TO DO THIS IN FRONT OF YOU, MASTER...
...BUT AFTER I USE MY POWER, ALL MY STRENGTH DISAP-PEARS...
THAT'S NOT VERY EFFI-CIENT!!
BUT...
...I'M THIS GIRL'S "MASTER"?
AND SHE WANTS TO RESTORE THE KATANA FAMILY?
......
HIS MIND WENT BLANK.
WELL...
FIRST...
I GUESS I BETTER FIND A NEW PLACE TO LIVE TO-MORROW...

Encounter Rebellion / End

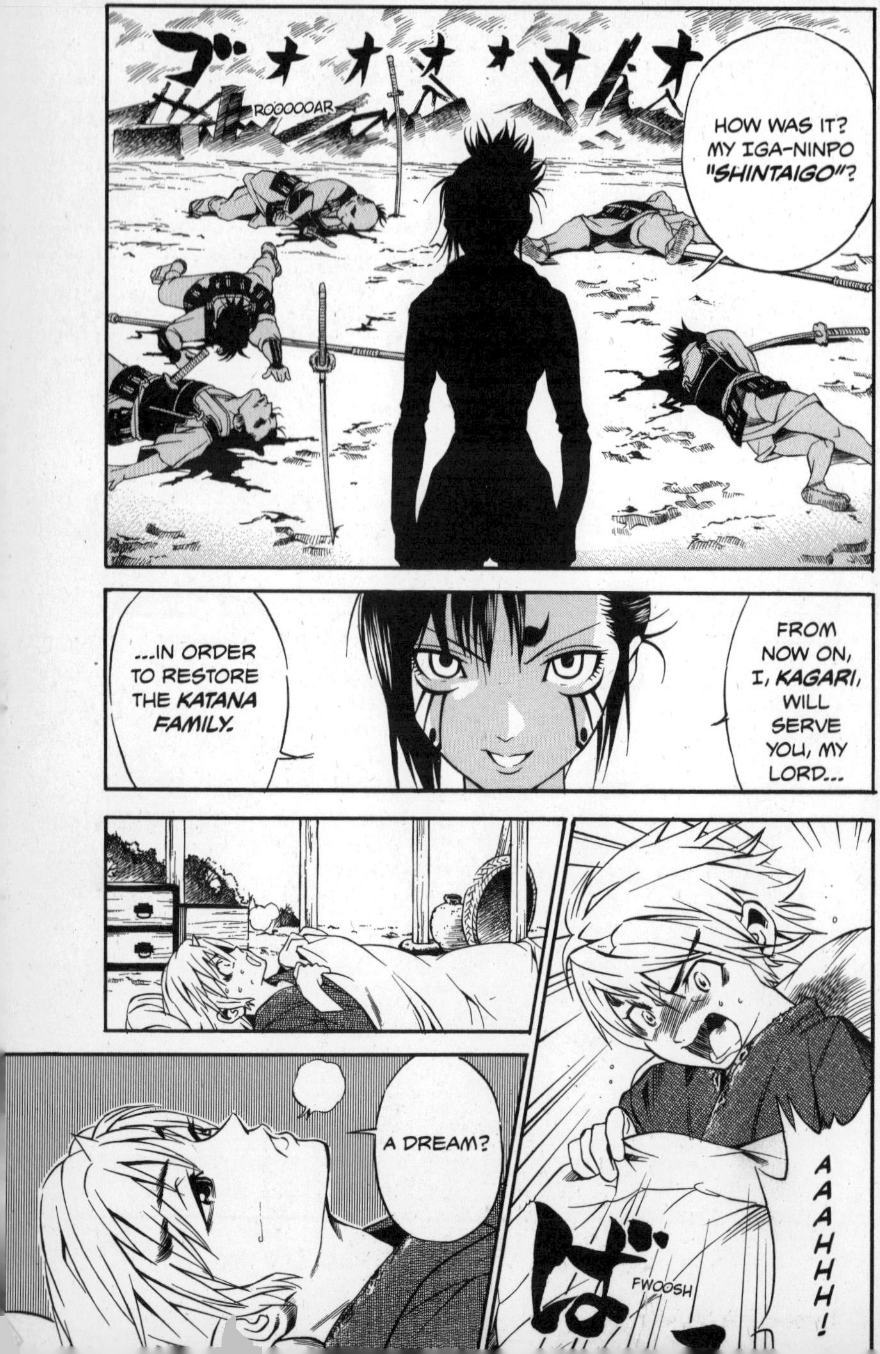
ROOOOOAR
HOW WAS IT? MY IGA-NINPO "SHINTAIGO"?
FROM NOW ON, I, KAGARI, WILL SERVE YOU, MY LORD...
...IN ORDER TO RESTORE THE KATANA FAMILY.
AAAAHHH!
FWOOSH
A DREAM?

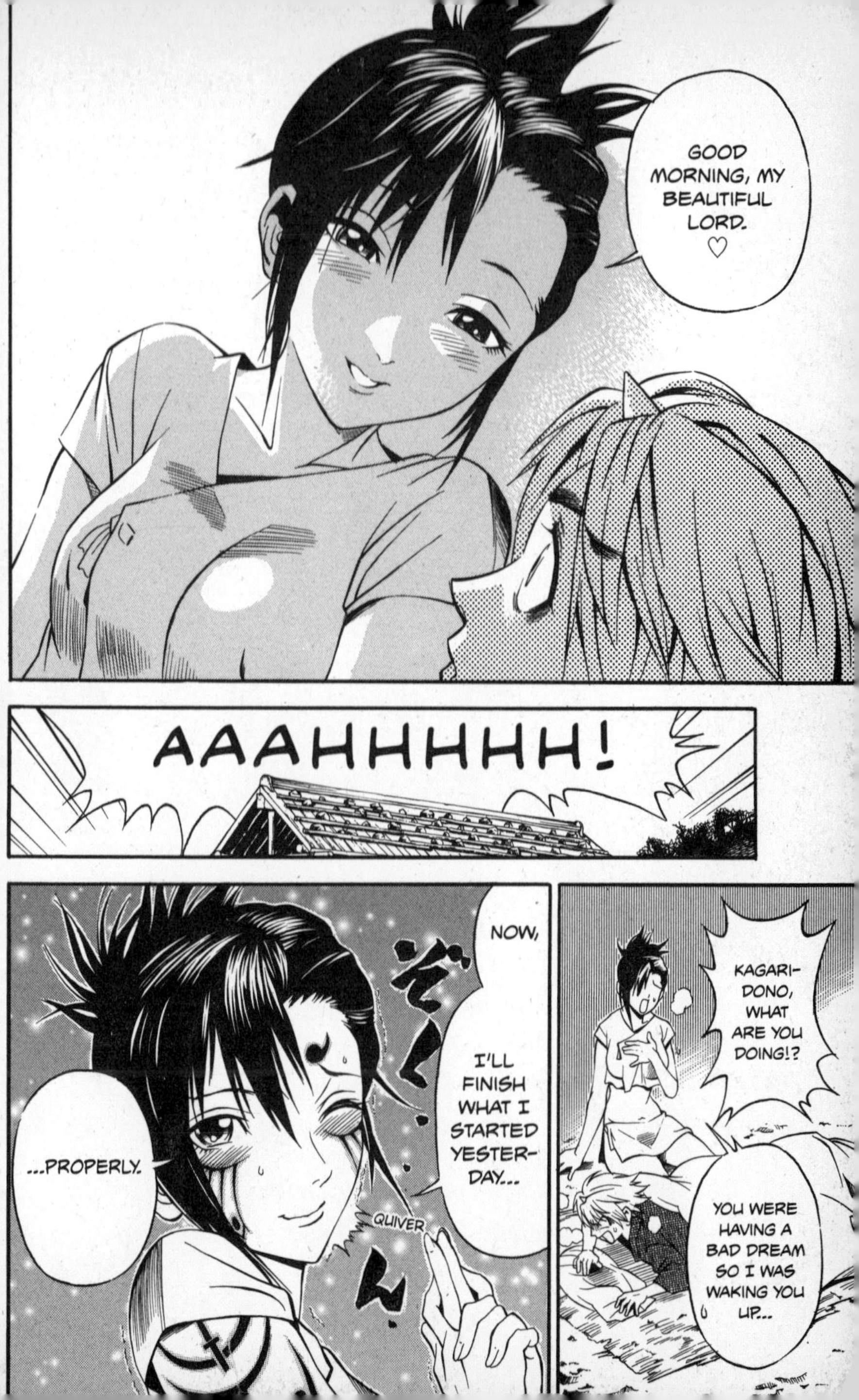
GOOD MORNING, MY BEAUTIFUL LORD. ♡
AAAHHHHH!
KAGARI-DONO, WHAT ARE YOU DOING!?
YOU WERE HAVING A BAD DREAM SO I WAS WAKING YOU UP...
NOW, I'LL FINISH WHAT I STARTED YESTER-DAY...
...PROPERLY.
QUIVER

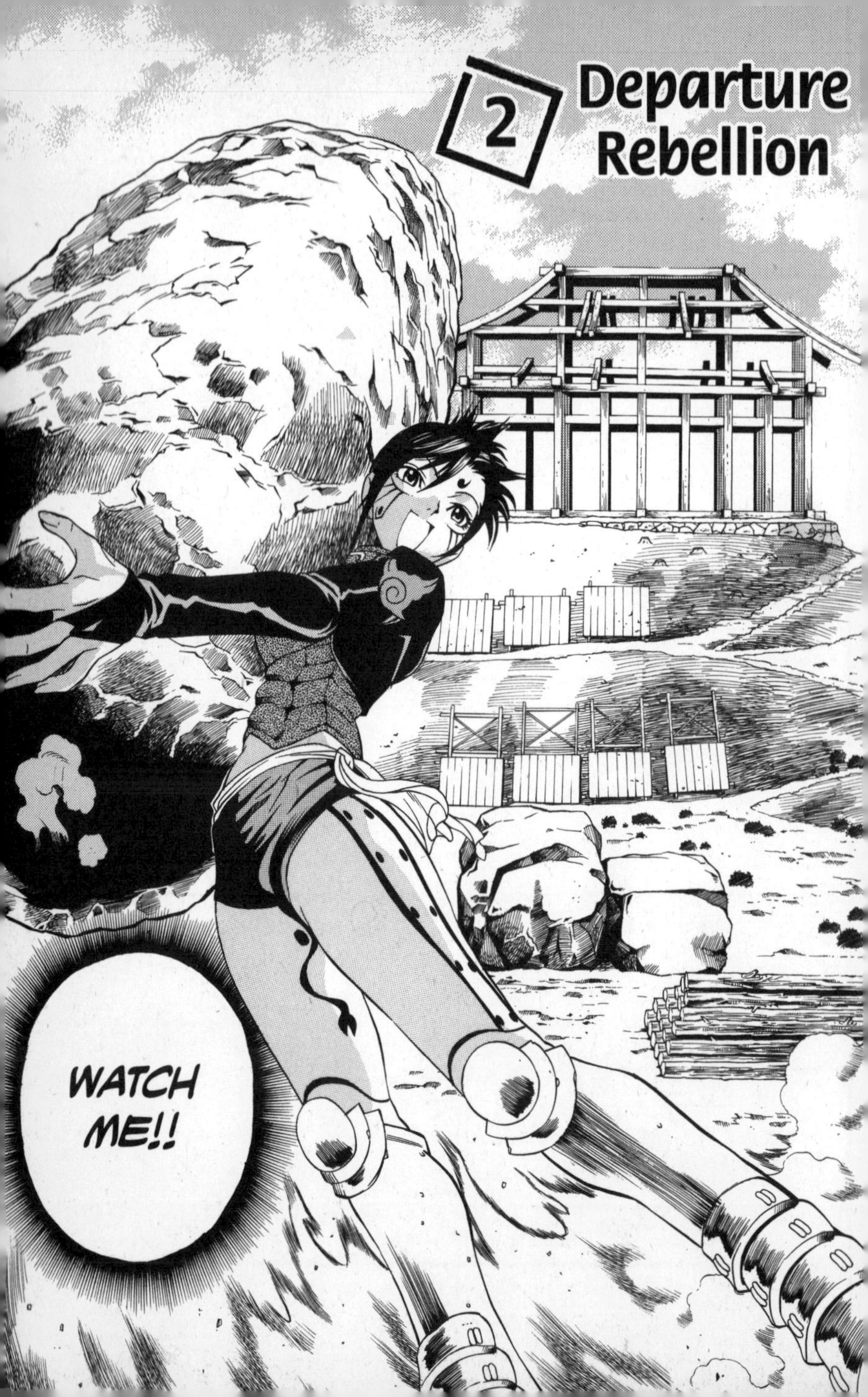
2
Departure Rebellion
WATCH ME!!

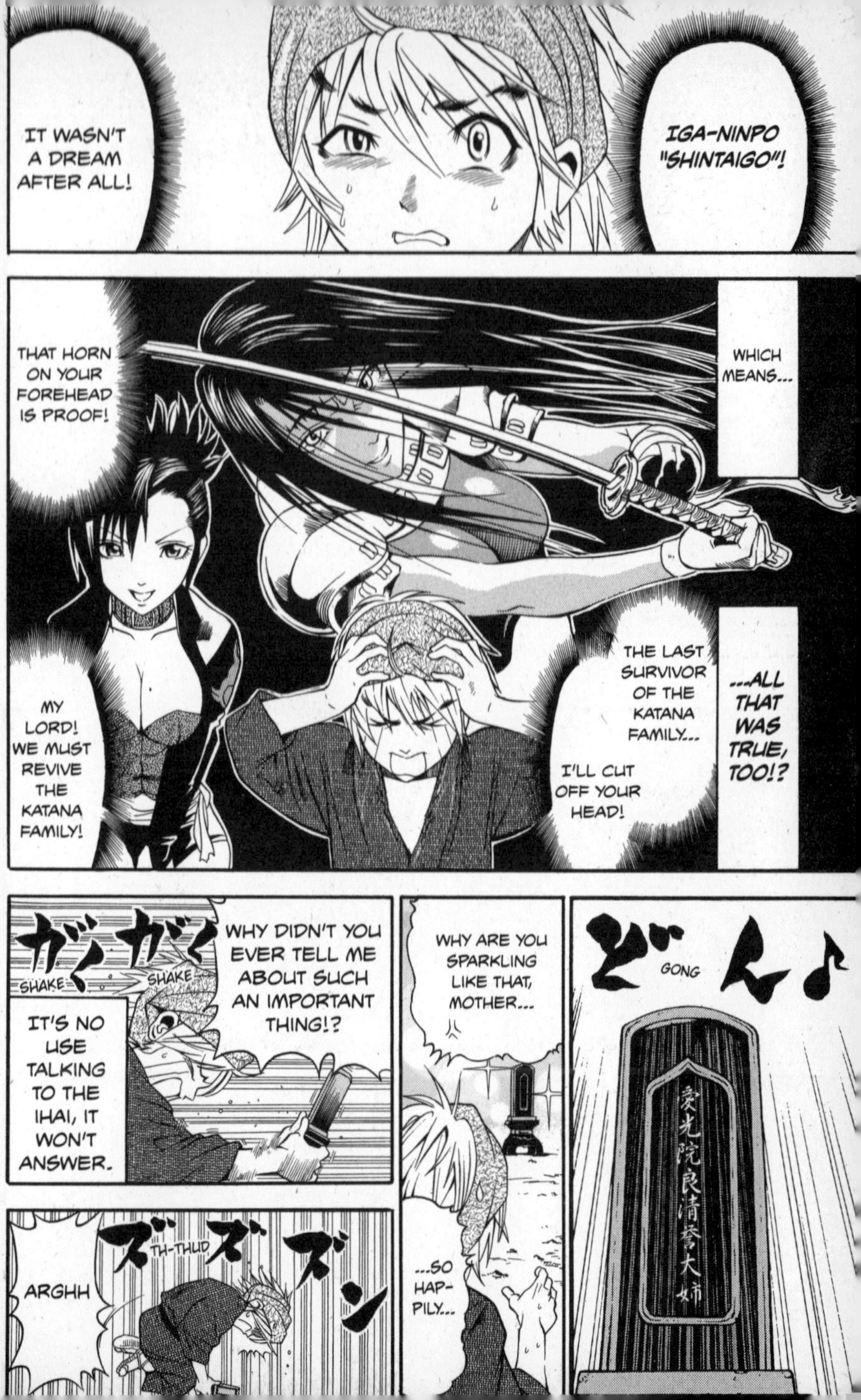
IGA-NINPO "SHINTAIGO"!
IT WASN'T A DREAM AFTER ALL!
WHICH MEANS...
...ALL THAT WAS TRUE, TOO!?
THAT HORN ON YOUR FOREHEAD IS PROOF!
THE LAST SURVIVOR OF THE KATANA FAMILY...
I'LL CUT OFF YOUR HEAD!
MY LORD! WE MUST REVIVE THE KATANA FAMILY!
どん♪
GONG
愛光院良清誉大姉
WHY ARE YOU SPARKLING LIKE THAT, MOTHER...
...SO HAPPILY...
がくがく
SHAKE
SHAKE
WHY DIDN'T YOU EVER TELL ME ABOUT SUCH AN IMPORTANT THING!?
IT'S NO USE TALKING TO THE IHAI, IT WON'T ANSWER.
ズズン
TH-THUD
ARGHH

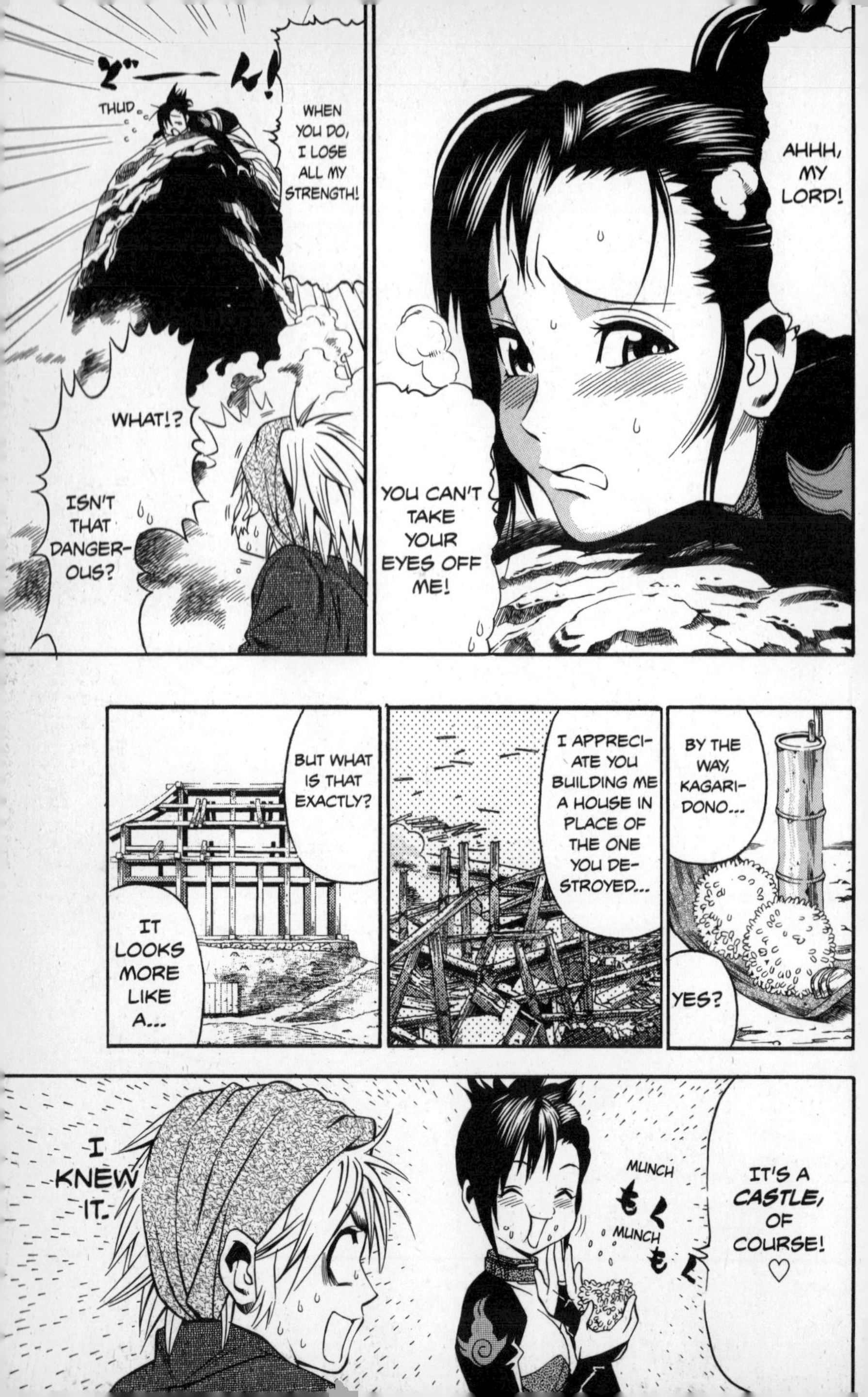
AHHH, MY LORD!
YOU CAN'T TAKE YOUR EYES OFF ME!
どーーん!
THUD
WHEN YOU DO, I LOSE ALL MY STRENGTH!
WHAT!?
ISN'T THAT DANGER-OUS?
BY THE WAY, KAGARI-DONO...
YES?
I APPRECI-ATE YOU BUILDING ME A HOUSE IN PLACE OF THE ONE YOU DE-STROYED...
BUT WHAT IS THAT EXACTLY?
IT LOOKS MORE LIKE A...
IT'S A *CASTLE,* OF COURSE! ♡
MUNCH もく
MUNCH もく
I KNEW IT.

KAGARI'S RESTORATION PLAN

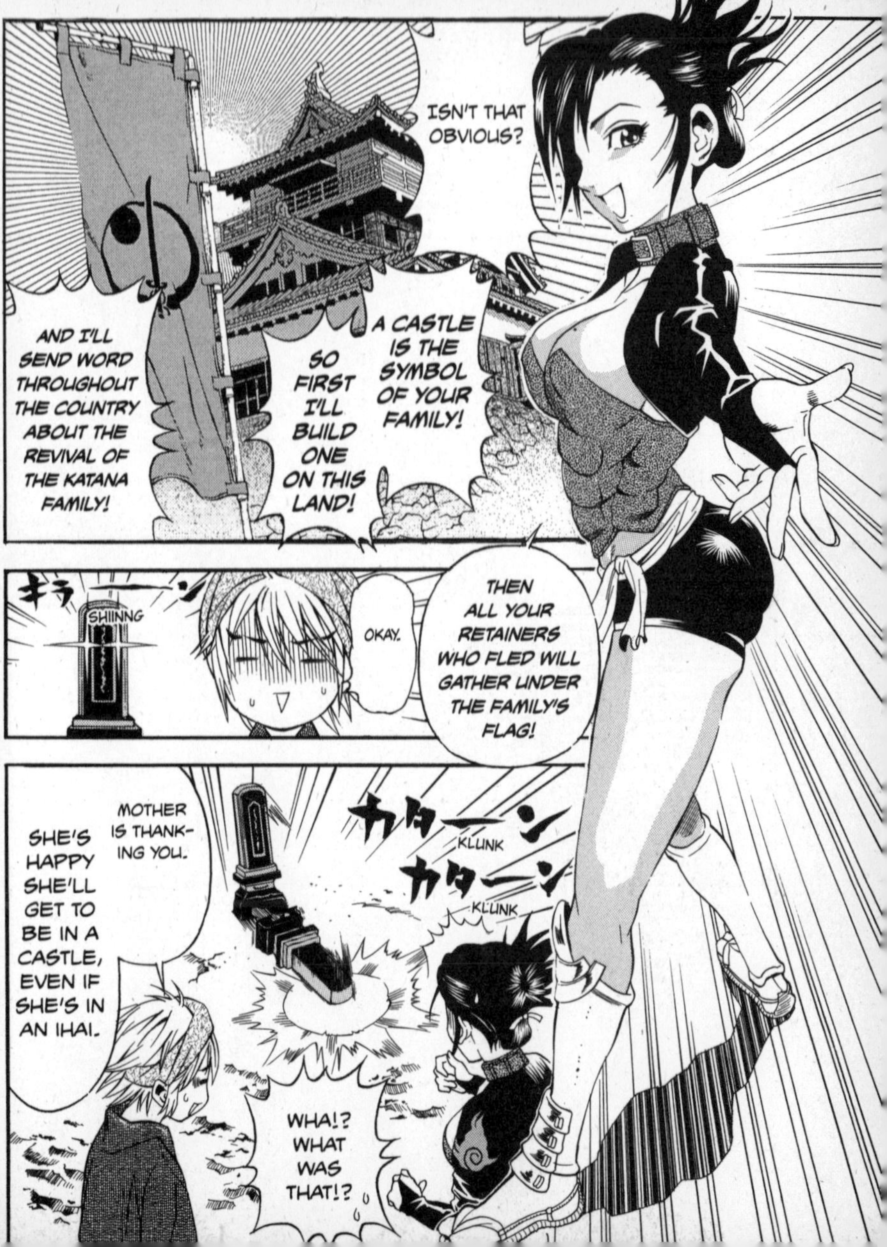
ISN'T THAT OBVIOUS?
A CASTLE IS THE SYMBOL OF YOUR FAMILY!
SO FIRST I'LL BUILD ONE ON THIS LAND!
AND I'LL SEND WORD THROUGHOUT THE COUNTRY ABOUT THE REVIVAL OF THE KATANA FAMILY!
THEN ALL YOUR RETAINERS WHO FLED WILL GATHER UNDER THE FAMILY'S FLAG!
OKAY.
キラーン
SHIINNG
カターン
KLUNK
カターン
KLUNK
MOTHER IS THANKING YOU.
SHE'S HAPPY SHE'LL GET TO BE IN A CASTLE, EVEN IF SHE'S IN AN IHAI.
WHA!? WHAT WAS THAT!?

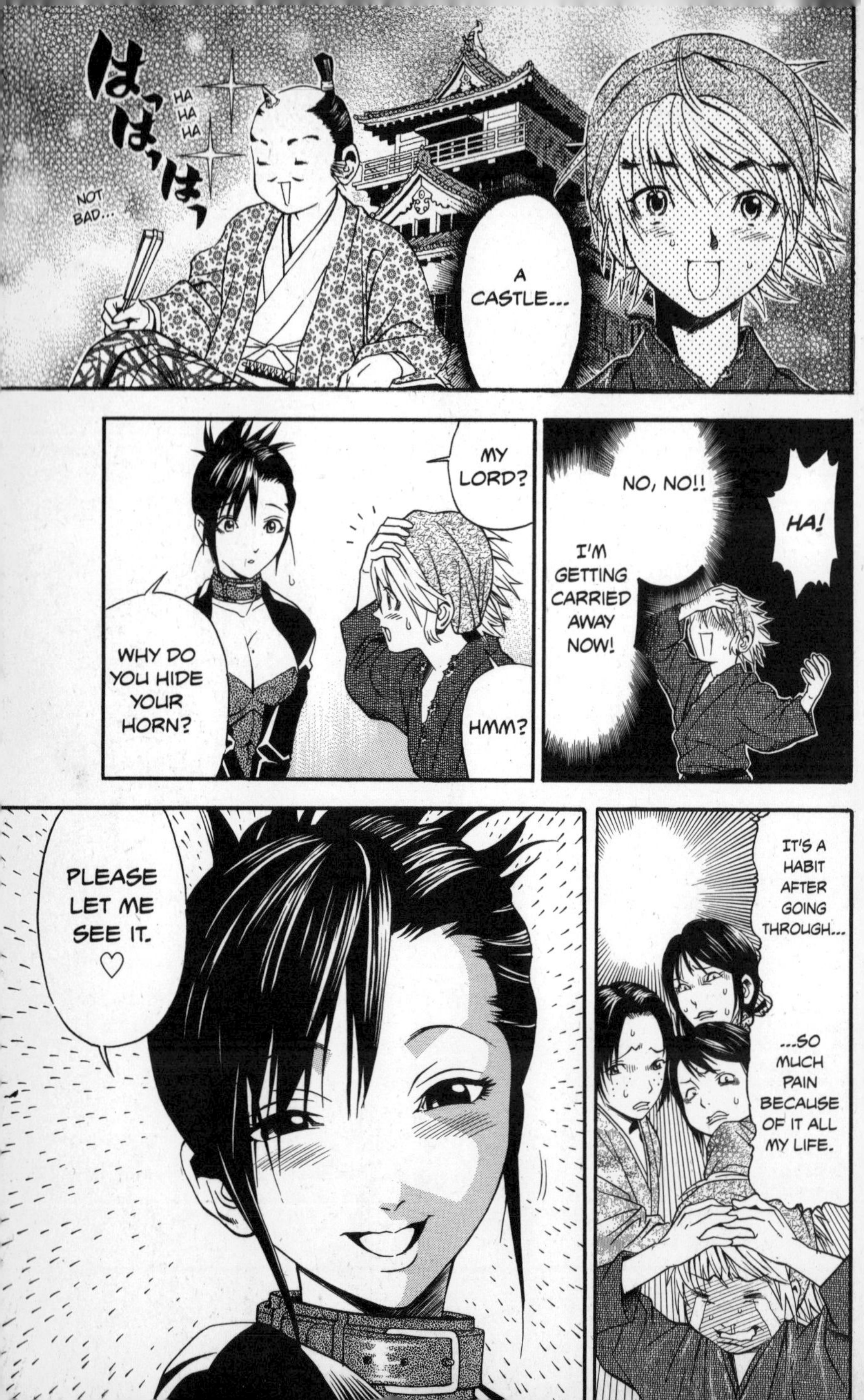
A CASTLE...
はっはっはっ
HA HA HA
NOT BAD...
HA!
NO, NO!!
I'M GETTING CARRIED AWAY NOW!
MY LORD?
HMM?
WHY DO YOU HIDE YOUR HORN?
IT'S A HABIT AFTER GOING THROUGH...
...SO MUCH PAIN BECAUSE OF IT ALL MY LIFE.
PLEASE LET ME SEE IT. ♡

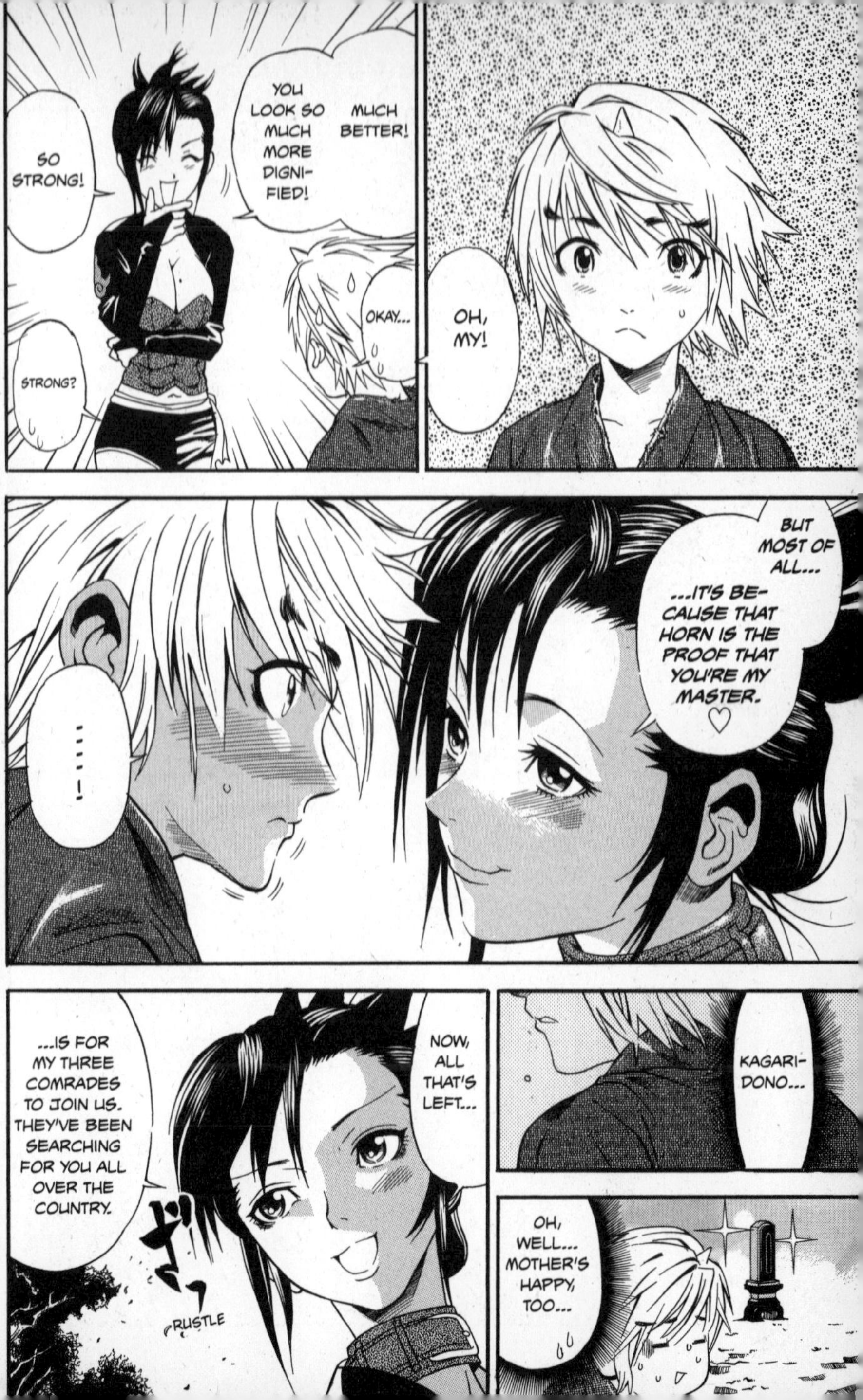
OH, MY!
MUCH BETTER!
YOU LOOK SO MUCH MORE DIGNI-FIED!
SO STRONG!
OKAY...
STRONG?
BUT MOST OF ALL...
...IT'S BE-CAUSE THAT HORN IS THE PROOF THAT YOU'RE MY MASTER. ♡
......!
KAGARI-DONO...
OH, WELL... MOTHER'S HAPPY, TOO...
NOW, ALL THAT'S LEFT...
...IS FOR MY THREE COMRADES TO JOIN US. THEY'VE BEEN SEARCHING FOR YOU ALL OVER THE COUNTRY.
RUSTLE

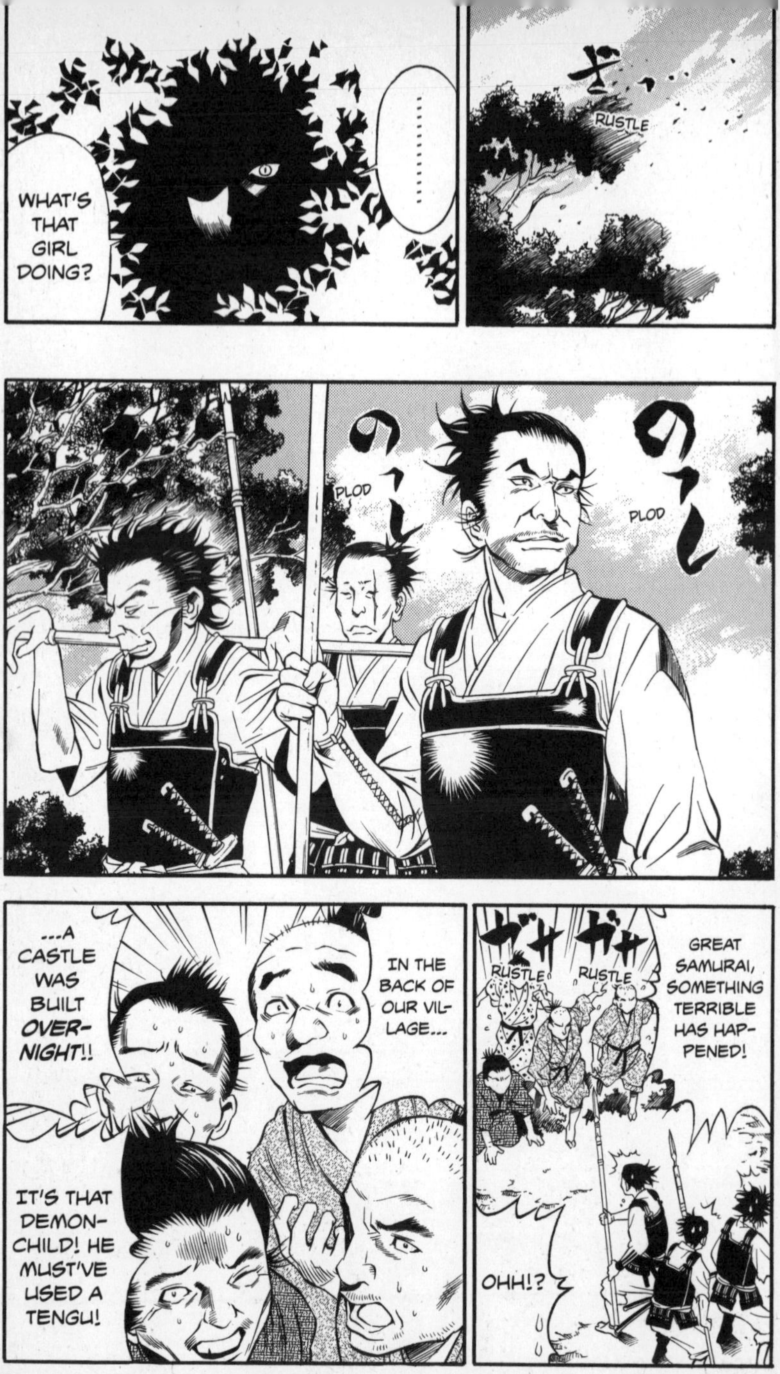

RUSTLE
......
WHAT'S THAT GIRL DOING?
のし
PLOD
のし
PLOD
ガサ
RUSTLE
ガサ
RUSTLE
GREAT SAMURAI, SOMETHING TERRIBLE HAS HAPPENED!
OHH!?
IN THE BACK OF OUR VIL-LAGE...
...A CASTLE WAS BUILT *OVER-NIGHT*!!
IT'S THAT DEMON-CHILD! HE MUST'VE USED A TENGU!

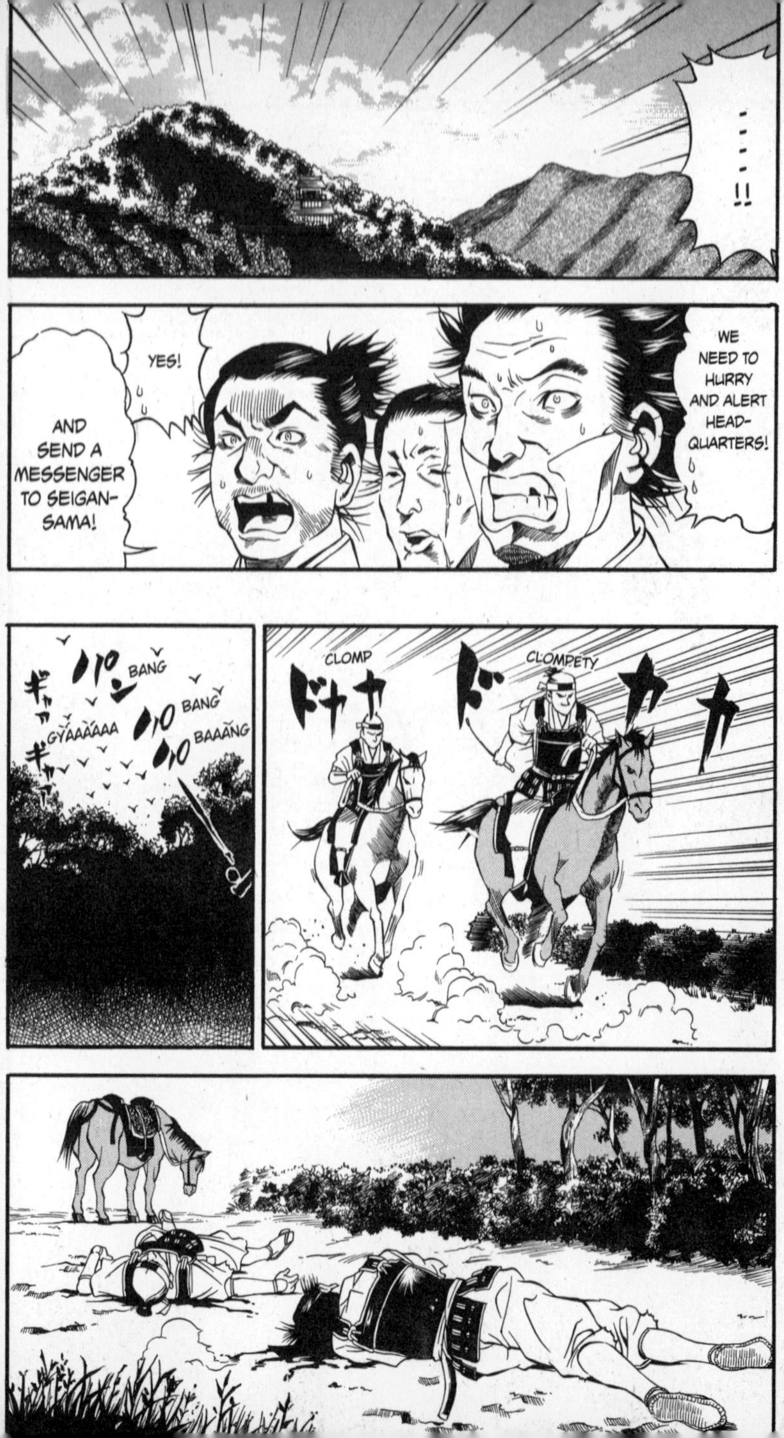

......!!
WE NEED TO HURRY AND ALERT HEAD-QUARTERS!
YES!
AND SEND A MESSENGER TO SEIGAN-SAMA!
CLOMPETY
CLOMP
BANG
BANG
BAAÄNG
GYAAÄAAA

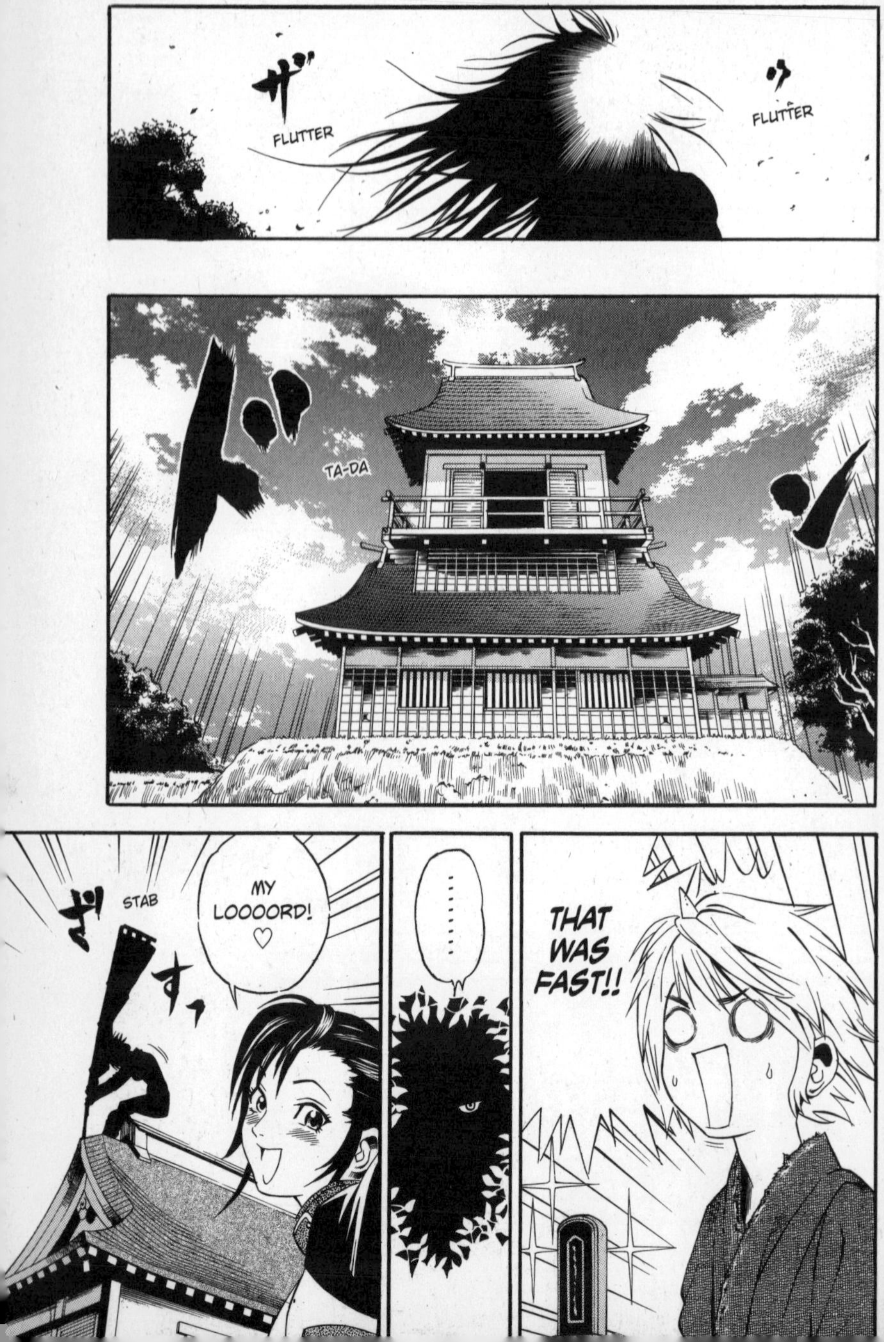
FLUTTER
FLUTTER
TA-DA
THAT WAS FAST!!
......
MY LOOOORD! ♡
STAB

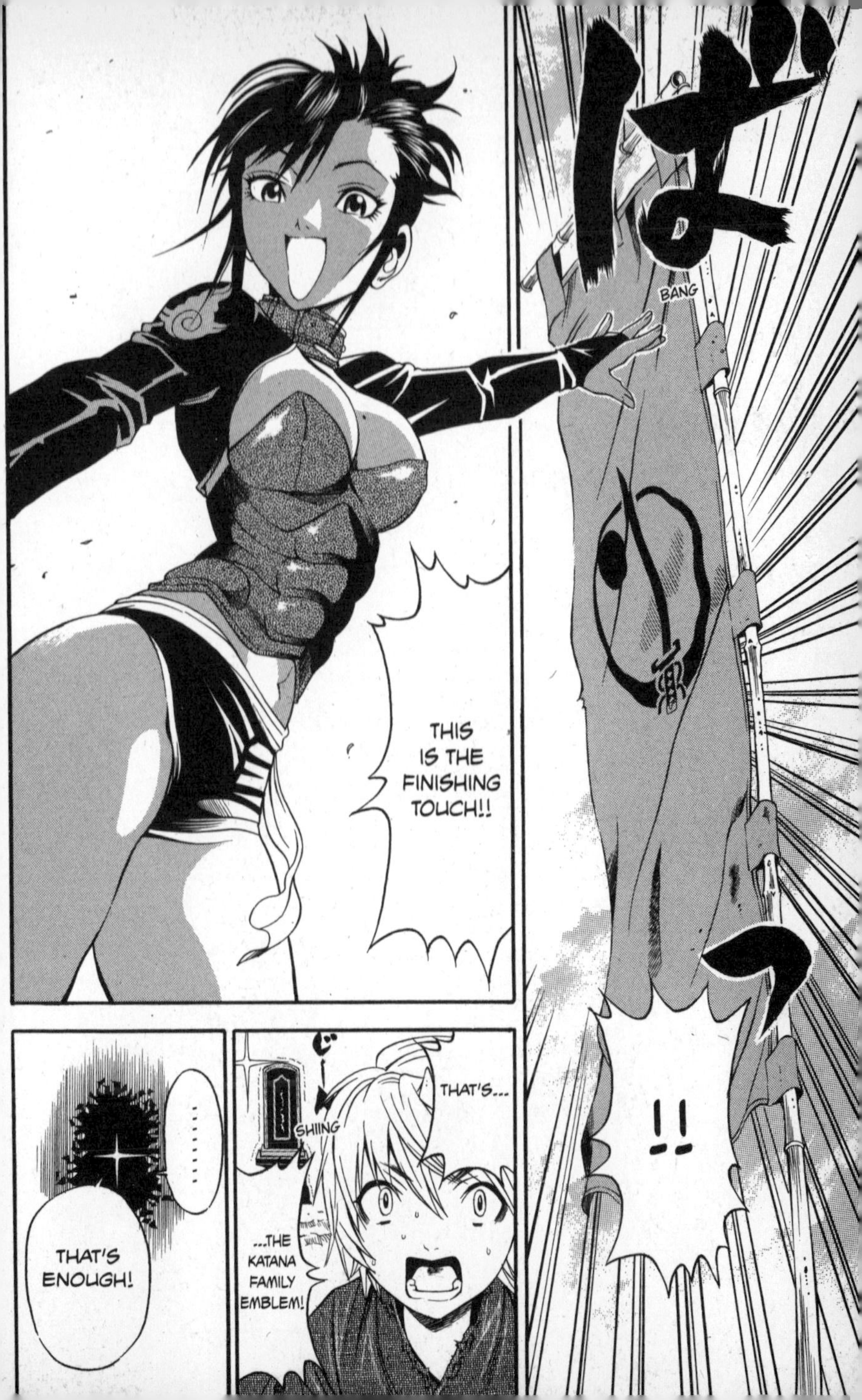
BANG
!!
THIS IS THE FINISHING TOUCH!!
SHIING
THAT'S...
...THE KATANA FAMILY EMBLEM!
......
THAT'S ENOUGH!

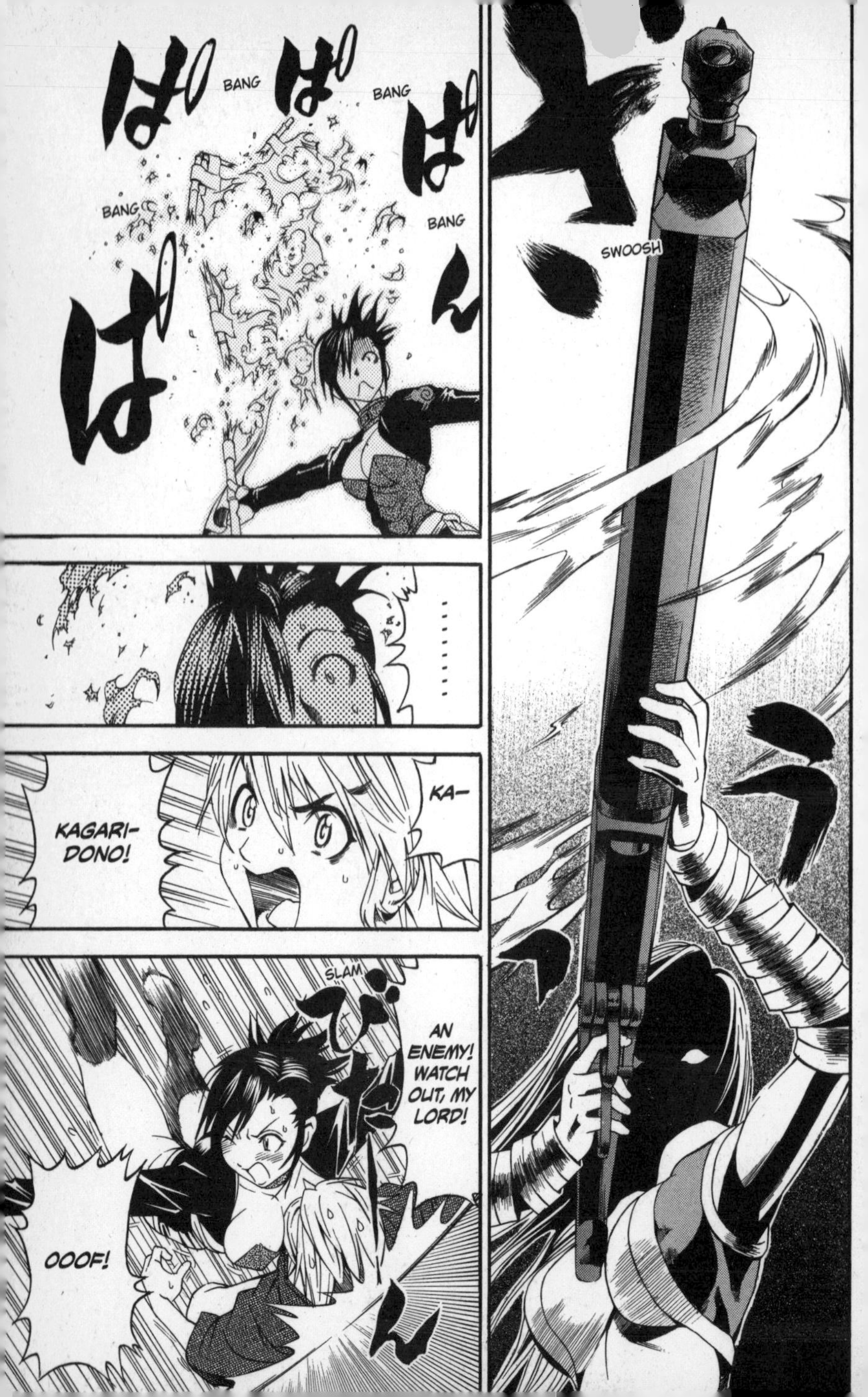
SWOOSH
BANG
BANG
BANG
BANG
......
KA-
KAGARI-DONO!
SLAM
AN ENEMY! WATCH OUT, MY LORD!
OOOF!

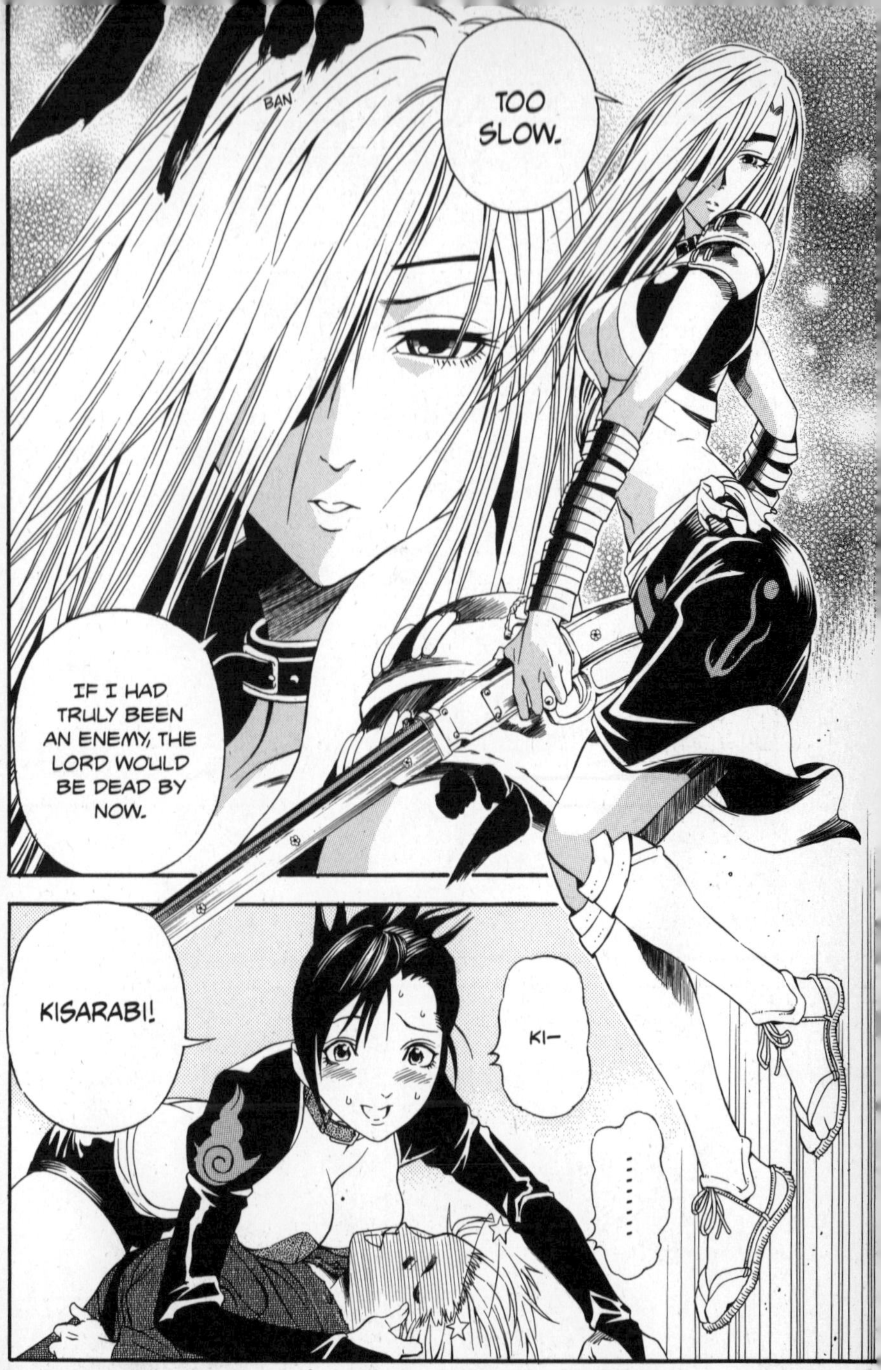
BAN
TOO SLOW.
IF I HAD TRULY BEEN AN ENEMY, THE LORD WOULD BE DEAD BY NOW.
KI—
......
KISARABI!

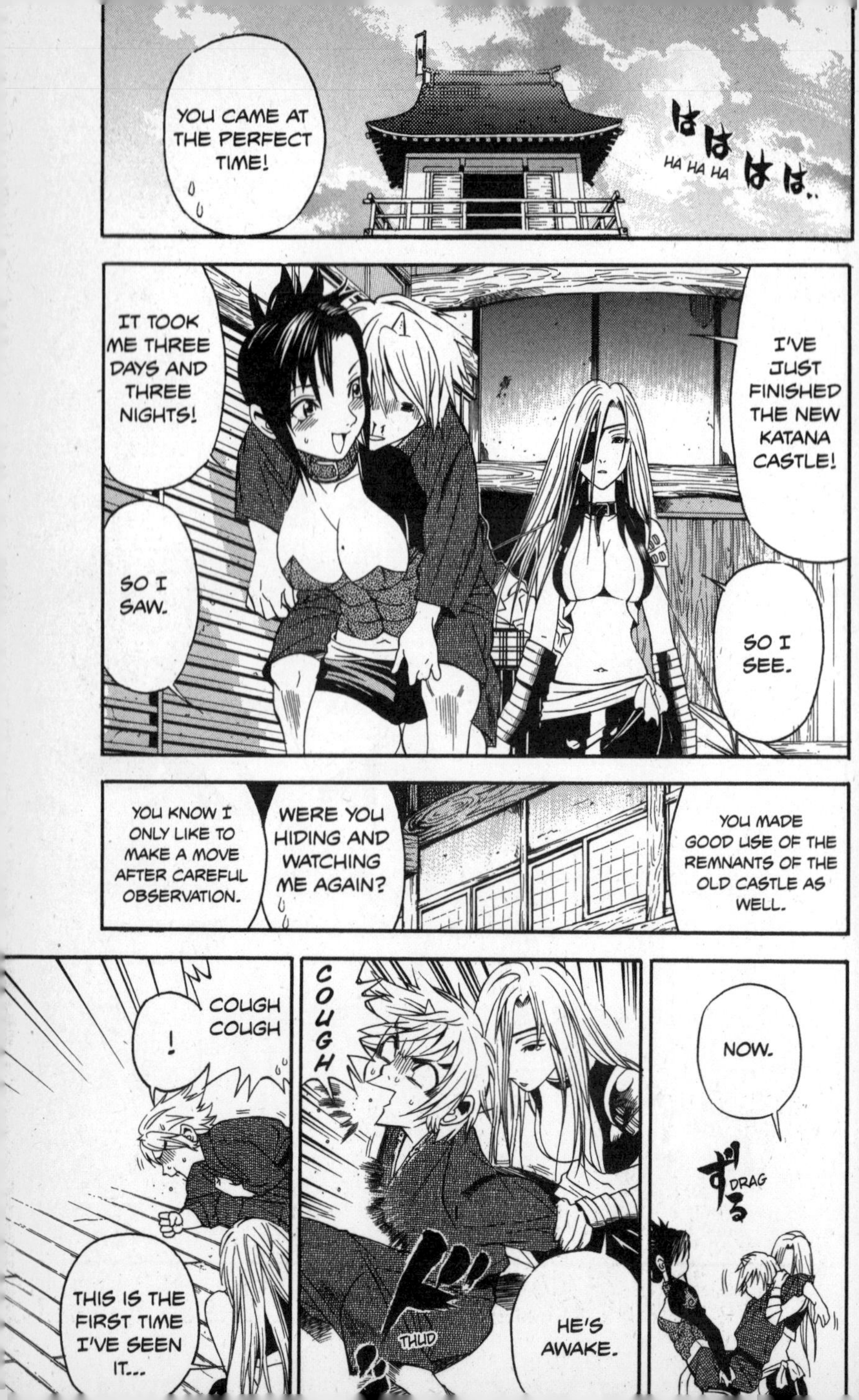
ははは.. HA HA HA
YOU CAME AT THE PERFECT TIME!
I'VE JUST FINISHED THE NEW KATANA CASTLE!
IT TOOK ME THREE DAYS AND THREE NIGHTS!
SO I SEE.
SO I SAW.
YOU MADE GOOD USE OF THE REMNANTS OF THE OLD CASTLE AS WELL.
WERE YOU HIDING AND WATCHING ME AGAIN?
YOU KNOW I ONLY LIKE TO MAKE A MOVE AFTER CAREFUL OBSERVATION.
NOW.
ずる DRAG
COUGH
HE'S AWAKE.
ド THUD
COUGH COUGH
!
THIS IS THE FIRST TIME I'VE SEEN IT...

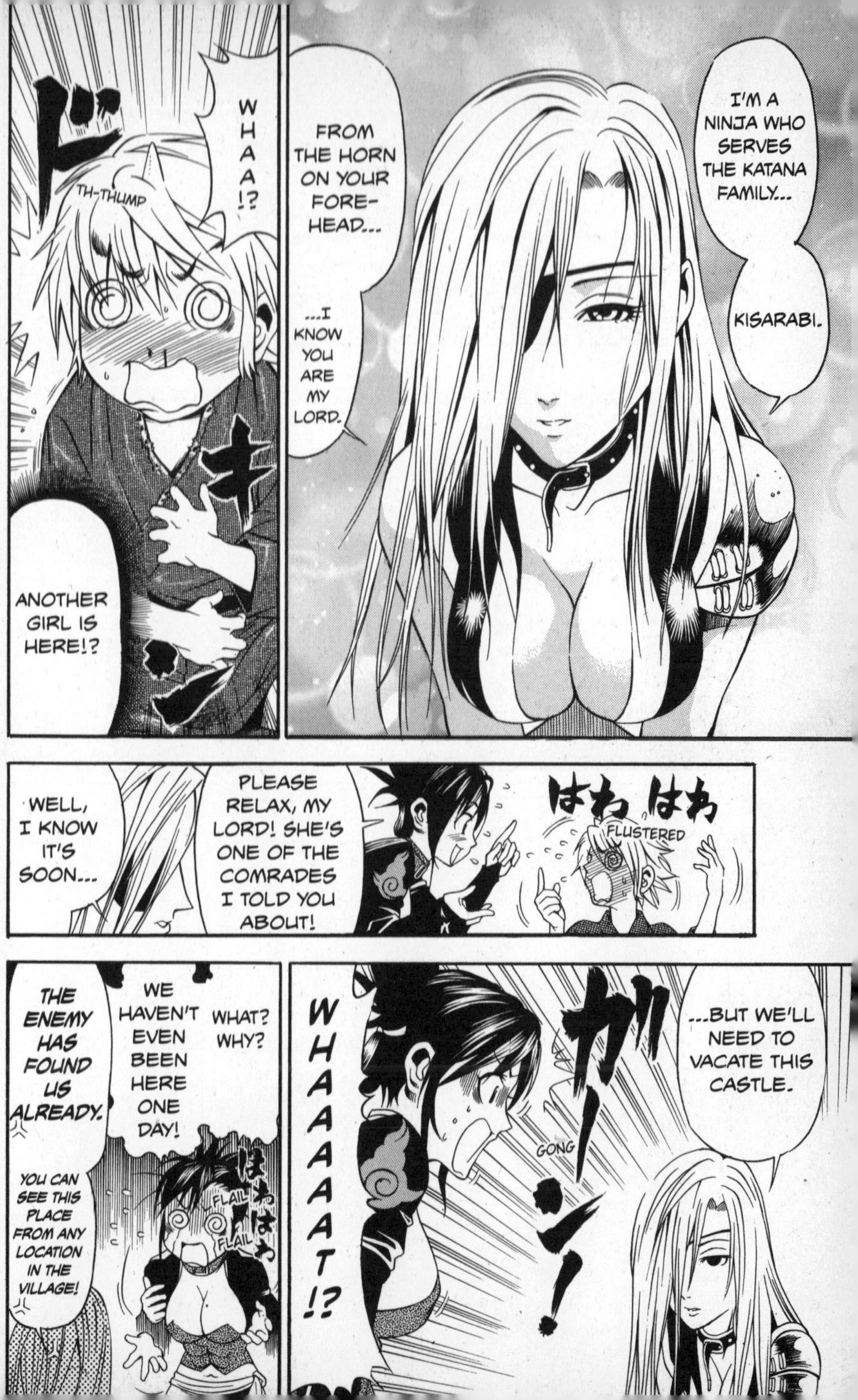
I'M A NINJA WHO SERVES THE KATANA FAMILY...
KISARABI.
FROM THE HORN ON YOUR FORE-HEAD...
...I KNOW YOU ARE MY LORD.
WHAA!?
TH-THUMP
ANOTHER GIRL IS HERE!?
はわ はわ
FLUSTERED
PLEASE RELAX, MY LORD! SHE'S ONE OF THE COMRADES I TOLD YOU ABOUT!
WELL, I KNOW IT'S SOON...
...BUT WE'LL NEED TO VACATE THIS CASTLE.
GONG
WHAAAAAAT!?
WHAT? WHY?
WE HAVEN'T EVEN BEEN HERE ONE DAY!
THE ENEMY HAS FOUND US ALREADY.
はわ はわ
FLAIL FLAIL
YOU CAN SEE THIS PLACE FROM ANY LOCATION IN THE VILLAGE!

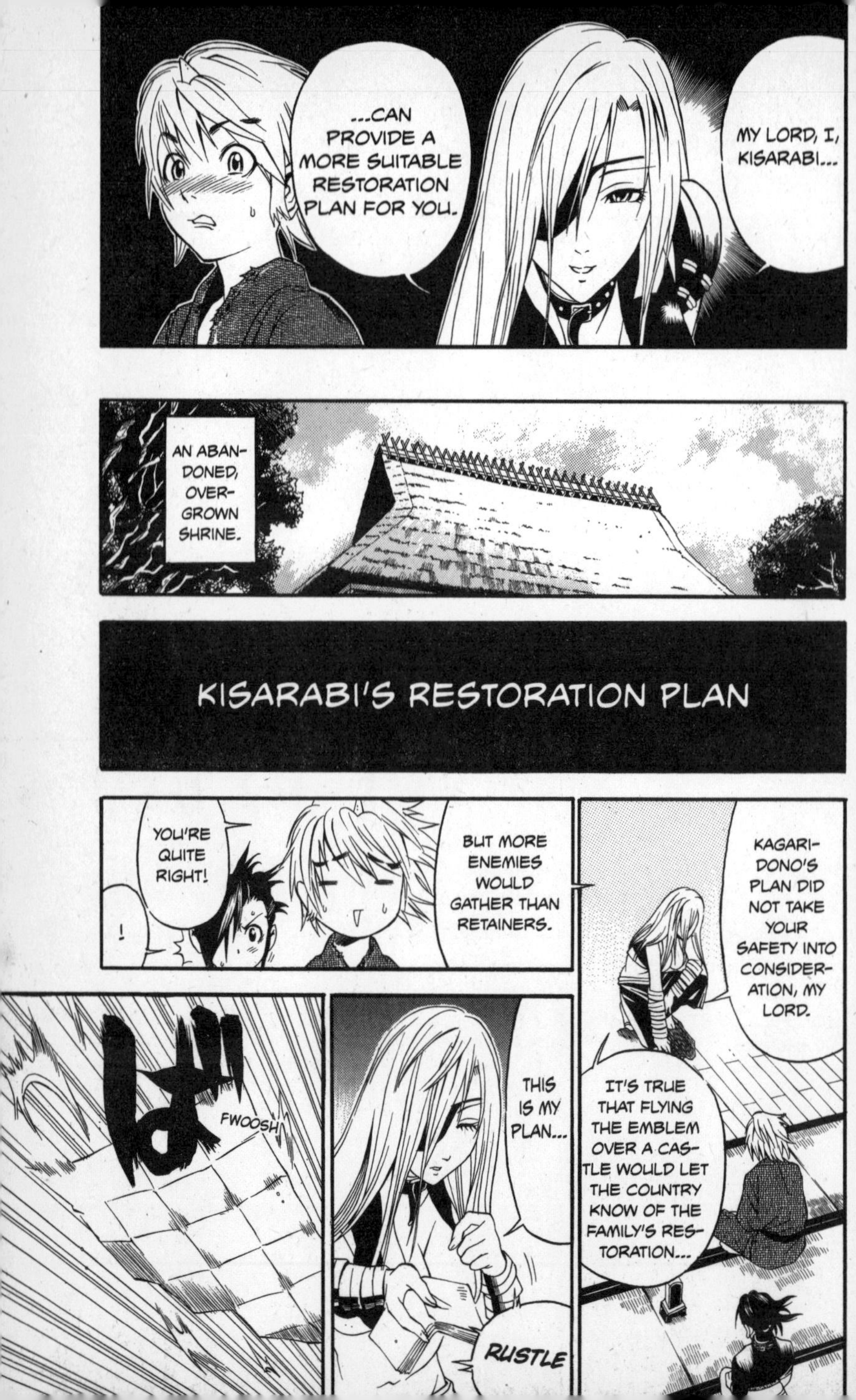

MY LORD, I, KISARABI...
...CAN PROVIDE A MORE SUITABLE RESTORATION PLAN FOR YOU.
AN ABANDONED, OVERGROWN SHRINE.
KISARABI'S RESTORATION PLAN
KAGARI-DONO'S PLAN DID NOT TAKE YOUR SAFETY INTO CONSIDERATION, MY LORD.
IT'S TRUE THAT FLYING THE EMBLEM OVER A CASTLE WOULD LET THE COUNTRY KNOW OF THE FAMILY'S RESTORATION...
BUT MORE ENEMIES WOULD GATHER THAN RETAINERS.
YOU'RE QUITE RIGHT!
!
THIS IS MY PLAN...
RUSTLE
FWOOSH

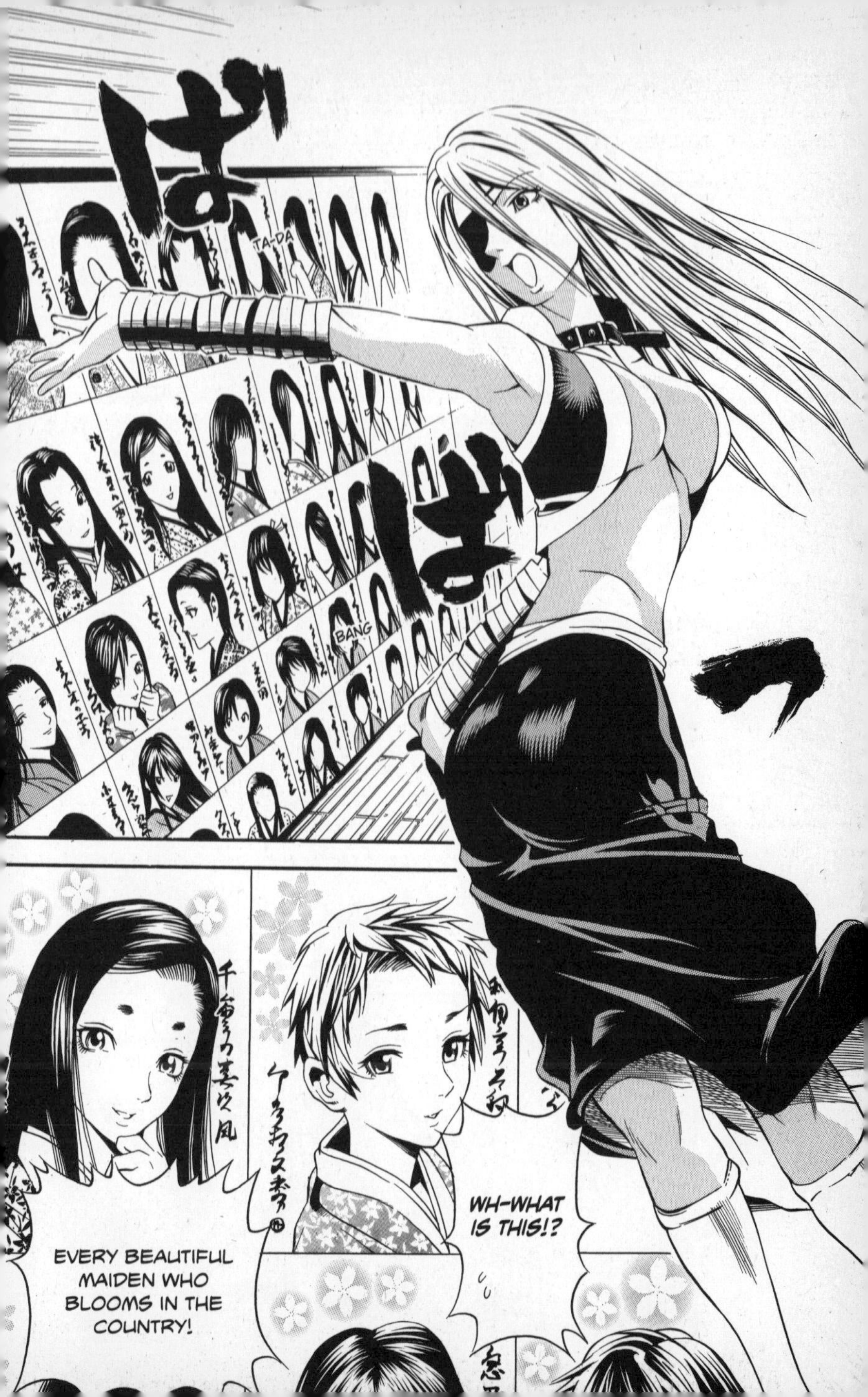
TA-DA
BANG
WH-WHAT IS THIS!?
EVERY BEAUTIFUL MAIDEN WHO BLOOMS IN THE COUNTRY!

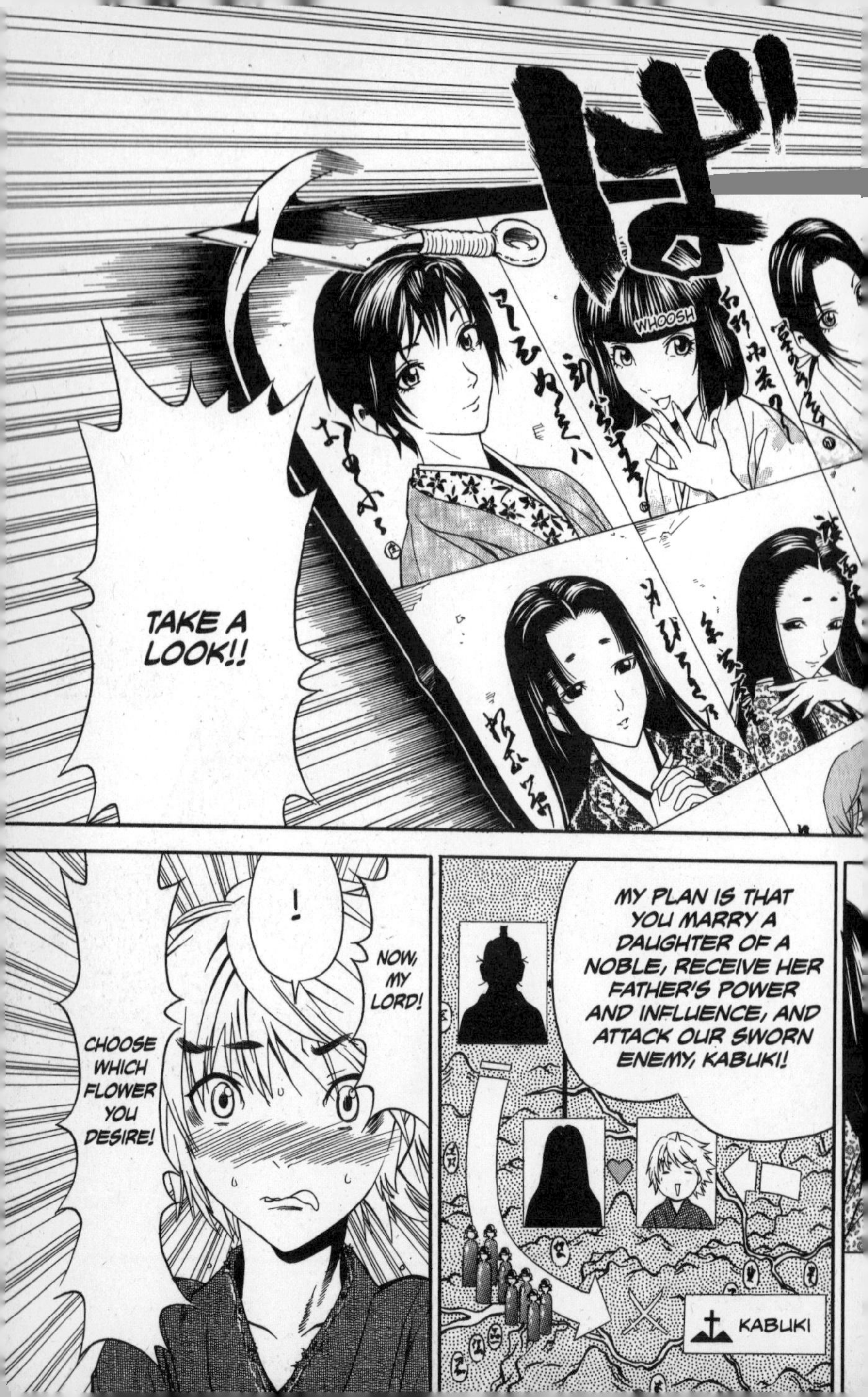
WHOOSH
TAKE A LOOK!!
MY PLAN IS THAT YOU MARRY A DAUGHTER OF A NOBLE, RECEIVE HER FATHER'S POWER AND INFLUENCE, AND ATTACK OUR SWORN ENEMY, KABUKI!
KABUKI
!
NOW, MY LORD!
CHOOSE WHICH FLOWER YOU DESIRE!

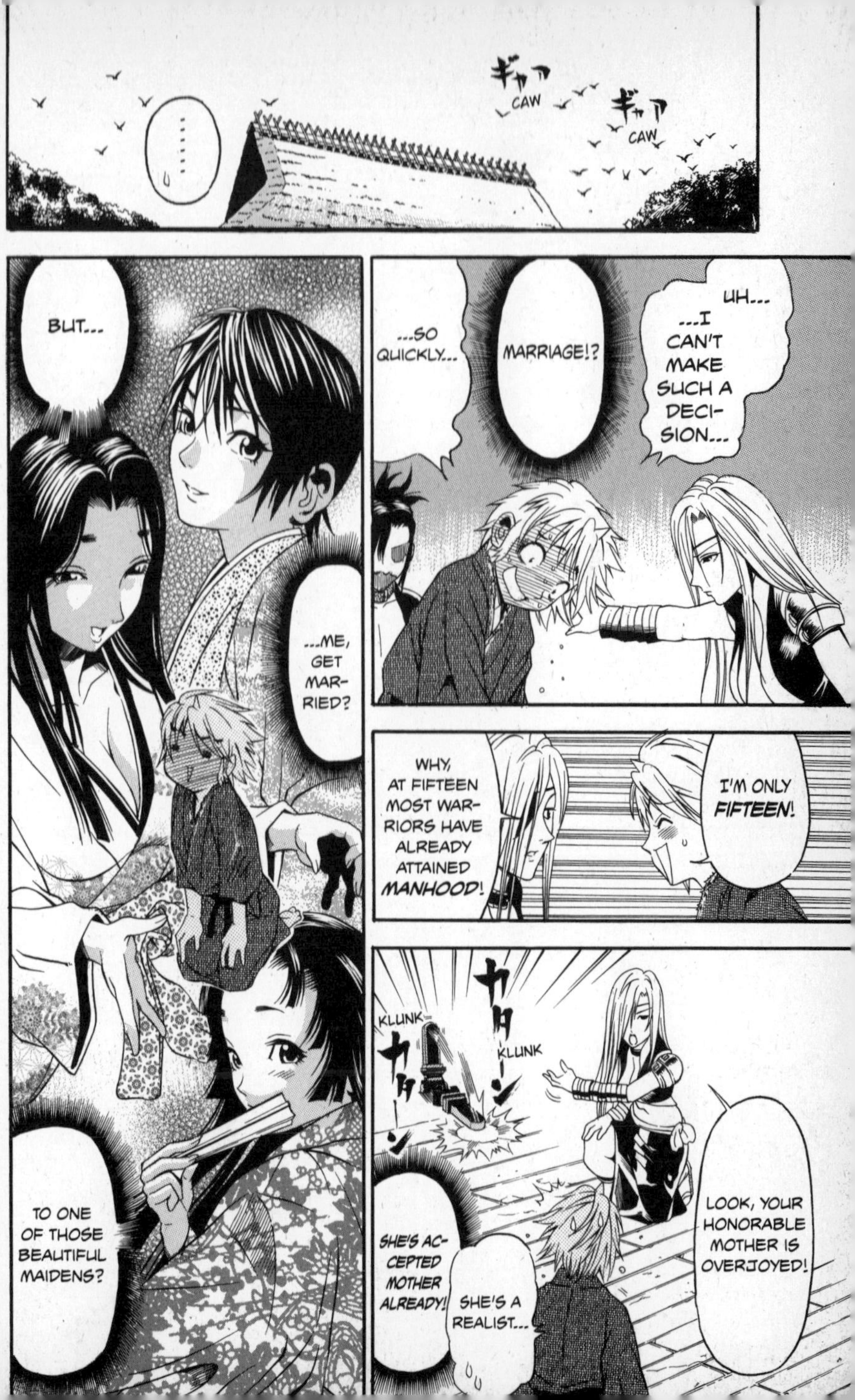

ギャア
CAW
ギャア
CAW
......
UH... ...I CAN'T MAKE SUCH A DECI-SION...
MARRIAGE!?
...SO QUICKLY...
I'M ONLY FIFTEEN!
WHY, AT FIFTEEN MOST WAR-RIORS HAVE ALREADY ATTAINED MANHOOD!
KLUNK
KLUNK
LOOK, YOUR HONORABLE MOTHER IS OVERJOYED!
SHE'S A REALIST...
SHE'S AC-CEPTED MOTHER ALREADY!
BUT...
...ME, GET MAR-RIED?
TO ONE OF THOSE BEAUTIFUL MAIDENS?

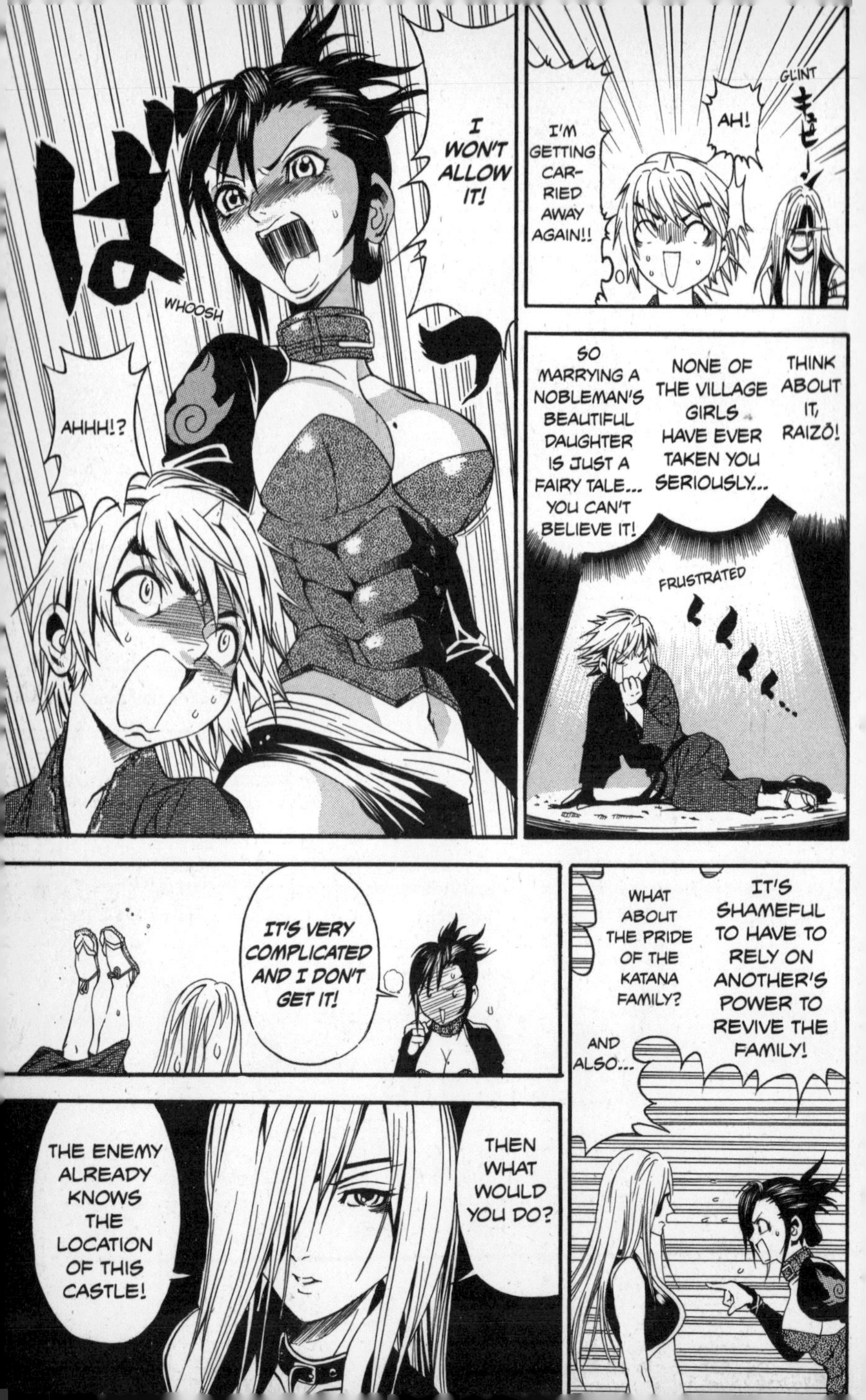
AH!
GLINT
I'M GETTING CAR-RIED AWAY AGAIN!!
THINK ABOUT IT, RAIZŌ!
NONE OF THE VILLAGE GIRLS HAVE EVER TAKEN YOU SERIOUSLY...
SO MARRYING A NOBLEMAN'S BEAUTIFUL DAUGHTER IS JUST A FAIRY TALE... YOU CAN'T BELIEVE IT!
FRUSTRATED
I WON'T ALLOW IT!
WHOOSH
AHHH!?
IT'S SHAMEFUL TO HAVE TO RELY ON ANOTHER'S POWER TO REVIVE THE FAMILY!
WHAT ABOUT THE PRIDE OF THE KATANA FAMILY?
AND ALSO...
IT'S VERY COMPLICATED AND I DON'T GET IT!
THEN WHAT WOULD YOU DO?
THE ENEMY ALREADY KNOWS THE LOCATION OF THIS CASTLE!

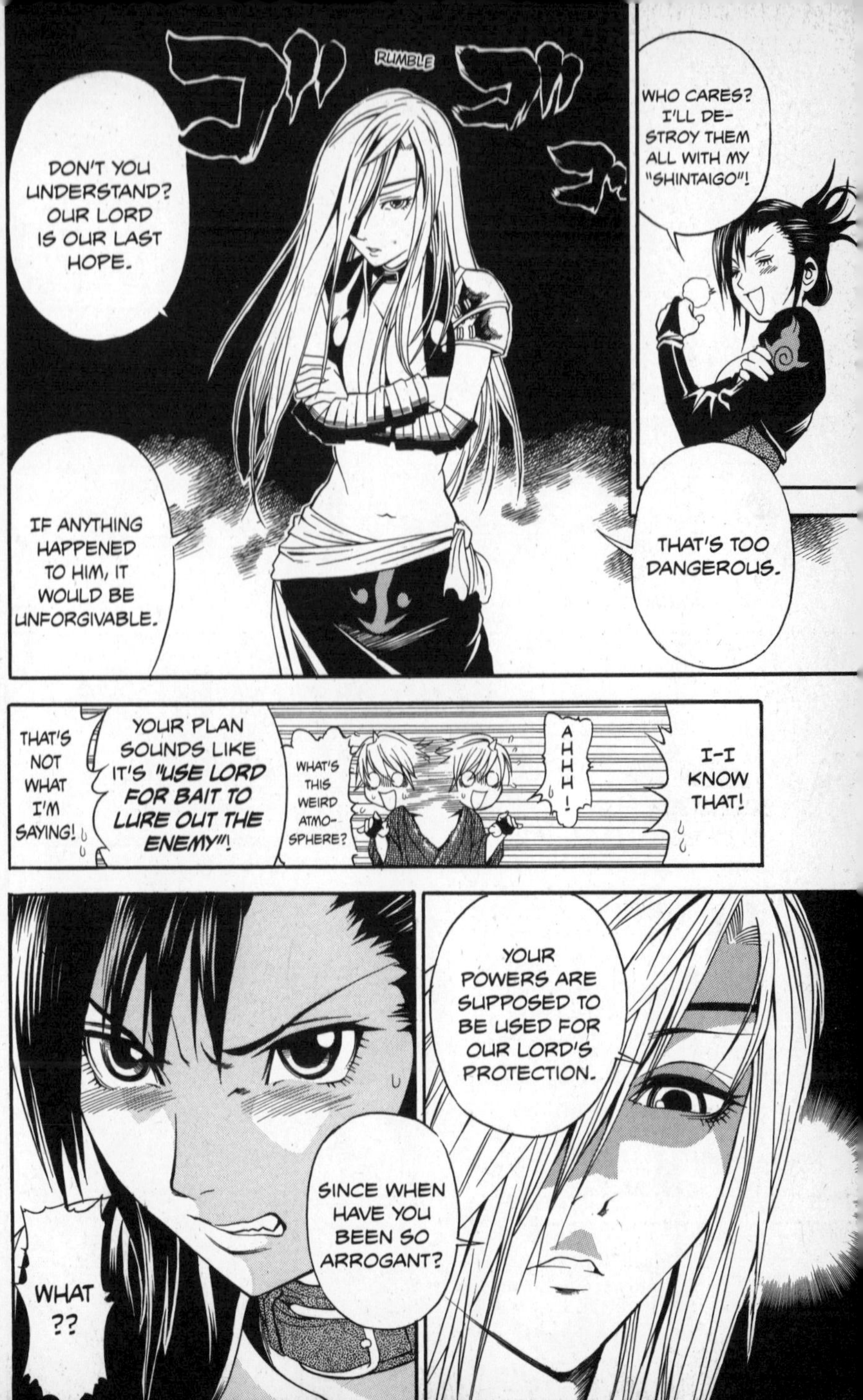
WHO CARES? I'LL DE-STROY THEM ALL WITH MY "SHINTAIGO"!
RUMBLE
THAT'S TOO DANGEROUS.
DON'T YOU UNDERSTAND? OUR LORD IS OUR LAST HOPE.
IF ANYTHING HAPPENED TO HIM, IT WOULD BE UNFORGIVABLE.
I-I KNOW THAT!
AHHH!
WHAT'S THIS WEIRD ATMO-SPHERE?
YOUR PLAN SOUNDS LIKE IT'S "USE LORD FOR BAIT TO LURE OUT THE ENEMY"!
THAT'S NOT WHAT I'M SAYING!
YOUR POWERS ARE SUPPOSED TO BE USED FOR OUR LORD'S PROTECTION.
SINCE WHEN HAVE YOU BEEN SO ARROGANT?
WHAT ??

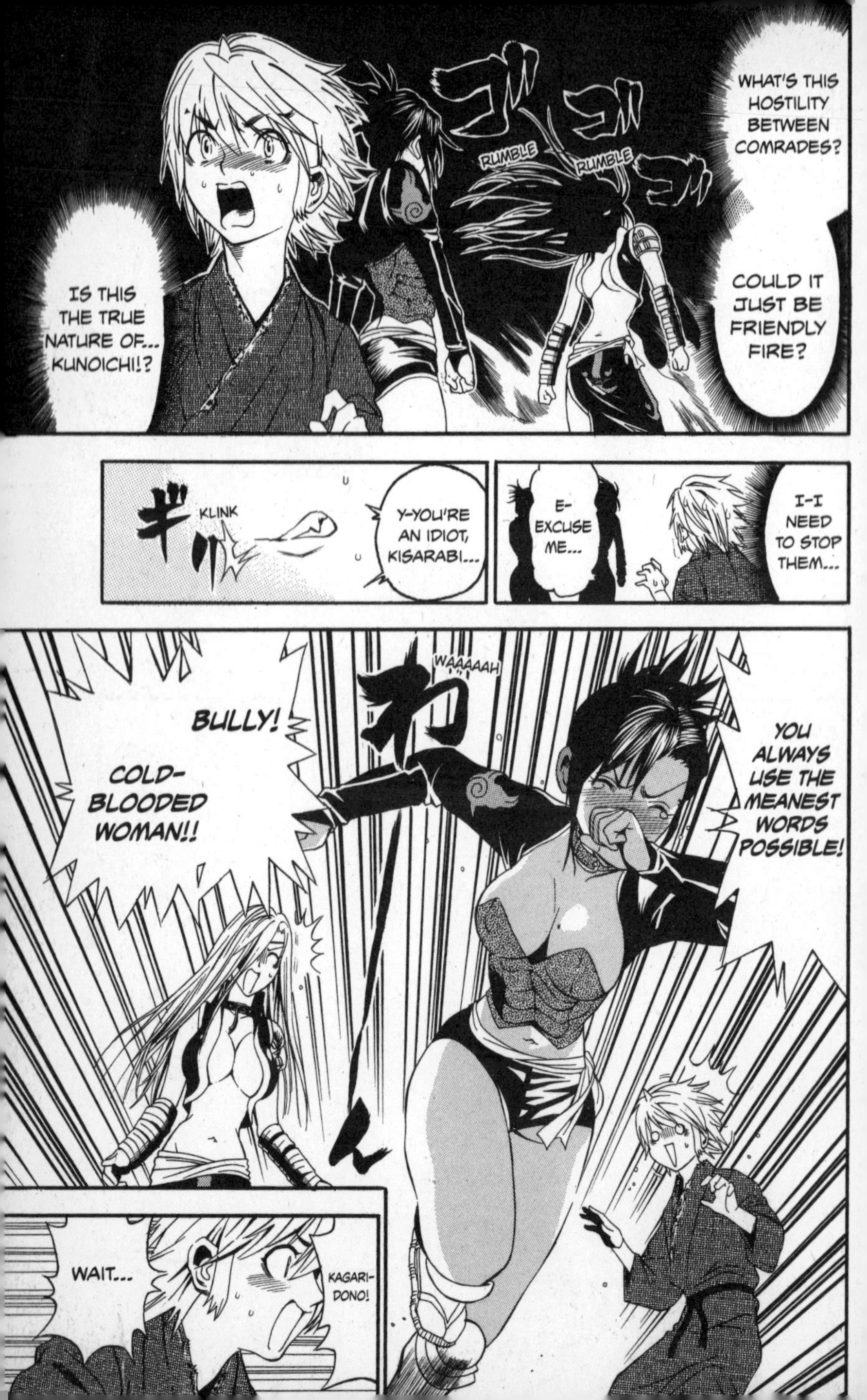
WHAT'S THIS HOSTILITY BETWEEN COMRADES?
COULD IT JUST BE FRIENDLY FIRE?
RUMBLE
RUMBLE
IS THIS THE TRUE NATURE OF... KUNOICHI!?
I-I NEED TO STOP THEM...
E-EXCUSE ME...
Y-YOU'RE AN IDIOT, KISARABI...
KLINK
YOU ALWAYS USE THE MEANEST WORDS POSSIBLE!
WAAAAAH
BULLY!
COLD-BLOODED WOMAN!!
KAGARI-DONO!
WAIT...

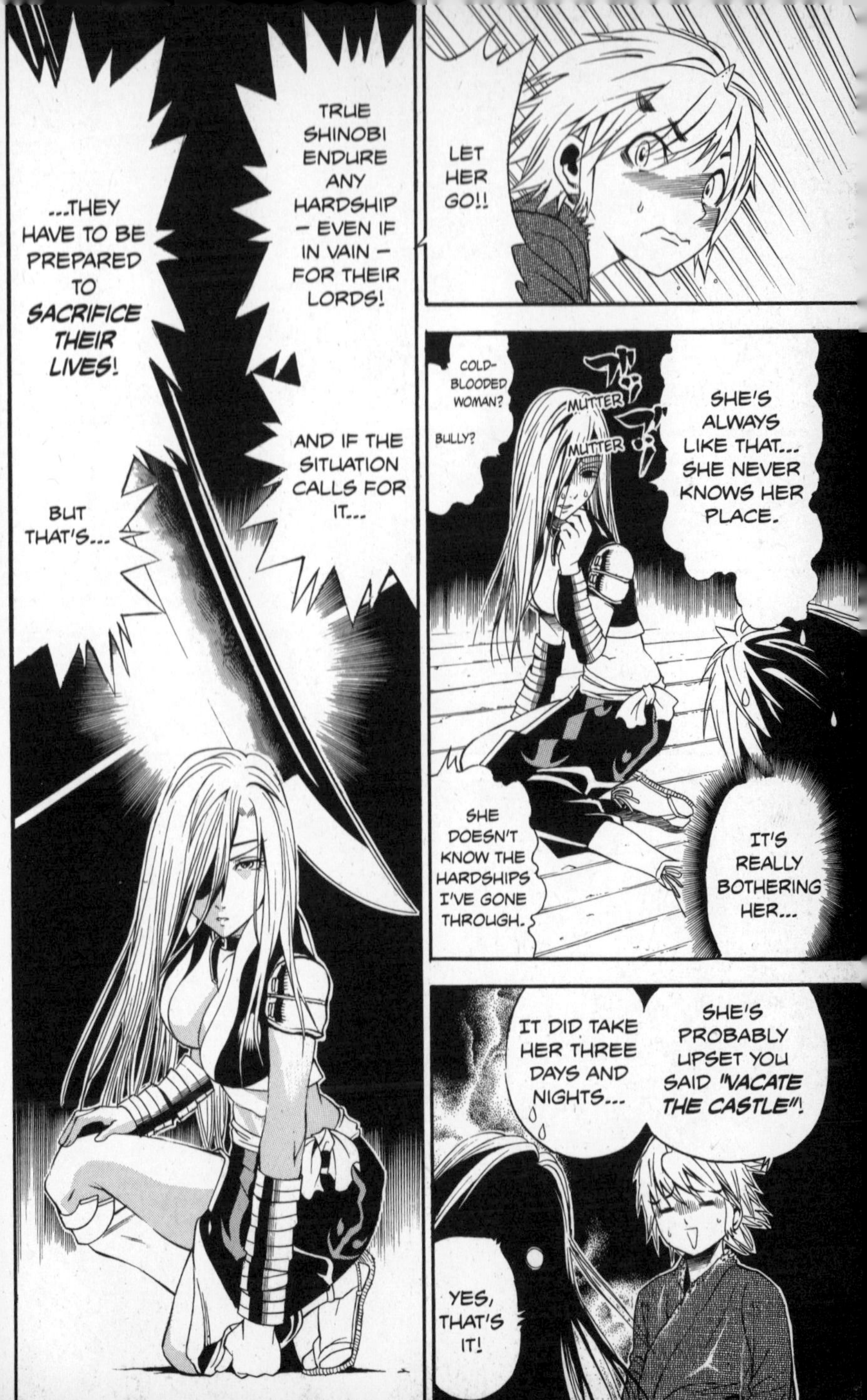
LET HER GO!!
SHE'S ALWAYS LIKE THAT... SHE NEVER KNOWS HER PLACE.
MUTTER
MUTTER
COLD-BLOODED WOMAN?
BULLY?
IT'S REALLY BOTHERING HER...
SHE DOESN'T KNOW THE HARDSHIPS I'VE GONE THROUGH.
SHE'S PROBABLY UPSET YOU SAID "VACATE THE CASTLE"!
IT DID TAKE HER THREE DAYS AND NIGHTS...
YES, THAT'S IT!
TRUE SHINOBI ENDURE ANY HARDSHIP – EVEN IF IN VAIN – FOR THEIR LORDS!
...THEY HAVE TO BE PREPARED TO SACRIFICE THEIR LIVES!
AND IF THE SITUATION CALLS FOR IT...
BUT THAT'S...

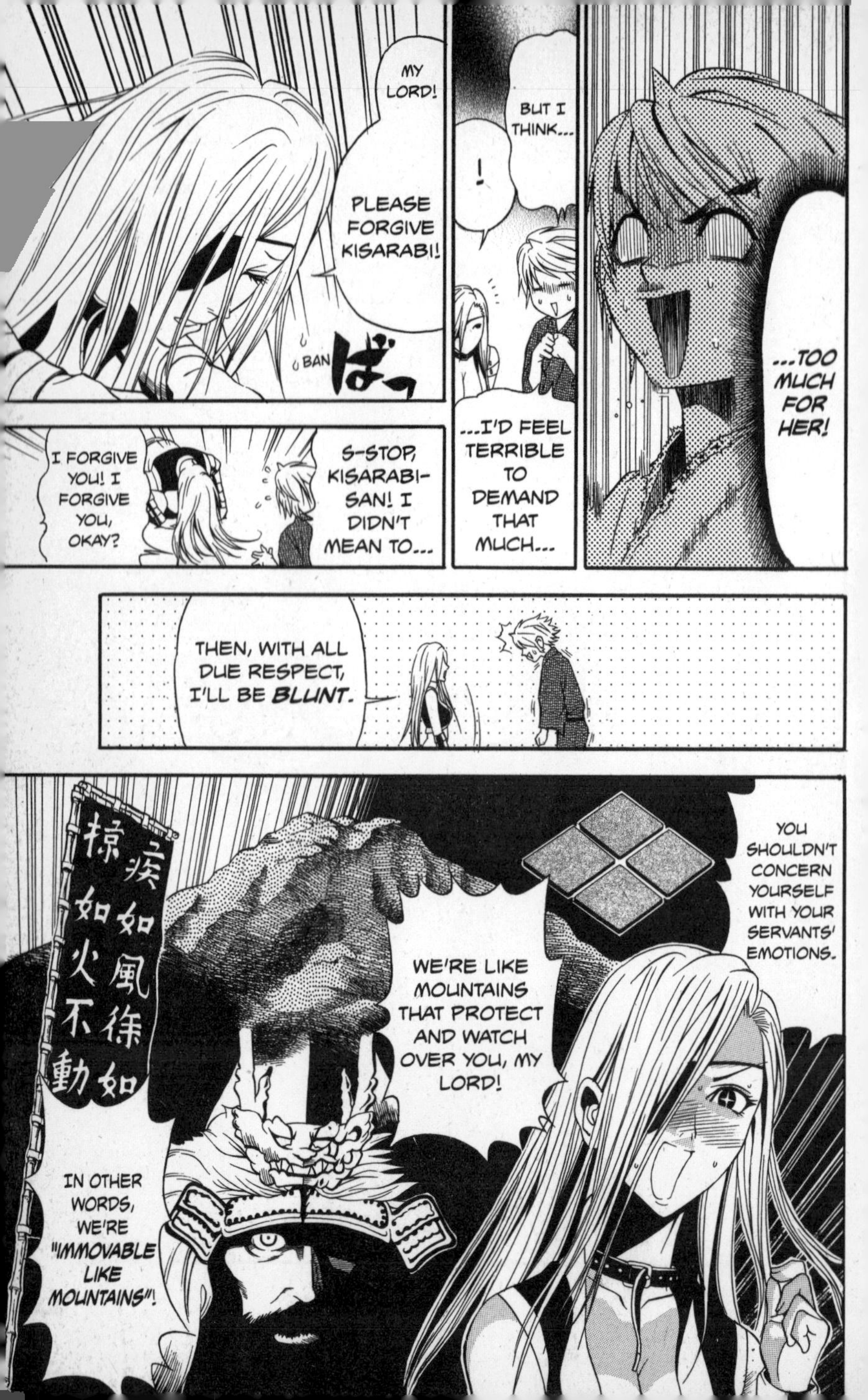
...TOO MUCH FOR HER!
!
BUT I THINK...
...I'D FEEL TERRIBLE TO DEMAND THAT MUCH...
MY LORD!
PLEASE FORGIVE KISARABI!
BAN ばっ
S-STOP, KISARABI-SAN! I DIDN'T MEAN TO...
I FORGIVE YOU! I FORGIVE YOU, OKAY?
THEN, WITH ALL DUE RESPECT, I'LL BE *BLUNT*.
YOU SHOULDN'T CONCERN YOURSELF WITH YOUR SERVANTS' EMOTIONS.
WE'RE LIKE MOUNTAINS THAT PROTECT AND WATCH OVER YOU, MY LORD!
疾如風徐如
掠如火不動如
IN OTHER WORDS, WE'RE "IMMOVABLE LIKE MOUNTAINS"!

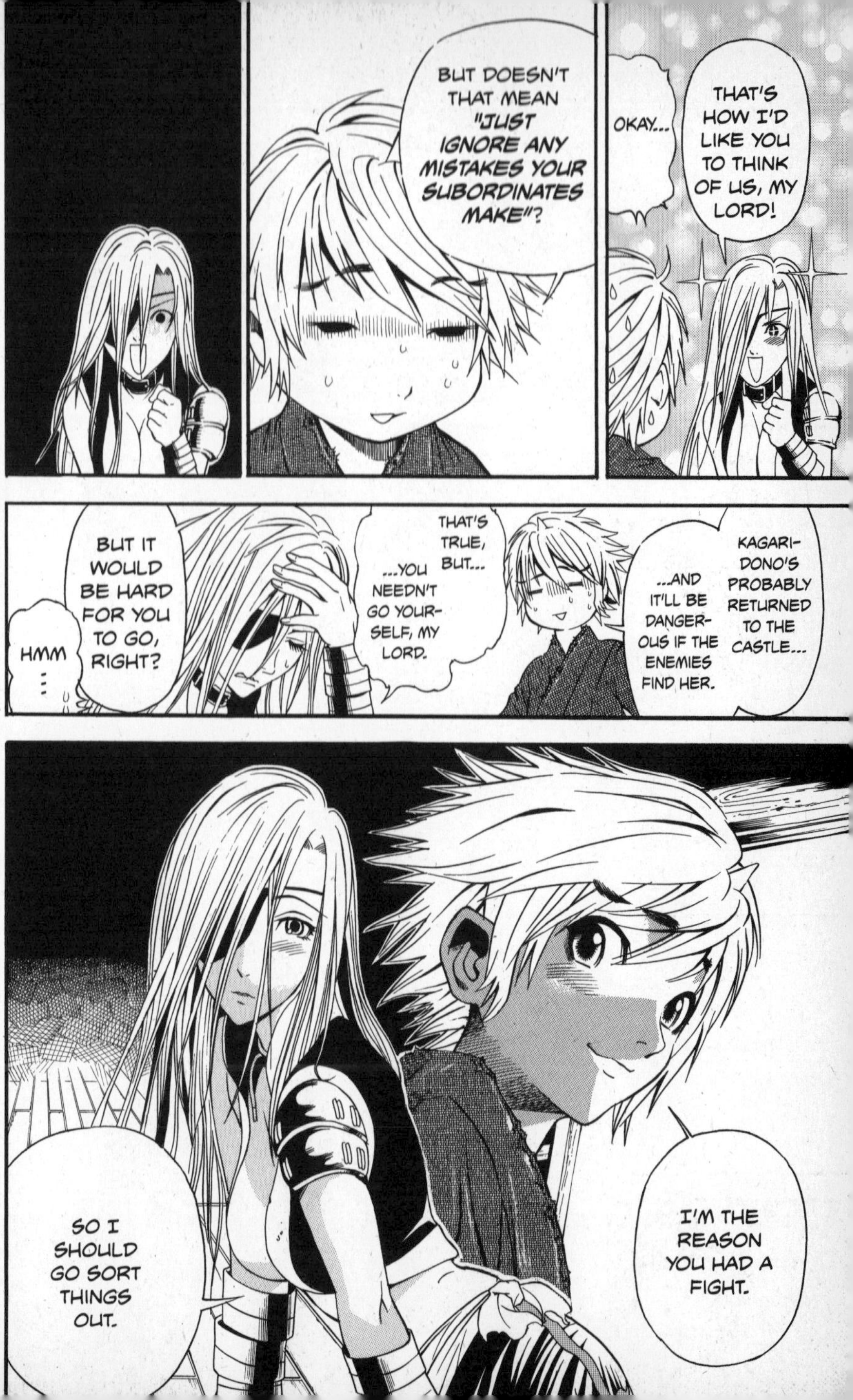
THAT'S HOW I'D LIKE YOU TO THINK OF US, MY LORD!
OKAY...
BUT DOESN'T THAT MEAN "JUST IGNORE ANY MISTAKES YOUR SUBORDINATES MAKE"?
KAGARI-DONO'S PROBABLY RETURNED TO THE CASTLE...
...AND IT'LL BE DANGER-OUS IF THE ENEMIES FIND HER.
THAT'S TRUE, BUT...
...YOU NEEDN'T GO YOUR-SELF, MY LORD.
BUT IT WOULD BE HARD FOR YOU TO GO, RIGHT?
HMM...
I'M THE REASON YOU HAD A FIGHT.
SO I SHOULD GO SORT THINGS OUT.

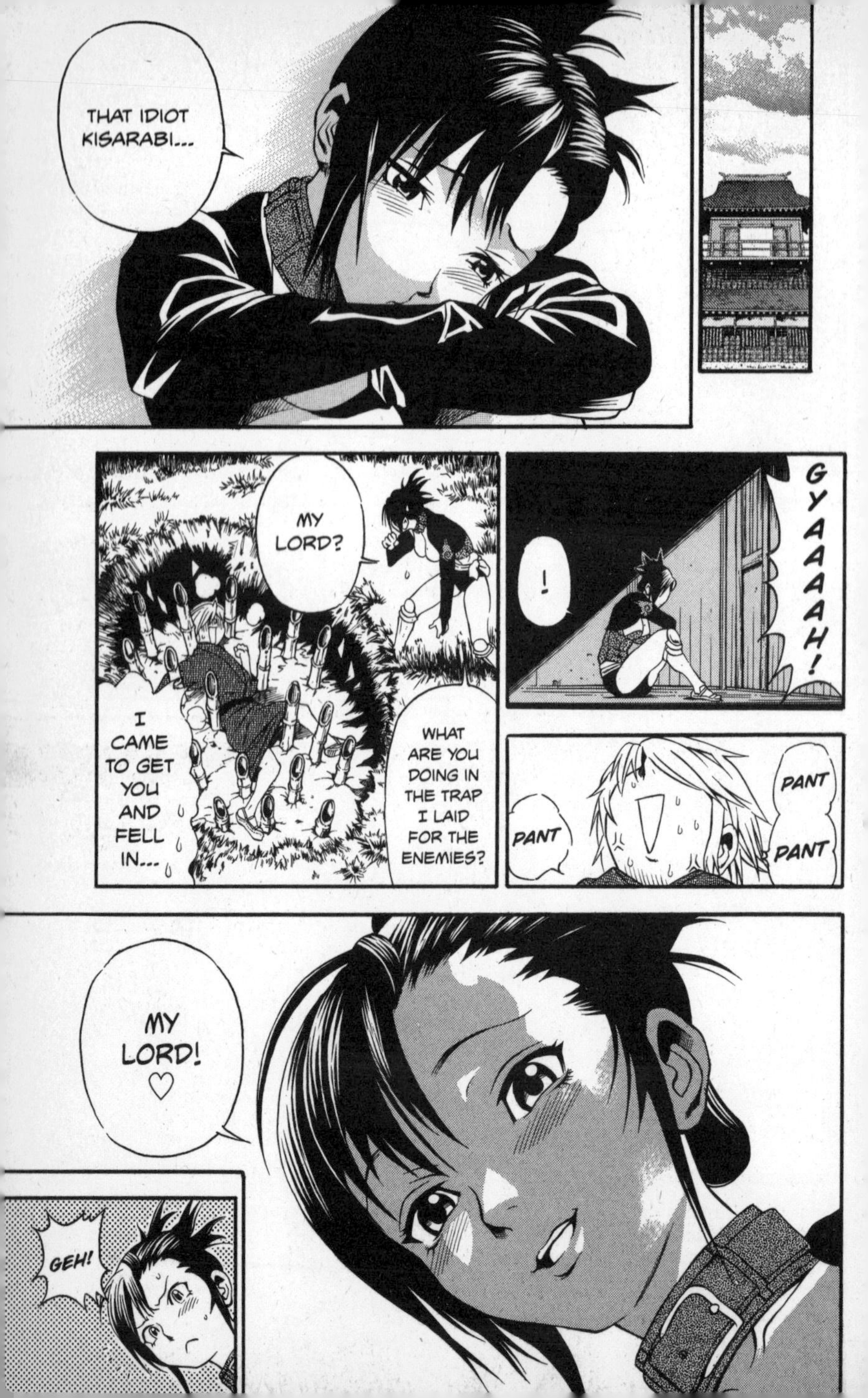
THAT IDIOT KISARABI...
GYAAAAAH!
!
PANT
PANT
PANT
MY LORD?
WHAT ARE YOU DOING IN THE TRAP I LAID FOR THE ENEMIES?
I CAME TO GET YOU AND FELL IN...
MY LORD! ♡
GEH!

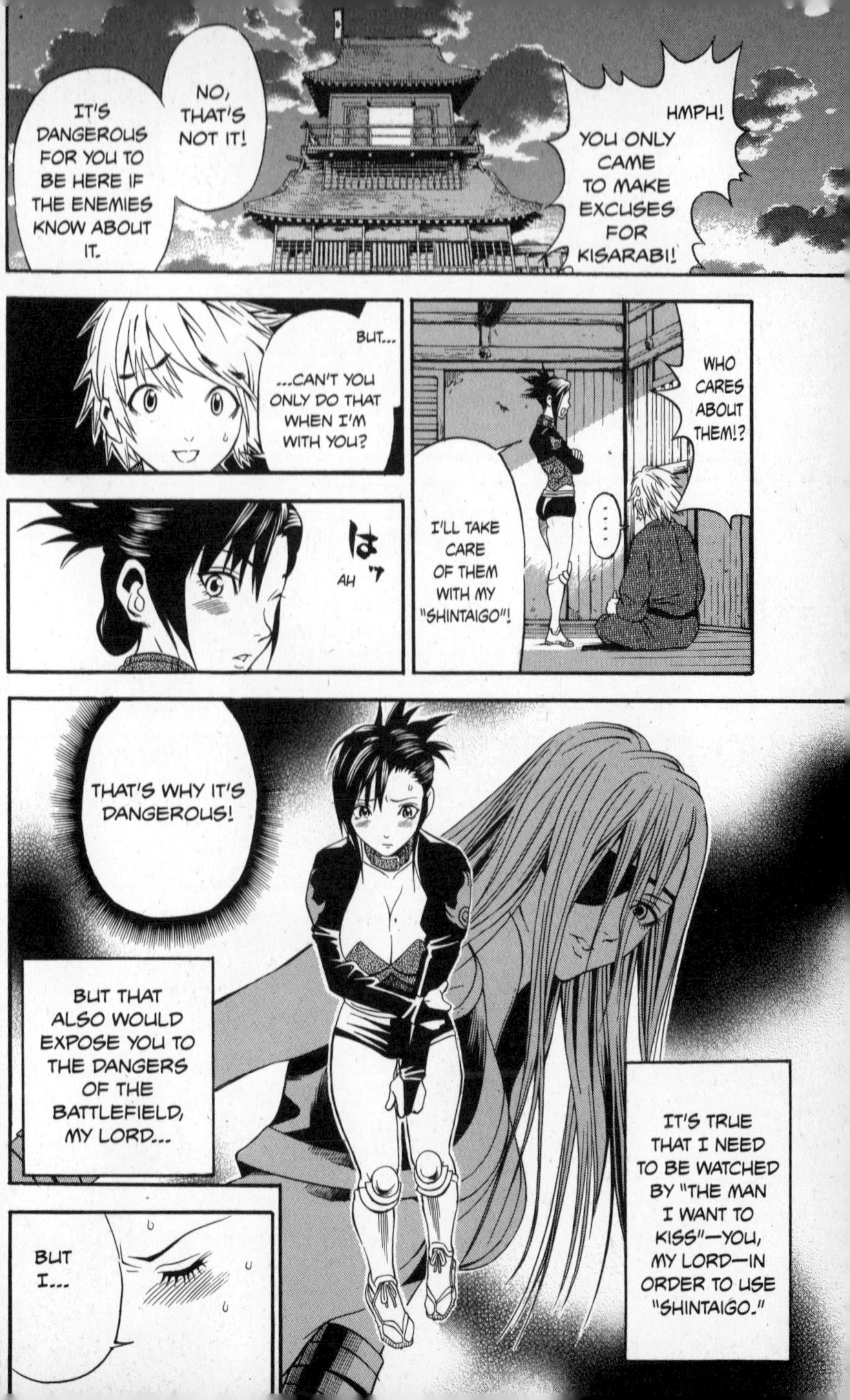
HMPH! YOU ONLY CAME TO MAKE EXCUSES FOR KISARABI!
NO, THAT'S NOT IT!
IT'S DANGEROUS FOR YOU TO BE HERE IF THE ENEMIES KNOW ABOUT IT.
WHO CARES ABOUT THEM!?
......
I'LL TAKE CARE OF THEM WITH MY "SHINTAIGO"!
BUT...
...CAN'T YOU ONLY DO THAT WHEN I'M WITH YOU?
はッ
AH
THAT'S WHY IT'S DANGEROUS!
IT'S TRUE THAT I NEED TO BE WATCHED BY "THE MAN I WANT TO KISS"—YOU, MY LORD—IN ORDER TO USE "SHINTAIGO."
BUT THAT ALSO WOULD EXPOSE YOU TO THE DANGERS OF THE BATTLEFIELD, MY LORD...
BUT I...

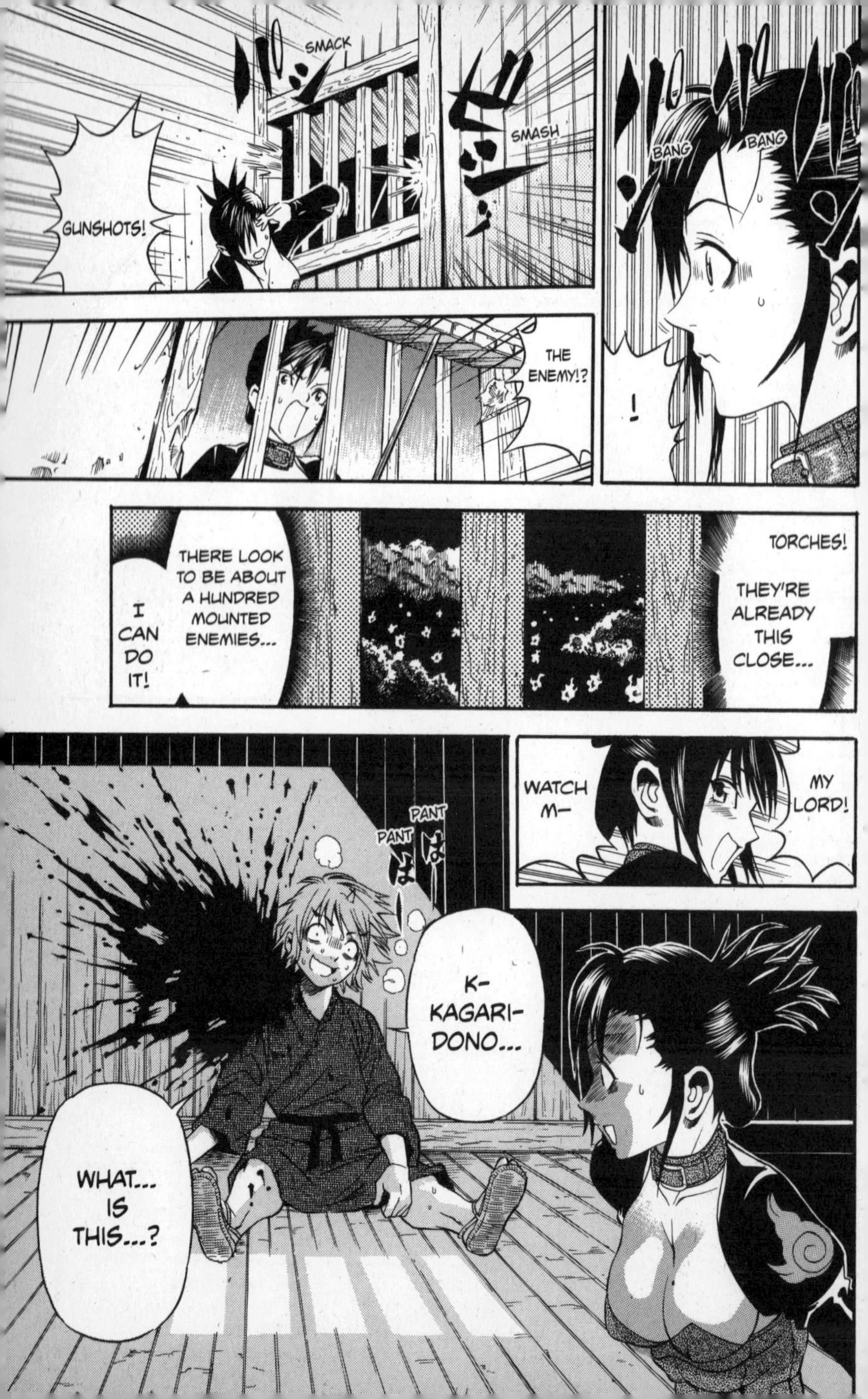
BANG
BANG
!
SMASH
SMACK
GUNSHOTS!
THE ENEMY!?
TORCHES!
THEY'RE ALREADY THIS CLOSE...
THERE LOOK TO BE ABOUT A HUNDRED MOUNTED ENEMIES...
I CAN DO IT!
MY LORD!
WATCH M—
PANT
PANT
K-KAGARI-DONO...
WHAT... IS THIS...?

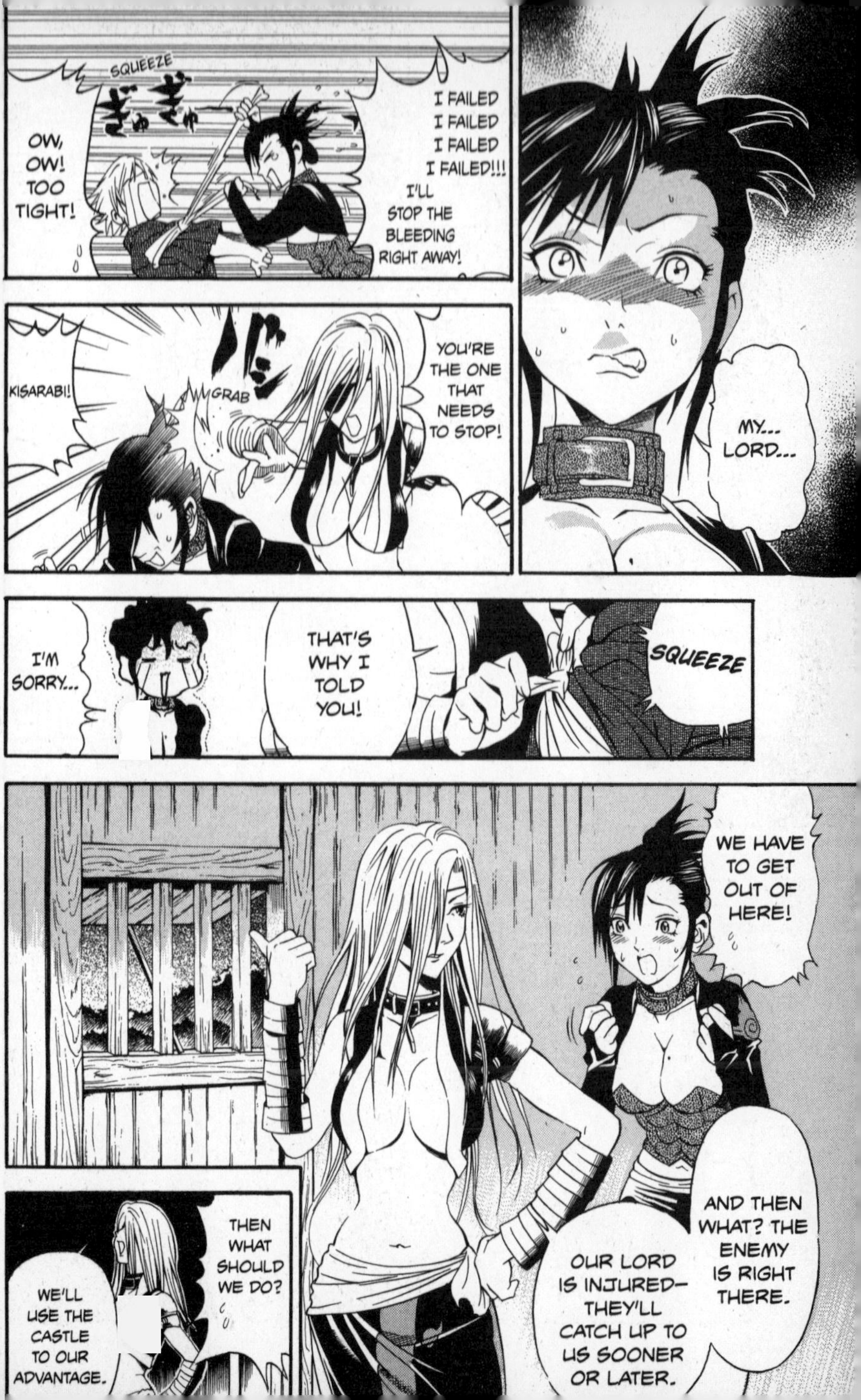
MY... LORD...
I FAILED I FAILED I FAILED I FAILED!!!
I'LL STOP THE BLEEDING RIGHT AWAY!
SQUEEZE
OW, OW! TOO TIGHT!
YOU'RE THE ONE THAT NEEDS TO STOP!
GRAB
KISARABI!
SQUEEZE
THAT'S WHY I TOLD YOU!
I'M SORRY...
WE HAVE TO GET OUT OF HERE!
AND THEN WHAT? THE ENEMY IS RIGHT THERE.
OUR LORD IS INJURED— THEY'LL CATCH UP TO US SOONER OR LATER.
THEN WHAT SHOULD WE DO?
WE'LL USE THE CASTLE TO OUR ADVANTAGE.

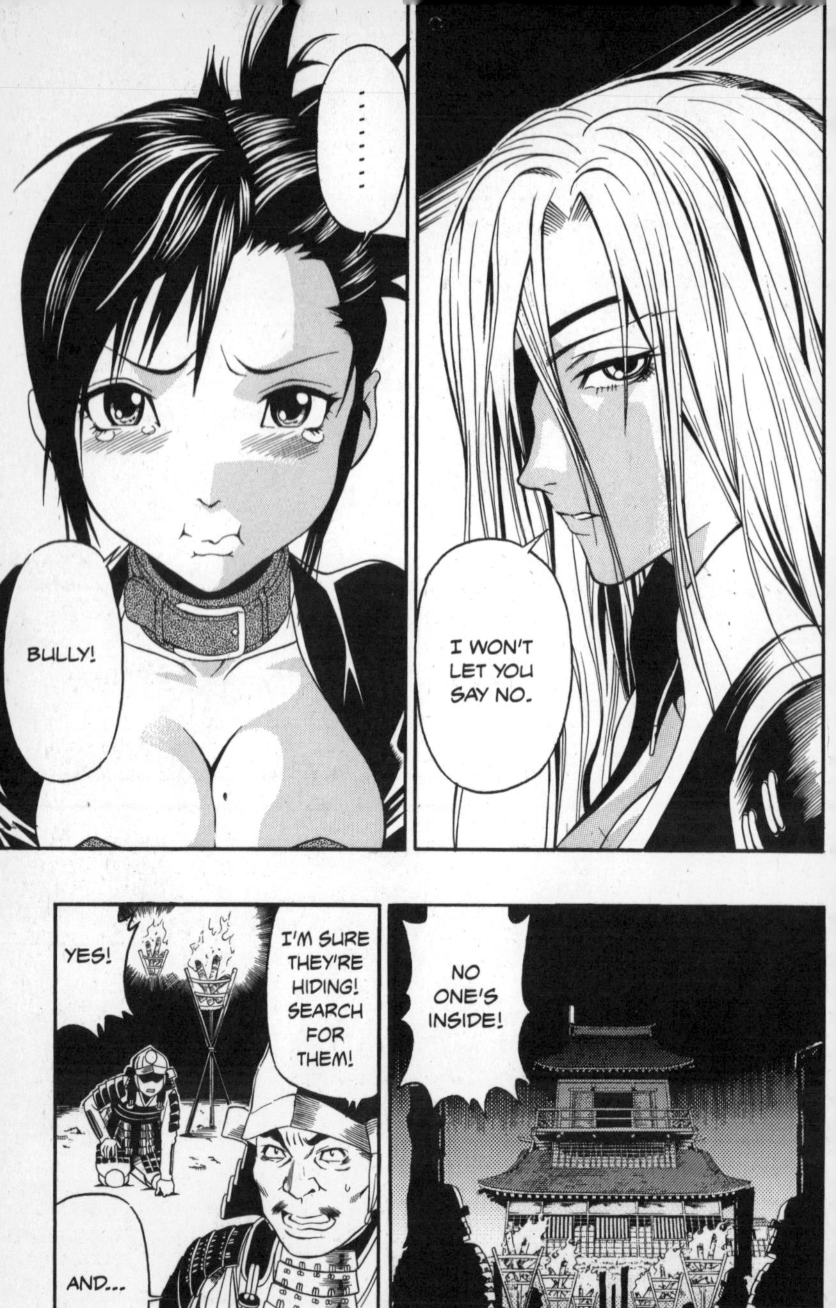
I WON'T LET YOU SAY NO.
......
BULLY!
NO ONE'S INSIDE!
I'M SURE THEY'RE HIDING! SEARCH FOR THEM!
YES!
AND...

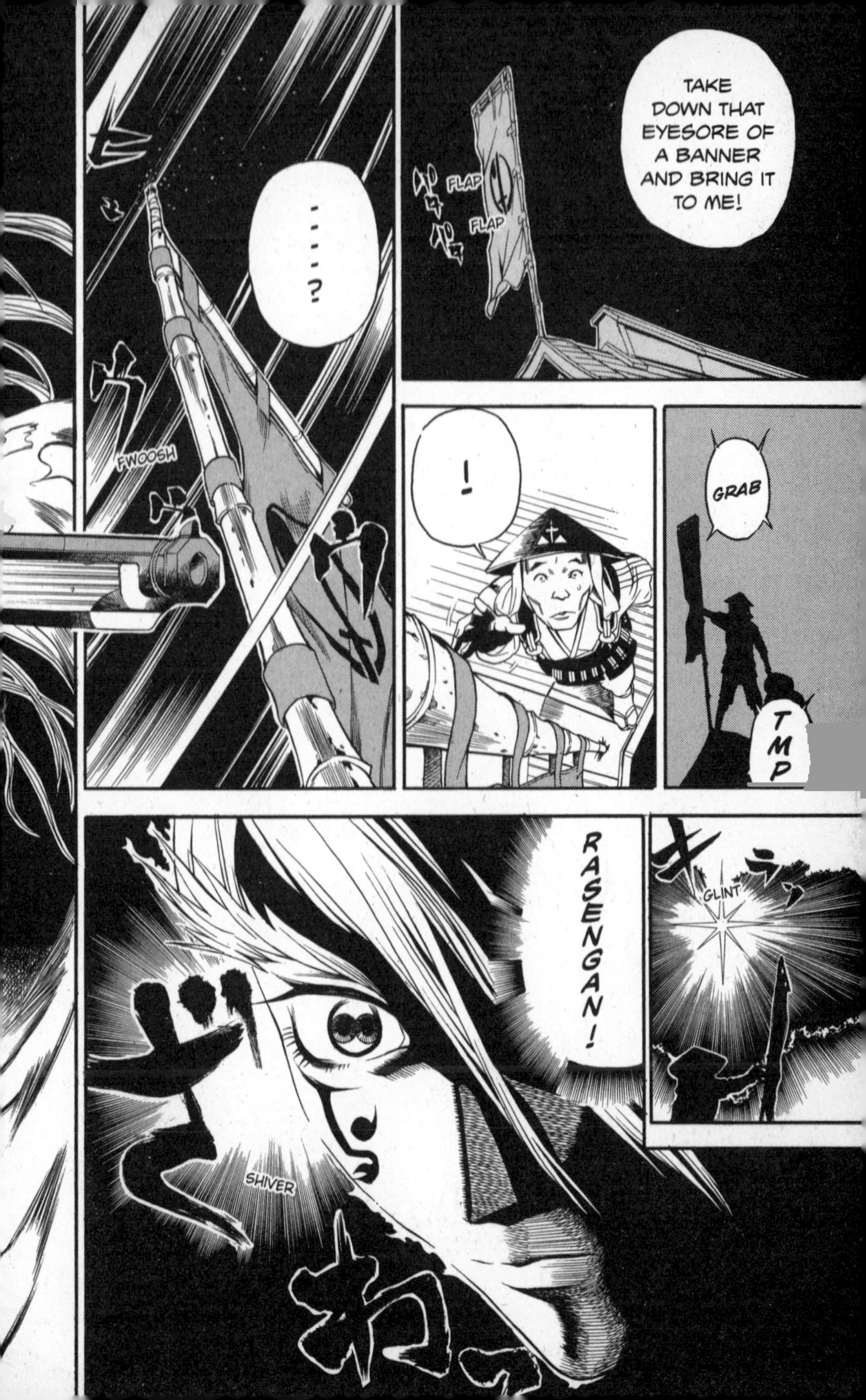
TAKE DOWN THAT EYESORE OF A BANNER AND BRING IT TO ME!
FLAP
FLAP
GRAB
TMP
!
......?
FWOOSH
GLINT
RASENGAN!
SHIVER

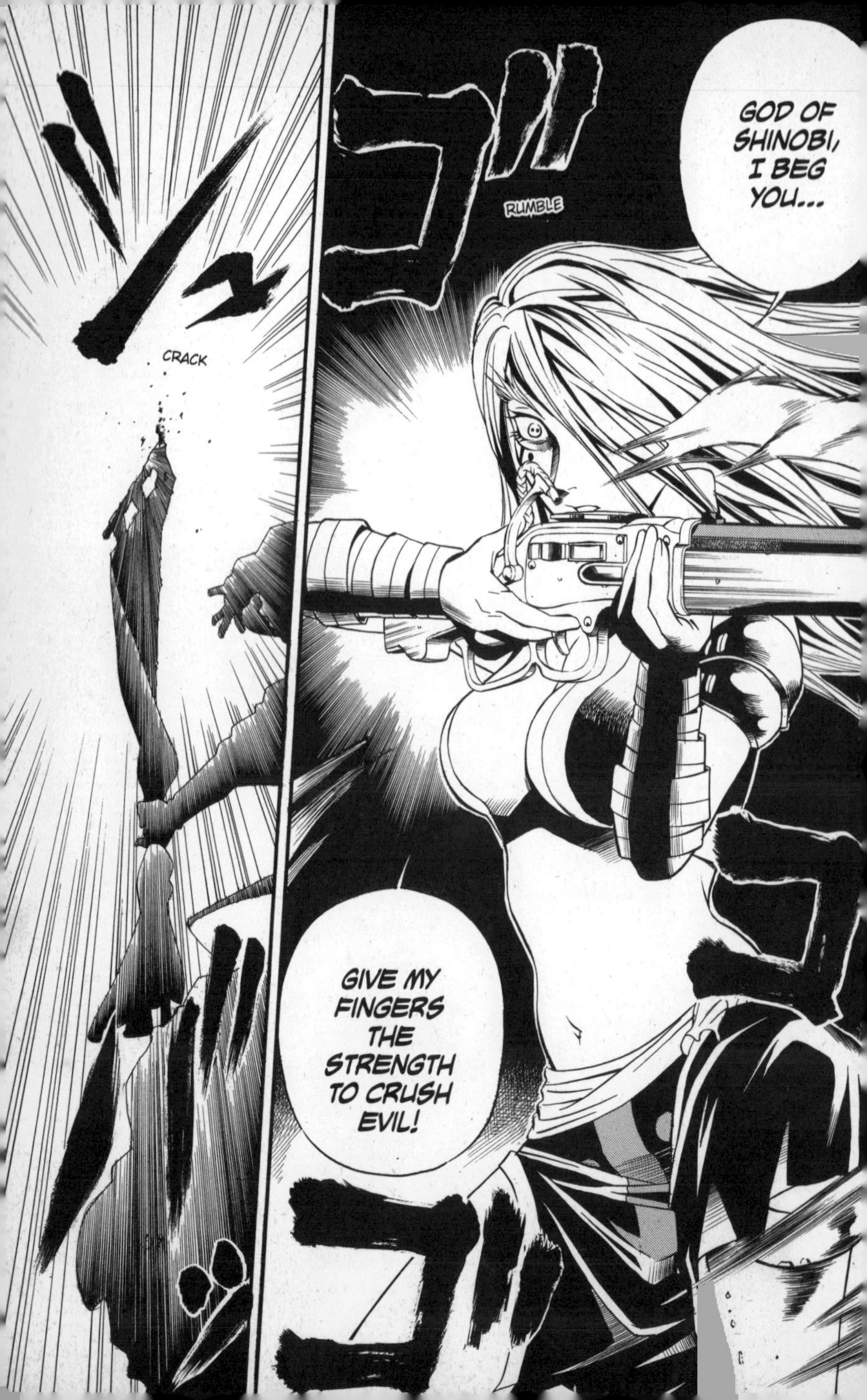
GOD OF SHINOBI, I BEG YOU...
RUMBLE
GIVE MY FINGERS THE STRENGTH TO CRUSH EVIL!
CRACK

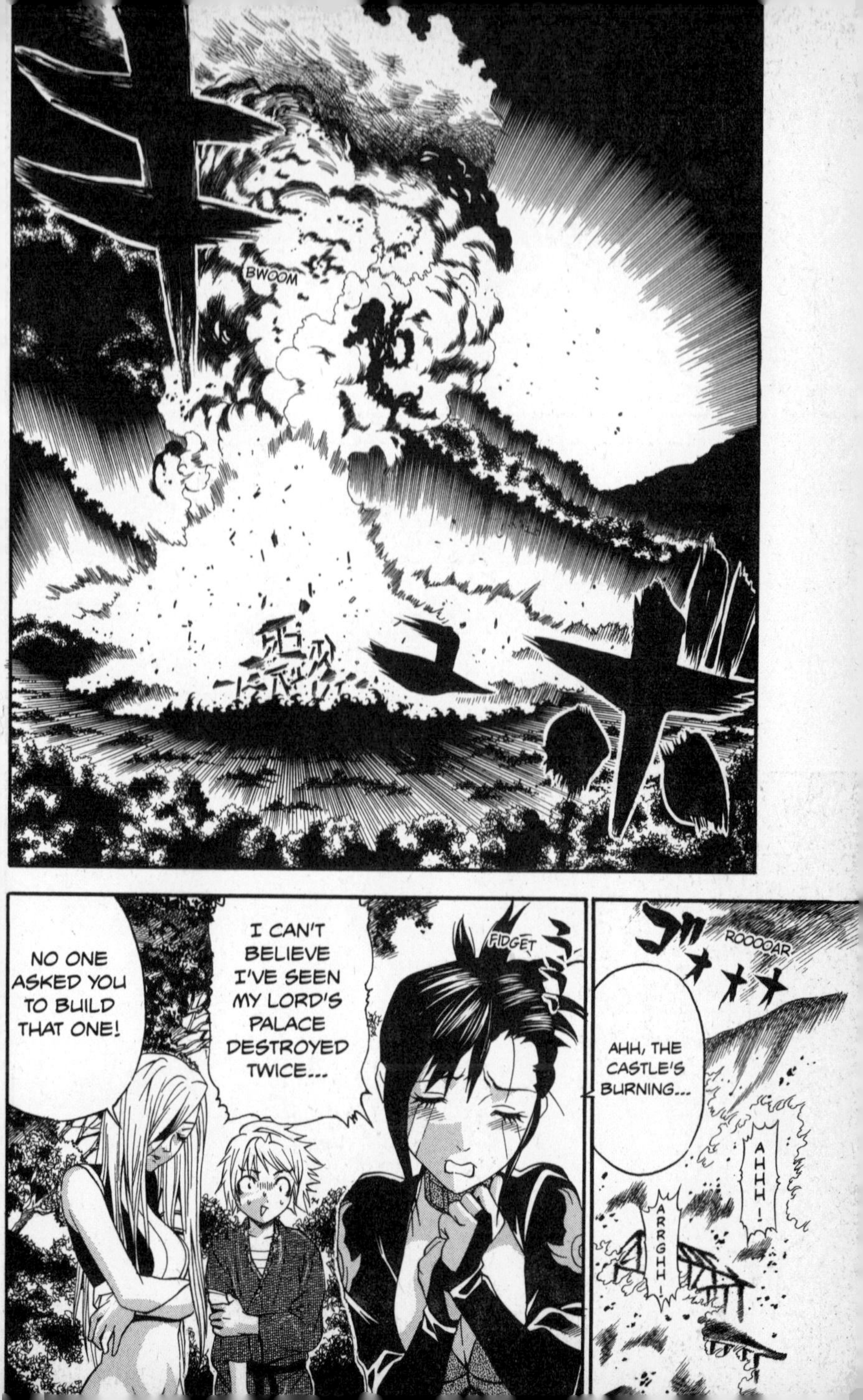
BWOOM
ROOOOAR
AHH, THE CASTLE'S BURNING...
AHHH!
ARRGHH!
FIDGET
I CAN'T BELIEVE I'VE SEEN MY LORD'S PALACE DESTROYED TWICE...
NO ONE ASKED YOU TO BUILD THAT ONE!

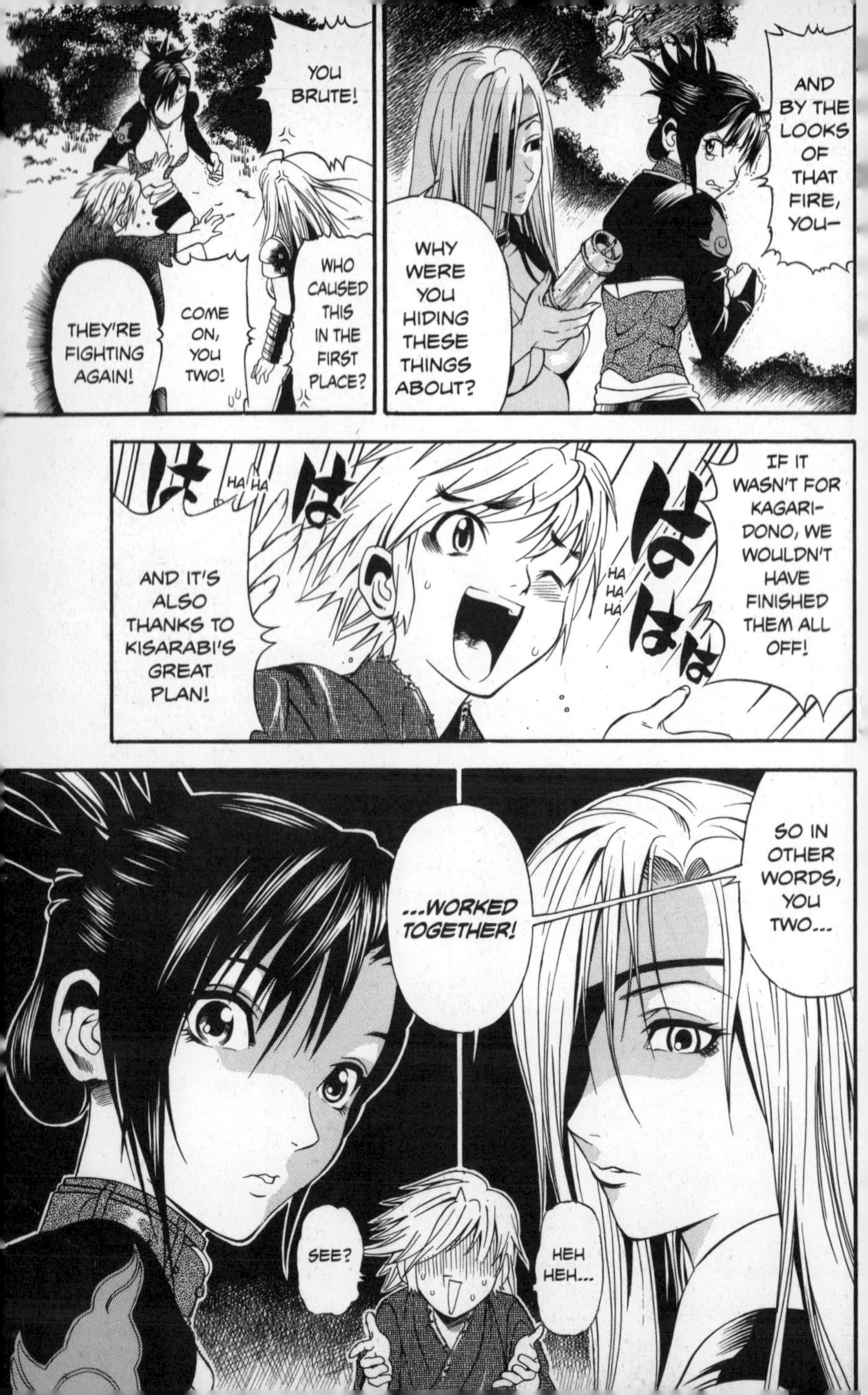
AND BY THE LOOKS OF THAT FIRE, YOU—
WHY WERE YOU HIDING THESE THINGS ABOUT?
YOU BRUTE!
WHO CAUSED THIS IN THE FIRST PLACE?
COME ON, YOU TWO!
THEY'RE FIGHTING AGAIN!
IF IT WASN'T FOR KAGARI-DONO, WE WOULDN'T HAVE FINISHED THEM ALL OFF!
HA HA HA
AND IT'S ALSO THANKS TO KISARABI'S GREAT PLAN!
HA HA
SO IN OTHER WORDS, YOU TWO...
...WORKED TOGETHER!
HEH HEH...
SEE?

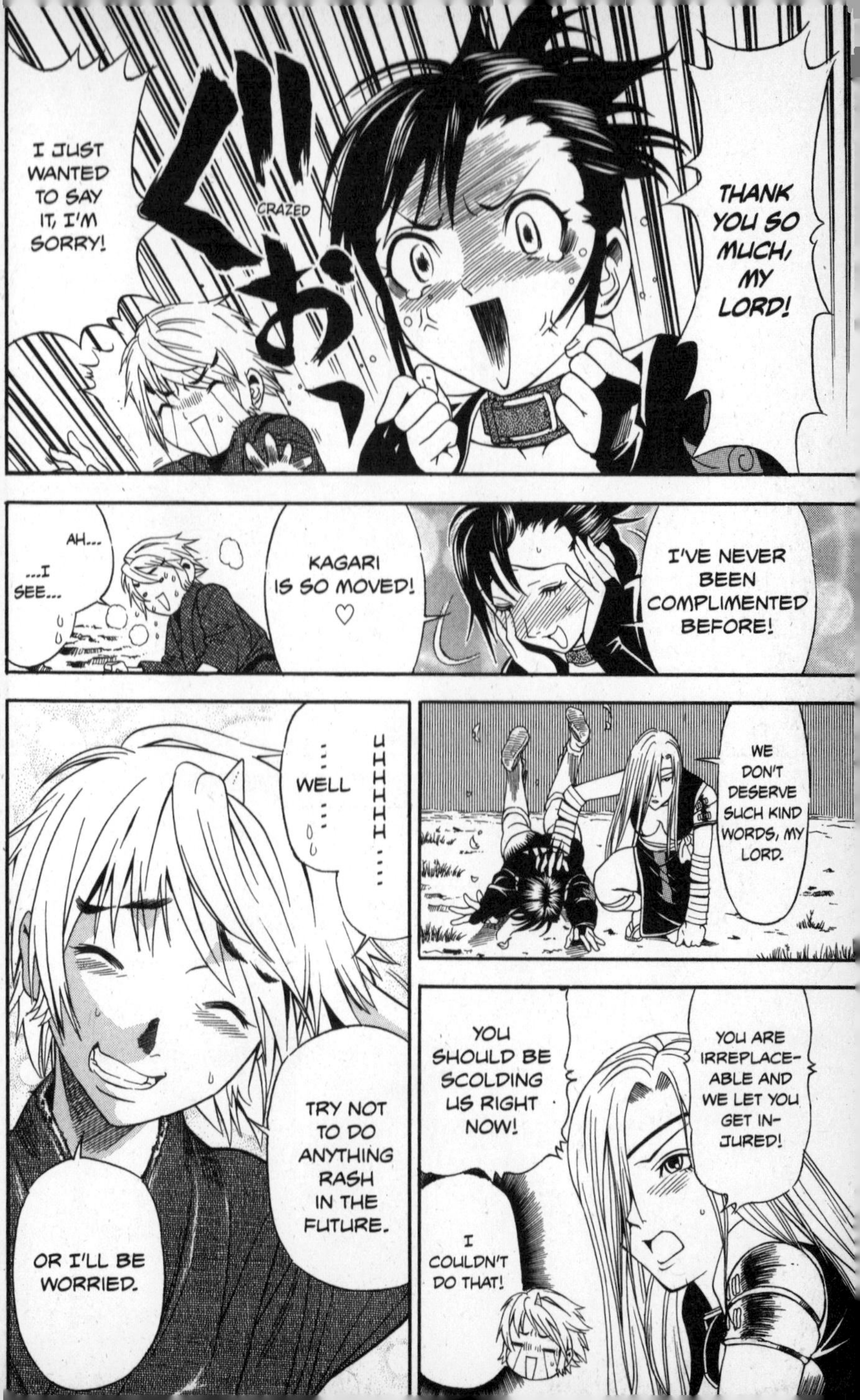
THANK YOU SO MUCH, MY LORD!
CRAZED
I JUST WANTED TO SAY IT, I'M SORRY!
I'VE NEVER BEEN COMPLIMENTED BEFORE!
KAGARI IS SO MOVED! ♡
AH... ...I SEE...
WE DON'T DESERVE SUCH KIND WORDS, MY LORD.
YOU ARE IRREPLACE-ABLE AND WE LET YOU GET IN-JURED!
YOU SHOULD BE SCOLDING US RIGHT NOW!
I COULDN'T DO THAT!
UHHHHH....
...WELL...
TRY NOT TO DO ANYTHING RASH IN THE FUTURE.
OR I'LL BE WORRIED.

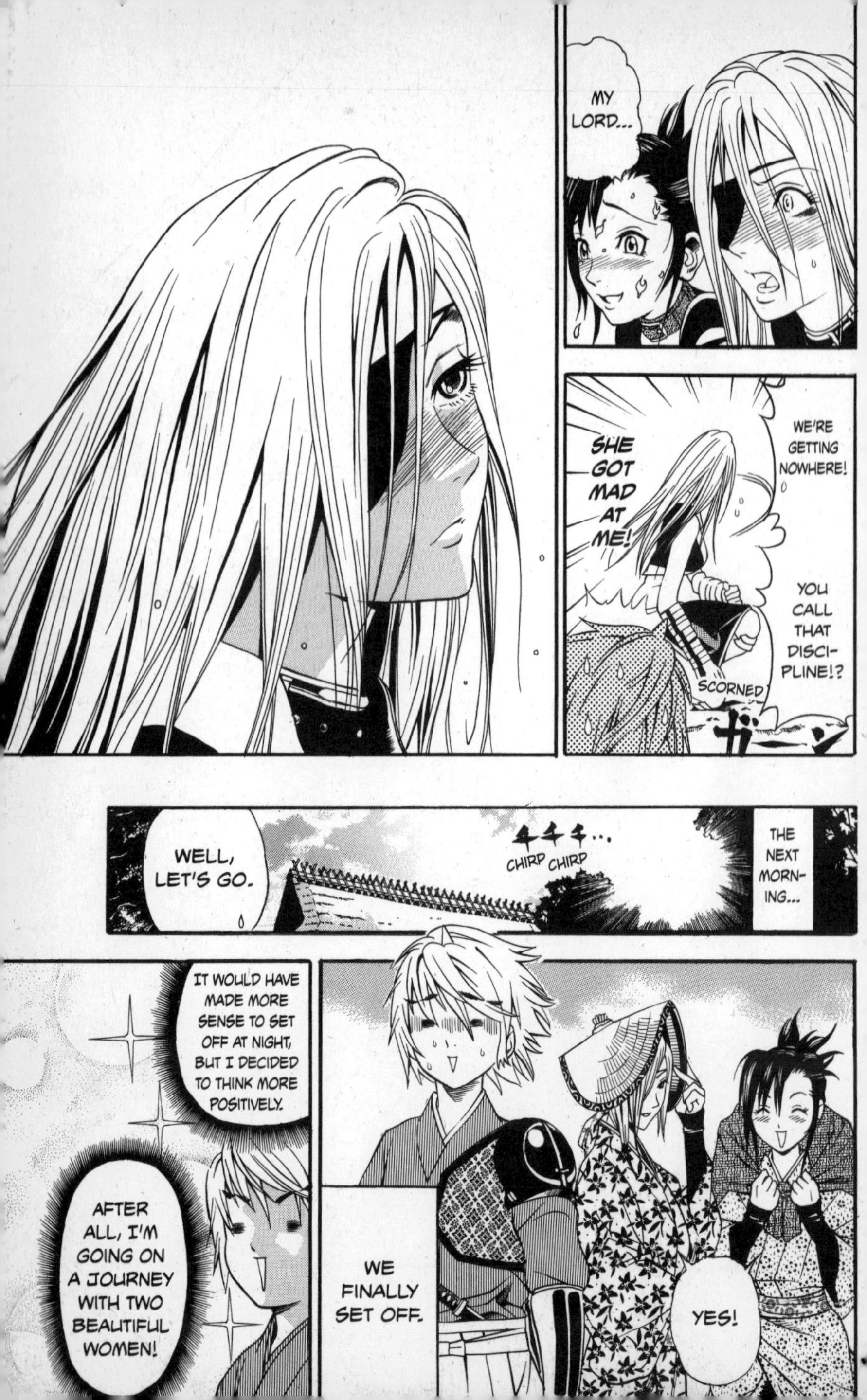
MY LORD...
WE'RE GETTING NOWHERE!
SHE GOT MAD AT ME!
YOU CALL THAT DISCI-PLINE!?
SCORNED
THE NEXT MORN-ING...
CHIRP CHIRP
WELL, LET'S GO.
YES!
WE FINALLY SET OFF.
IT WOULD HAVE MADE MORE SENSE TO SET OFF AT NIGHT, BUT I DECIDED TO THINK MORE POSITIVELY.
AFTER ALL, I'M GOING ON A JOURNEY WITH TWO BEAUTIFUL WOMEN!

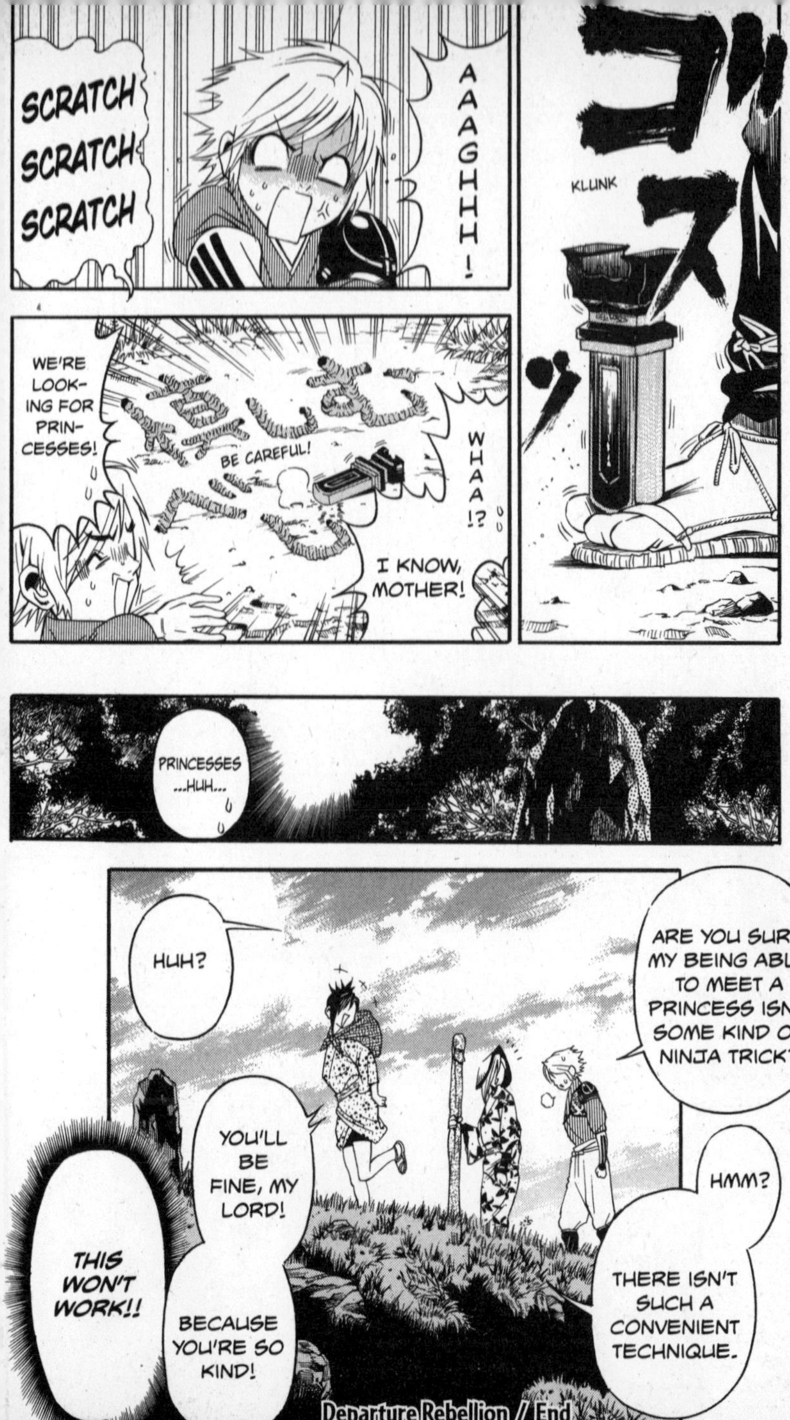
KLUNK
AAAGHHH!
SCRATCH SCRATCH SCRATCH
WHAA!?
BE CAREFUL!
WE'RE LOOKING FOR PRINCESSES!
I KNOW, MOTHER!
PRINCESSES ...HUH...
ARE YOU SURE MY BEING ABLE TO MEET A PRINCESS ISN'T SOME KIND OF NINJA TRICK?
HUH?
HMM?
THERE ISN'T SUCH A CONVENIENT TECHNIQUE.
YOU'LL BE FINE, MY LORD!
BECAUSE YOU'RE SO KIND!
THIS WON'T WORK!!

Departure Rebellion / End

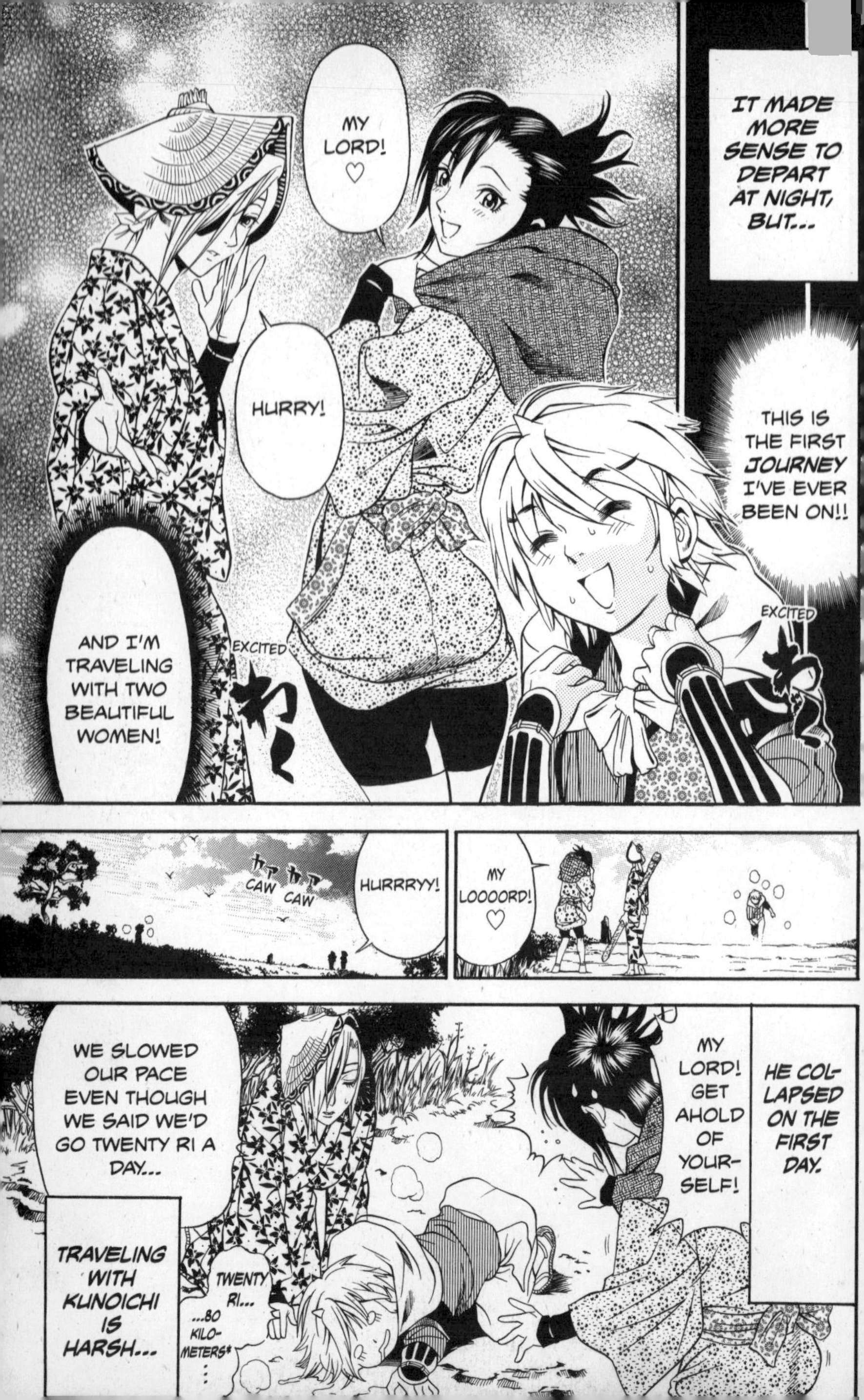
IT MADE MORE SENSE TO DEPART AT NIGHT, BUT...
THIS IS THE FIRST JOURNEY I'VE EVER BEEN ON!!
EXCITED
MY LORD! ♡
HURRY!
EXCITED
AND I'M TRAVELING WITH TWO BEAUTIFUL WOMEN!
MY LOOOORD! ♡
HURRRYY!
CAW CAW
HE COL-LAPSED ON THE FIRST DAY.
MY LORD! GET AHOLD OF YOUR-SELF!
WE SLOWED OUR PACE EVEN THOUGH WE SAID WE'D GO TWENTY RI A DAY...
TWENTY RI...
...80 KILO-METERS*...
TRAVELING WITH KUNOICHI IS HARSH...

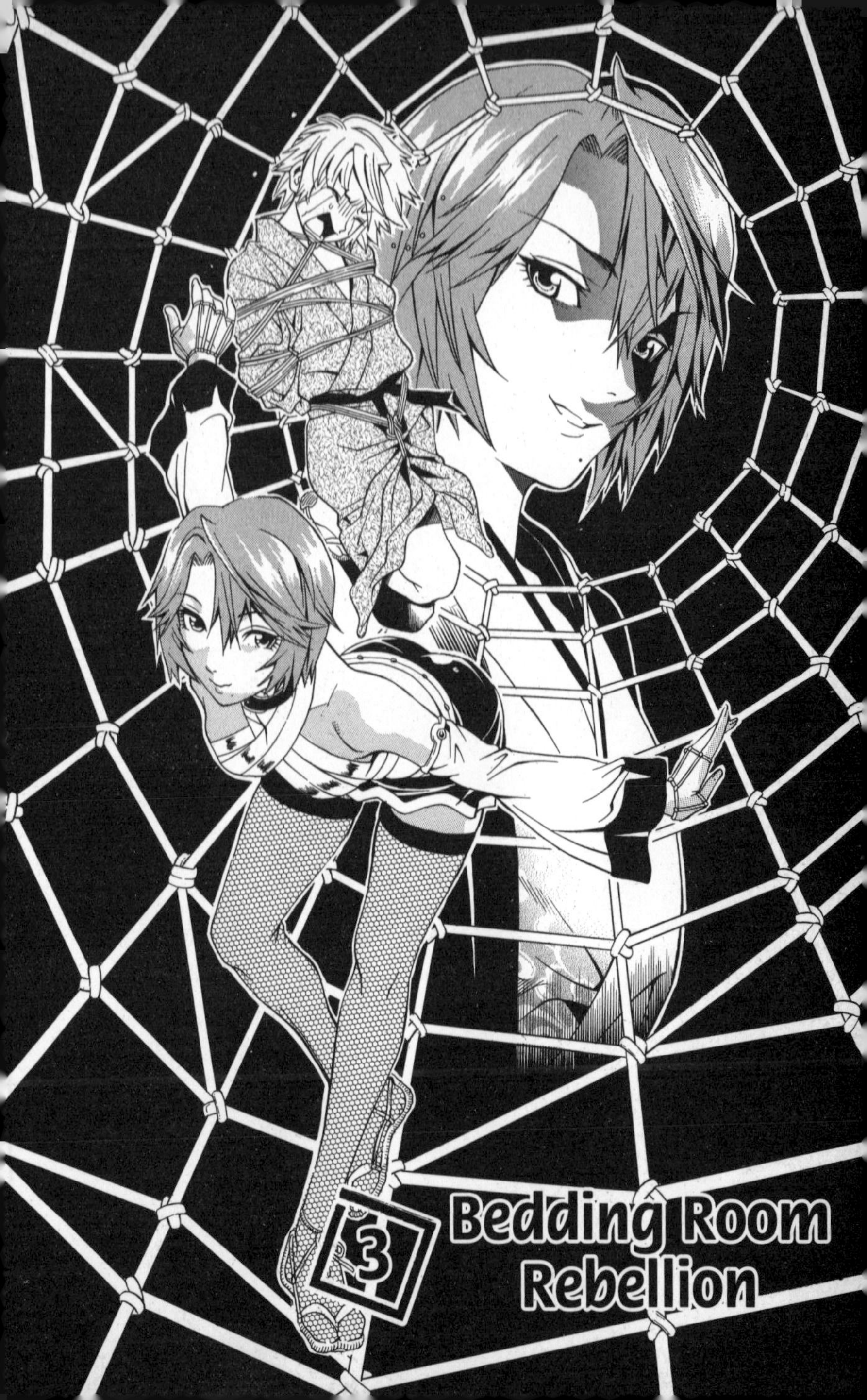
3
Bedding Room
Rebellion

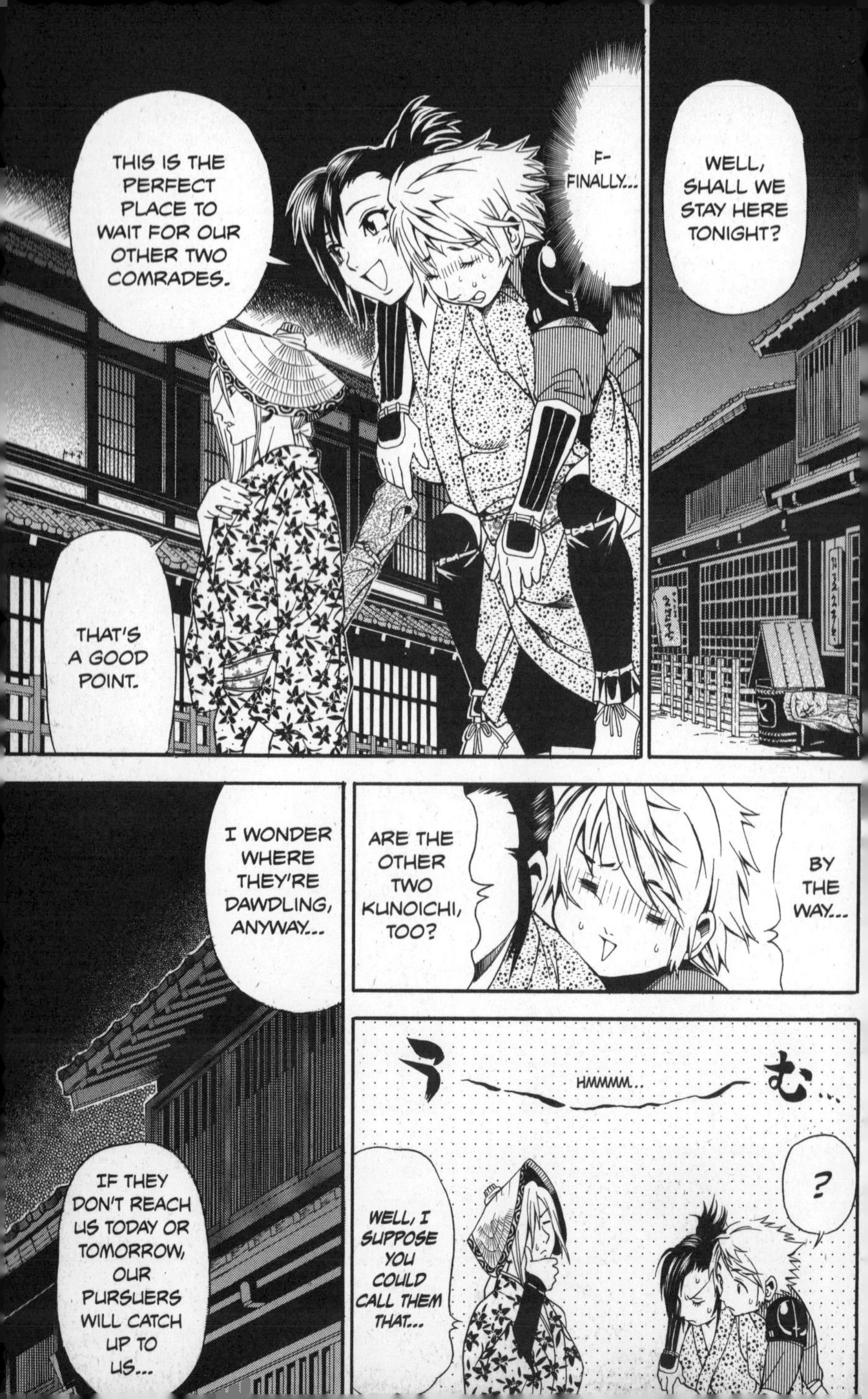

WELL, SHALL WE STAY HERE TONIGHT?
F- FINALLY...
THIS IS THE PERFECT PLACE TO WAIT FOR OUR OTHER TWO COMRADES.
THAT'S A GOOD POINT.
BY THE WAY...
ARE THE OTHER TWO KUNOICHI, TOO?
う HMMMM... む...
?
WELL, I SUPPOSE YOU COULD CALL THEM THAT...
I WONDER WHERE THEY'RE DAWDLING, ANYWAY...
IF THEY DON'T REACH US TODAY OR TOMORROW, OUR PURSUERS WILL CATCH UP TO US...

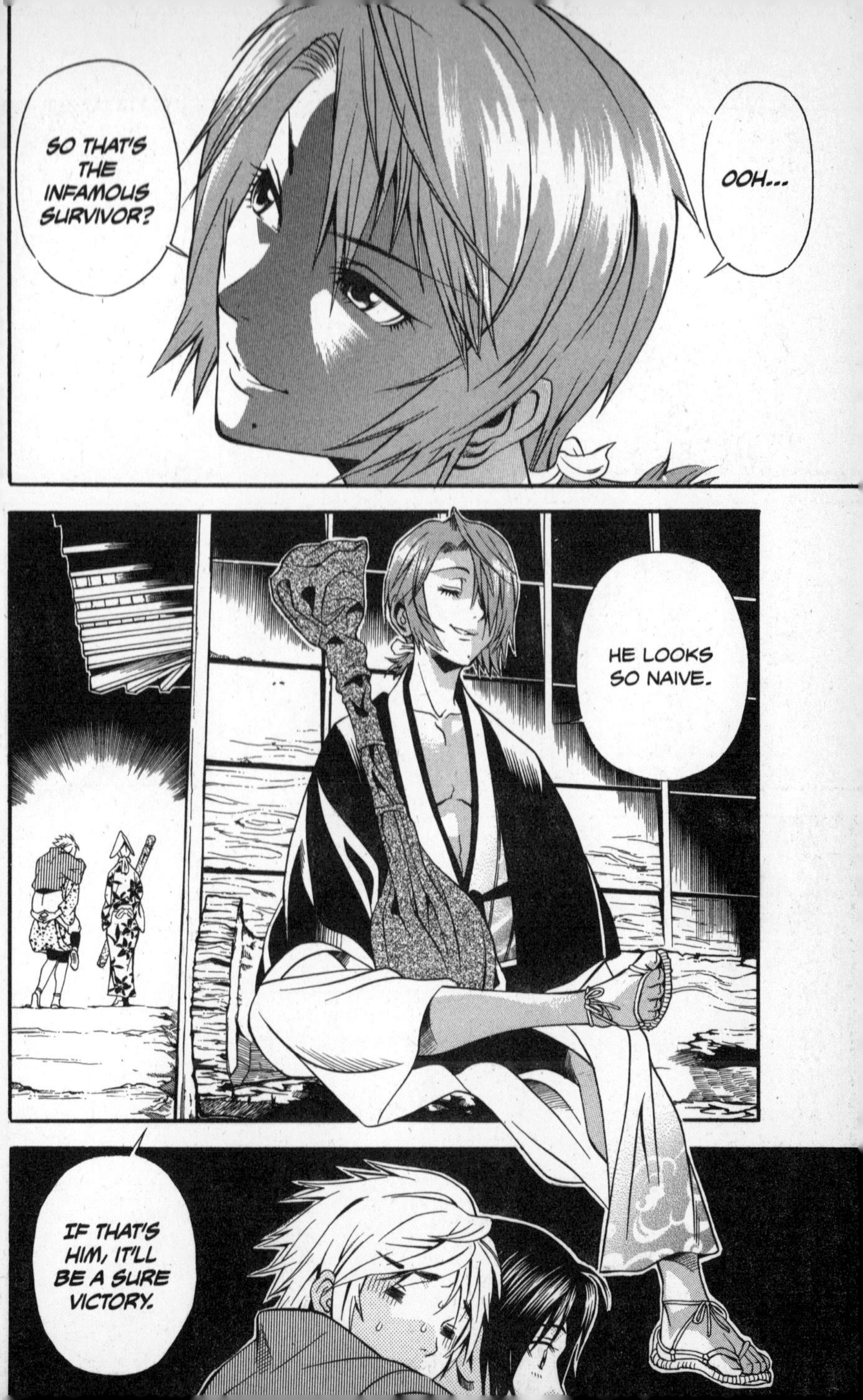
OOH...
SO THAT'S THE INFAMOUS SURVIVOR?
HE LOOKS SO NAIVE.
IF THAT'S HIM, IT'LL BE A SURE VICTORY.

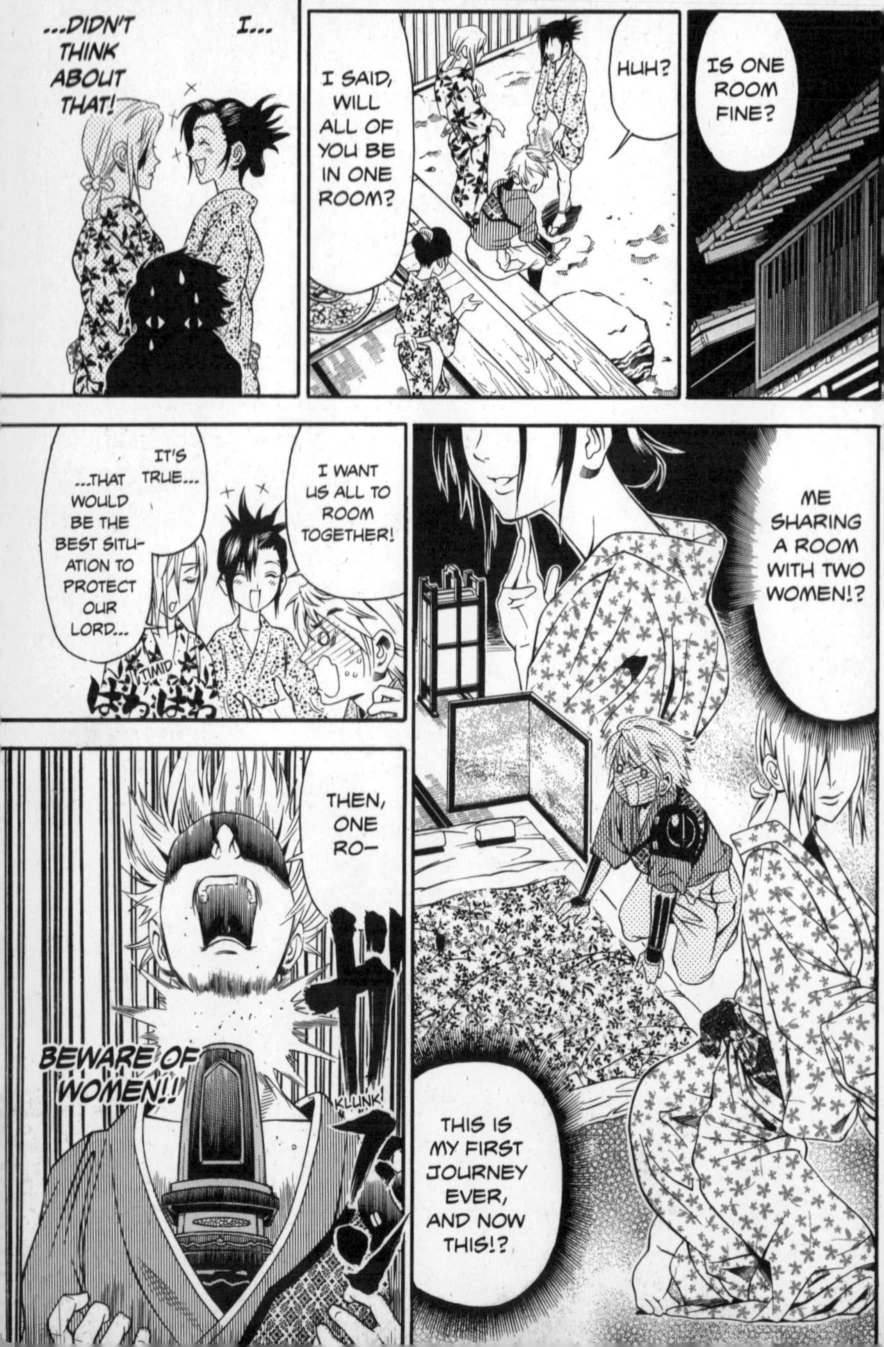
IS ONE ROOM FINE?
HUH?
I SAID, WILL ALL OF YOU BE IN ONE ROOM?
I...
...DIDN'T THINK ABOUT THAT!
ME SHARING A ROOM WITH TWO WOMEN!?
THIS IS MY FIRST JOURNEY EVER, AND NOW THIS!?
I WANT US ALL TO ROOM TOGETHER!
IT'S TRUE...
...THAT WOULD BE THE BEST SITUATION TO PROTECT OUR LORD...
TIMID
THEN, ONE RO—
KLUNK!
BEWARE OF WOMEN!!

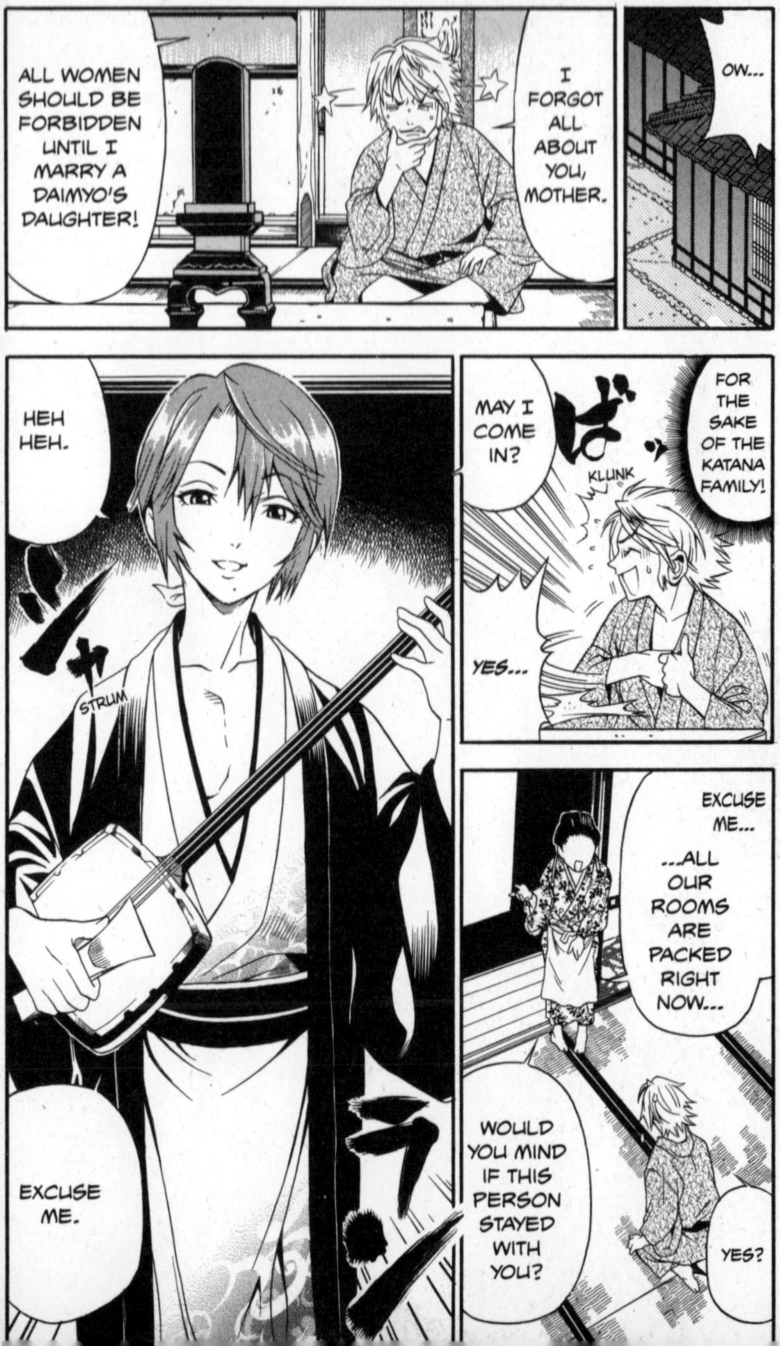
OW...
I FORGOT ALL ABOUT YOU, MOTHER.
ALL WOMEN SHOULD BE FORBIDDEN UNTIL I MARRY A DAIMYO'S DAUGHTER!
FOR THE SAKE OF THE KATANA FAMILY!
ば
KLUNK
MAY I COME IN?
YES...
EXCUSE ME...
...ALL OUR ROOMS ARE PACKED RIGHT NOW...
WOULD YOU MIND IF THIS PERSON STAYED WITH YOU?
YES?
HEH HEH.
STRUM
EXCUSE ME.

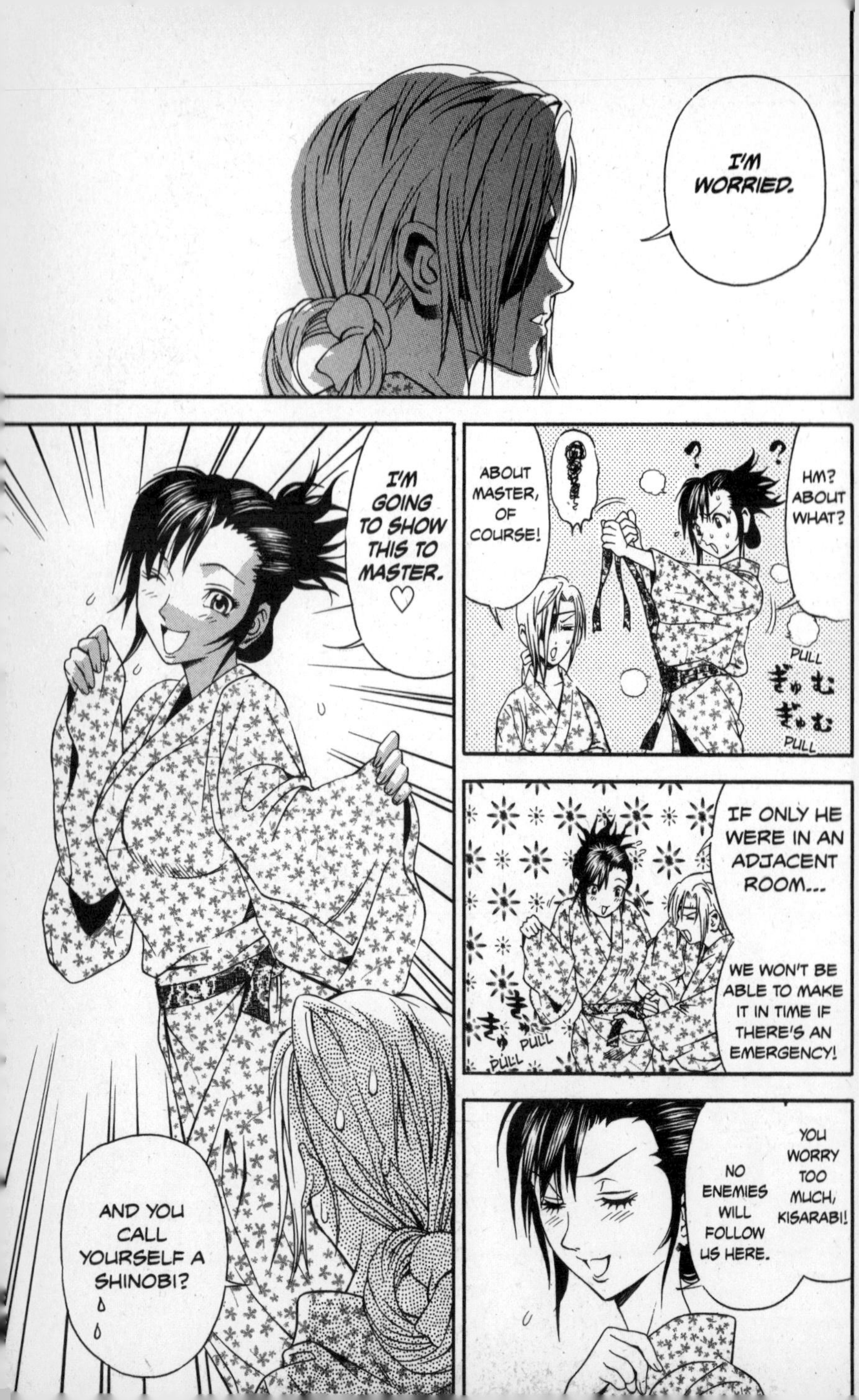
I'M WORRIED.
HM? ABOUT WHAT?
ABOUT MASTER, OF COURSE!
PULL
ぎゅむ
ぎゅむ
PULL
IF ONLY HE WERE IN AN ADJACENT ROOM...
WE WON'T BE ABLE TO MAKE IT IN TIME IF THERE'S AN EMERGENCY!
きゅ
PULL
きゅ
PULL
YOU WORRY TOO MUCH, KISARABI!
NO ENEMIES WILL FOLLOW US HERE.
I'M GOING TO SHOW THIS TO MASTER. ♡
AND YOU CALL YOURSELF A SHINOBI?

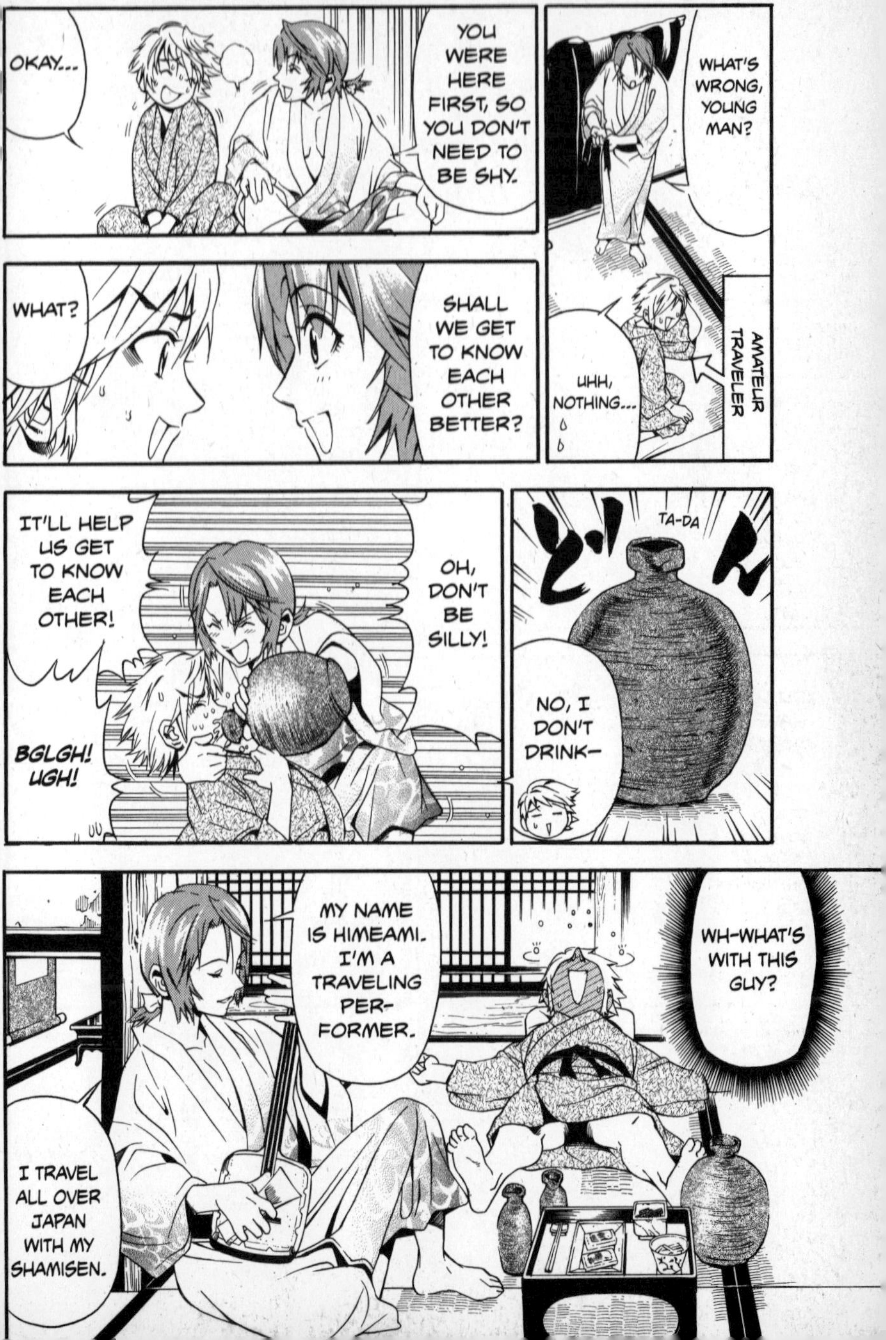
WHAT'S WRONG, YOUNG MAN?
UHH, NOTHING...
AMATEUR TRAVELER
YOU WERE HERE FIRST, SO YOU DON'T NEED TO BE SHY.
OKAY...
SHALL WE GET TO KNOW EACH OTHER BETTER?
WHAT?
TA-DA
NO, I DON'T DRINK—
OH, DON'T BE SILLY!
IT'LL HELP US GET TO KNOW EACH OTHER!
BGLGH! UGH!
WH-WHAT'S WITH THIS GUY?
MY NAME IS HIMEAMI. I'M A TRAVELING PER-FORMER.
I TRAVEL ALL OVER JAPAN WITH MY SHAMISEN.

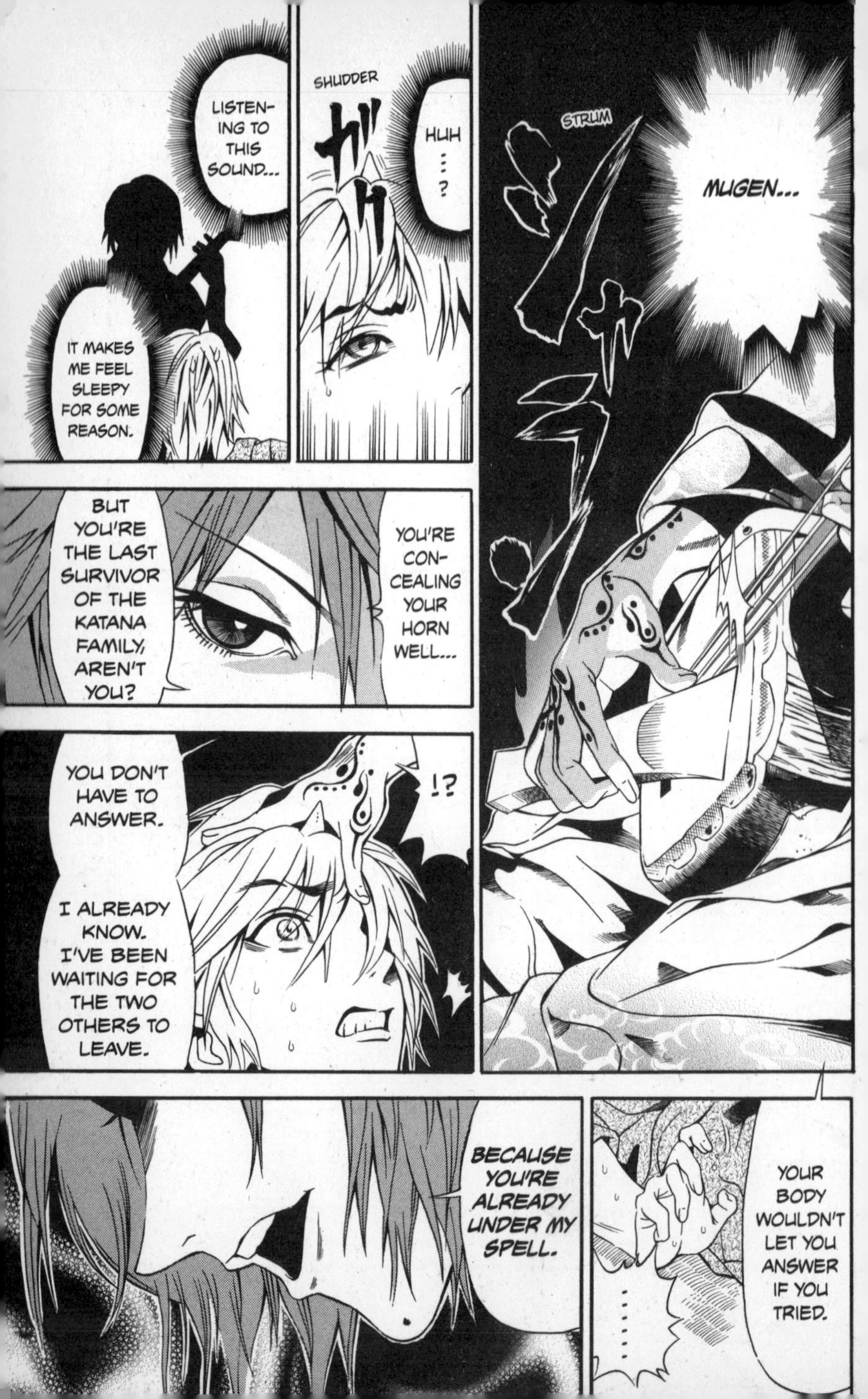
STRUM
MUGEN...
SHUDDER
HUH...?
LISTENING TO THIS SOUND...
IT MAKES ME FEEL SLEEPY FOR SOME REASON.
YOU'RE CONCEALING YOUR HORN WELL...
BUT YOU'RE THE LAST SURVIVOR OF THE KATANA FAMILY, AREN'T YOU?
!?
YOU DON'T HAVE TO ANSWER.
I ALREADY KNOW. I'VE BEEN WAITING FOR THE TWO OTHERS TO LEAVE.
YOUR BODY WOULDN'T LET YOU ANSWER IF YOU TRIED.
......
BECAUSE YOU'RE ALREADY UNDER MY SPELL.

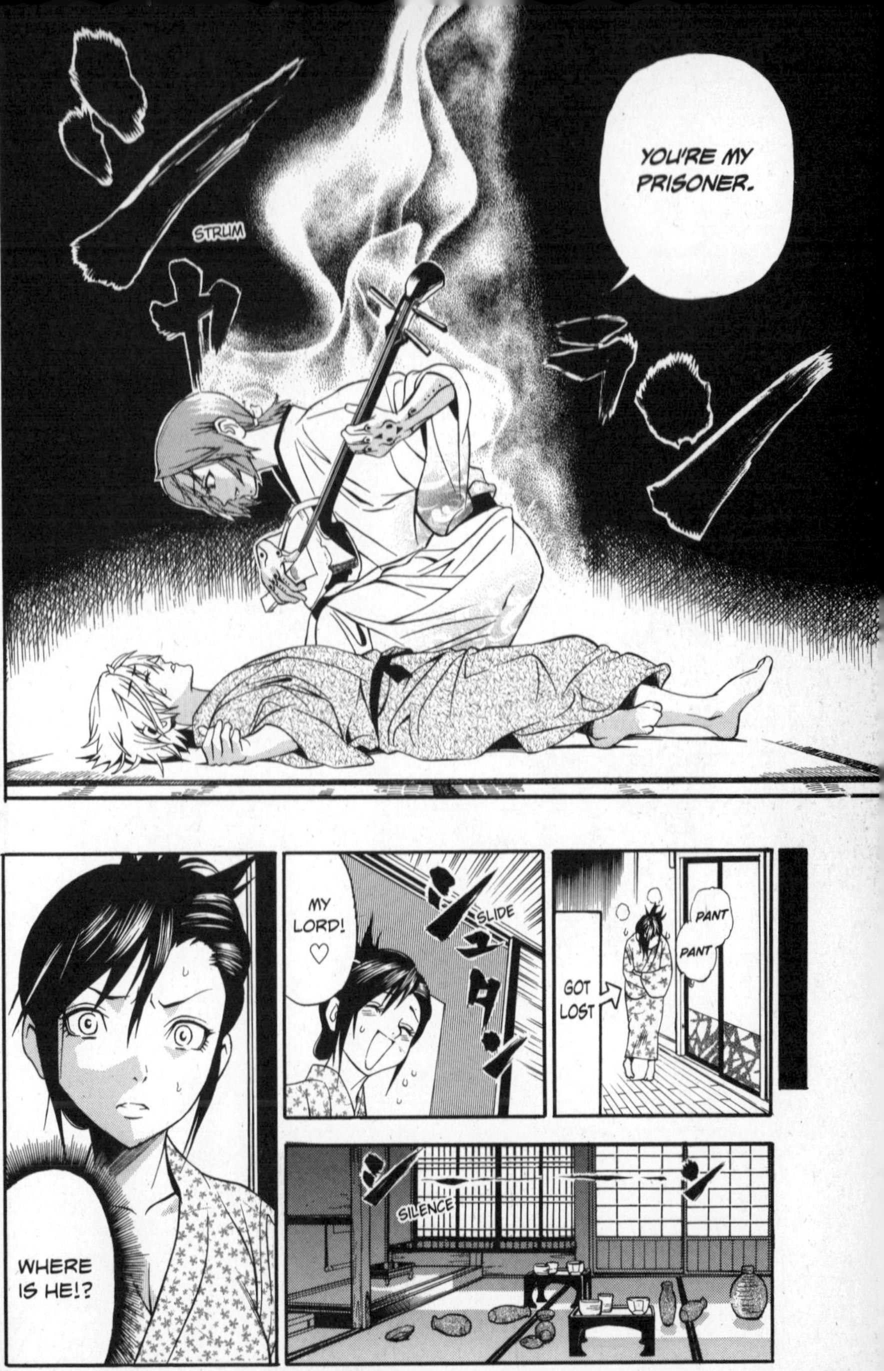
YOU'RE MY PRISONER.
STRUM
PANT
PANT
GOT LOST
SLIDE
MY LORD! ♡
SILENCE
WHERE IS HE!?

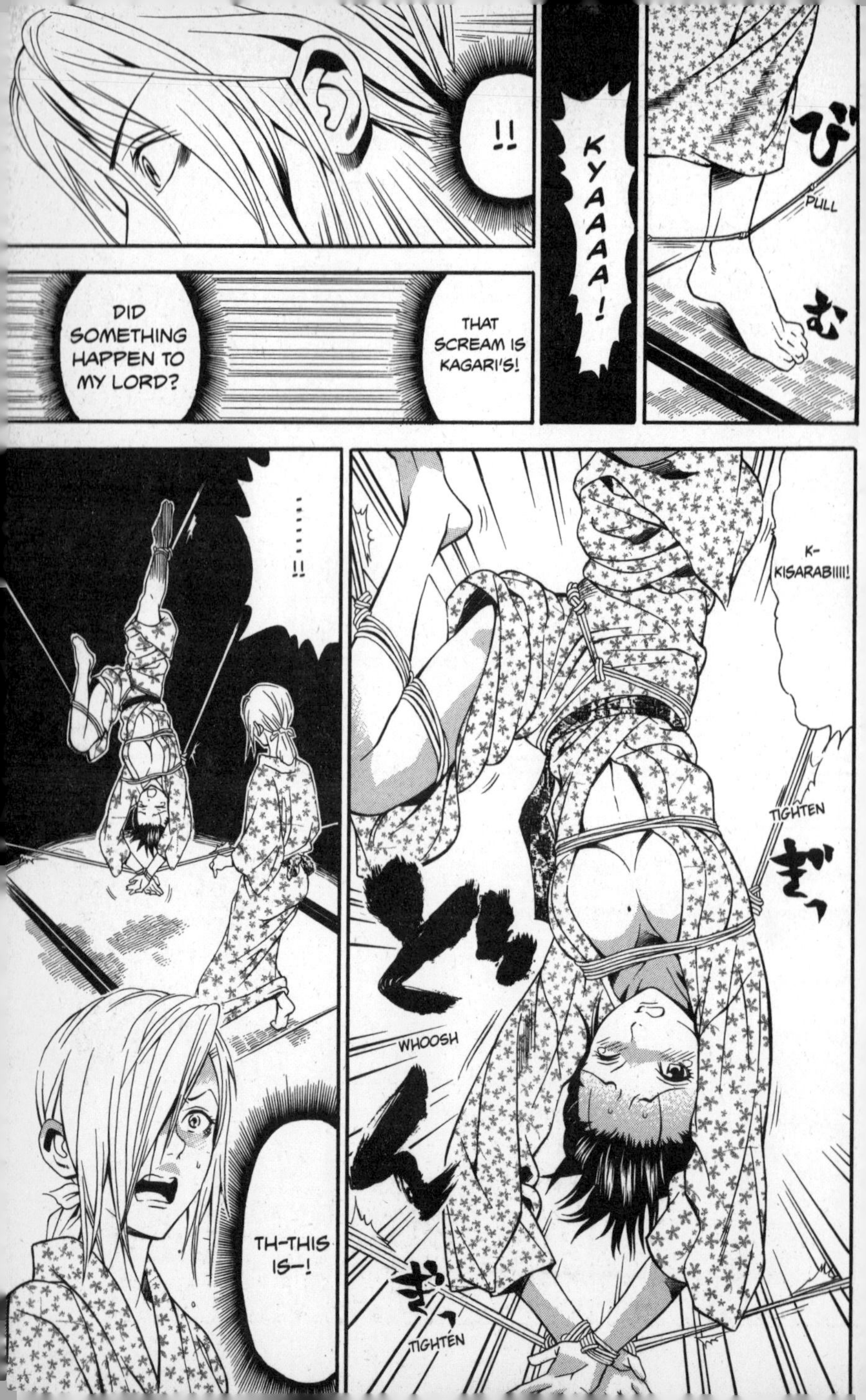
PULL
KYAAAAA!
!!
THAT SCREAM IS KAGARI'S!
DID SOMETHING HAPPEN TO MY LORD?
K-KISARABIIIII!
TIGHTEN
WHOOSH
TIGHTEN
......!!
TH-THIS IS—!

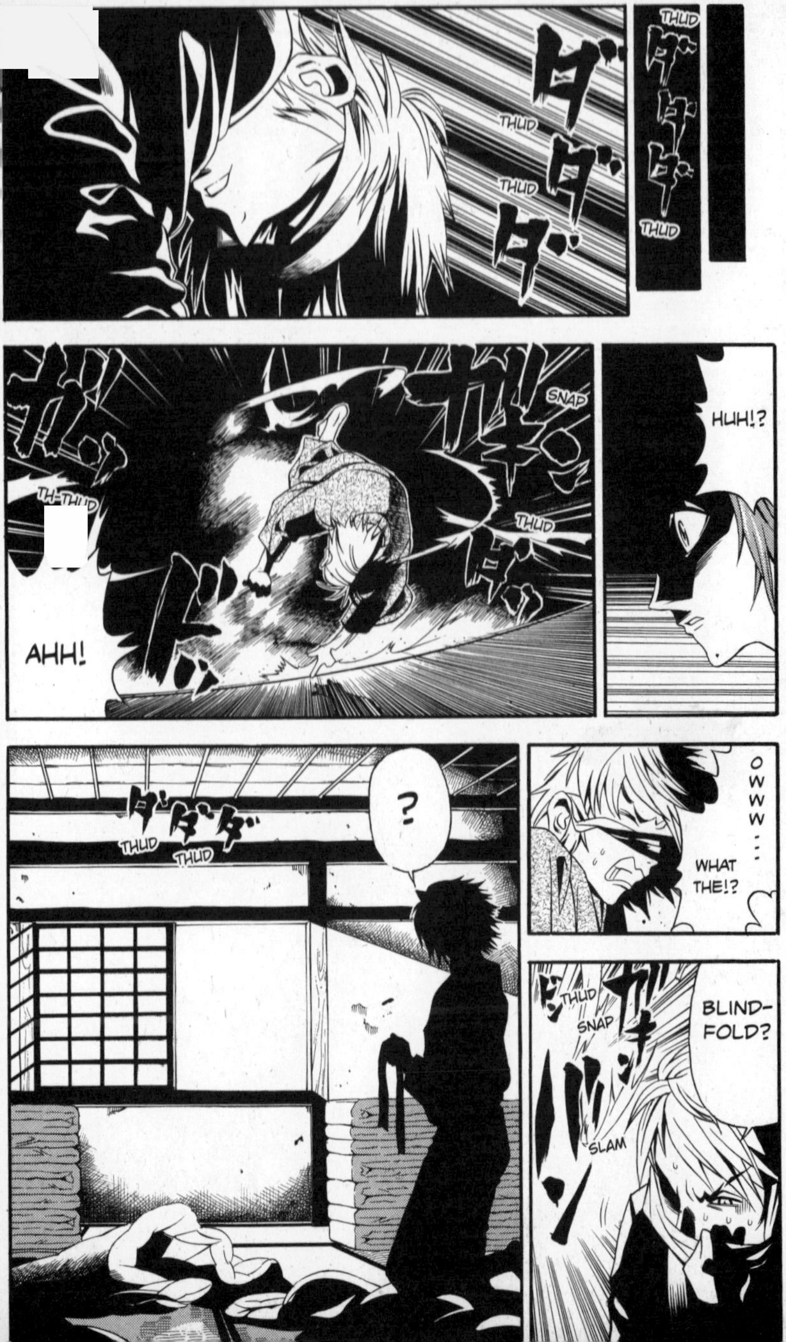
THUD
THUD
THUD
THUD
HUH!?
SNAP
THUD
TH-THUD
AHH!
OWWW...
WHAT THE!?
THUD
SNAP
SLAM
BLIND-FOLD?
THUD
THUD
?

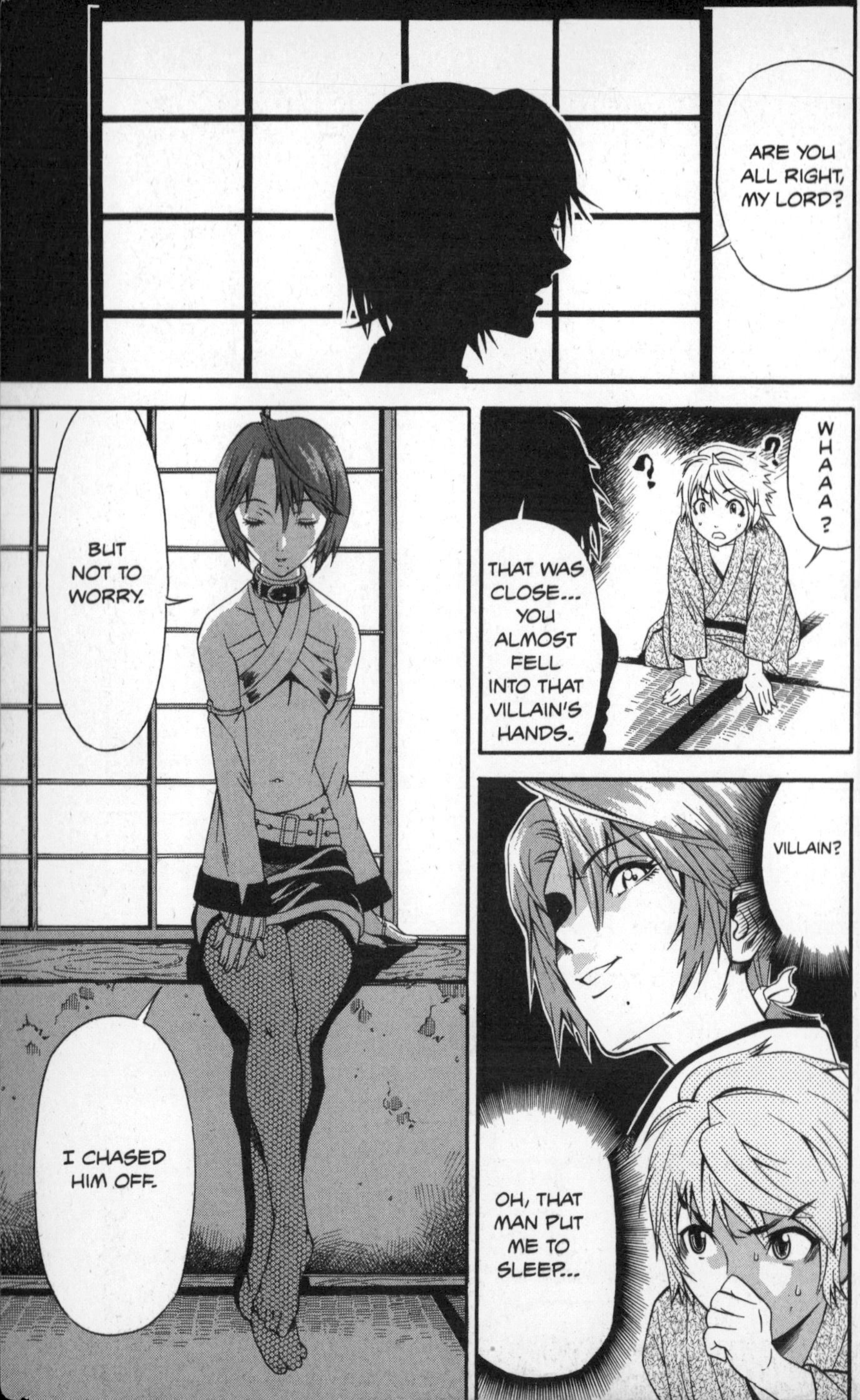
ARE YOU ALL RIGHT, MY LORD?
WHAAA?
THAT WAS CLOSE... YOU ALMOST FELL INTO THAT VILLAIN'S HANDS.
VILLAIN?
OH, THAT MAN PUT ME TO SLEEP...
BUT NOT TO WORRY.
I CHASED HIM OFF.

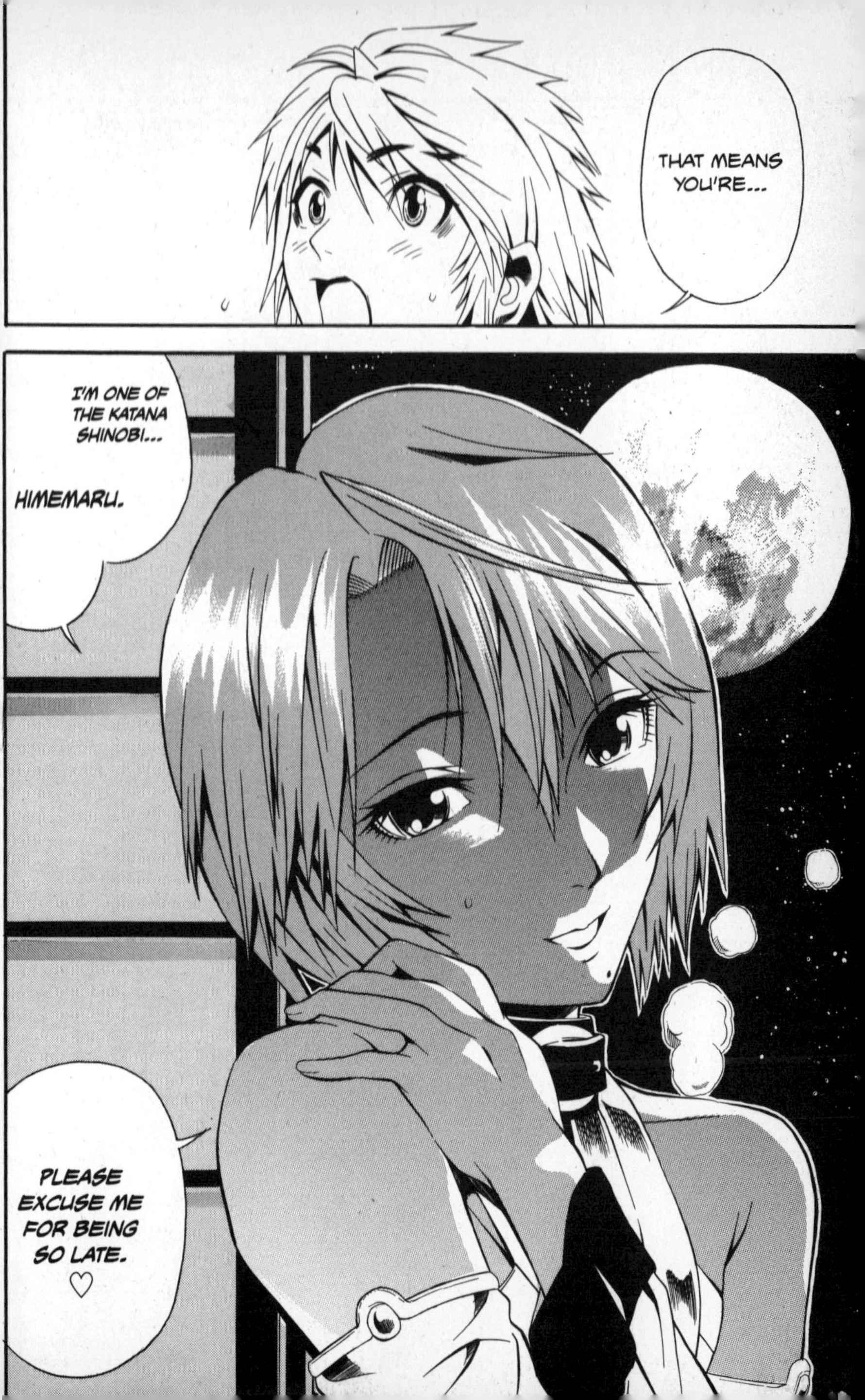
THAT MEANS YOU'RE...
I'M ONE OF THE KATANA SHINOBI...
HIMEMARU.
PLEASE EXCUSE ME FOR BEING SO LATE. ♡

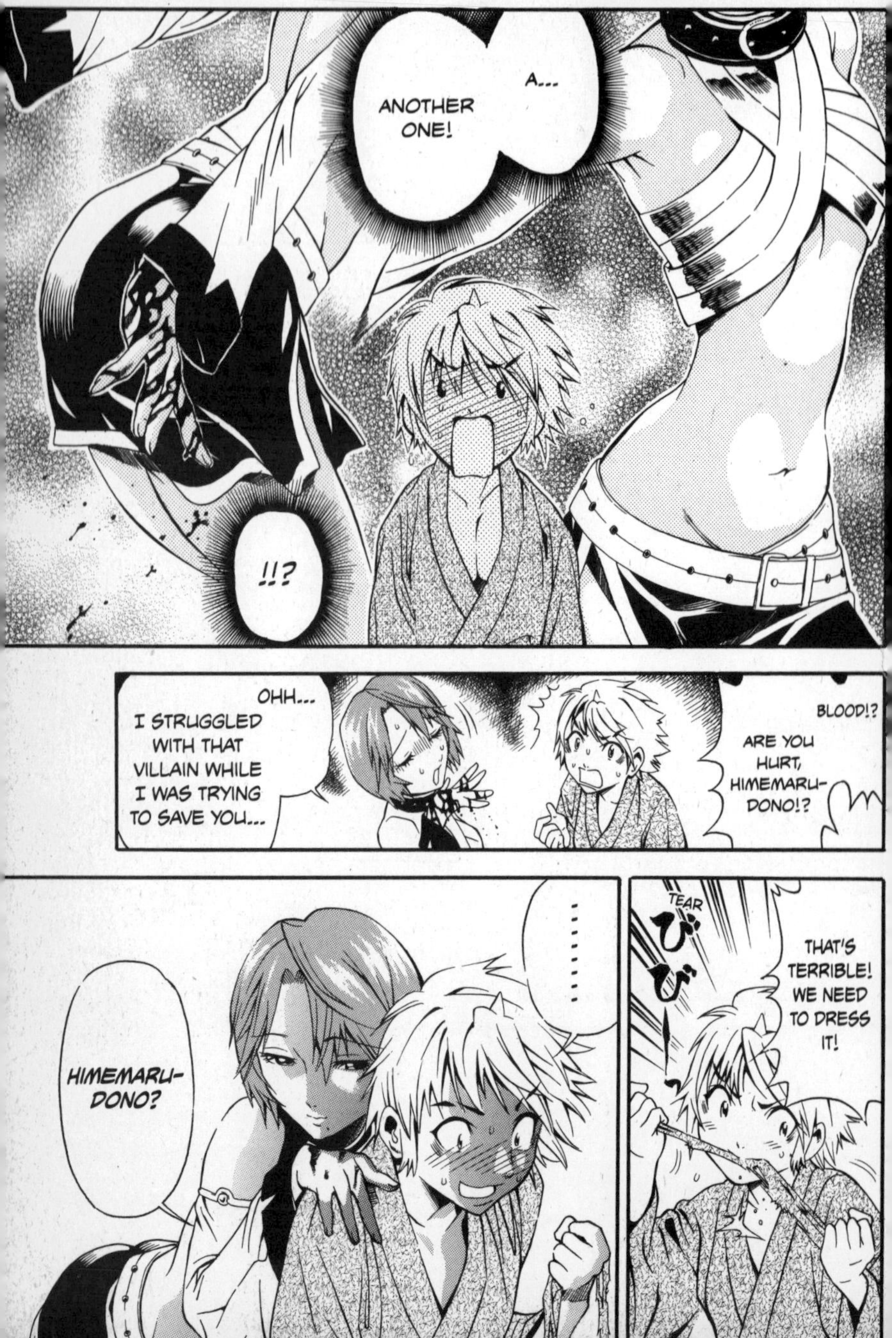

A...
ANOTHER ONE!
!!?
BLOOD!?
ARE YOU HURT, HIMEMARU-DONO!?
OHH...
I STRUGGLED WITH THAT VILLAIN WHILE I WAS TRYING TO SAVE YOU...
TEAR
THAT'S TERRIBLE! WE NEED TO DRESS IT!
......
HIMEMARU-DONO?

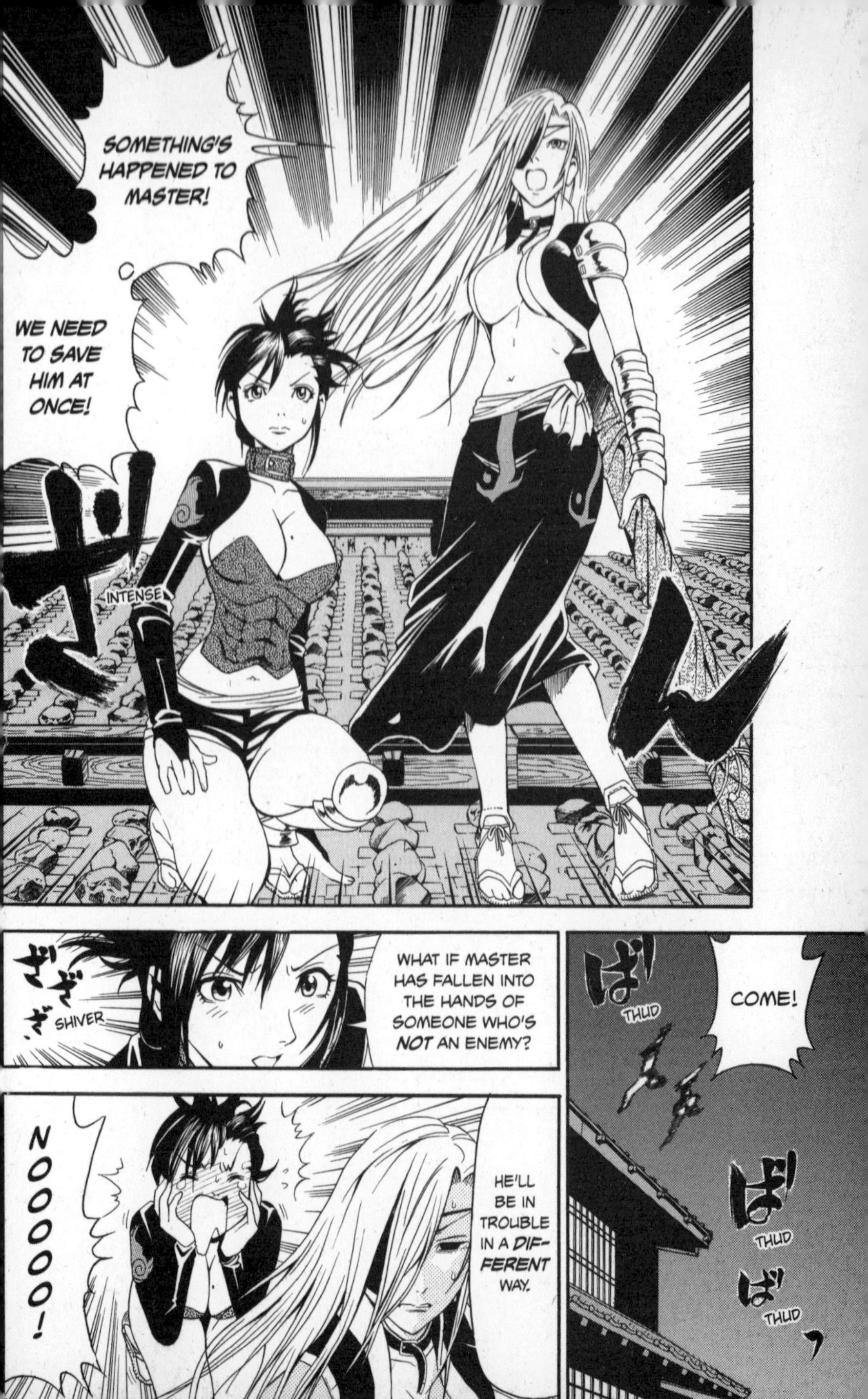
SOMETHING'S HAPPENED TO MASTER!
WE NEED TO SAVE HIM AT ONCE!
INTENSE
COME!
THUD
THUD
THUD
WHAT IF MASTER HAS FALLEN INTO THE HANDS OF SOMEONE WHO'S *NOT* AN ENEMY?
SHIVER
HE'LL BE IN TROUBLE IN A *DIFFERENT* WAY.
NOOOOOO!

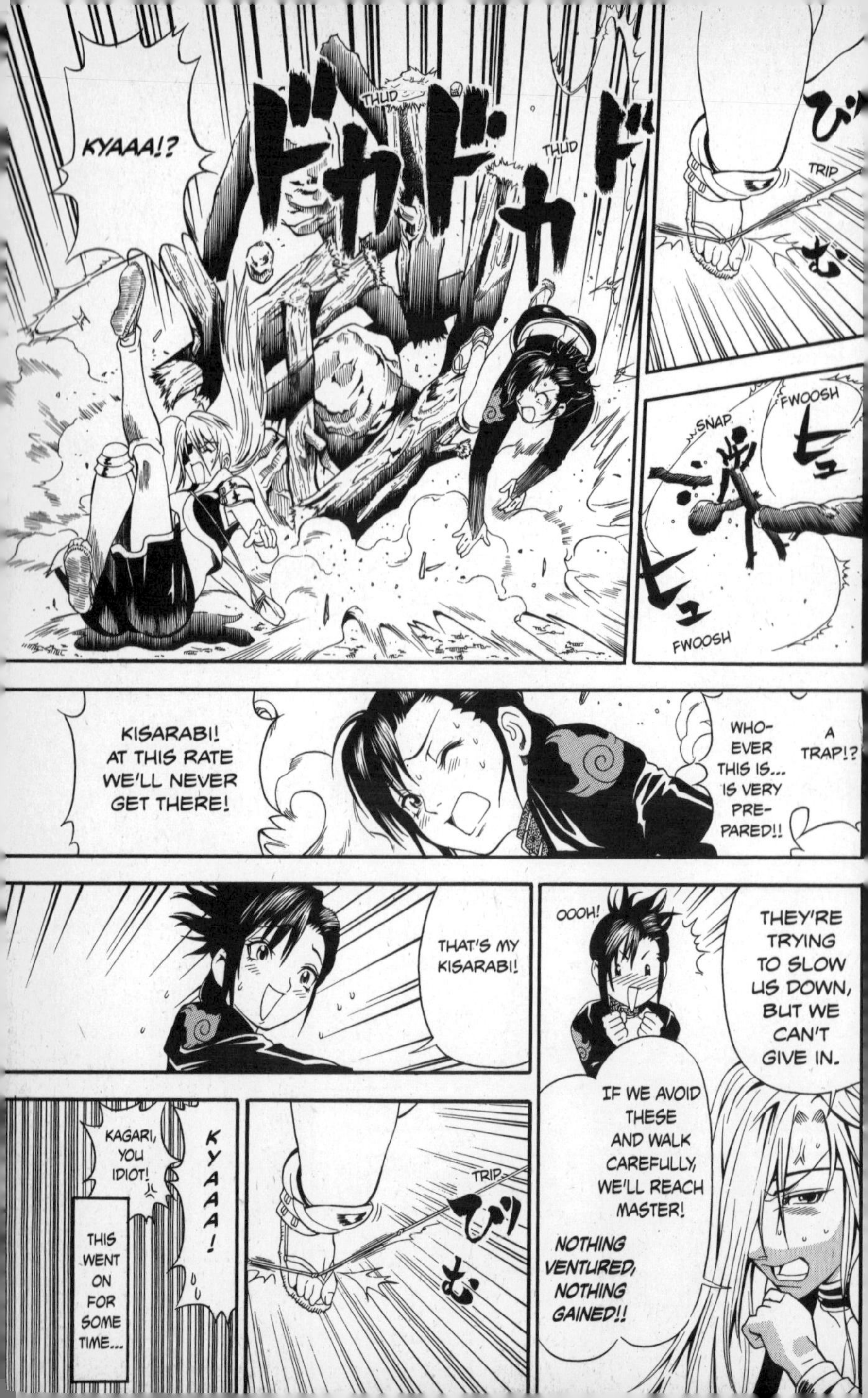
TRIP
SNAP
FWOOSH
FWOOSH
THUD
THUD
KYAAA!?
A TRAP!?
WHO-EVER THIS IS... IS VERY PRE-PARED!!
KISARABI! AT THIS RATE WE'LL NEVER GET THERE!
THEY'RE TRYING TO SLOW US DOWN, BUT WE CAN'T GIVE IN.
OOOH!
IF WE AVOID THESE AND WALK CAREFULLY, WE'LL REACH MASTER!
NOTHING VENTURED, NOTHING GAINED!!
THAT'S MY KISARABI!
TRIP
KYAAA!
KAGARI, YOU IDIOT!
THIS WENT ON FOR SOME TIME...

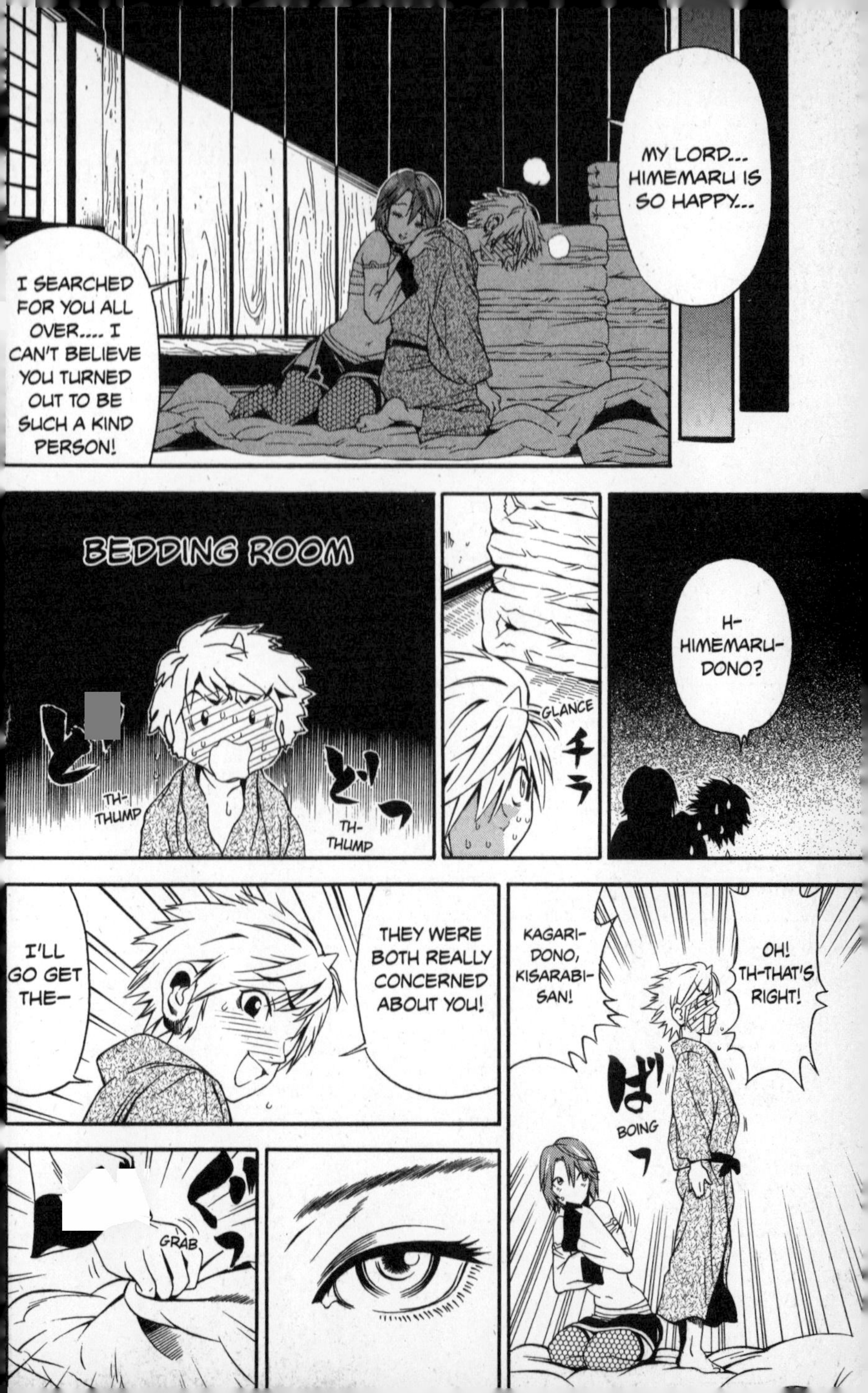
MY LORD... HIMEMARU IS SO HAPPY...
I SEARCHED FOR YOU ALL OVER.... I CAN'T BELIEVE YOU TURNED OUT TO BE SUCH A KIND PERSON!
H-HIMEMARU-DONO?
GLANCE
チラ
BEDDING ROOM
どっ
TH-THUMP
TH-THUMP
OH! TH-THAT'S RIGHT!
KAGARI-DONO, KISARABI-SAN!
ば
BOING
THEY WERE BOTH REALLY CONCERNED ABOUT YOU!
I'LL GO GET THE—
GRAB

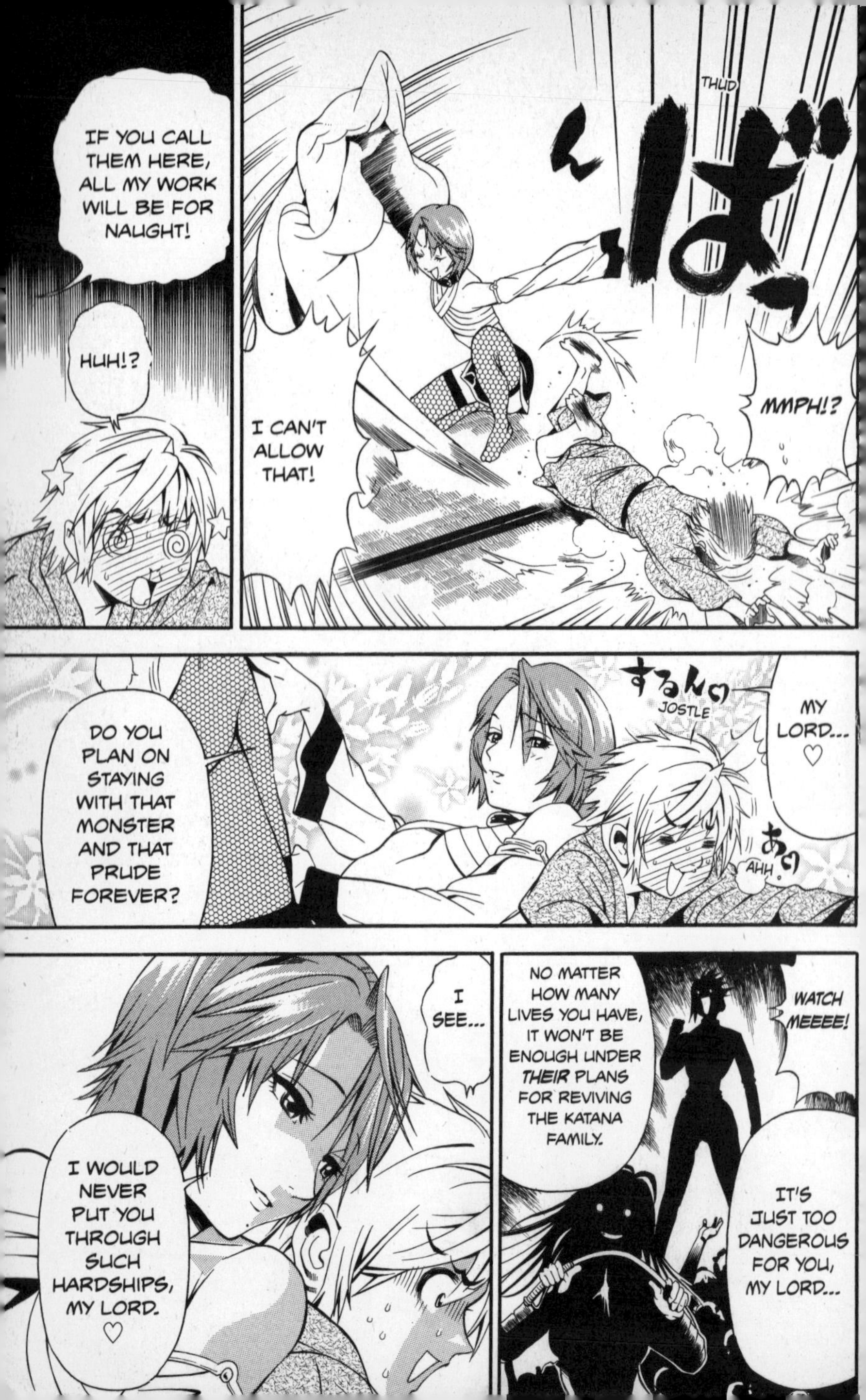
MMPH!?
THUD
I CAN'T ALLOW THAT!
IF YOU CALL THEM HERE, ALL MY WORK WILL BE FOR NAUGHT!
HUH!?
MY LORD... ♡
JOSTLE
AHH
DO YOU PLAN ON STAYING WITH THAT MONSTER AND THAT PRUDE FOREVER?
WATCH MEEEE!
NO MATTER HOW MANY LIVES YOU HAVE, IT WON'T BE ENOUGH UNDER *THEIR* PLANS FOR REVIVING THE KATANA FAMILY.
IT'S JUST TOO DANGEROUS FOR YOU, MY LORD...
I SEE...
I WOULD NEVER PUT YOU THROUGH SUCH HARDSHIPS, MY LORD. ♡

HIMEMARU'S RESTORATION PLAN

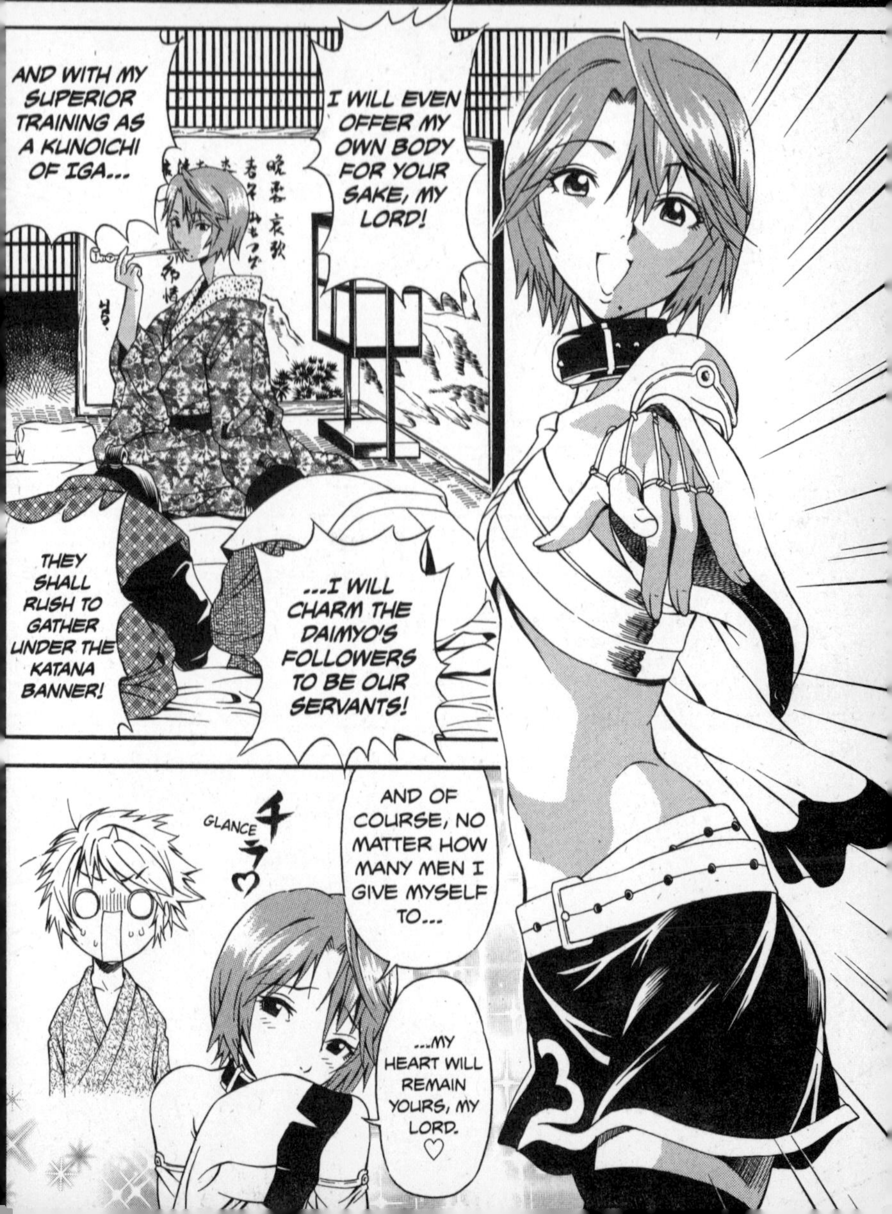
AND WITH MY SUPERIOR TRAINING AS A KUNOICHI OF IGA...
...I WILL CHARM THE DAIMYO'S FOLLOWERS TO BE OUR SERVANTS!
THEY SHALL RUSH TO GATHER UNDER THE KATANA BANNER!
I WILL EVEN OFFER MY OWN BODY FOR YOUR SAKE, MY LORD!
GLANCE
AND OF COURSE, NO MATTER HOW MANY MEN I GIVE MYSELF TO...
...MY HEART WILL REMAIN YOURS, MY LORD. ♡

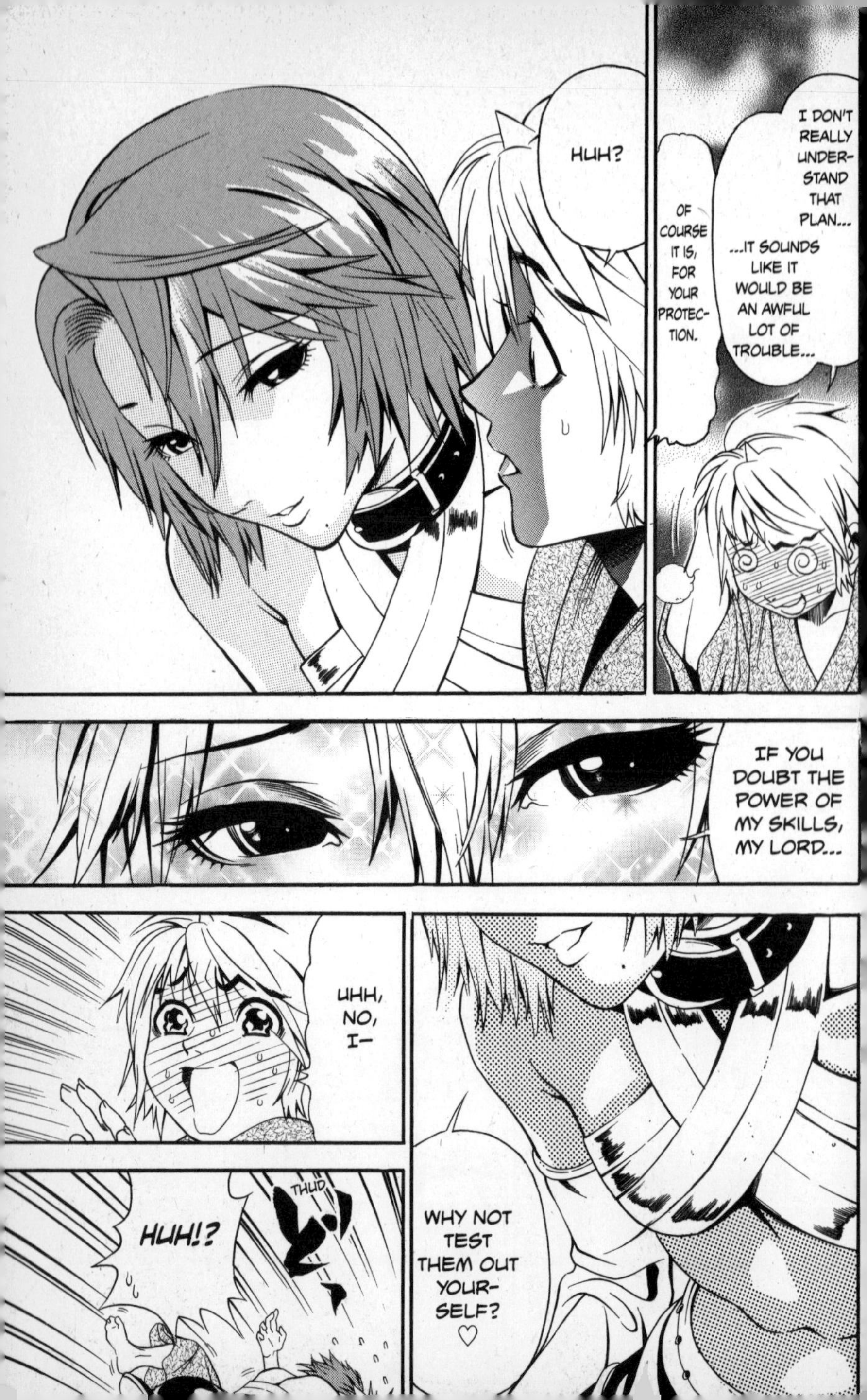
I DON'T REALLY UNDER-STAND THAT PLAN...
...IT SOUNDS LIKE IT WOULD BE AN AWFUL LOT OF TROUBLE...
OF COURSE IT IS, FOR YOUR PROTEC-TION.
HUH?
IF YOU DOUBT THE POWER OF MY SKILLS, MY LORD...
WHY NOT TEST THEM OUT YOUR-SELF? ♡
UHH, NO, I—
THUD
HUH!?

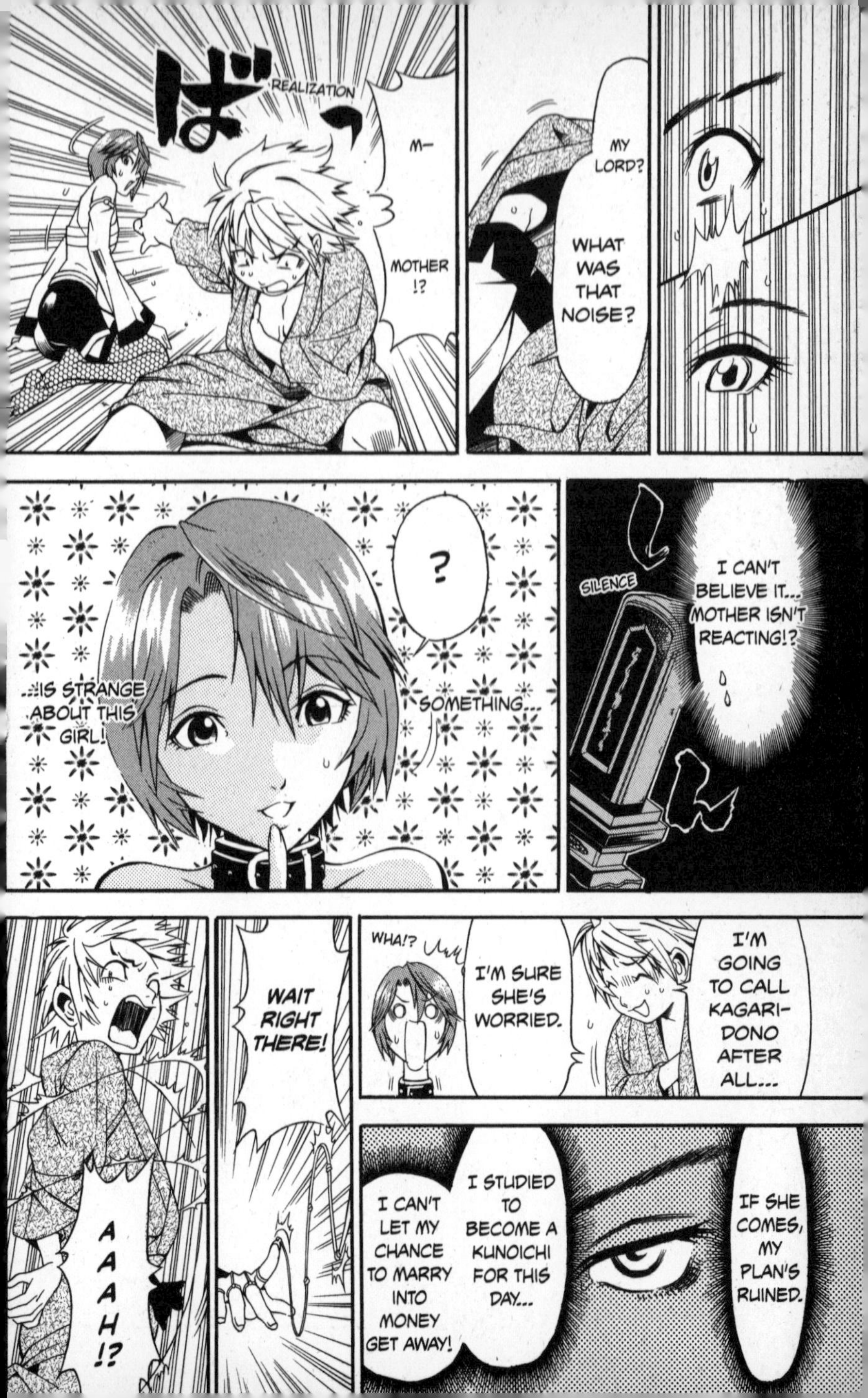
MY LORD?
WHAT WAS THAT NOISE?
ばっ
REALIZATION
M—
MOTHER!?
しん
SILENCE
I CAN'T BELIEVE IT... MOTHER ISN'T REACTING!?
?
SOMETHING...
...IS STRANGE ABOUT THIS GIRL!
I'M GOING TO CALL KAGARI-DONO AFTER ALL...
I'M SURE SHE'S WORRIED.
WHA!?
IF SHE COMES, MY PLAN'S RUINED.
I STUDIED TO BECOME A KUNOICHI FOR THIS DAY...
I CAN'T LET MY CHANCE TO MARRY INTO MONEY GET AWAY!
WAIT RIGHT THERE!
AAAAH!?

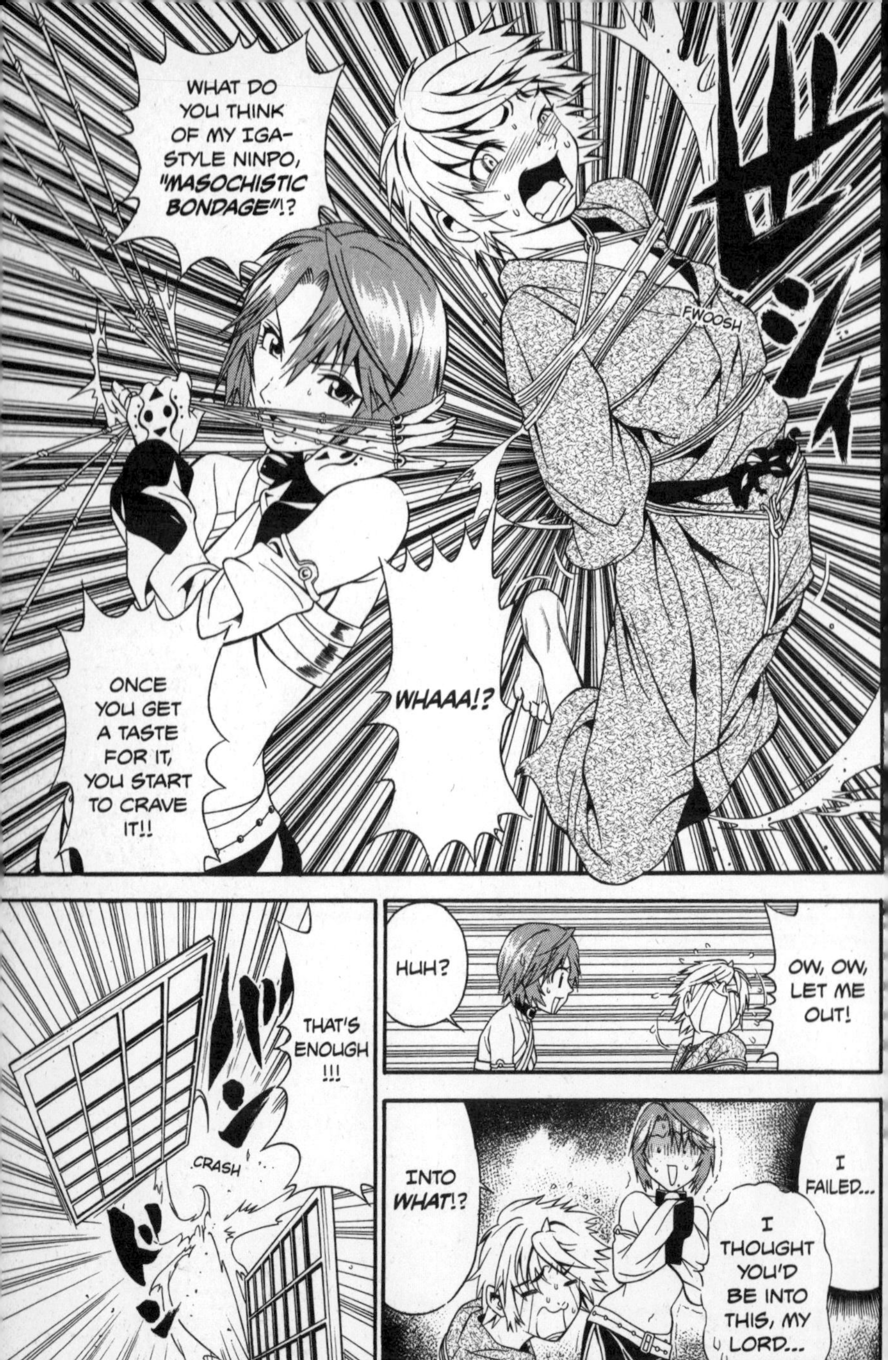
WHAT DO YOU THINK OF MY IGA-STYLE NINPO, "MASOCHISTIC BONDAGE"!?
FWOOSH
WHAAA!?
ONCE YOU GET A TASTE FOR IT, YOU START TO CRAVE IT!!
OW, OW, LET ME OUT!
HUH?
I FAILED...
I THOUGHT YOU'D BE INTO THIS, MY LORD...
INTO WHAT!?
THAT'S ENOUGH!!!
CRASH

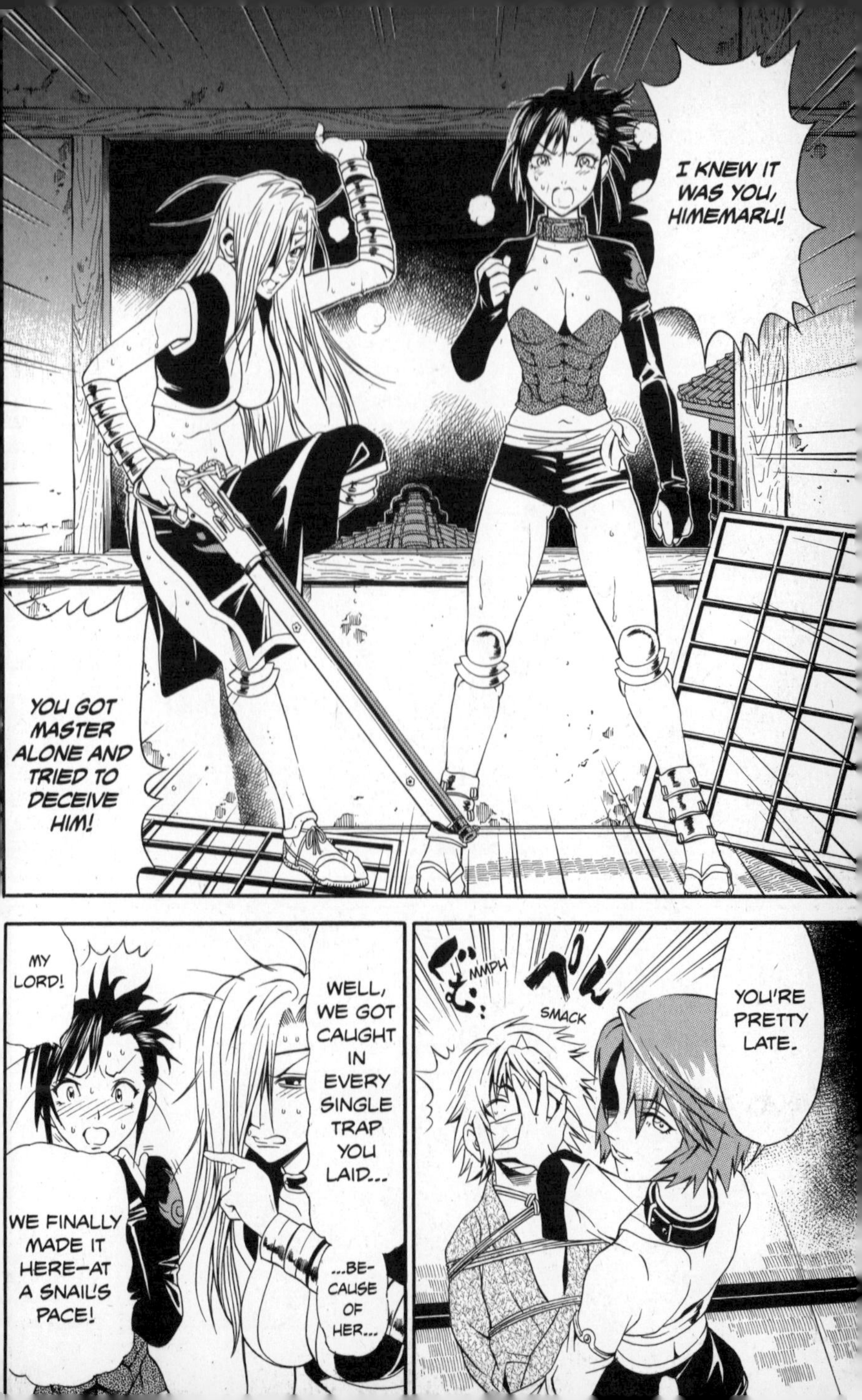
I KNEW IT WAS YOU, HIMEMARU!
YOU GOT MASTER ALONE AND TRIED TO DECEIVE HIM!
MMPH
SMACK
YOU'RE PRETTY LATE.
WELL, WE GOT CAUGHT IN EVERY SINGLE TRAP YOU LAID...
MY LORD!
WE FINALLY MADE IT HERE—AT A SNAIL'S PACE!
...BE-CAUSE OF HER...

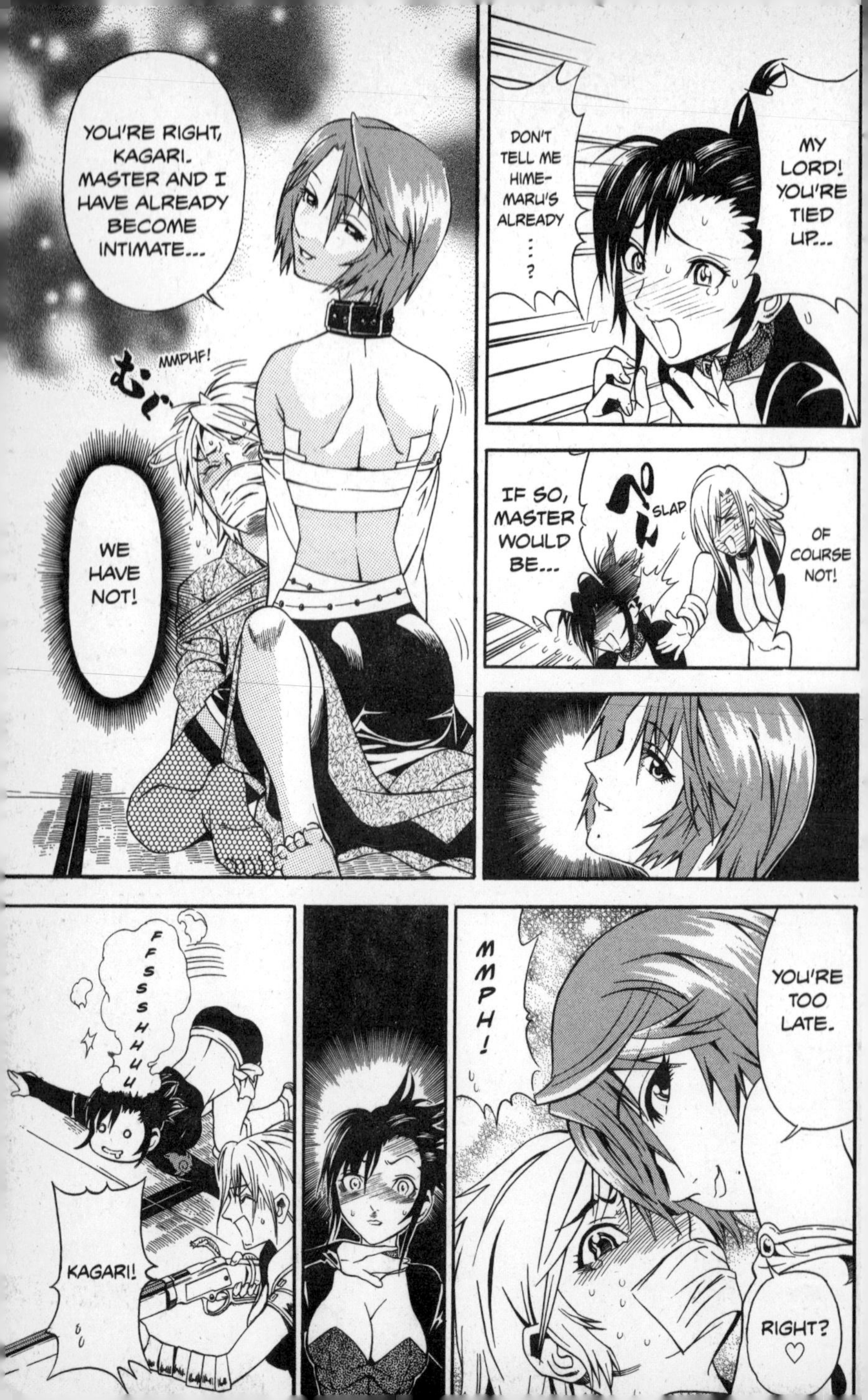
MY LORD! YOU'RE TIED UP...
DON'T TELL ME HIME-MARU'S ALREADY ...?
IF SO, MASTER WOULD BE...
SLAP
OF COURSE NOT!
YOU'RE RIGHT, KAGARI. MASTER AND I HAVE ALREADY BECOME INTIMATE...
むぐ
MMPHF!
WE HAVE NOT!
YOU'RE TOO LATE.
MMPH!
RIGHT? ♡
FFSSSHHUUU
KAGARI!

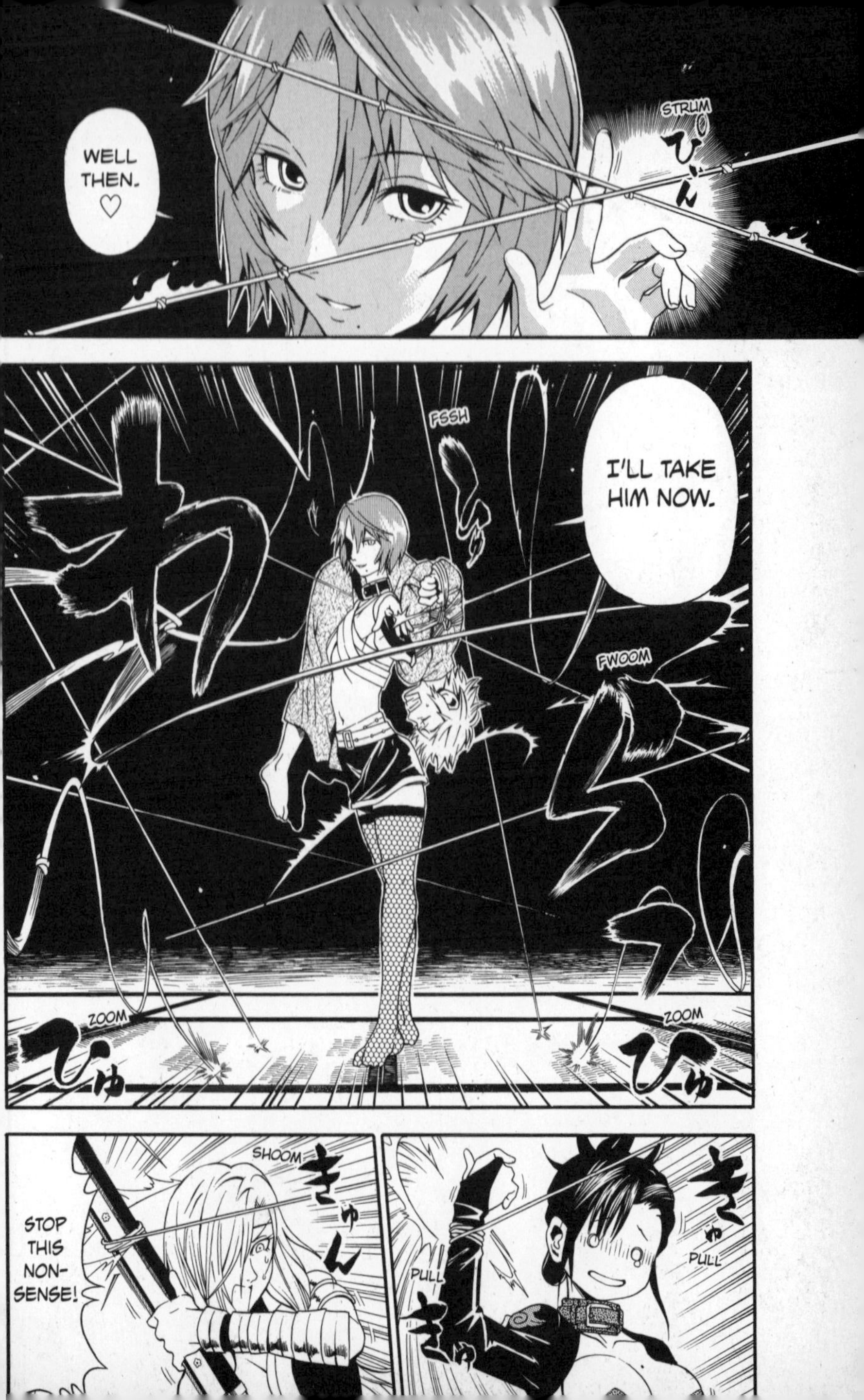
STRUM
びん
WELL THEN. ♡
I'LL TAKE HIM NOW.
FSSH
FWOOM
ZOOM
ひゅ
ZOOM
ひゅ
きゅ
PULL
PULL
きゅ
SHOOM
きゅん
STOP THIS NON-SENSE!

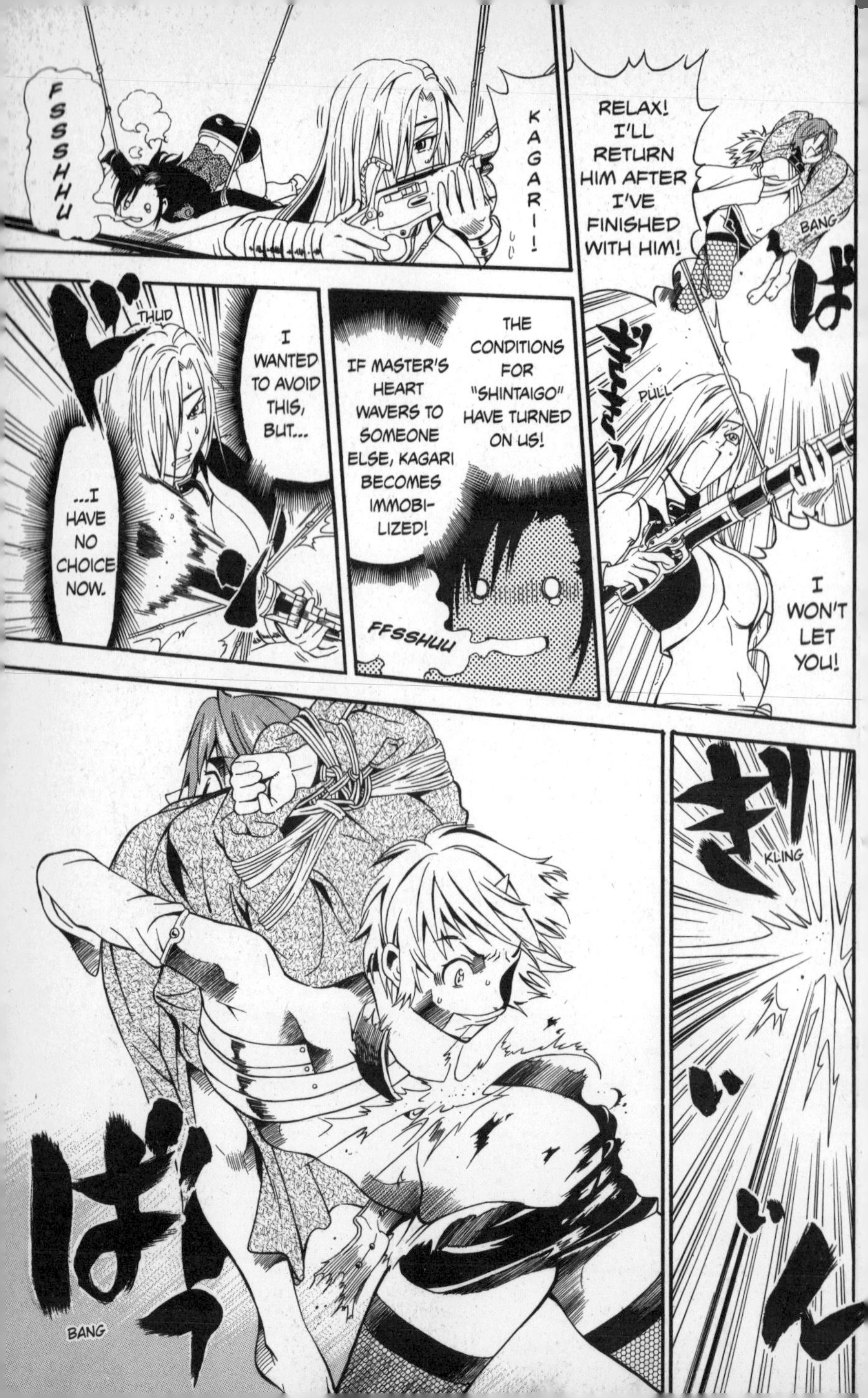

RELAX! I'LL RETURN HIM AFTER I'VE FINISHED WITH HIM!
BANG
PULL
I WON'T LET YOU!
KAGARI!!
FSSSHHU
THE CONDITIONS FOR "SHINTAIGO" HAVE TURNED ON US!
IF MASTER'S HEART WAVERS TO SOMEONE ELSE, KAGARI BECOMES IMMOBI-LIZED!
FFSSHUU
I WANTED TO AVOID THIS, BUT...
...I HAVE NO CHOICE NOW.
THUD
KLING
BANG

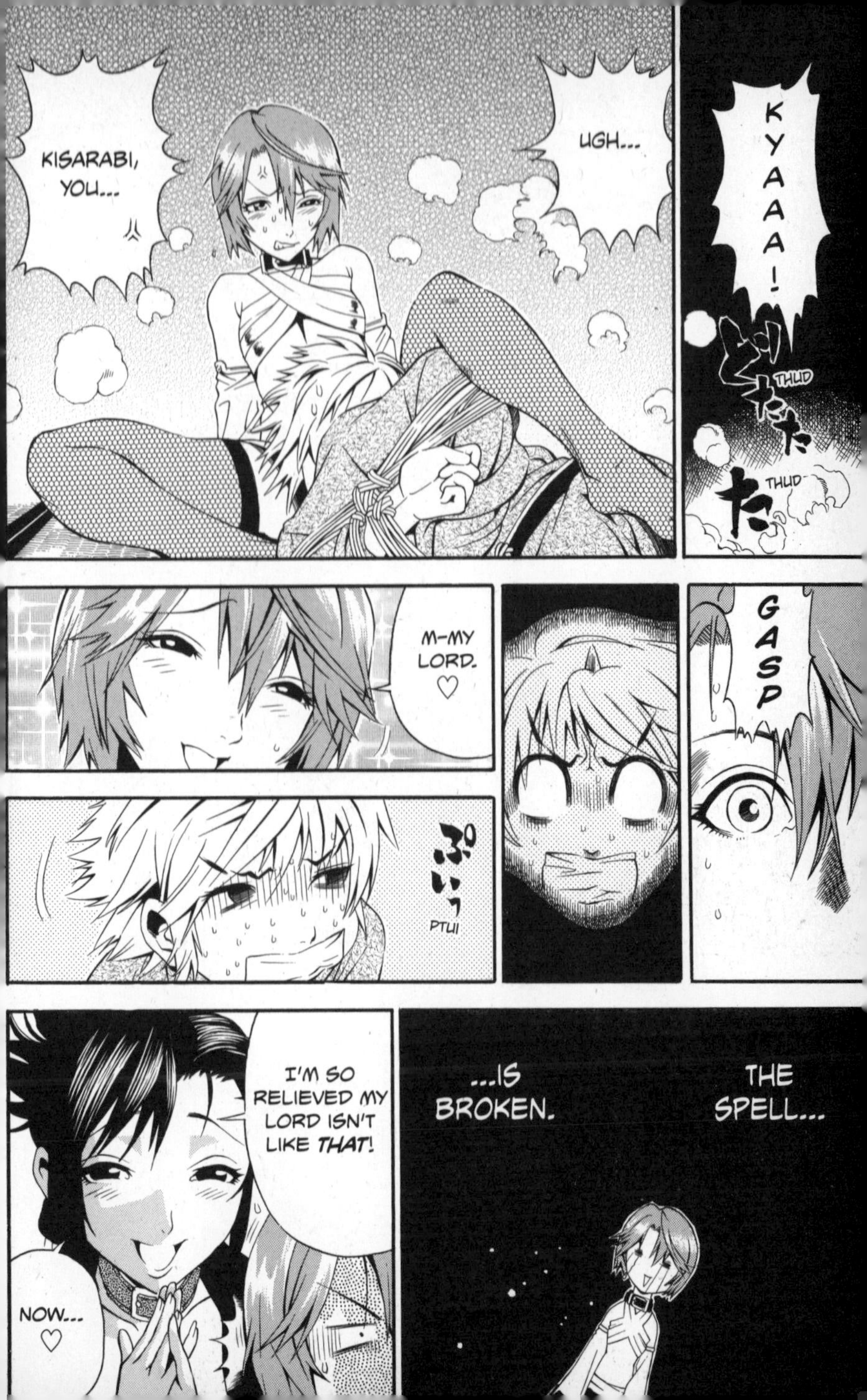
KYAAA!
THUD
THUD
UGH...
KISARABI, YOU...
GASP
M-MY LORD. ♡
ぷいっ
PTUI
THE SPELL...
...IS BROKEN.
I'M SO RELIEVED MY LORD ISN'T LIKE *THAT*!
NOW... ♡

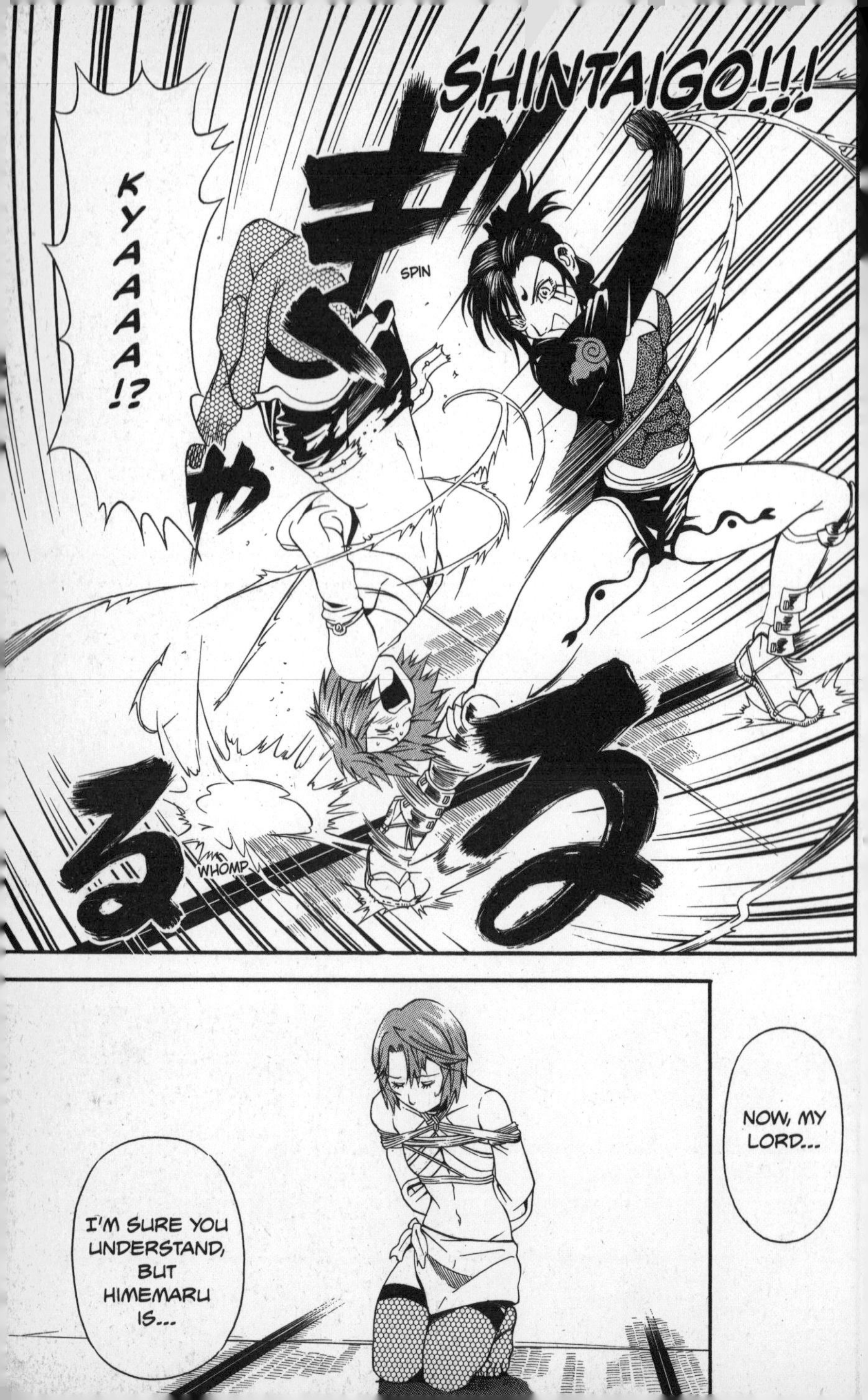
SHINTAIGO!!!
KYAAAAA!?
SPIN
WHOMP
NOW, MY LORD...
I'M SURE YOU UNDERSTAND, BUT HIMEMARU IS...

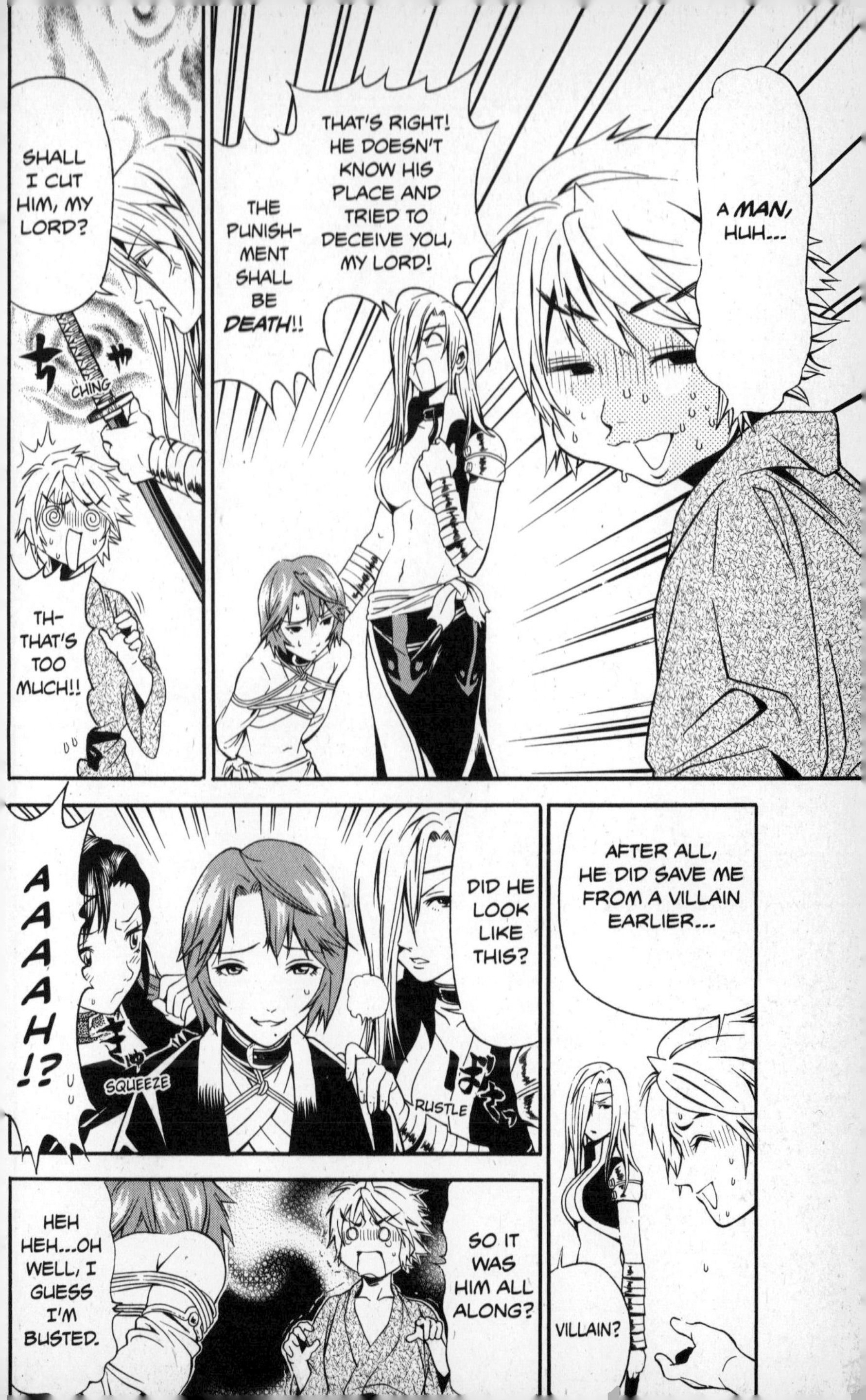
A MAN, HUH...
THAT'S RIGHT! HE DOESN'T KNOW HIS PLACE AND TRIED TO DECEIVE YOU, MY LORD!
THE PUNISHMENT SHALL BE DEATH!!
SHALL I CUT HIM, MY LORD?
CHING
TH-THAT'S TOO MUCH!!
AFTER ALL, HE DID SAVE ME FROM A VILLAIN EARLIER...
VILLAIN?
DID HE LOOK LIKE THIS?
RUSTLE
SQUEEZE
AAAAAH!?
SO IT WAS HIM ALL ALONG?
HEH HEH...OH WELL, I GUESS I'M BUSTED.

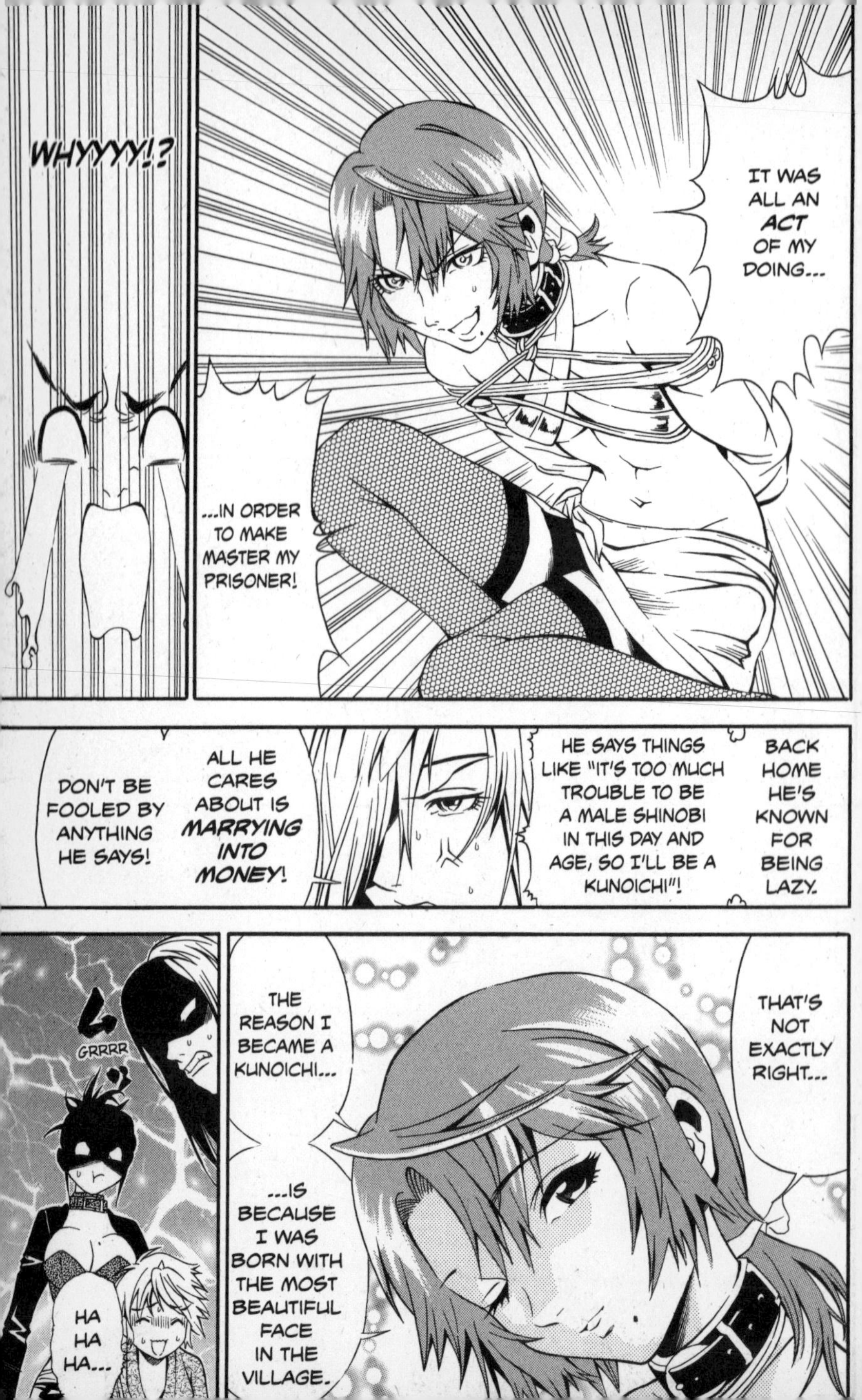
IT WAS ALL AN ACT OF MY DOING...
...IN ORDER TO MAKE MASTER MY PRISONER!
WHYYYY!?
BACK HOME HE'S KNOWN FOR BEING LAZY.
HE SAYS THINGS LIKE "IT'S TOO MUCH TROUBLE TO BE A MALE SHINOBI IN THIS DAY AND AGE, SO I'LL BE A KUNOICHI"!
ALL HE CARES ABOUT IS MARRYING INTO MONEY!
DON'T BE FOOLED BY ANYTHING HE SAYS!
THAT'S NOT EXACTLY RIGHT...
THE REASON I BECAME A KUNOICHI...
...IS BECAUSE I WAS BORN WITH THE MOST BEAUTIFUL FACE IN THE VILLAGE.
GRRRR
HA HA HA...

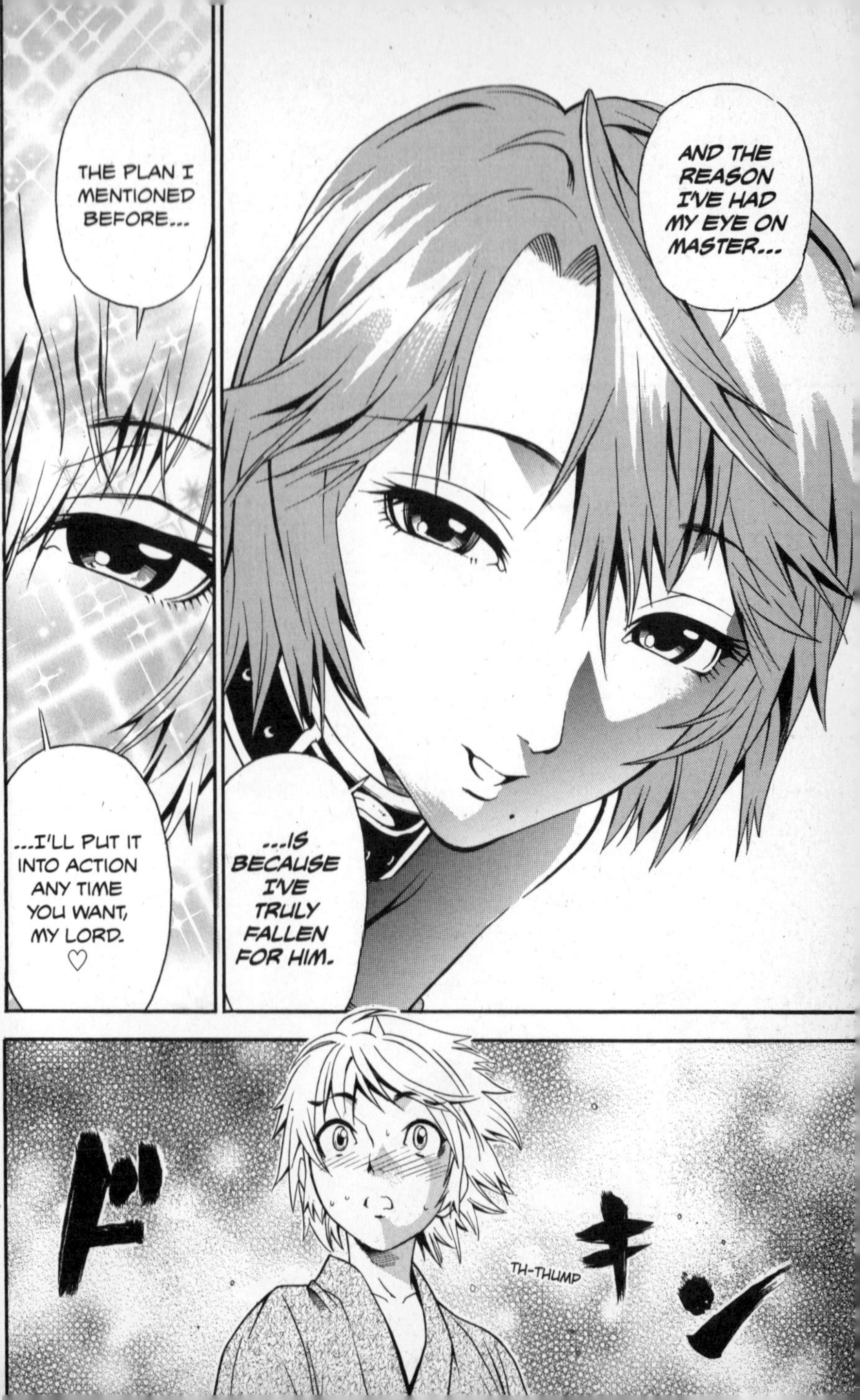
AND THE REASON I'VE HAD MY EYE ON MASTER...
...IS BECAUSE I'VE TRULY FALLEN FOR HIM.
THE PLAN I MENTIONED BEFORE...
...I'LL PUT IT INTO ACTION ANY TIME YOU WANT, MY LORD. ♡
ドキン
TH-THUMP

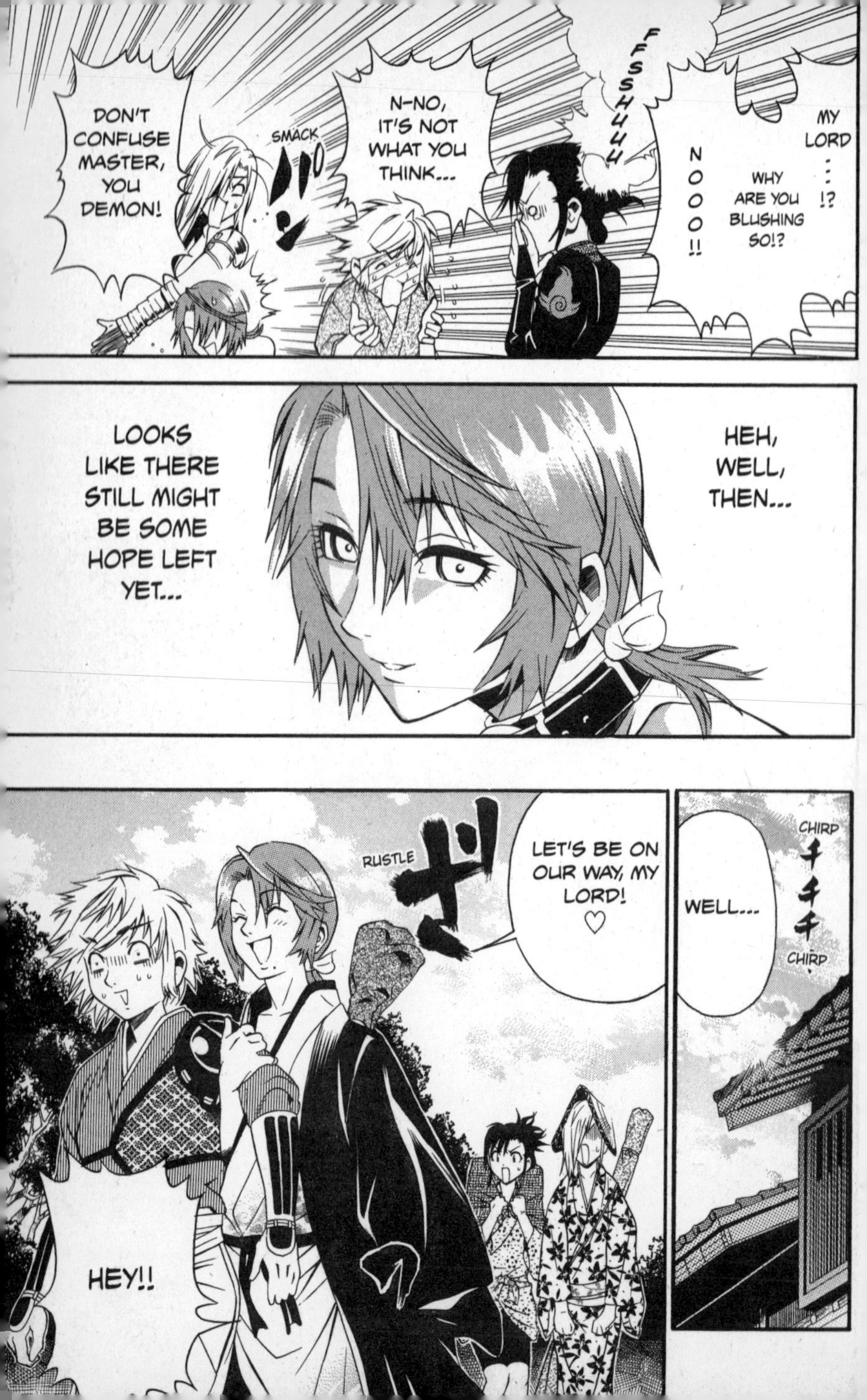
MY LORD ... !?
WHY ARE YOU BLUSHING SO!?
NOOOO!!
FFSSHUUU
N-NO, IT'S NOT WHAT YOU THINK...
SMACK
DON'T CONFUSE MASTER, YOU DEMON!
HEH, WELL, THEN...
LOOKS LIKE THERE STILL MIGHT BE SOME HOPE LEFT YET...
CHIRP
CHIRP
WELL...
LET'S BE ON OUR WAY, MY LORD! ♡
RUSTLE
HEY!!

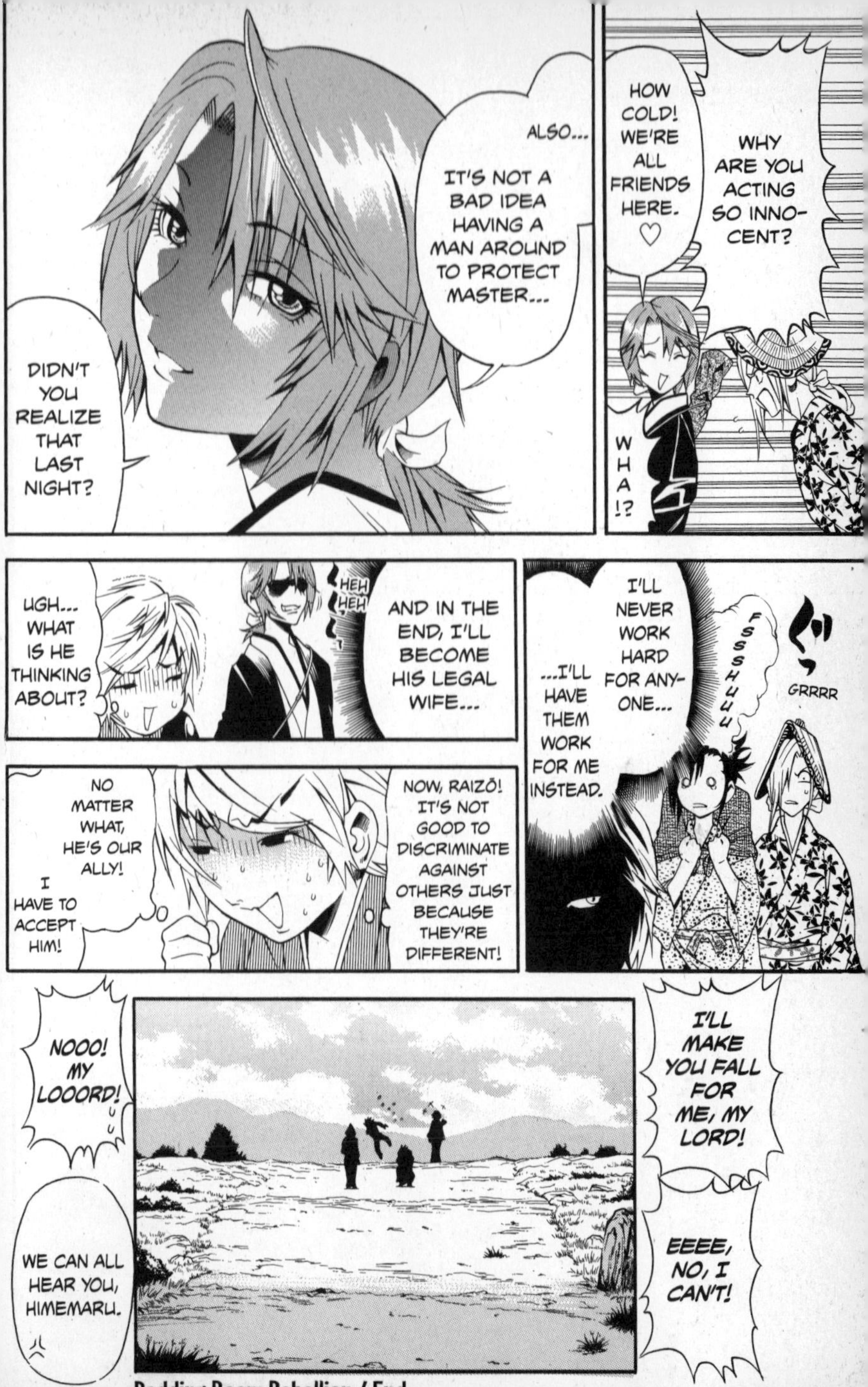
WHY ARE YOU ACTING SO INNOCENT?
HOW COLD! WE'RE ALL FRIENDS HERE. ♡
WHA!?
ALSO...
IT'S NOT A BAD IDEA HAVING A MAN AROUND TO PROTECT MASTER...
DIDN'T YOU REALIZE THAT LAST NIGHT?
GRRRR
FSSSHUUU
I'LL NEVER WORK HARD FOR ANYONE...
...I'LL HAVE THEM WORK FOR ME INSTEAD.
HEH HEH
AND IN THE END, I'LL BECOME HIS LEGAL WIFE...
UGH... WHAT IS HE THINKING ABOUT?
NOW, RAIZŌ! IT'S NOT GOOD TO DISCRIMINATE AGAINST OTHERS JUST BECAUSE THEY'RE DIFFERENT!
NO MATTER WHAT, HE'S OUR ALLY!
I HAVE TO ACCEPT HIM!
I'LL MAKE YOU FALL FOR ME, MY LORD!
EEEE, NO, I CAN'T!
NOOO! MY LOOORD!
WE CAN ALL HEAR YOU, HIMEMARU.
Bedding Room Rebellion / End

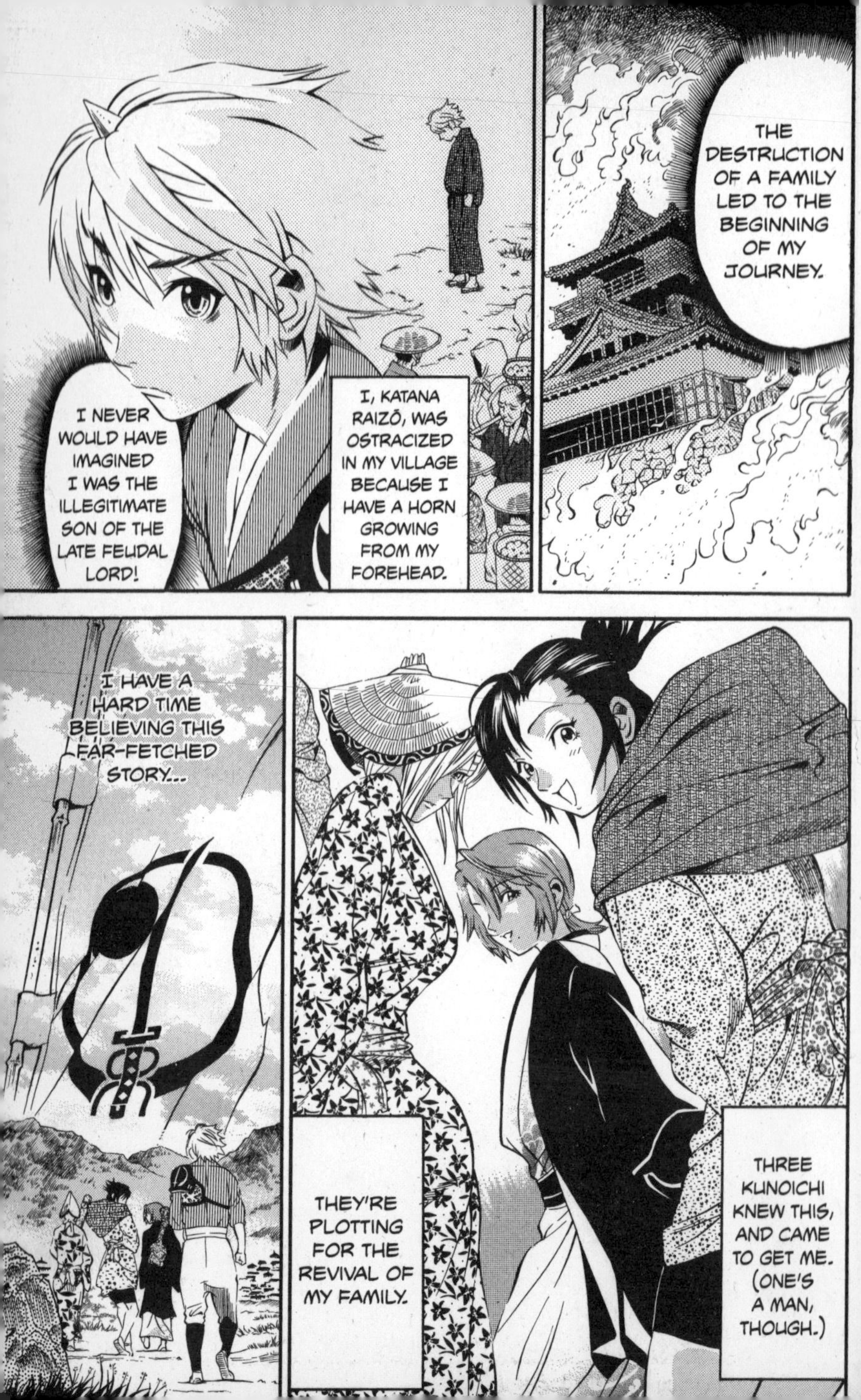
THE DESTRUCTION OF A FAMILY LED TO THE BEGINNING OF MY JOURNEY.
I, KATANA RAIZŌ, WAS OSTRACIZED IN MY VILLAGE BECAUSE I HAVE A HORN GROWING FROM MY FOREHEAD.
I NEVER WOULD HAVE IMAGINED I WAS THE ILLEGITIMATE SON OF THE LATE FEUDAL LORD!
THREE KUNOICHI KNEW THIS, AND CAME TO GET ME. (ONE'S A MAN, THOUGH.)
THEY'RE PLOTTING FOR THE REVIVAL OF MY FAMILY.
I HAVE A HARD TIME BELIEVING THIS FAR-FETCHED STORY...

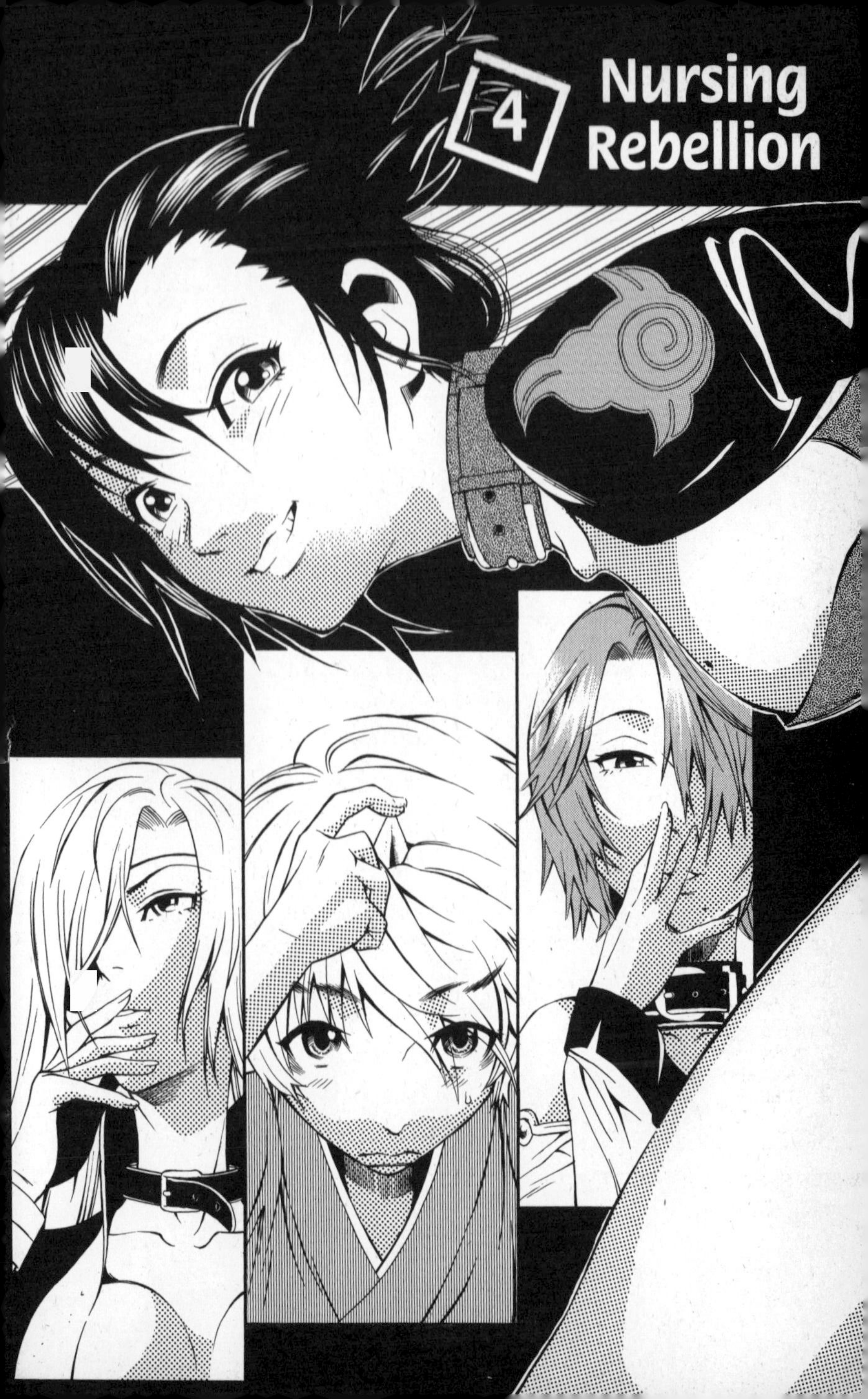
4
Nursing Rebellion

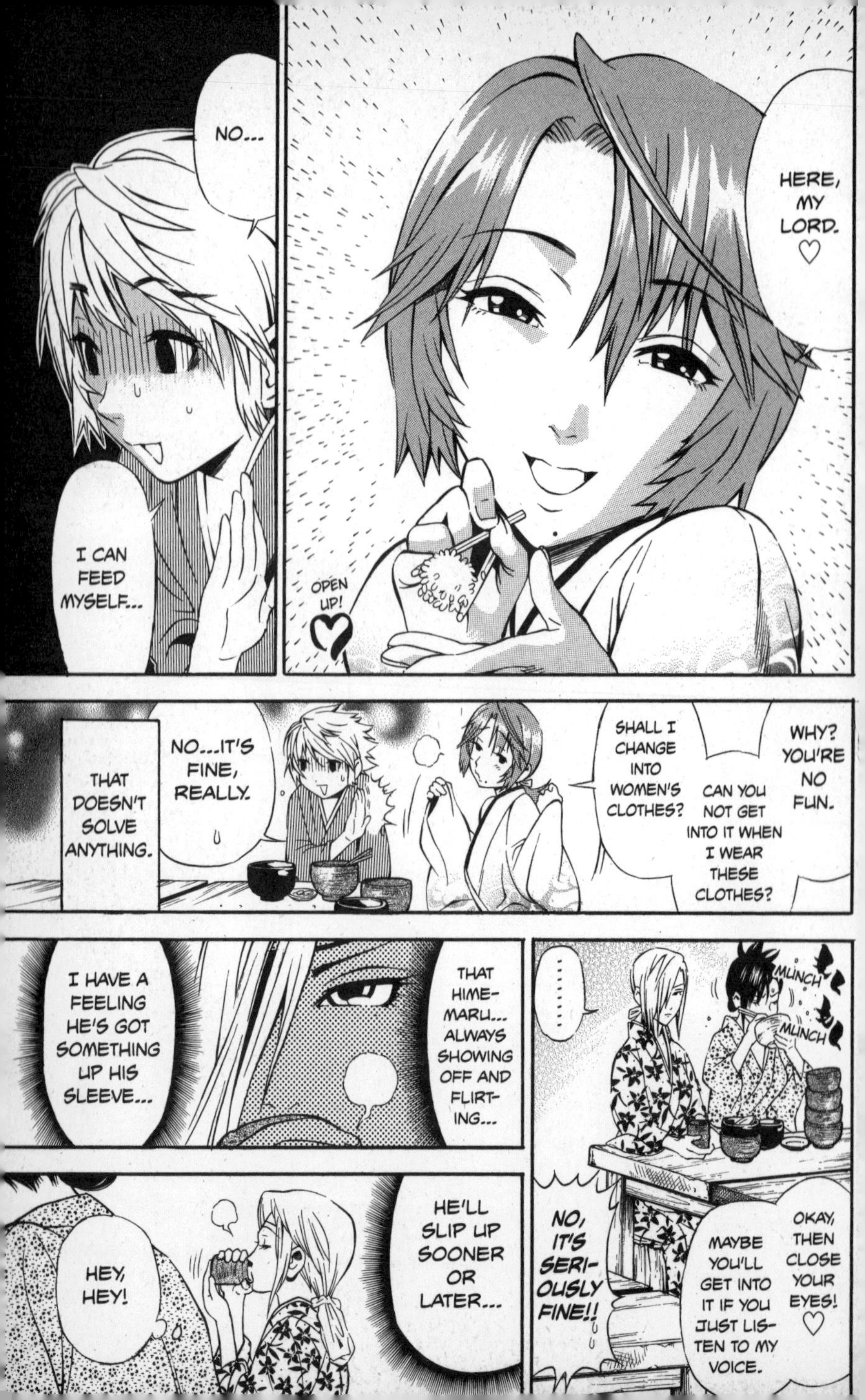
HERE, MY LORD. ♡
OPEN UP! ♡
NO...
I CAN FEED MYSELF...
WHY? YOU'RE NO FUN.
CAN YOU NOT GET INTO IT WHEN I WEAR THESE CLOTHES?
SHALL I CHANGE INTO WOMEN'S CLOTHES?
NO...IT'S FINE, REALLY.
THAT DOESN'T SOLVE ANYTHING.
MUNCH
MUNCH
......
OKAY, THEN CLOSE YOUR EYES! ♡
MAYBE YOU'LL GET INTO IT IF YOU JUST LIS-TEN TO MY VOICE.
NO, IT'S SERI-OUSLY FINE!!
THAT HIME-MARU... ALWAYS SHOWING OFF AND FLIRT-ING...
I HAVE A FEELING HE'S GOT SOMETHING UP HIS SLEEVE...
HE'LL SLIP UP SOONER OR LATER...
HEY, HEY!

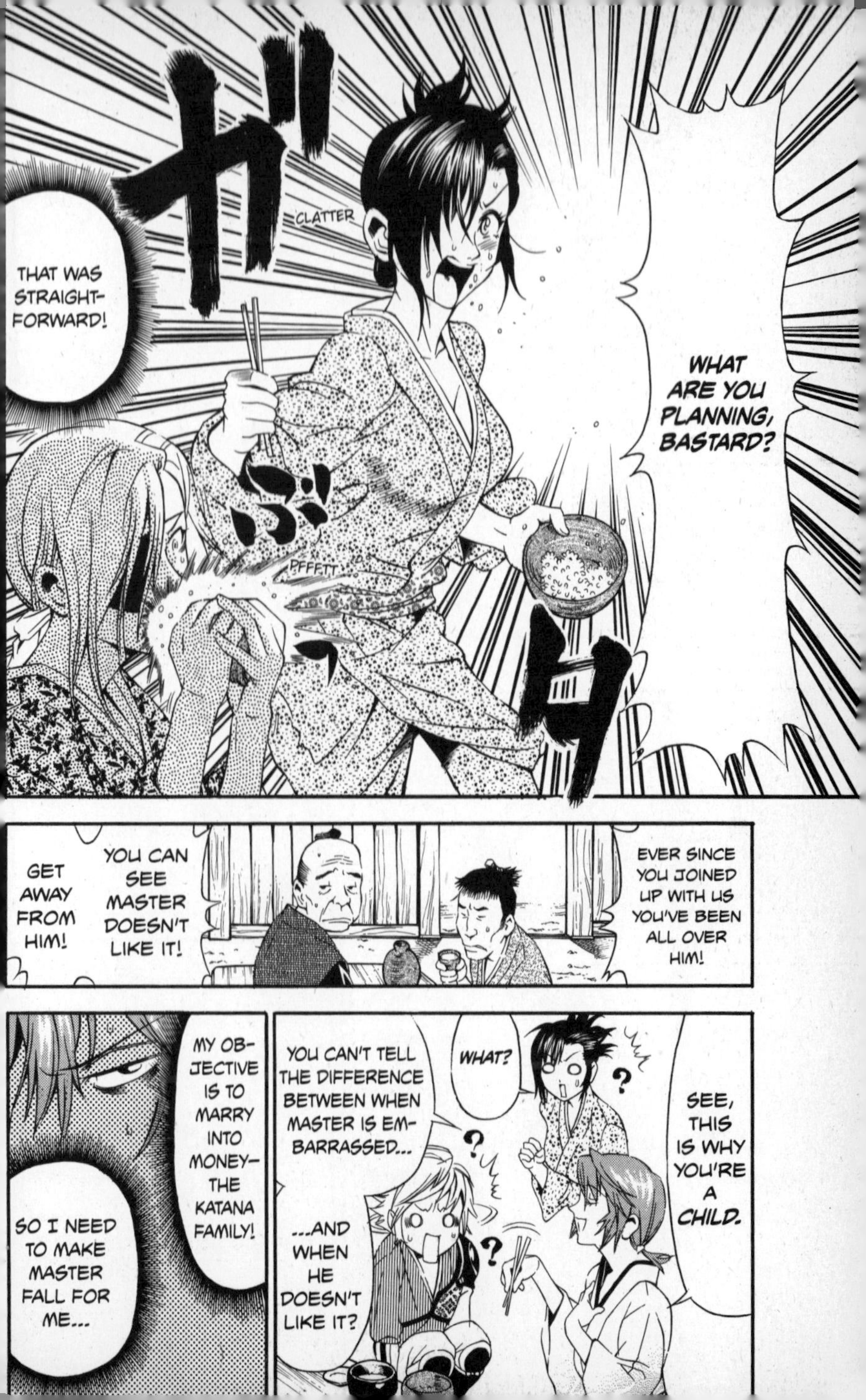
WHAT ARE YOU PLANNING, BASTARD?
CLATTER
THAT WAS STRAIGHT-FORWARD!
PFFFTT
EVER SINCE YOU JOINED UP WITH US YOU'VE BEEN ALL OVER HIM!
YOU CAN SEE MASTER DOESN'T LIKE IT!
GET AWAY FROM HIM!
WHAT?
SEE, THIS IS WHY YOU'RE A CHILD.
YOU CAN'T TELL THE DIFFERENCE BETWEEN WHEN MASTER IS EM-BARRASSED...
...AND WHEN HE DOESN'T LIKE IT?
MY OB-JECTIVE IS TO MARRY INTO MONEY—THE KATANA FAMILY!
SO I NEED TO MAKE MASTER FALL FOR ME...

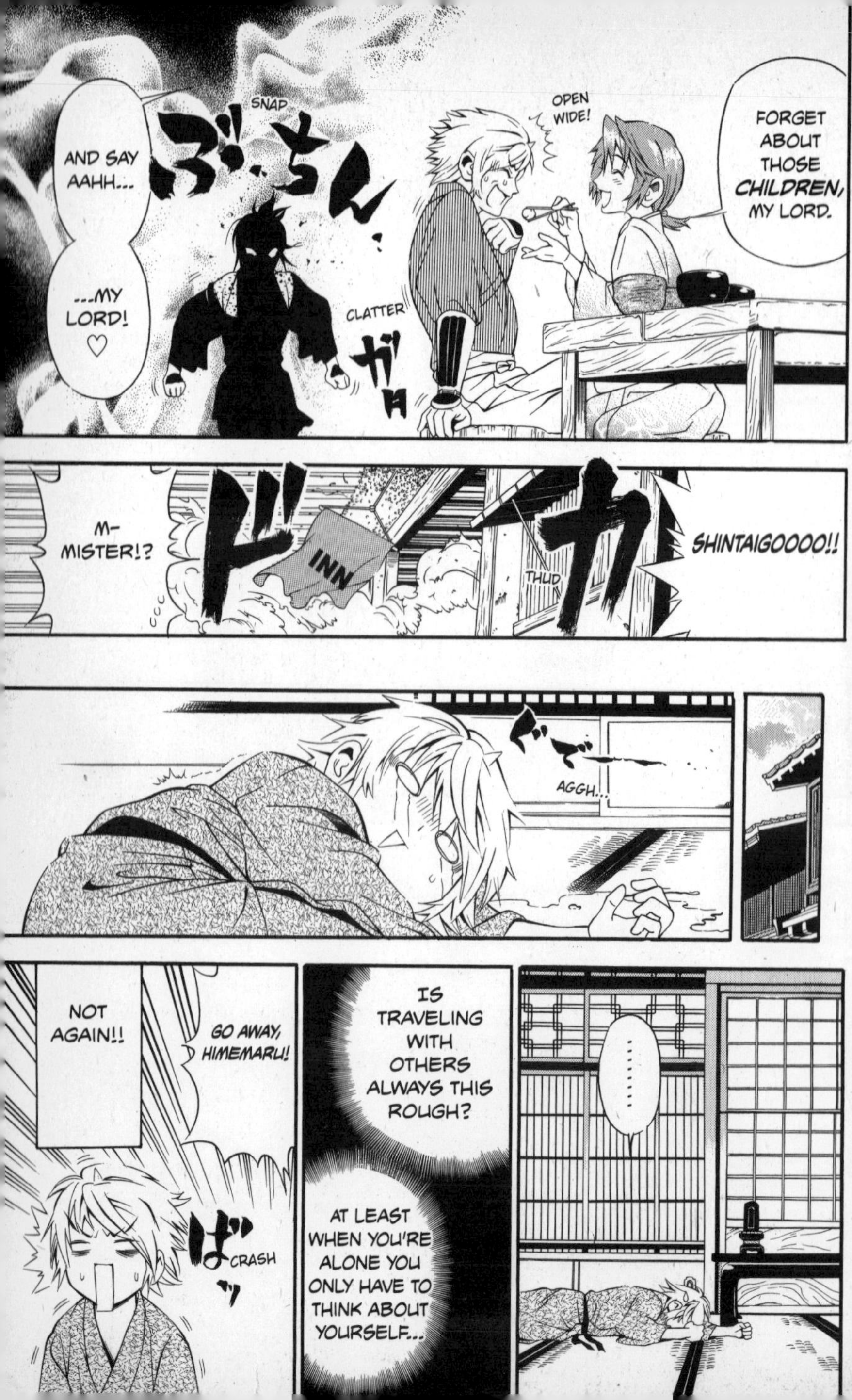
FORGET ABOUT THOSE CHILDREN, MY LORD.
OPEN WIDE!
SNAP
AND SAY AAHH...
CLATTER
...MY LORD! ♡
SHINTAIGOOOO!!
THUD
INN
M-MISTER!?
AGGH...
......
IS TRAVELING WITH OTHERS ALWAYS THIS ROUGH?
AT LEAST WHEN YOU'RE ALONE YOU ONLY HAVE TO THINK ABOUT YOURSELF...
GO AWAY, HIMEMARU!
NOT AGAIN!!
CRASH

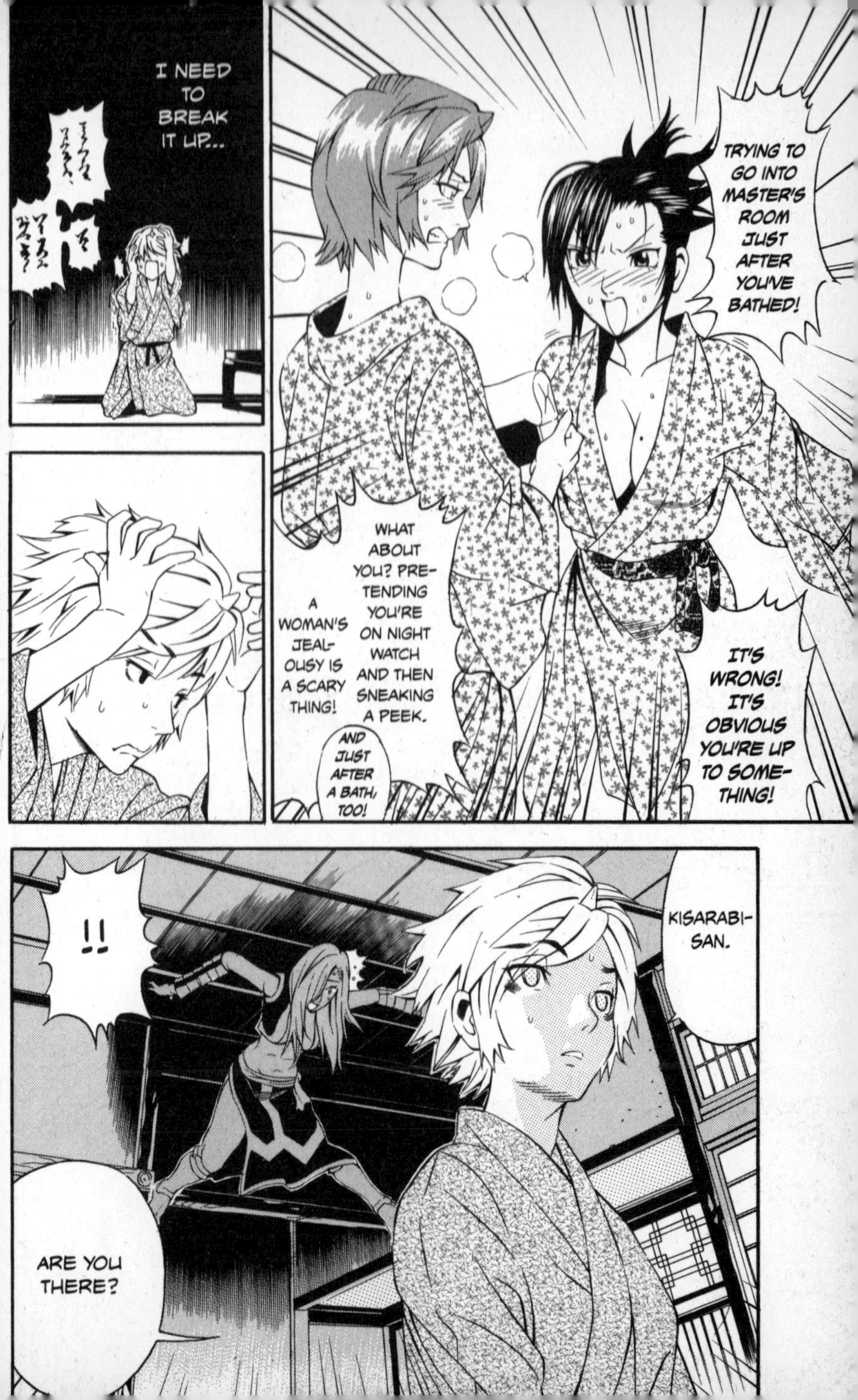

TRYING TO GO INTO MASTER'S ROOM JUST AFTER YOU'VE BATHED!
IT'S WRONG! IT'S OBVIOUS YOU'RE UP TO SOME-THING!
WHAT ABOUT YOU? PRE-TENDING YOU'RE ON NIGHT WATCH AND THEN SNEAKING A PEEK.
AND JUST AFTER A BATH, TOO!
A WOMAN'S JEAL-OUSY IS A SCARY THING!
I NEED TO BREAK IT UP...
KISARABI-SAN.
!!
ARE YOU THERE?

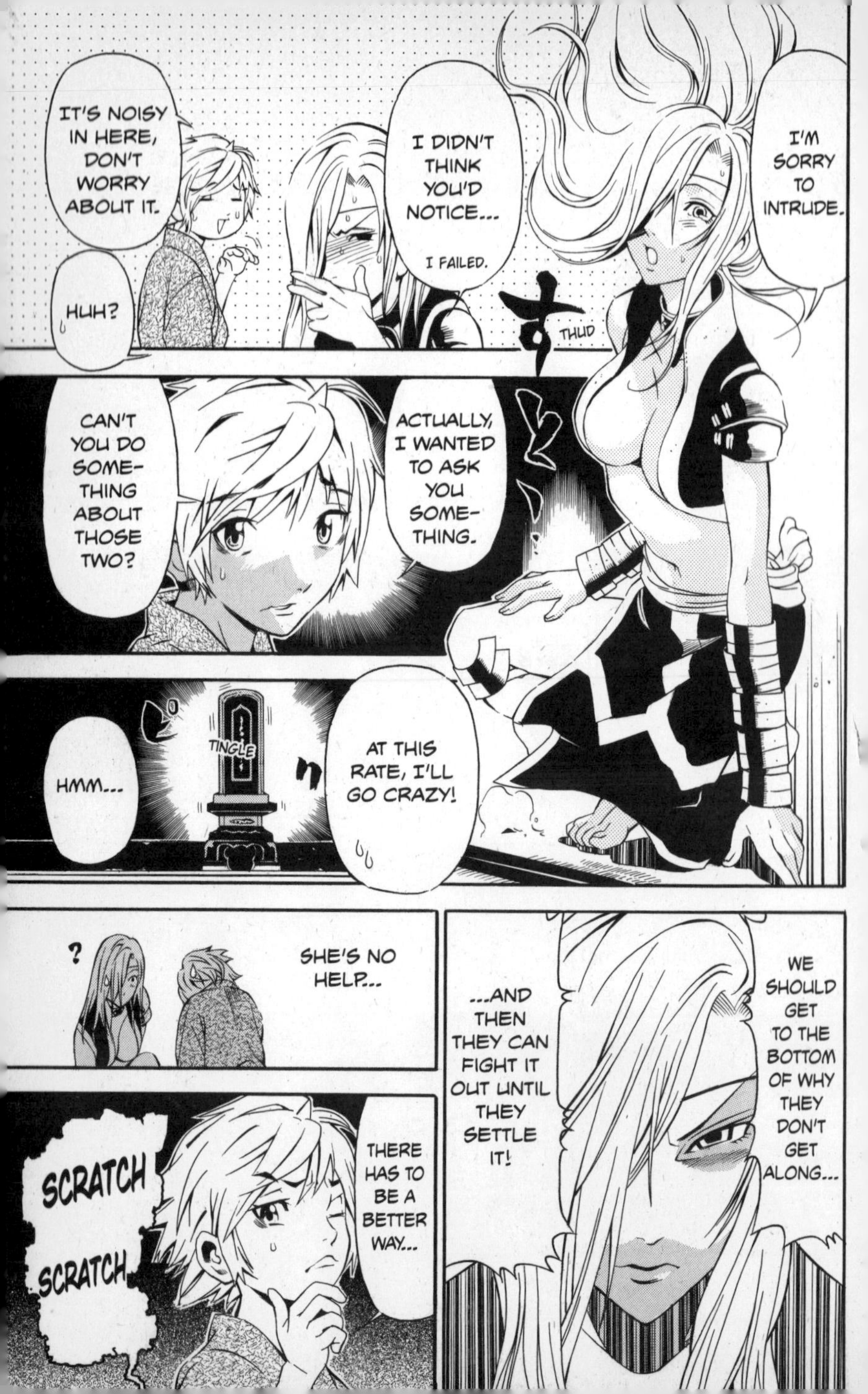
I'M SORRY TO INTRUDE.
THUD
I DIDN'T THINK YOU'D NOTICE...
I FAILED.
IT'S NOISY IN HERE, DON'T WORRY ABOUT IT.
HUH?
ACTUALLY, I WANTED TO ASK YOU SOMETHING.
CAN'T YOU DO SOMETHING ABOUT THOSE TWO?
AT THIS RATE, I'LL GO CRAZY!
TINGLE
HMM...
WE SHOULD GET TO THE BOTTOM OF WHY THEY DON'T GET ALONG...
...AND THEN THEY CAN FIGHT IT OUT UNTIL THEY SETTLE IT!
SHE'S NO HELP...
?
THERE HAS TO BE A BETTER WAY...
SCRATCH
SCRATCH

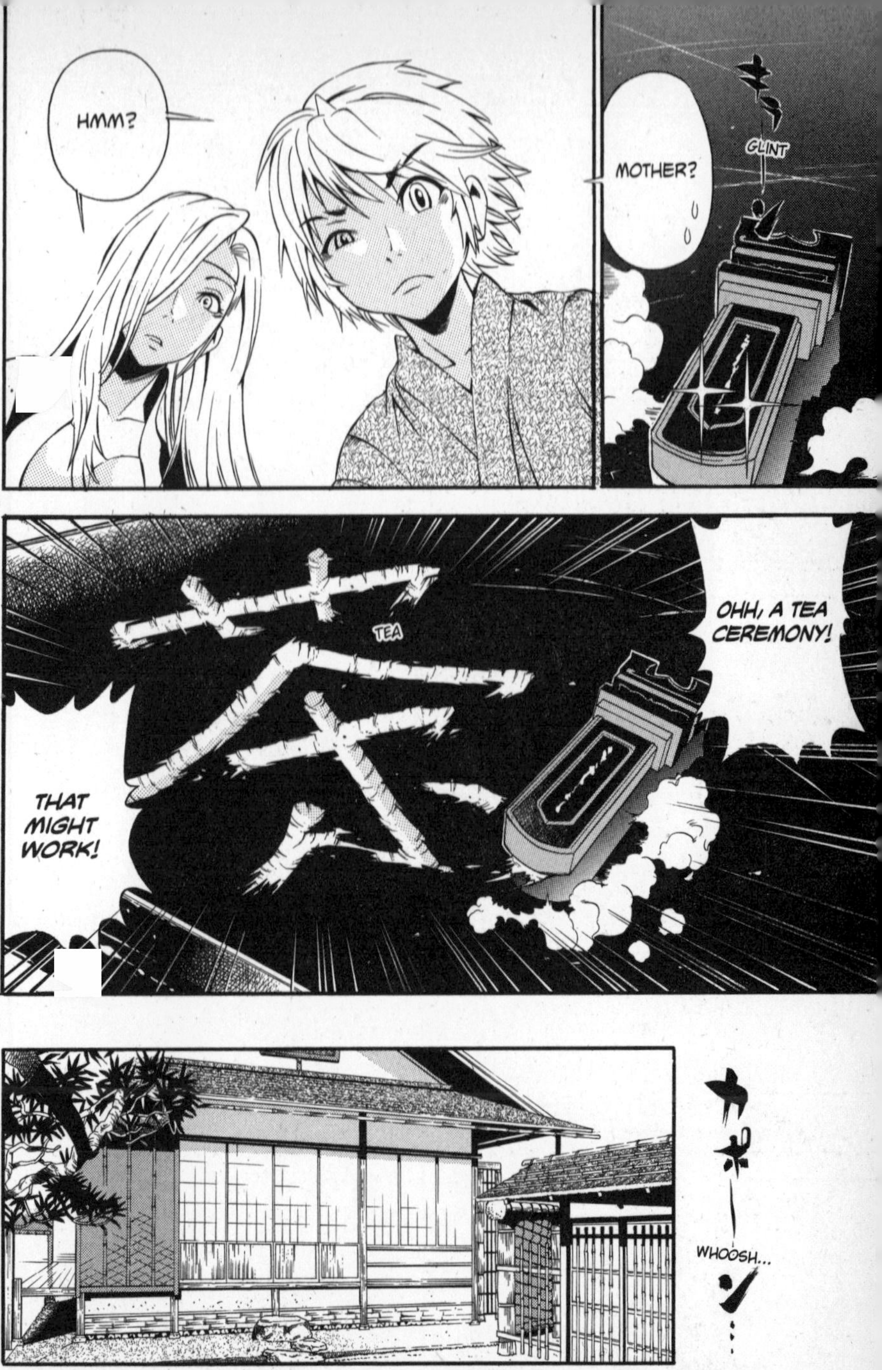
GLINT
MOTHER?
HMM?
OHH, A TEA CEREMONY!
TEA
THAT MIGHT WORK!
WHOOSH...

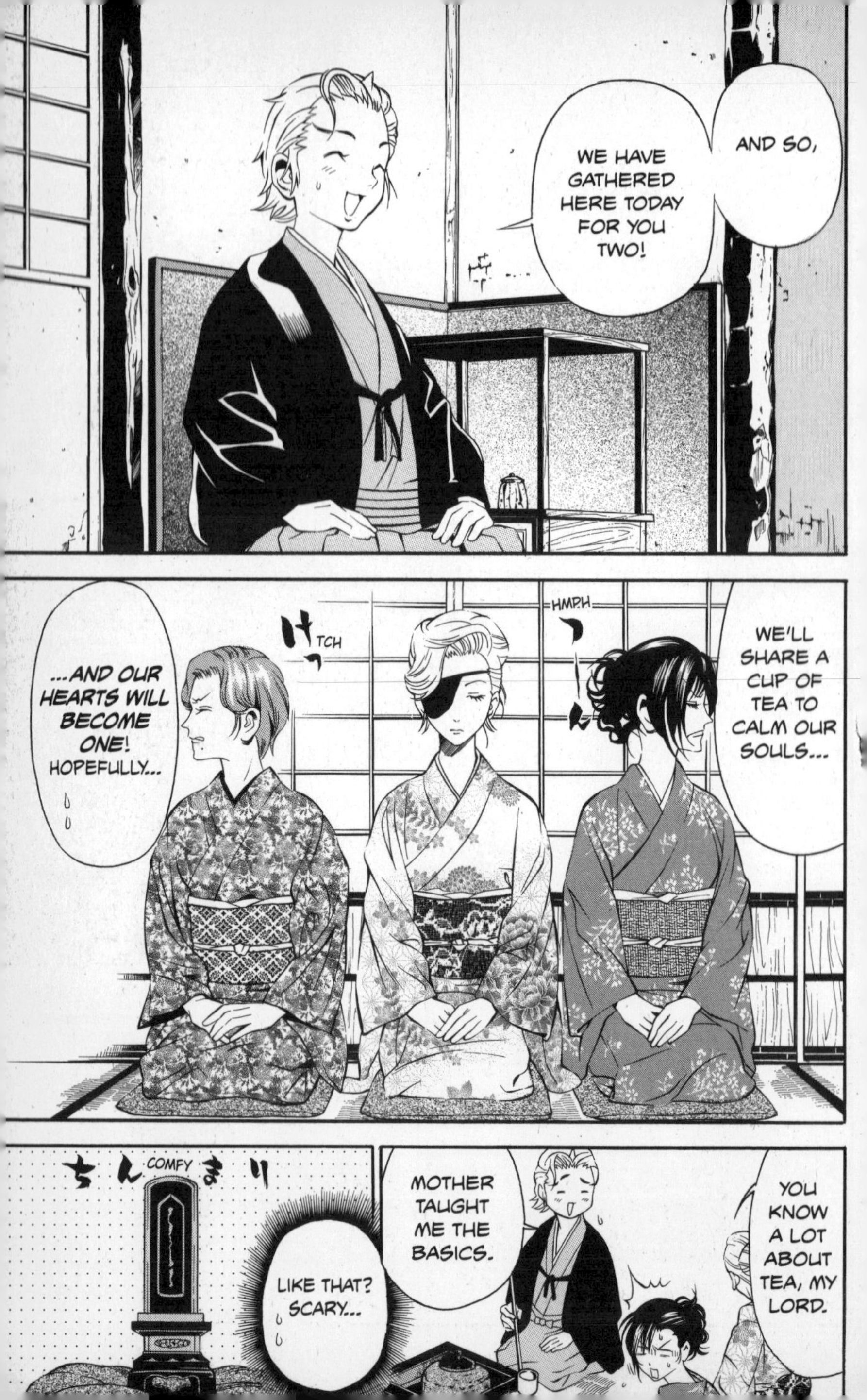
AND SO,
WE HAVE GATHERED HERE TODAY FOR YOU TWO!
WE'LL SHARE A CUP OF TEA TO CALM OUR SOULS...
HMPH
け TCH
...AND OUR HEARTS WILL BECOME ONE! HOPEFULLY...
YOU KNOW A LOT ABOUT TEA, MY LORD.
MOTHER TAUGHT ME THE BASICS.
LIKE THAT? SCARY...
ちんまり COMFY

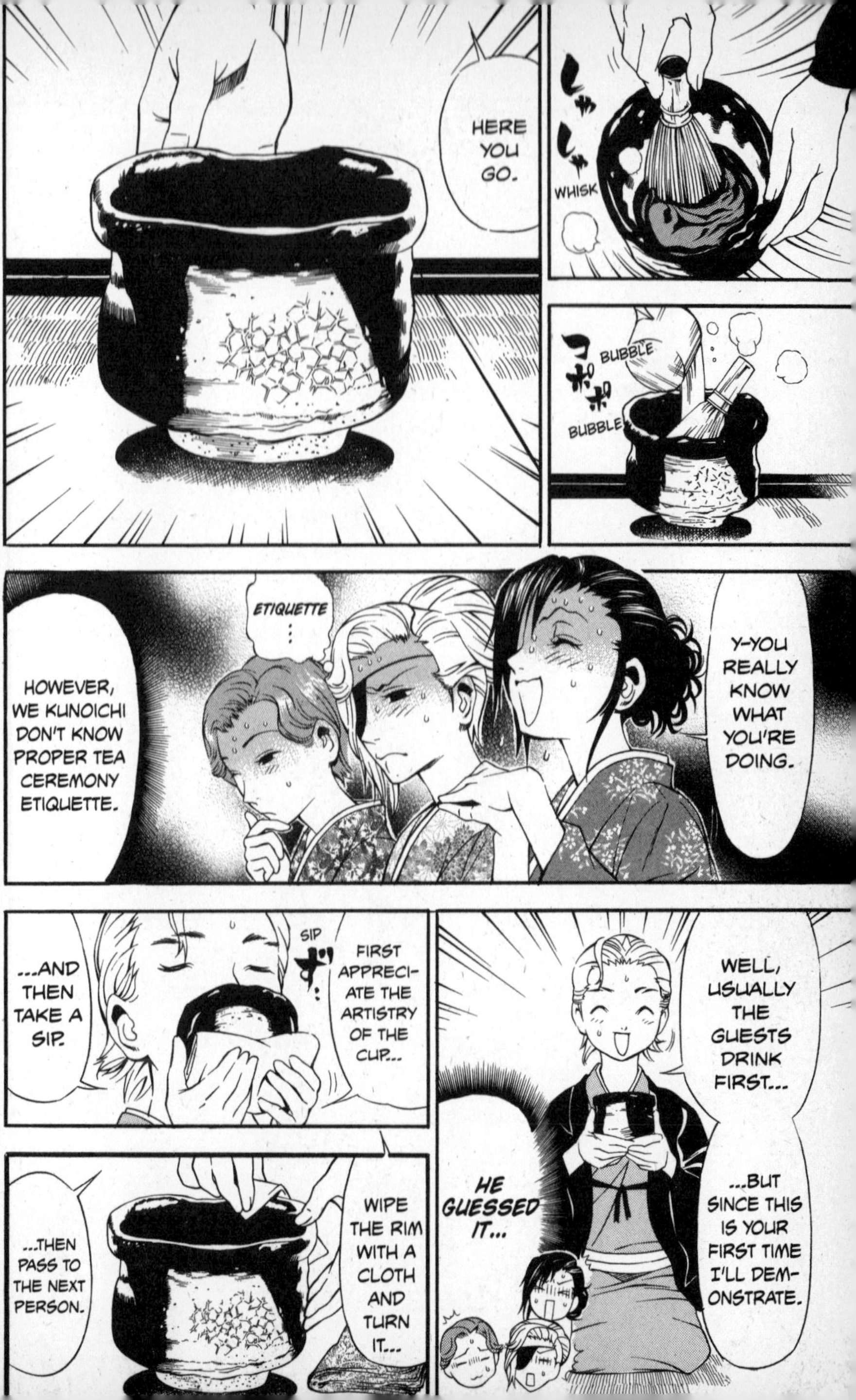
WHISK
BUBBLE
BUBBLE
HERE YOU GO.
Y-YOU REALLY KNOW WHAT YOU'RE DOING.
ETIQUETTE...
HOWEVER, WE KUNOICHI DON'T KNOW PROPER TEA CEREMONY ETIQUETTE.
WELL, USUALLY THE GUESTS DRINK FIRST...
...BUT SINCE THIS IS YOUR FIRST TIME I'LL DEM-ONSTRATE.
HE GUESSED IT...
FIRST APPRECI-ATE THE ARTISTRY OF THE CUP...
SIP
...AND THEN TAKE A SIP.
WIPE THE RIM WITH A CLOTH AND TURN IT...
...THEN PASS TO THE NEXT PERSON.

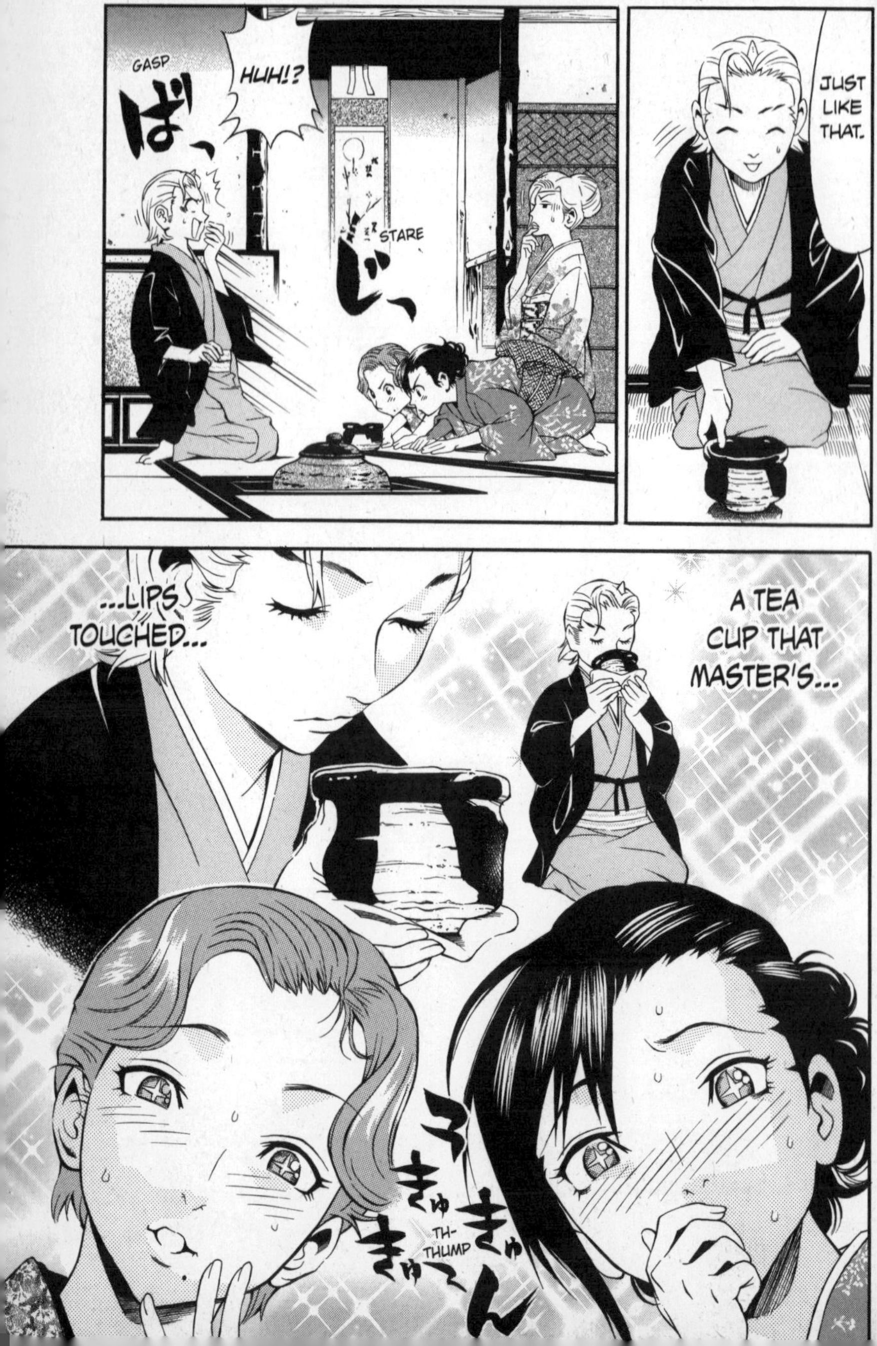
JUST LIKE THAT.
GASP
HUH!?
STARE
A TEA CUP THAT MASTER'S...
...LIPS TOUCHED...
TH-THUMP

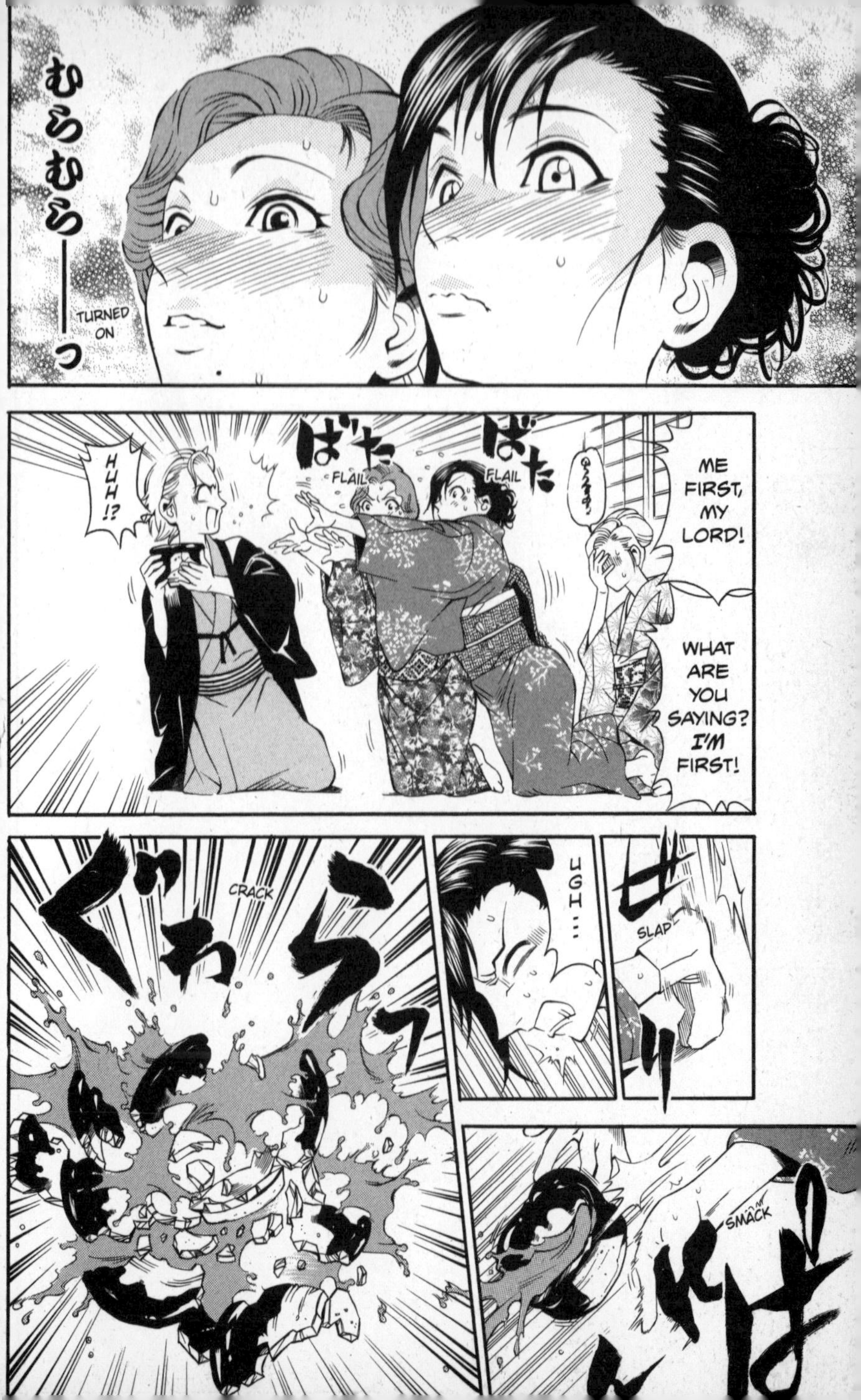
むらむらーっ
TURNED ON
ME FIRST, MY LORD!
WHAT ARE YOU SAYING? I'M FIRST!
ばた
FLAIL
ばた
FLAIL
HUH!?
SLAP
UGH...
SMACK
CRACK

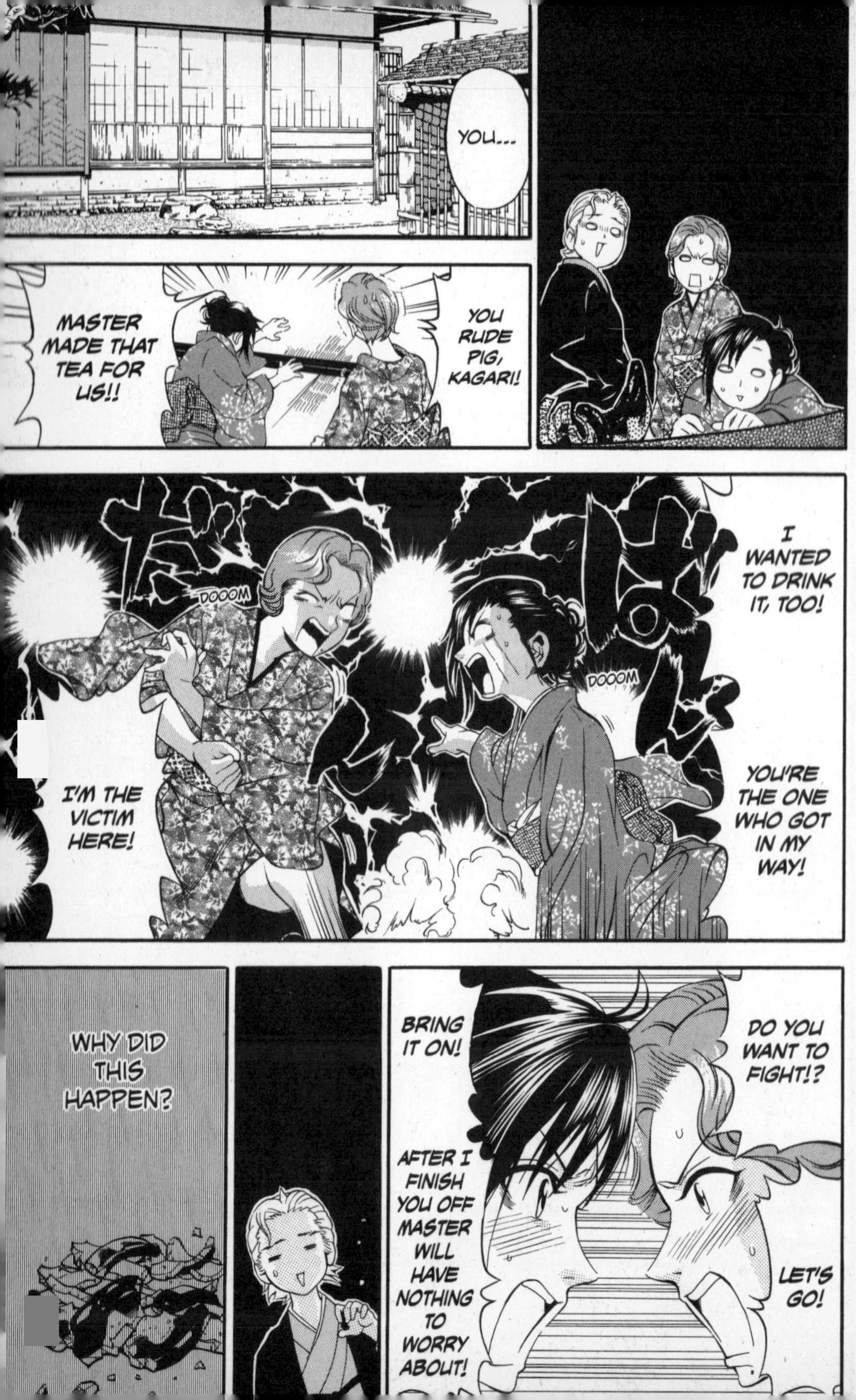
YOU...
YOU RUDE PIG, KAGARI!
MASTER MADE THAT TEA FOR US!!
I WANTED TO DRINK IT, TOO!
DOOOM
YOU'RE THE ONE WHO GOT IN MY WAY!
DOOOM
I'M THE VICTIM HERE!
DO YOU WANT TO FIGHT!?
BRING IT ON!
LET'S GO!
AFTER I FINISH YOU OFF MASTER WILL HAVE NOTHING TO WORRY ABOUT!
WHY DID THIS HAPPEN?

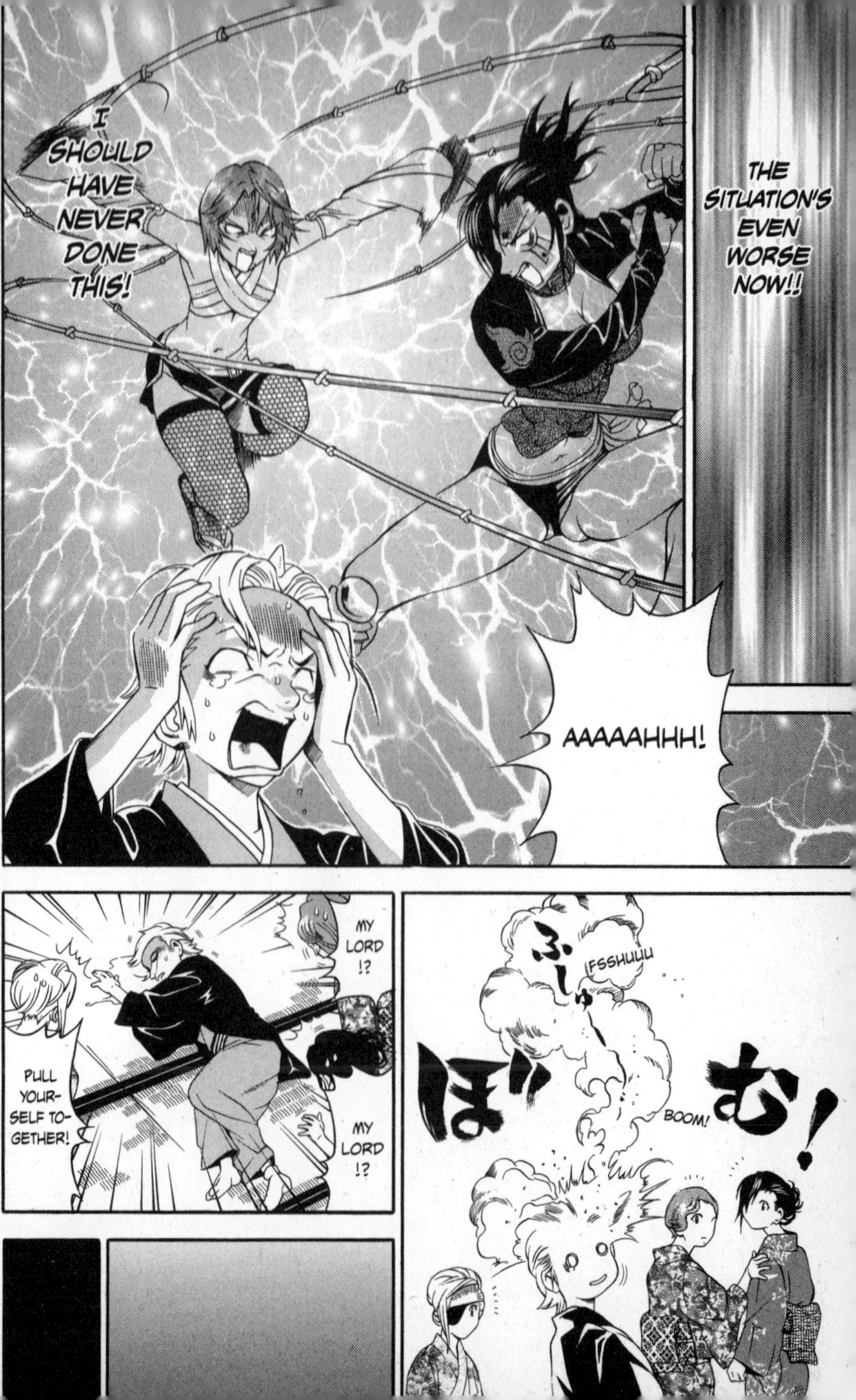
THE SITUATION'S EVEN WORSE NOW!!
I SHOULD HAVE NEVER DONE THIS!
AAAAAHHH!
ふしゅ
FSSHUUU
ぼむ!
BOOM!
MY LORD !?
MY LORD !?
PULL YOUR-SELF TO-GETHER!

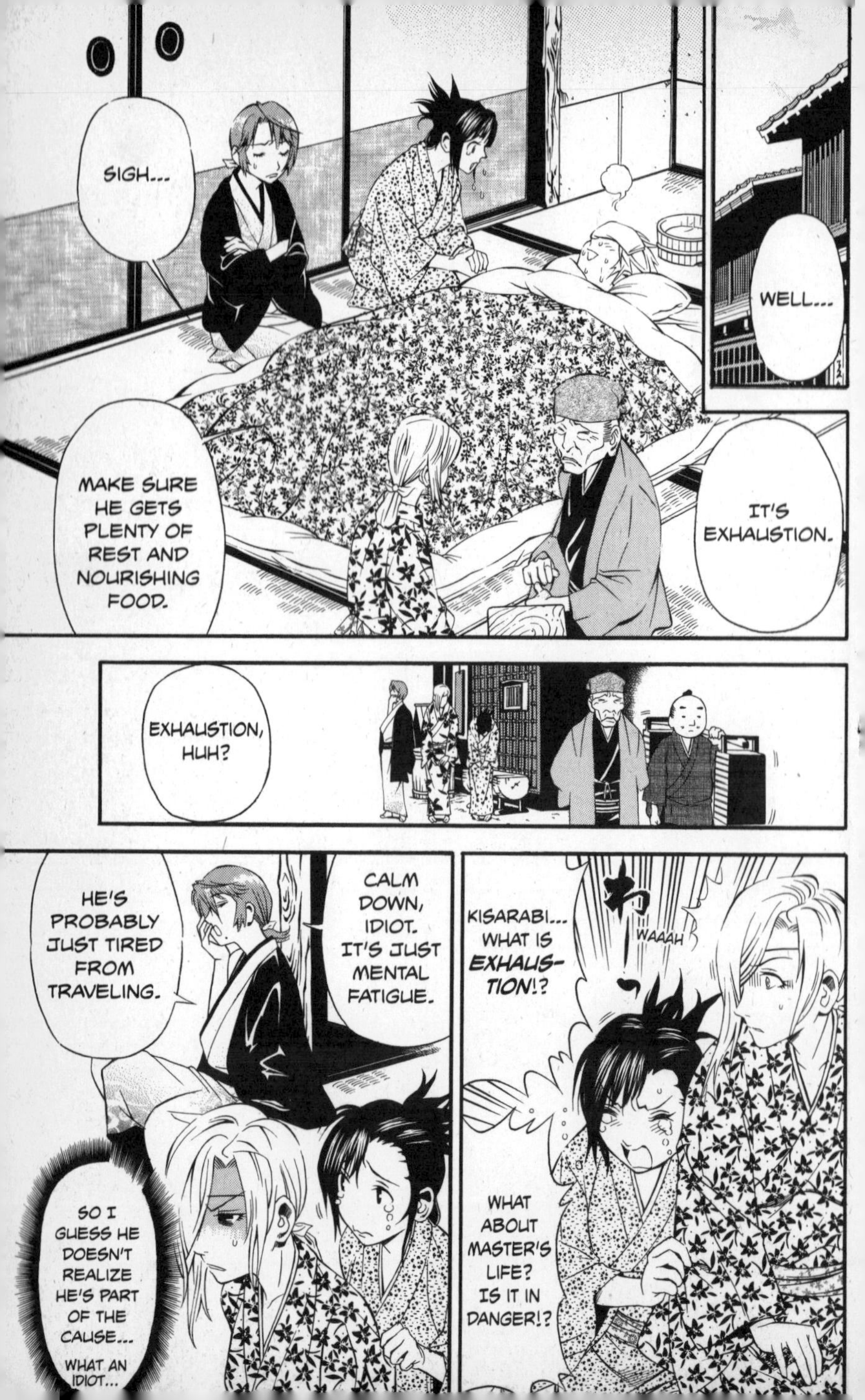
WELL...
SIGH...
IT'S EXHAUSTION.
MAKE SURE HE GETS PLENTY OF REST AND NOURISHING FOOD.
EXHAUSTION, HUH?
KISARABI... WHAT IS EXHAUSTION!?
WAAAH
WHAT ABOUT MASTER'S LIFE? IS IT IN DANGER!?
CALM DOWN, IDIOT. IT'S JUST MENTAL FATIGUE.
HE'S PROBABLY JUST TIRED FROM TRAVELING.
SO I GUESS HE DOESN'T REALIZE HE'S PART OF THE CAUSE...
WHAT AN IDIOT...

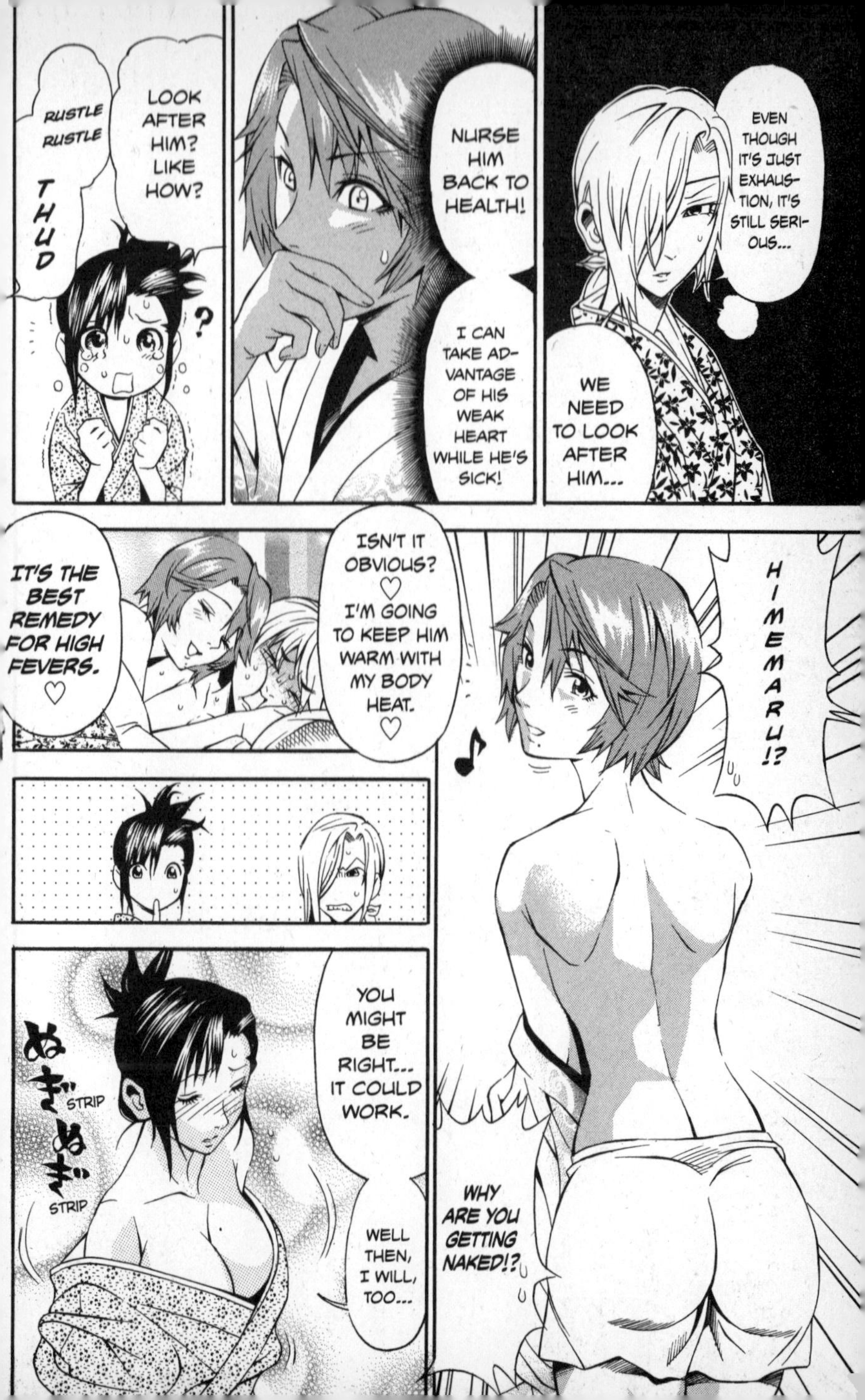
EVEN THOUGH IT'S JUST EXHAUSTION, IT'S STILL SERIOUS...
WE NEED TO LOOK AFTER HIM...
NURSE HIM BACK TO HEALTH!
I CAN TAKE ADVANTAGE OF HIS WEAK HEART WHILE HE'S SICK!
LOOK AFTER HIM? LIKE HOW?
RUSTLE RUSTLE
THUD
HIMEMARU!?
WHY ARE YOU GETTING NAKED!?
ISN'T IT OBVIOUS? ♡ I'M GOING TO KEEP HIM WARM WITH MY BODY HEAT. ♡
IT'S THE BEST REMEDY FOR HIGH FEVERS. ♡
YOU MIGHT BE RIGHT... IT COULD WORK.
WELL THEN, I WILL, TOO...
ぬぎ STRIP
ぬぎ STRIP

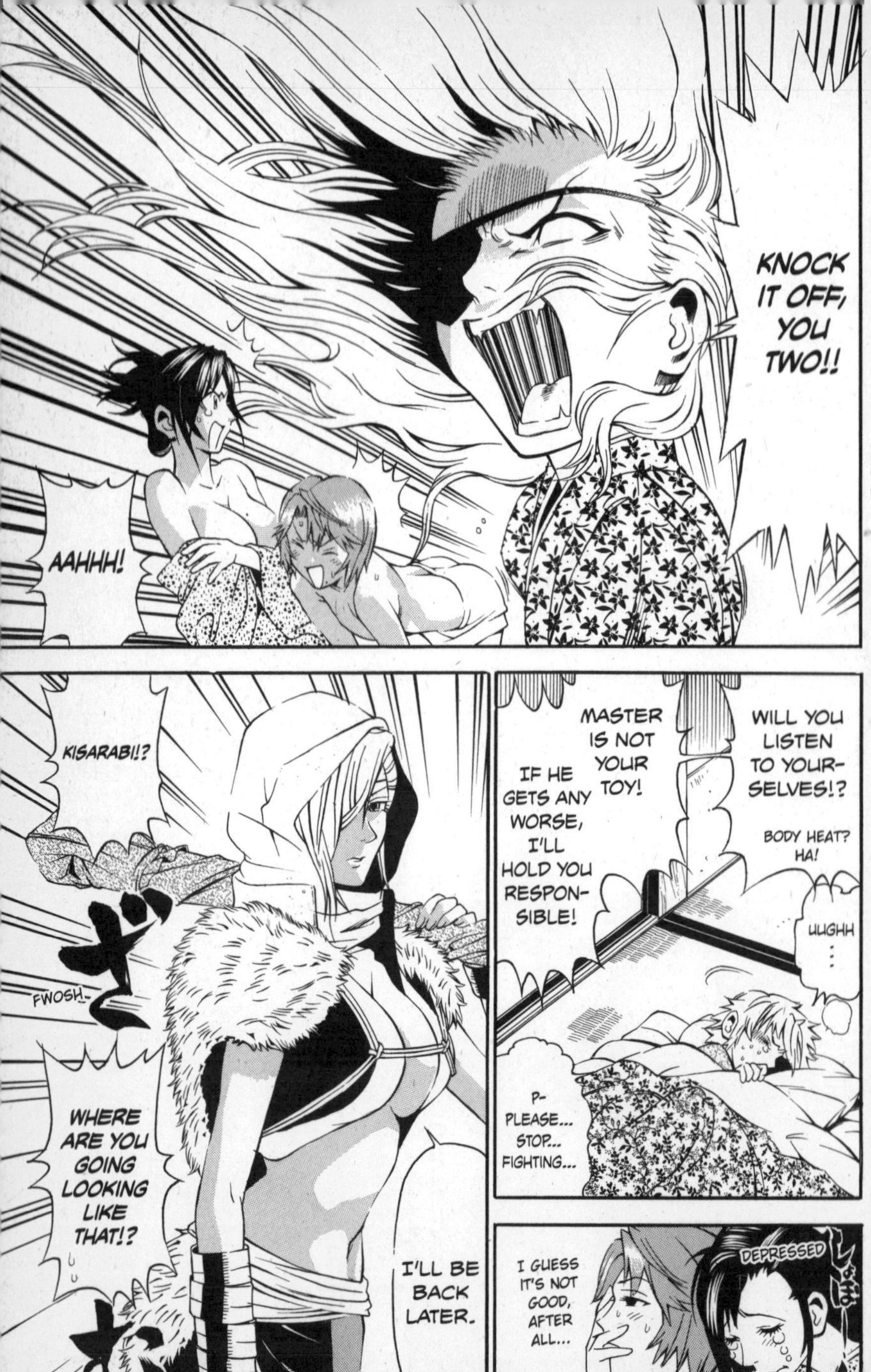
KNOCK IT OFF, YOU TWO!!
AAHHH!
WILL YOU LISTEN TO YOURSELVES!?
MASTER IS NOT YOUR TOY!
IF HE GETS ANY WORSE, I'LL HOLD YOU RESPONSIBLE!
BODY HEAT? HA!
UUGHH ...
P-PLEASE... STOP... FIGHTING...
DEPRESSED
I GUESS IT'S NOT GOOD, AFTER ALL...
KISARABI!?
FWOSH_
WHERE ARE YOU GOING LOOKING LIKE THAT!?
I'LL BE BACK LATER.

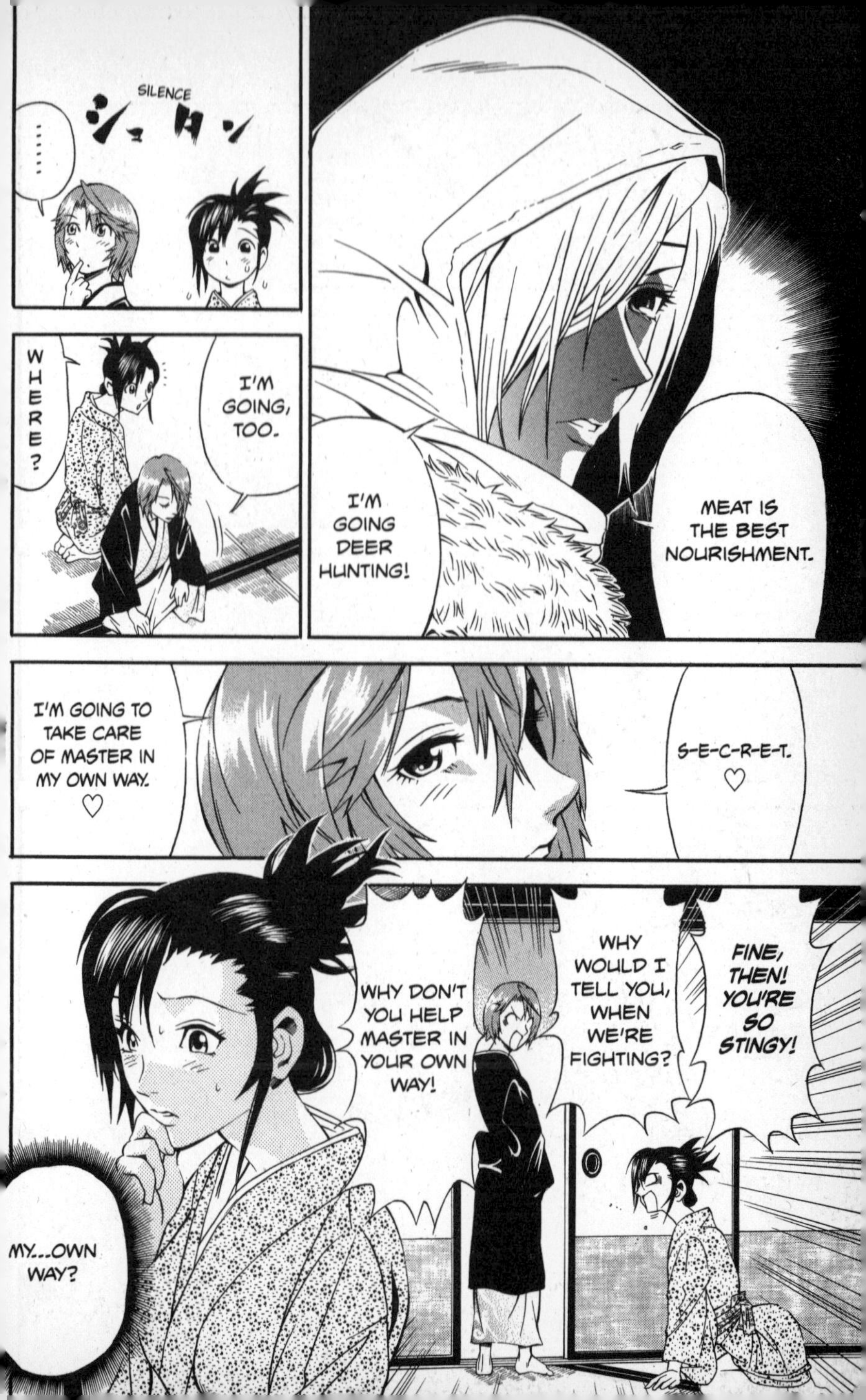
MEAT IS THE BEST NOURISHMENT.
I'M GOING DEER HUNTING!
SILENCE
シュタン
......
I'M GOING, TOO.
WHERE?
S-E-C-R-E-T. ♡
I'M GOING TO TAKE CARE OF MASTER IN MY OWN WAY. ♡
FINE, THEN! YOU'RE SO STINGY!
WHY WOULD I TELL YOU, WHEN WE'RE FIGHTING?
WHY DON'T YOU HELP MASTER IN YOUR OWN WAY!
MY...OWN WAY?

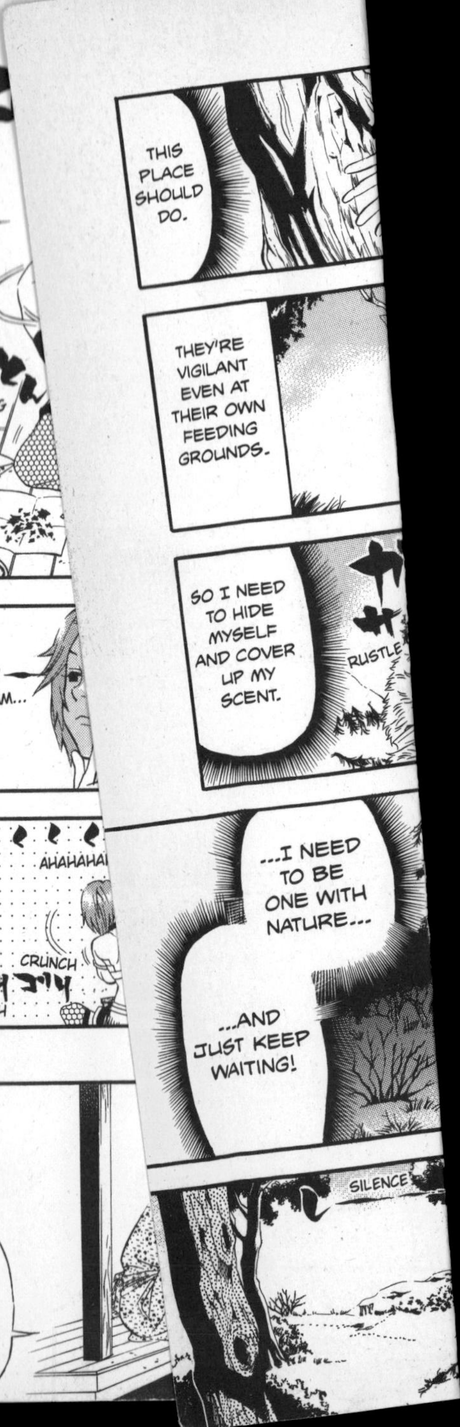
THIS PLACE SHOULD DO.
THEY'RE VIGILANT EVEN AT THEIR OWN FEEDING GROUNDS.
SO I NEED TO HIDE MYSELF AND COVER UP MY SCENT.
RUSTLE
...I NEED TO BE ONE WITH NATURE...
...AND JUST KEEP WAITING!
SILENCE

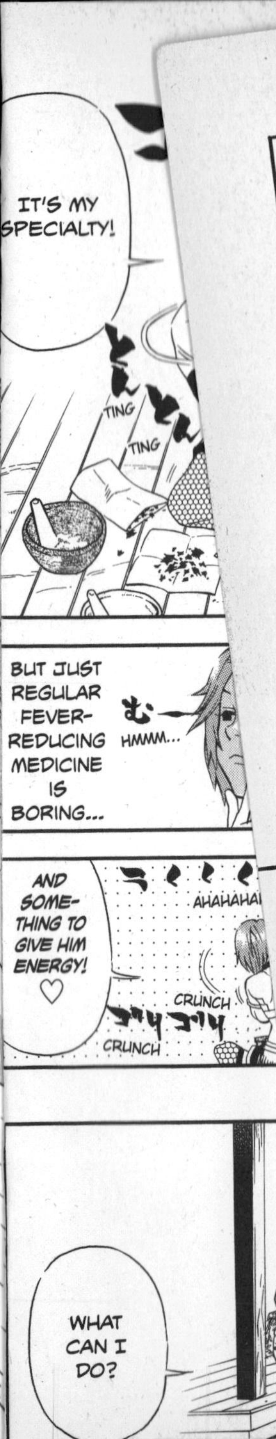
IT'S MY SPECIALTY!
TING
TING
HMMM...
BUT JUST REGULAR FEVER-REDUCING MEDICINE IS BORING...
AHAHAHA
AND SOME-THING TO GIVE HIM ENERGY! ♡
CRUNCH
CRUNCH
WHAT CAN I DO?

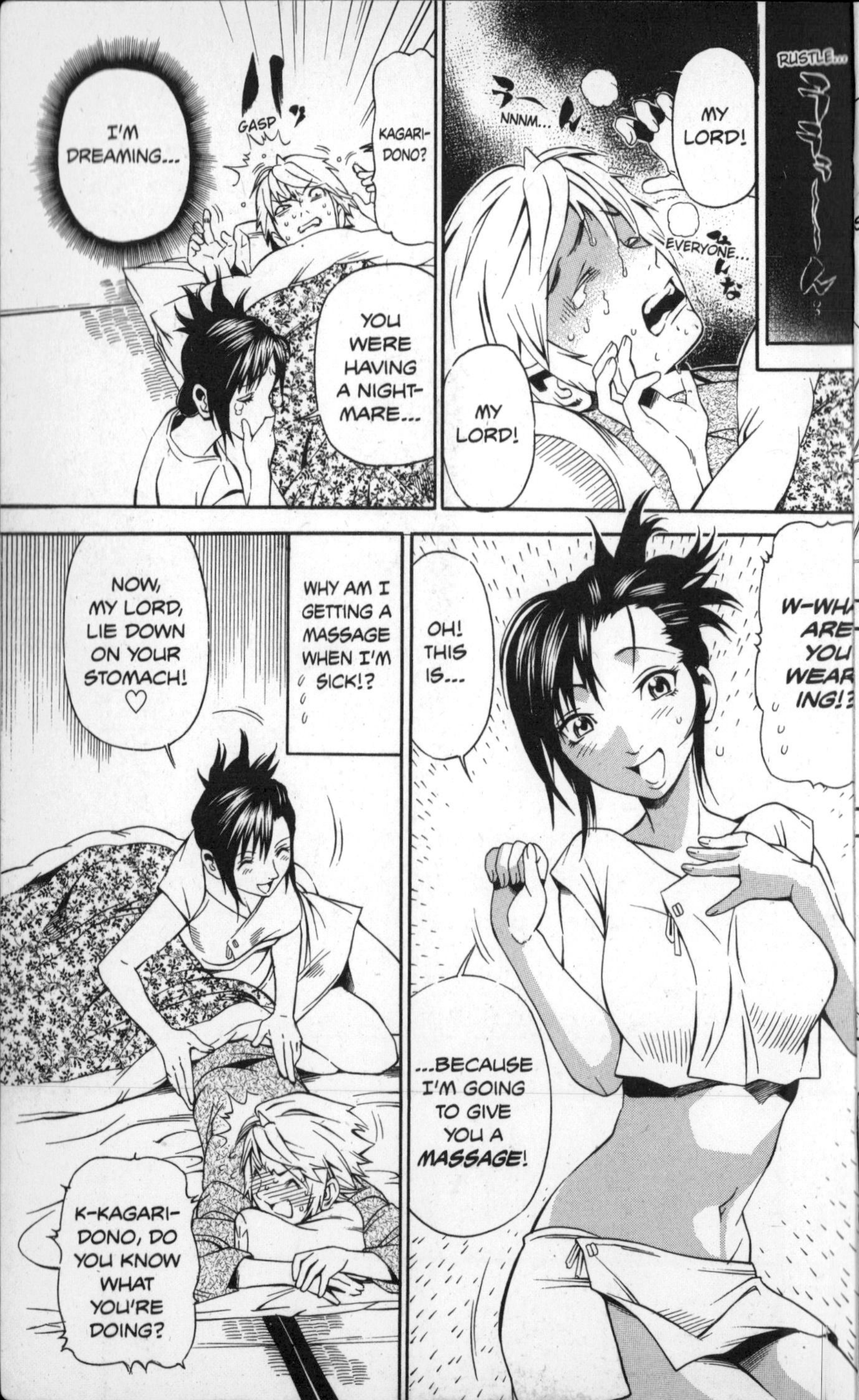
RUSTLE...
MY LORD!
NNNM...
EVERYONE...
MY LORD!
KAGARI-DONO?
GASP
I'M DREAMING...
YOU WERE HAVING A NIGHT-MARE...
W-WHA ARE YOU WEAR ING!?
OH! THIS IS...
...BECAUSE I'M GOING TO GIVE YOU A MASSAGE!
WHY AM I GETTING A MASSAGE WHEN I'M SICK!?
NOW, MY LORD, LIE DOWN ON YOUR STOMACH! ♡
K-KAGARI-DONO, DO YOU KNOW WHAT YOU'RE DOING?

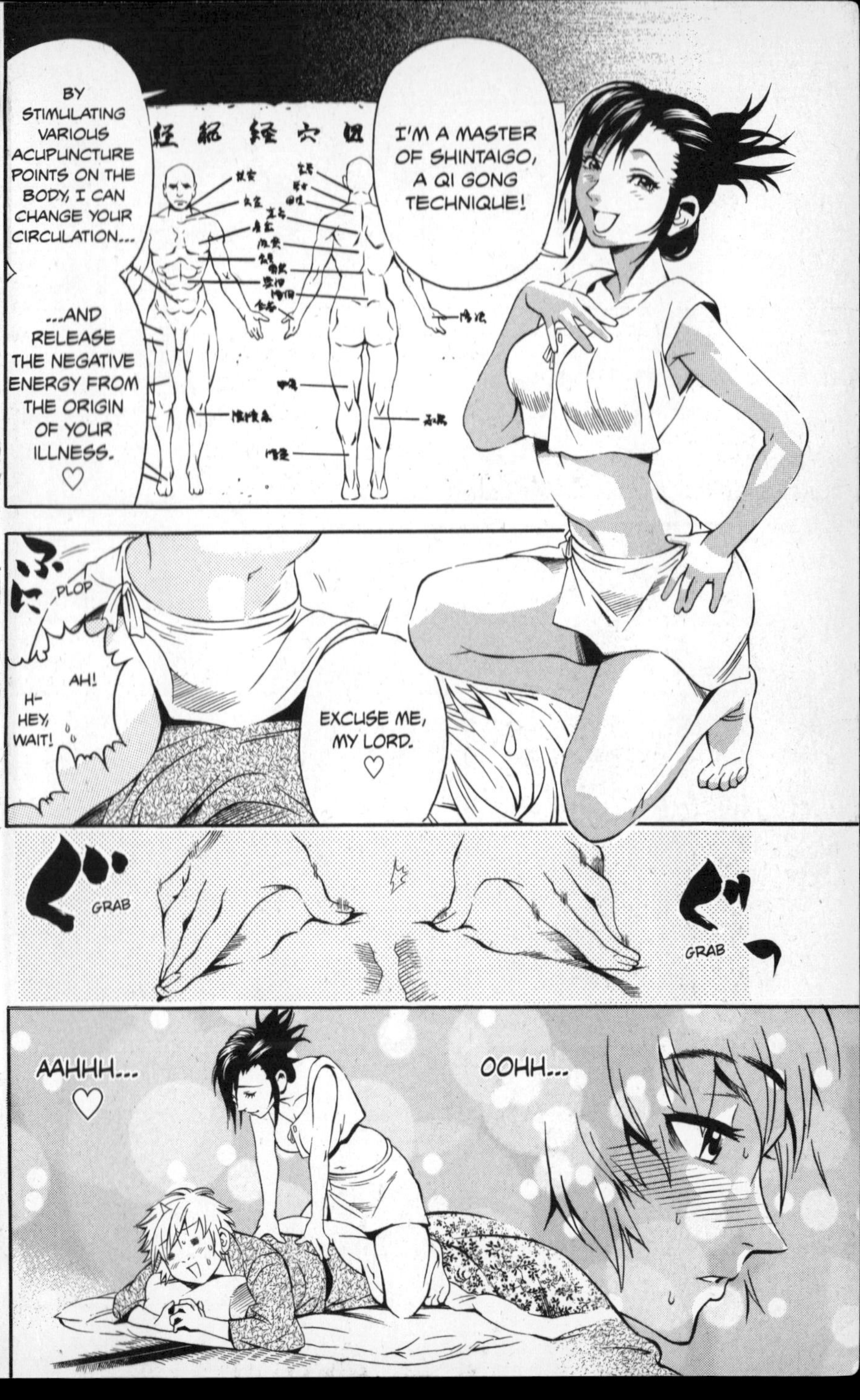
I'M A MASTER OF SHINTAIGO, A QI GONG TECHNIQUE!
BY STIMULATING VARIOUS ACUPUNCTURE POINTS ON THE BODY, I CAN CHANGE YOUR CIRCULATION...
...AND RELEASE THE NEGATIVE ENERGY FROM THE ORIGIN OF YOUR ILLNESS. ♡
EXCUSE ME, MY LORD. ♡
AH!
H-HEY, WAIT!
PLOP
GRAB
GRAB
OOHH...
AAHHH... ♡

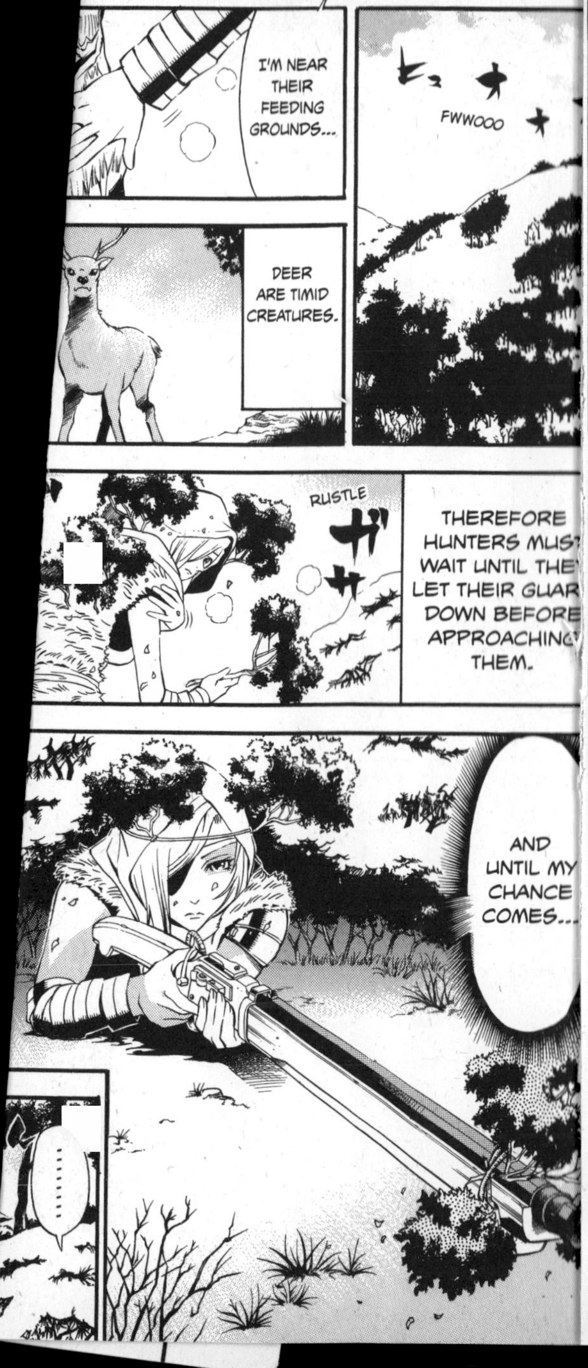
FWWOOO
I'M NEAR THEIR FEEDING GROUNDS...
DEER ARE TIMID CREATURES.
THEREFORE HUNTERS MUS WAIT UNTIL THE LET THEIR GUAR DOWN BEFORE APPROACHING THEM.
RUSTLE
AND UNTIL MY CHANCE COMES...
......

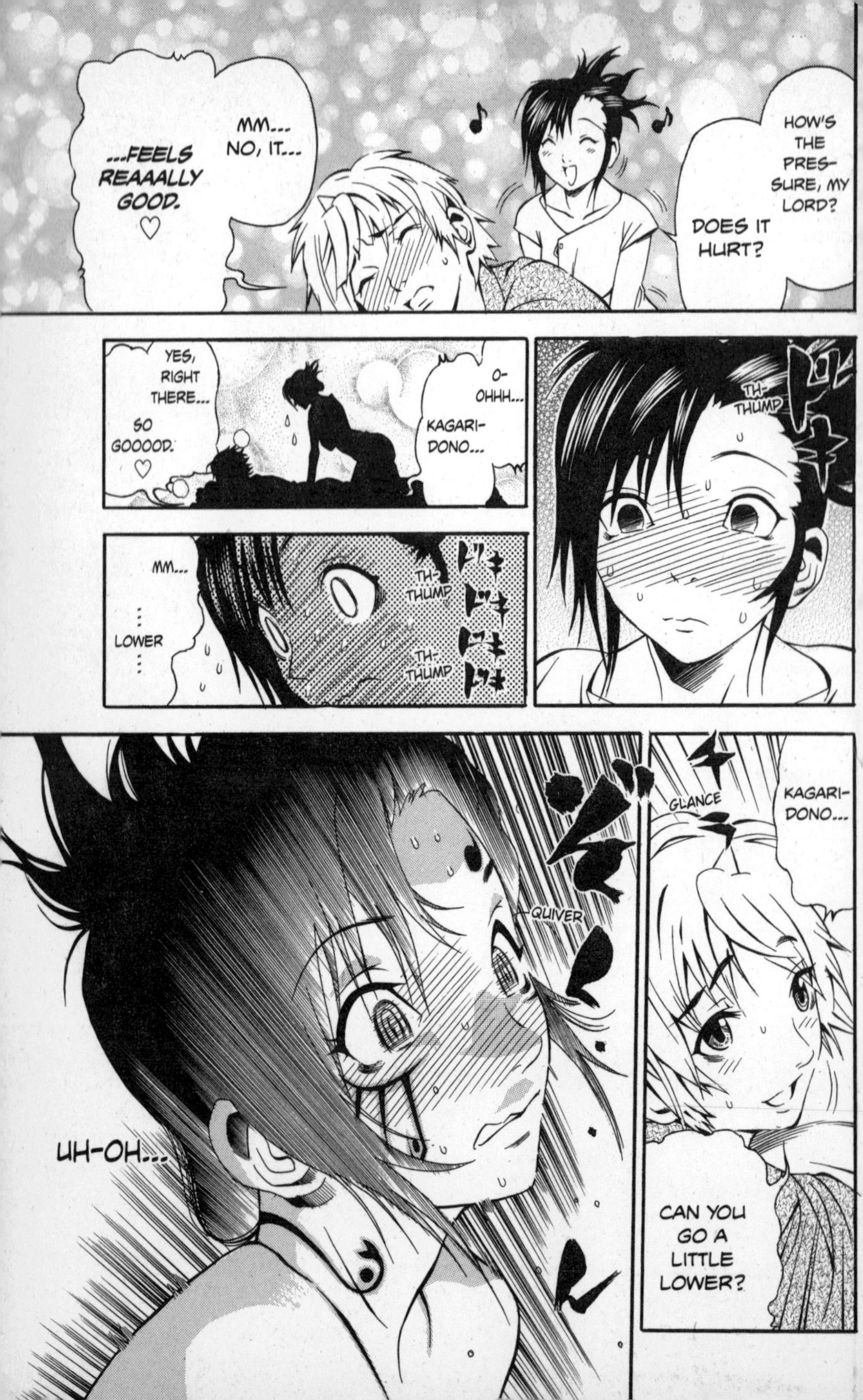
HOW'S THE PRES-SURE, MY LORD?
DOES IT HURT?
MM... NO, IT...
...FEELS REAAALLY GOOD. ♡
TH-THUMP
O-OHHH... KAGARI-DONO...
YES, RIGHT THERE... SO GOOOOD. ♡
TH-THUMP
TH-THUMP
MM... ...LOWER ...
GLANCE
KAGARI-DONO...
CAN YOU GO A LITTLE LOWER?
QUIVER
UH-OH...

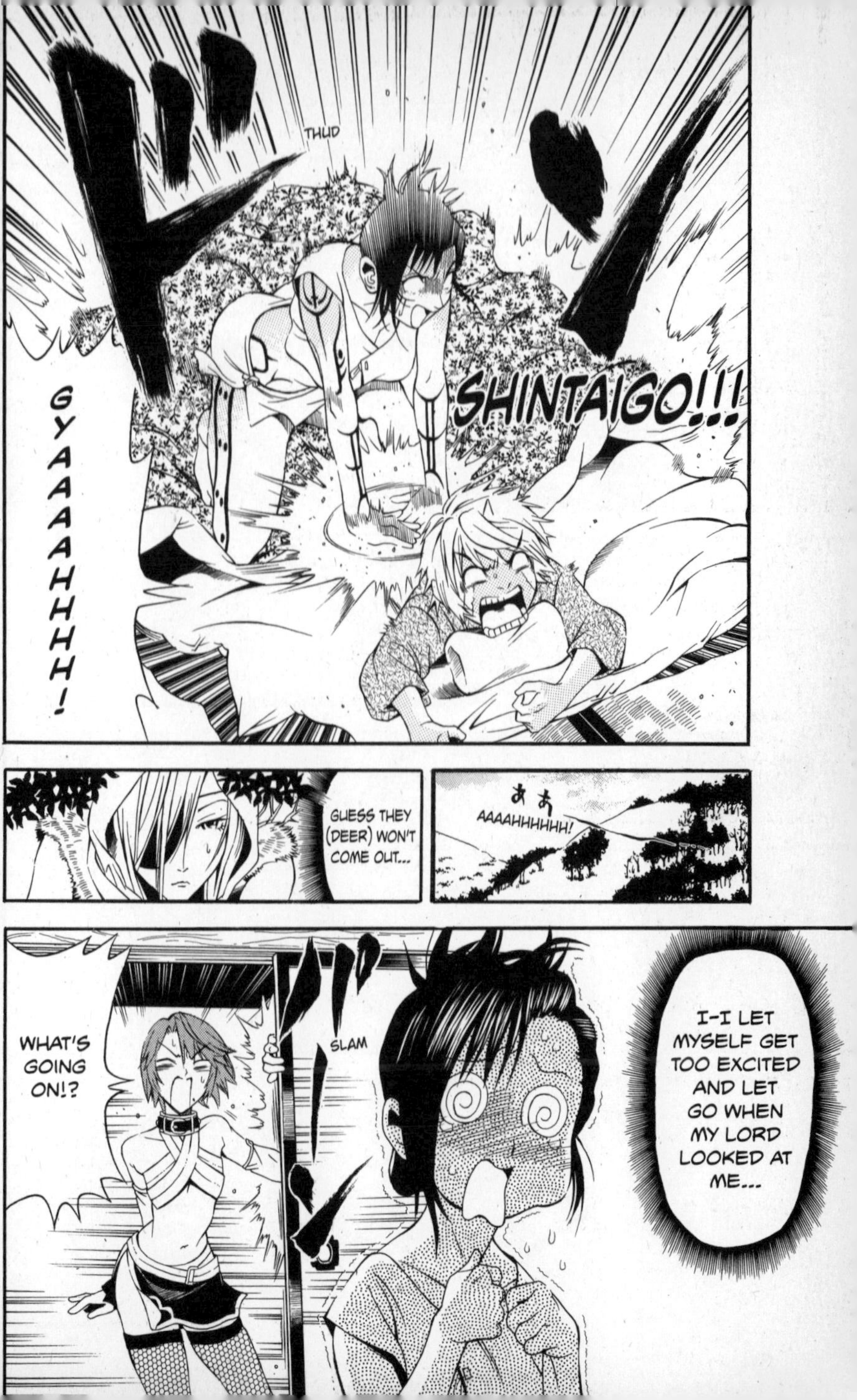
THUD
SHINTAIGO!!!
GYAAAAAHHHHH!
ああ
AAAAHHHHHH!
GUESS THEY (DEER) WON'T COME OUT...
I-I LET MYSELF GET TOO EXCITED AND LET GO WHEN MY LORD LOOKED AT ME...
SLAM
WHAT'S GOING ON!?

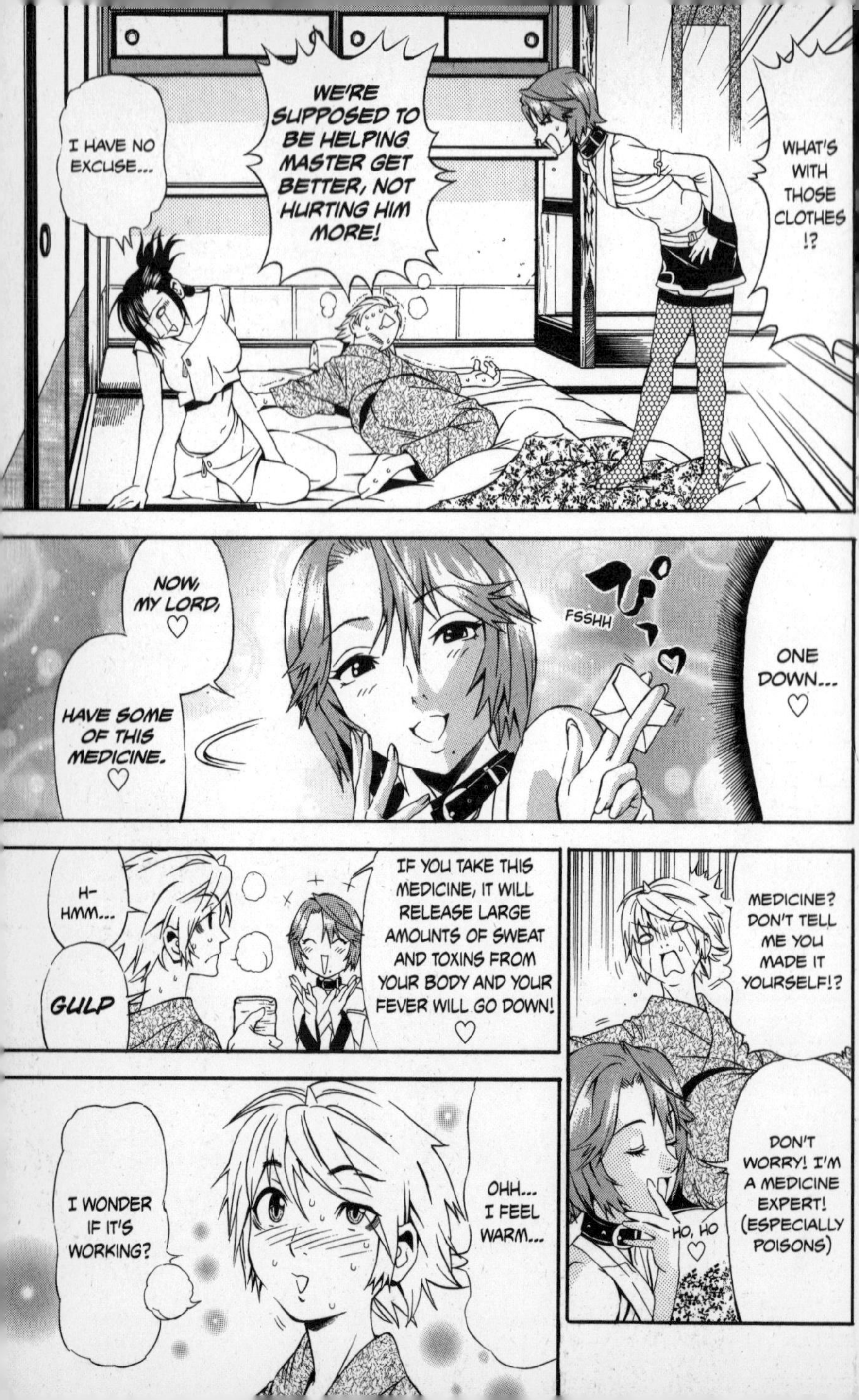
WHAT'S WITH THOSE CLOTHES !?
WE'RE SUPPOSED TO BE HELPING MASTER GET BETTER, NOT HURTING HIM MORE!
I HAVE NO EXCUSE...
ONE DOWN... ♡
FSSHH
NOW, MY LORD, ♡
HAVE SOME OF THIS MEDICINE. ♡
MEDICINE? DON'T TELL ME YOU MADE IT YOURSELF!?
DON'T WORRY! I'M A MEDICINE EXPERT! (ESPECIALLY POISONS)
HO, HO ♡
IF YOU TAKE THIS MEDICINE, IT WILL RELEASE LARGE AMOUNTS OF SWEAT AND TOXINS FROM YOUR BODY AND YOUR FEVER WILL GO DOWN! ♡
H-HMM...
GULP
OHH... I FEEL WARM...
I WONDER IF IT'S WORKING?

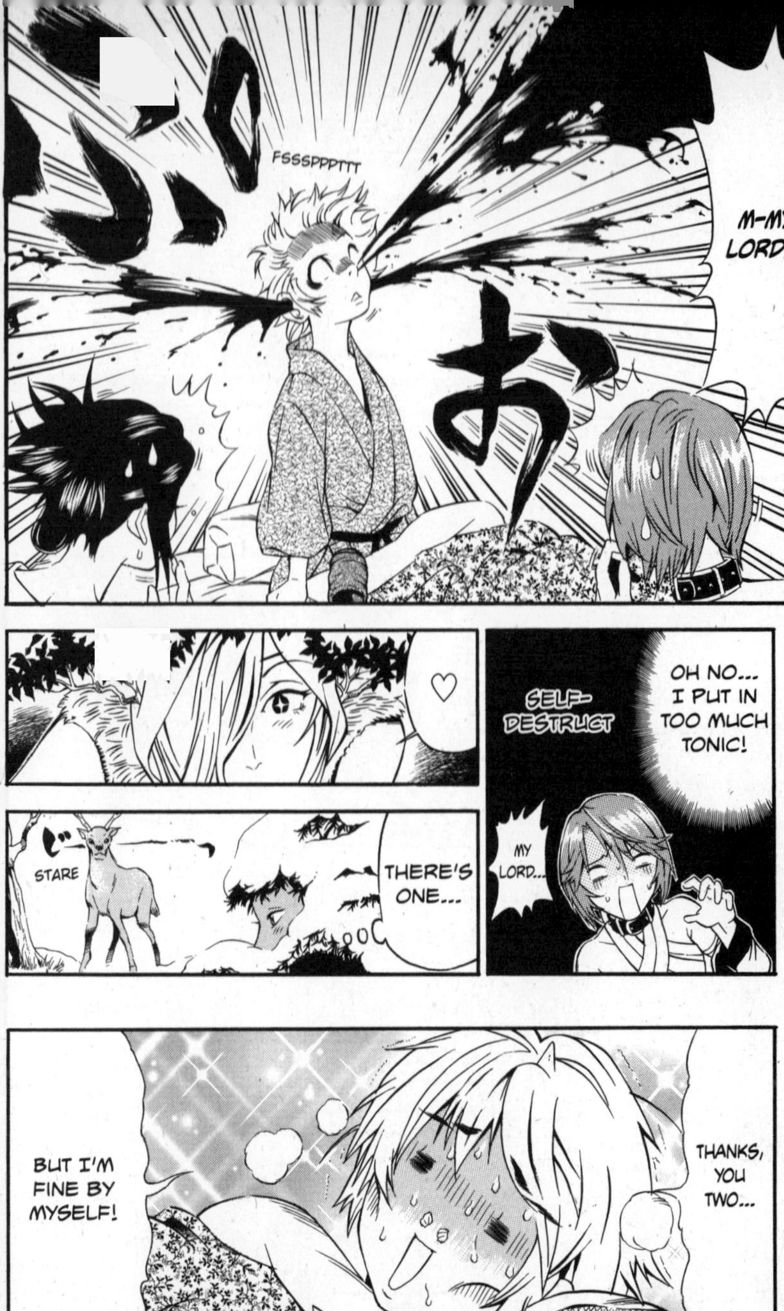
M-MY LORD!?
FSSSPPPTTT
お
OH NO... I PUT IN TOO MUCH TONIC!
SELF-DESTRUCT
MY LORD...
♥
THERE'S ONE...
STARE
THANKS, YOU TWO...
BUT I'M FINE BY MYSELF!

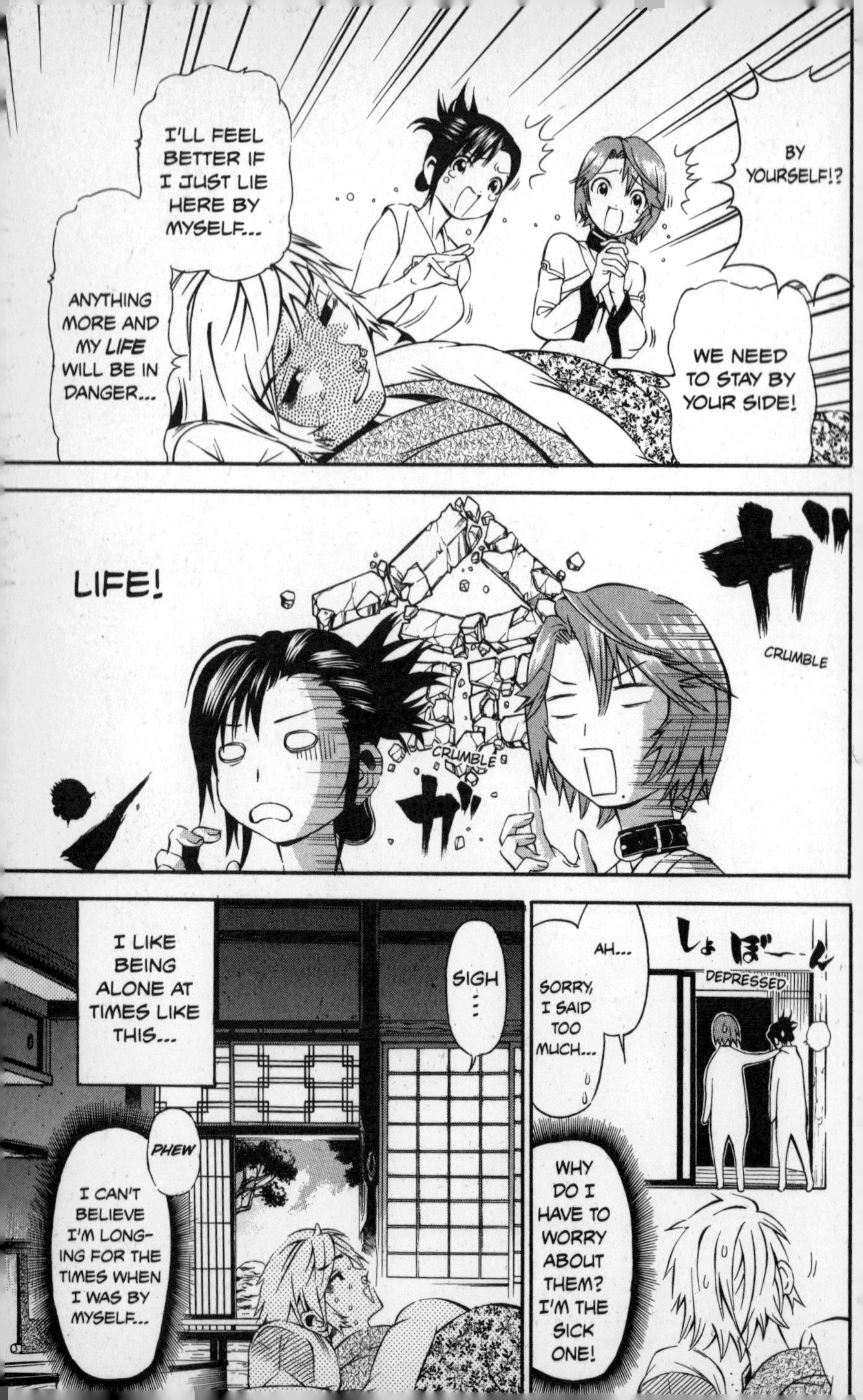
BY YOURSELF!?
WE NEED TO STAY BY YOUR SIDE!
I'LL FEEL BETTER IF I JUST LIE HERE BY MYSELF...
ANYTHING MORE AND MY *LIFE* WILL BE IN DANGER...
ガ
CRUMBLE
LIFE!
CRUMBLE
ガ
しょぼーん
DEPRESSED
AH...
SORRY, I SAID TOO MUCH...
WHY DO I HAVE TO WORRY ABOUT THEM? I'M THE SICK ONE!
SIGH...
I LIKE BEING ALONE AT TIMES LIKE THIS...
PHEW
I CAN'T BELIEVE I'M LONG-ING FOR THE TIMES WHEN I WAS BY MYSELF...

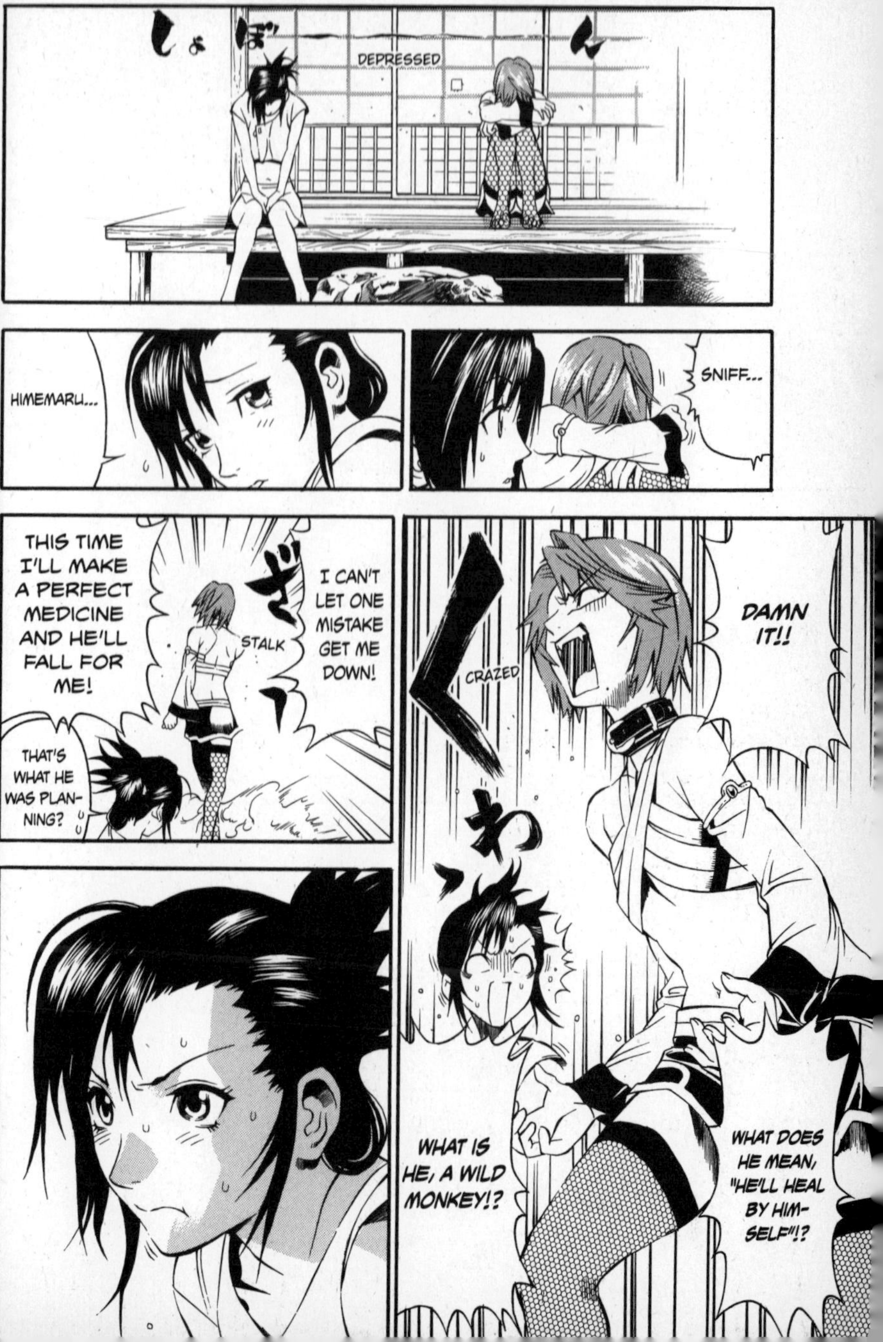

しょぼーん
DEPRESSED
SNIFF...
HIMEMARU...
くわっ
CRAZED
DAMN IT!!
WHAT DOES HE MEAN, "HE'LL HEAL BY HIMSELF"!?
WHAT IS HE, A WILD MONKEY!?
STALK
I CAN'T LET ONE MISTAKE GET ME DOWN!
THIS TIME I'LL MAKE A PERFECT MEDICINE AND HE'LL FALL FOR ME!
THAT'S WHAT HE WAS PLANNING?

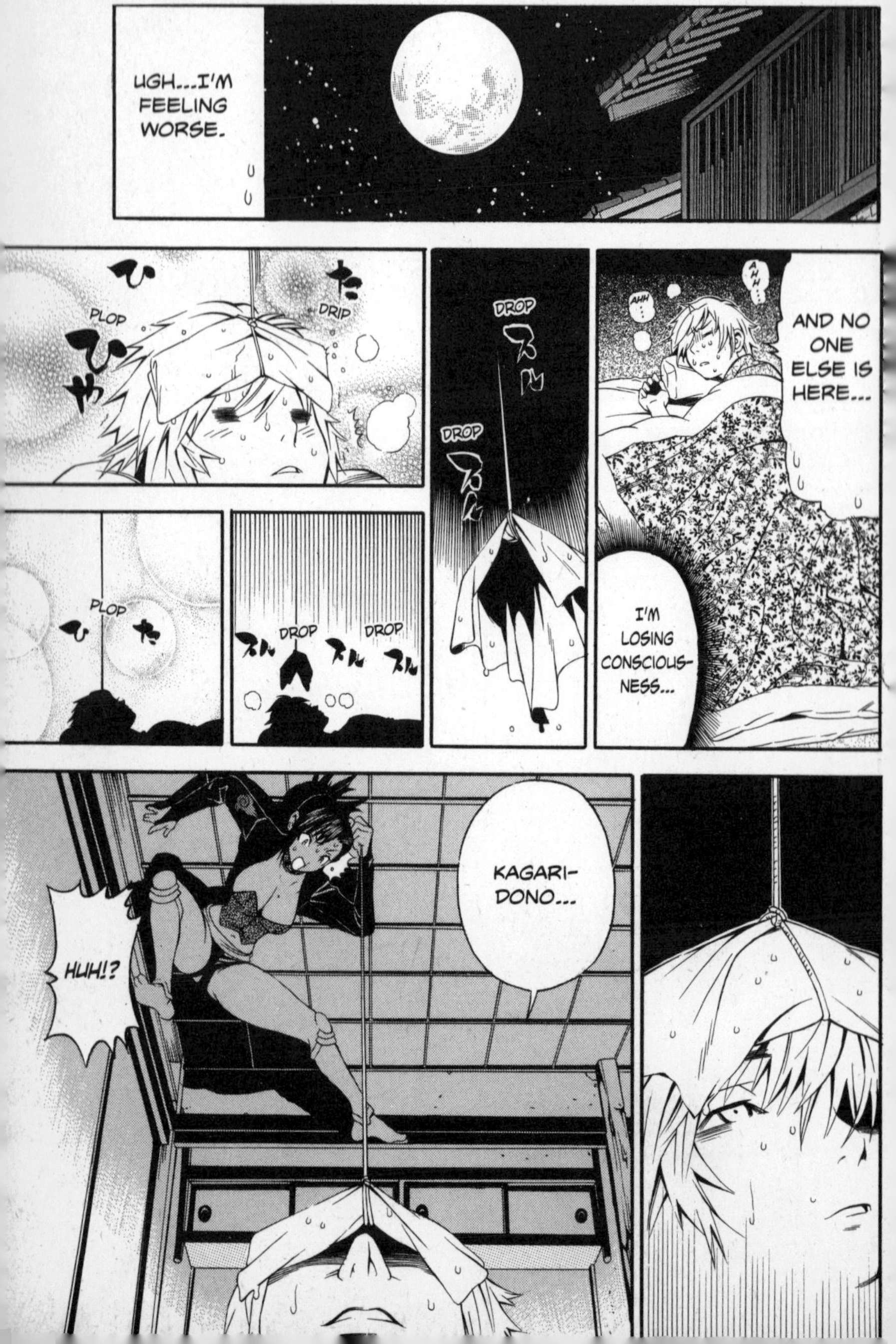
UGH...I'M FEELING WORSE.
AHH...
AHH...
AND NO ONE ELSE IS HERE...
I'M LOSING CONSCIOUS-NESS...
DROP
DROP
DRIP
PLOP
DROP
DROP
PLOP
KAGARI-DONO...
HUH!?

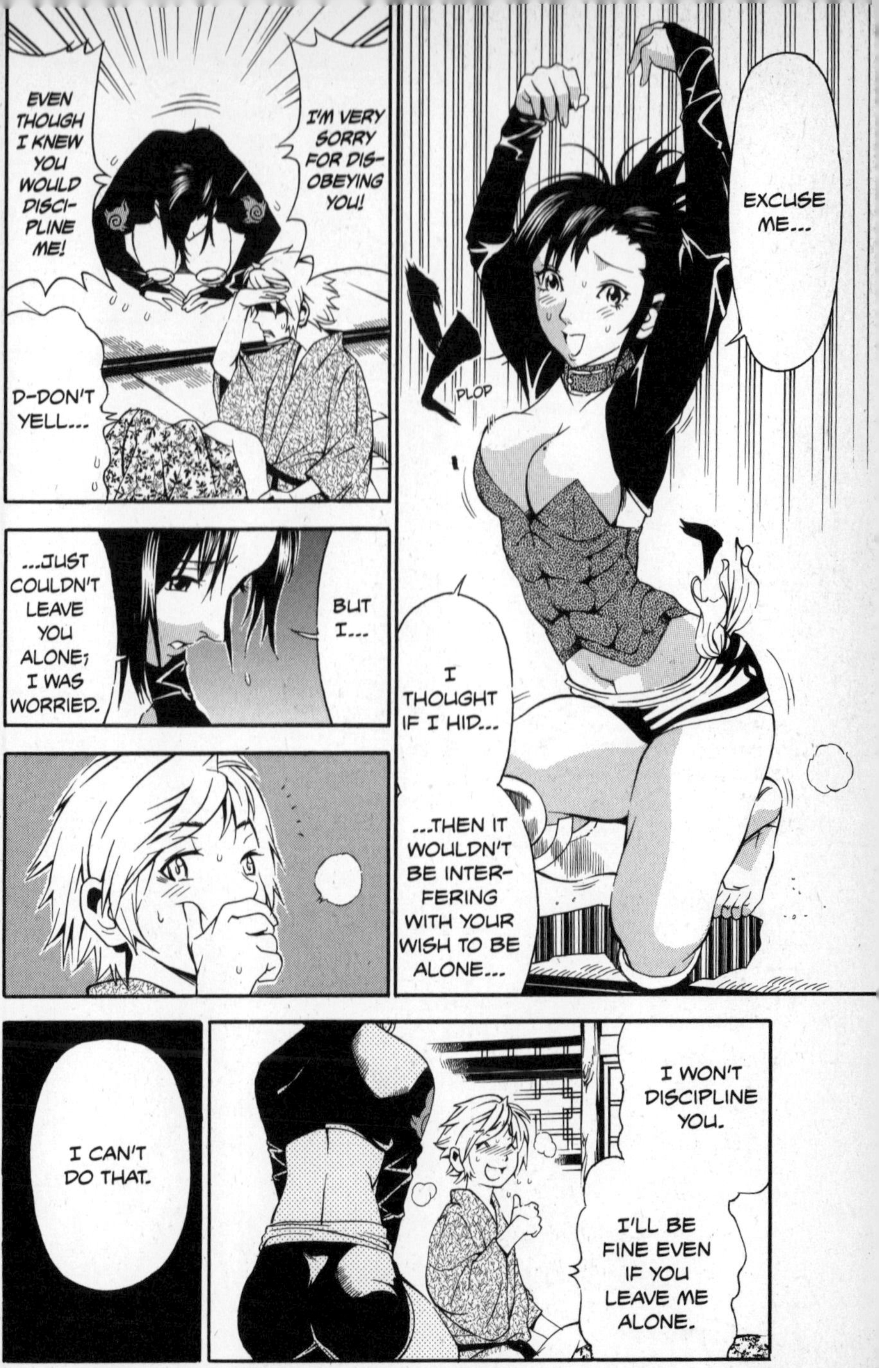
EXCUSE ME...
PLOP
I THOUGHT IF I HID...
...THEN IT WOULDN'T BE INTERFERING WITH YOUR WISH TO BE ALONE...
I'M VERY SORRY FOR DIS-OBEYING YOU!
EVEN THOUGH I KNEW YOU WOULD DISCI-PLINE ME!
D-DON'T YELL...
BUT I...
...JUST COULDN'T LEAVE YOU ALONE; I WAS WORRIED.
I WON'T DISCIPLINE YOU.
I'LL BE FINE EVEN IF YOU LEAVE ME ALONE.
I CAN'T DO THAT.

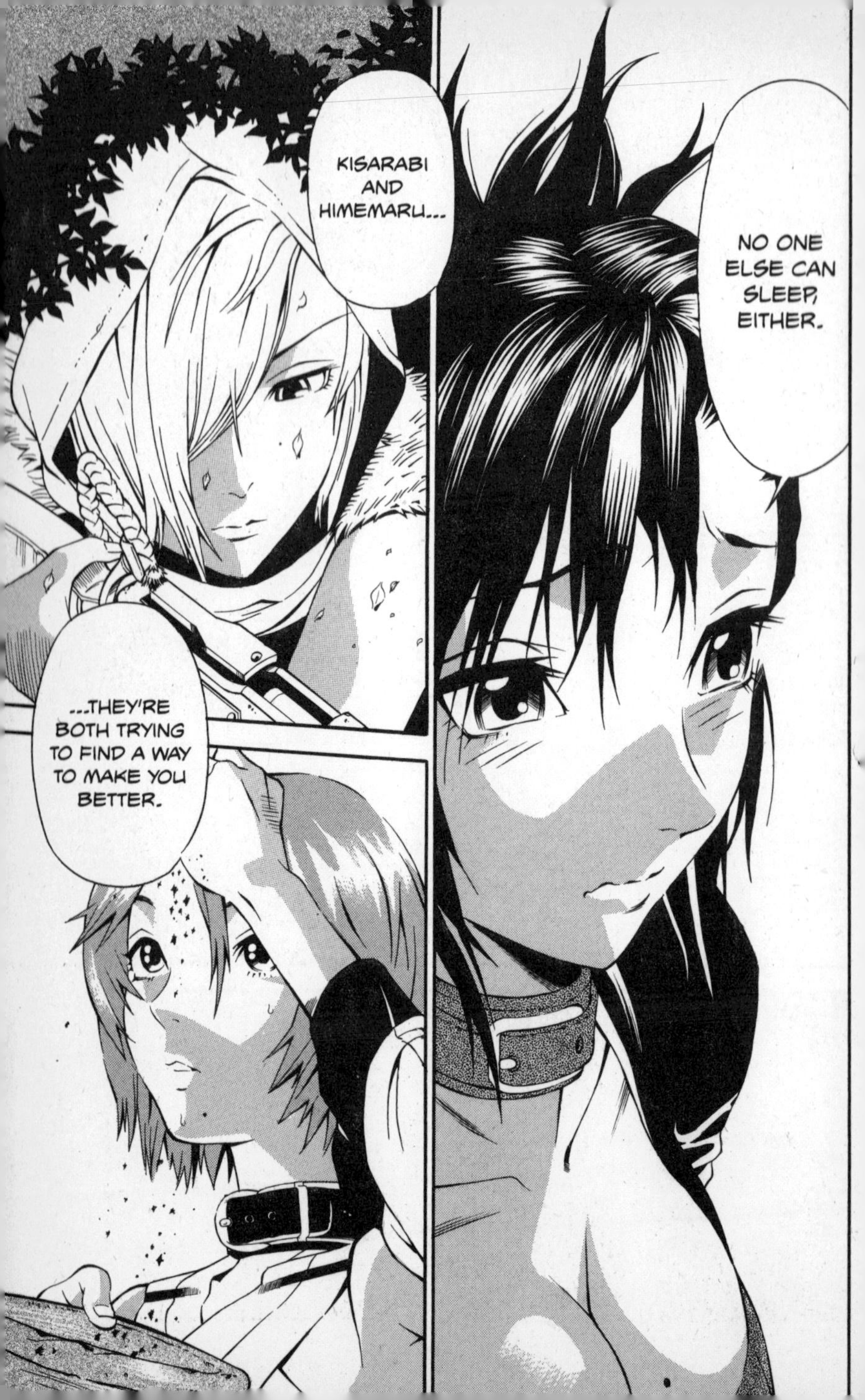
NO ONE ELSE CAN SLEEP, EITHER.
KISARABI AND HIMEMARU...
...THEY'RE BOTH TRYING TO FIND A WAY TO MAKE YOU BETTER.

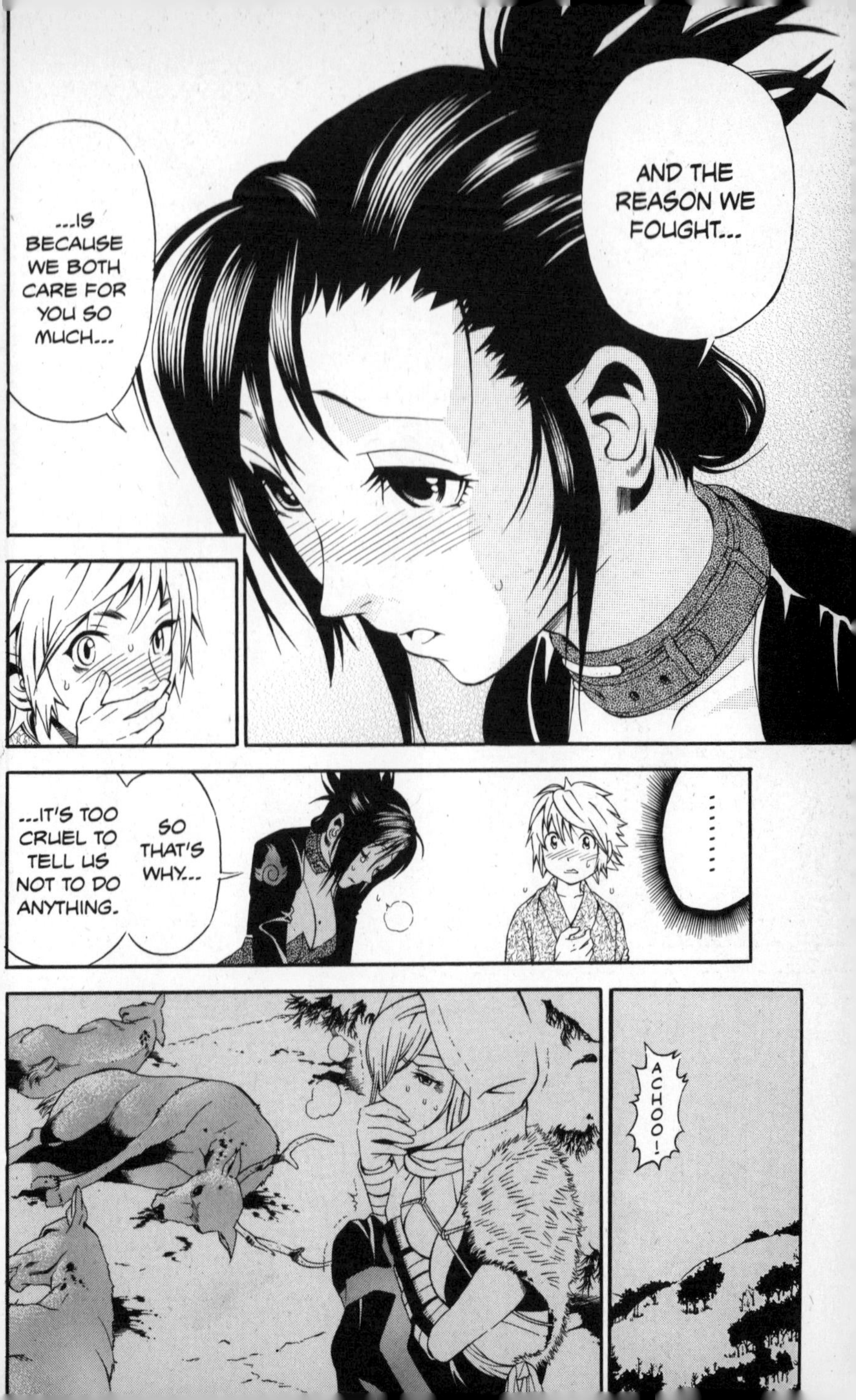
AND THE REASON WE FOUGHT...
...IS BECAUSE WE BOTH CARE FOR YOU SO MUCH...
....
SO THAT'S WHY...
...IT'S TOO CRUEL TO TELL US NOT TO DO ANYTHING.
ACHOO!

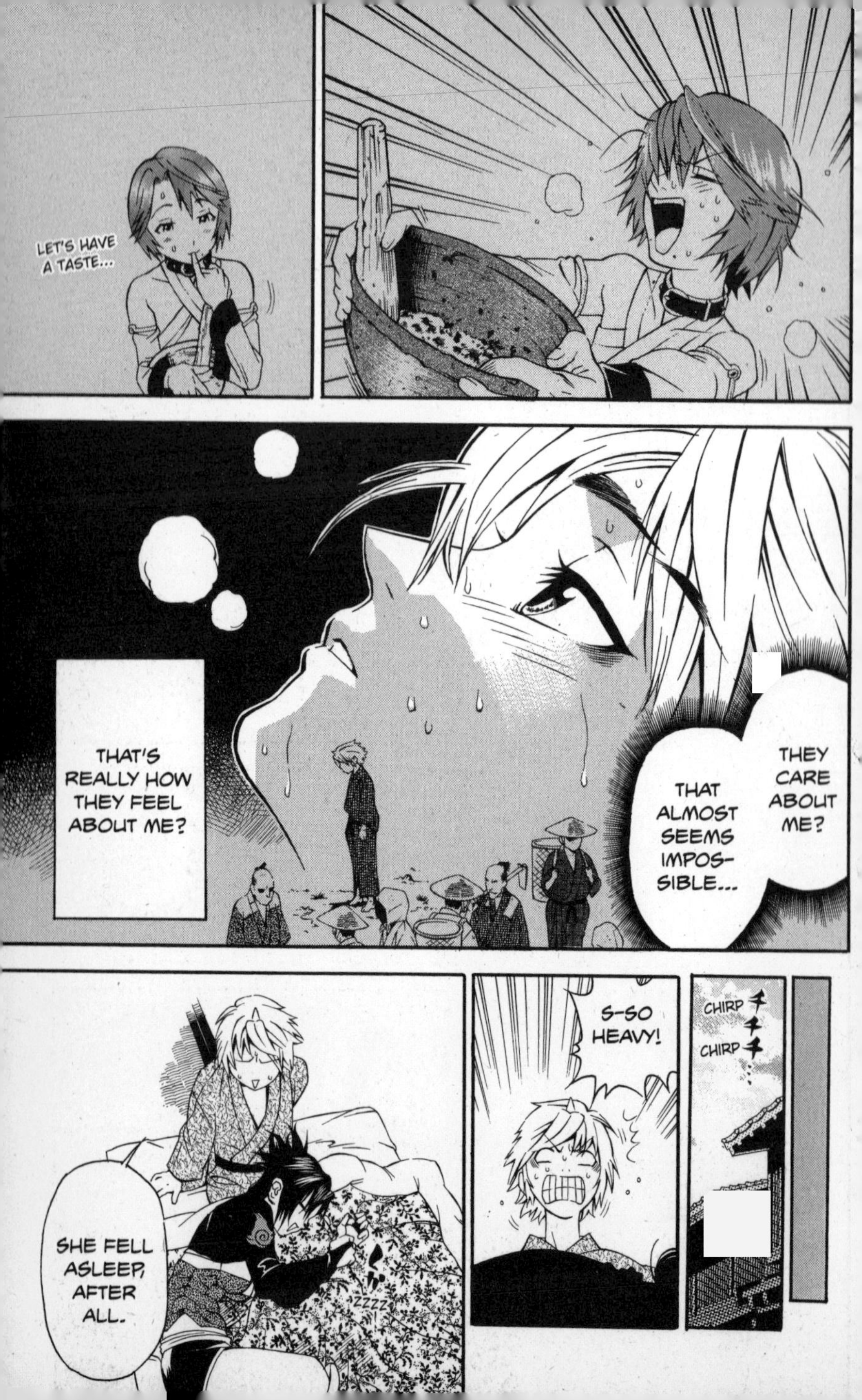
LET'S HAVE A TASTE...
THEY CARE ABOUT ME?
THAT ALMOST SEEMS IMPOSSIBLE...
THAT'S REALLY HOW THEY FEEL ABOUT ME?
CHIRP
CHIRP
S-SO HEAVY!
SHE FELL ASLEEP, AFTER ALL.
ZZZZ

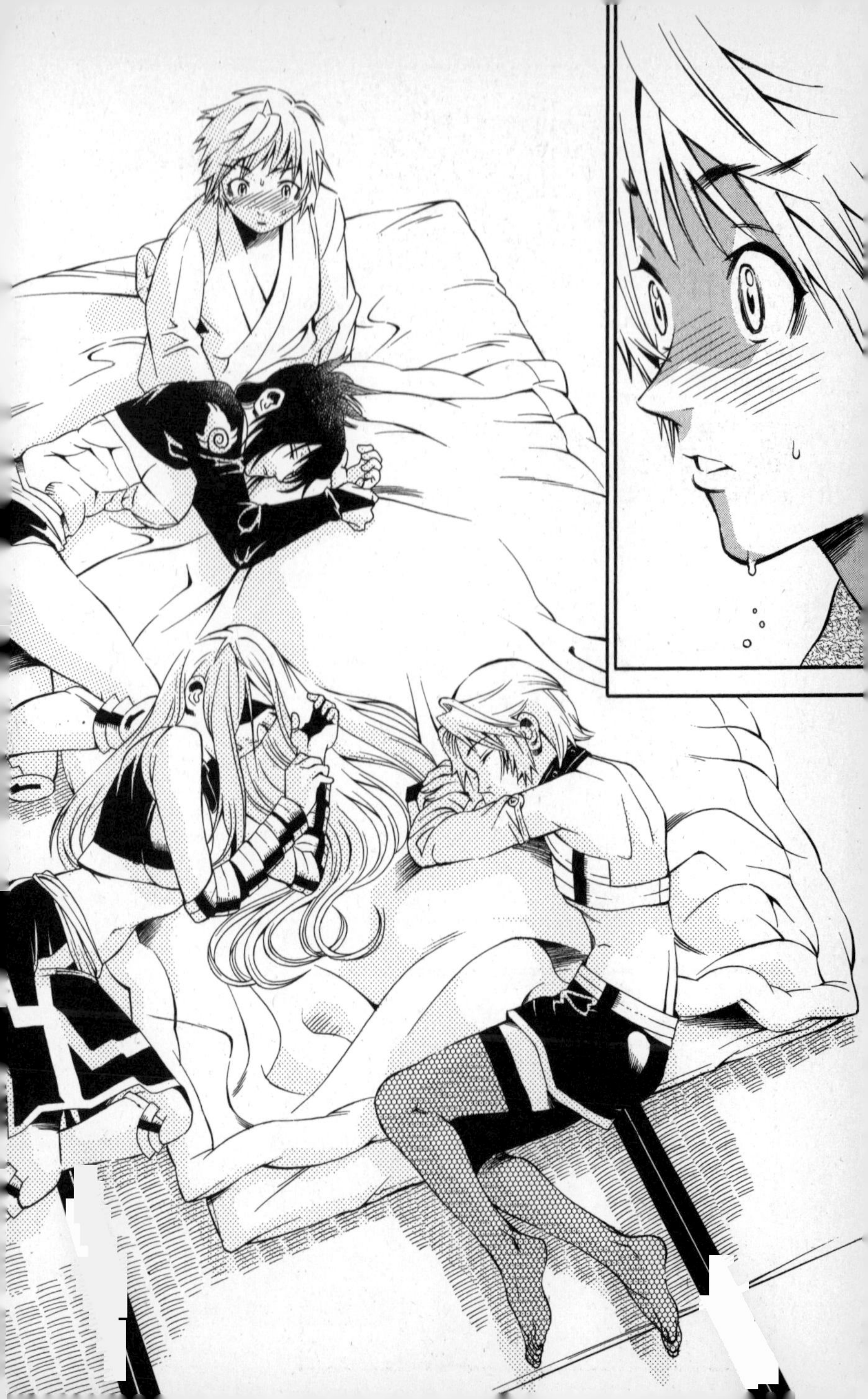

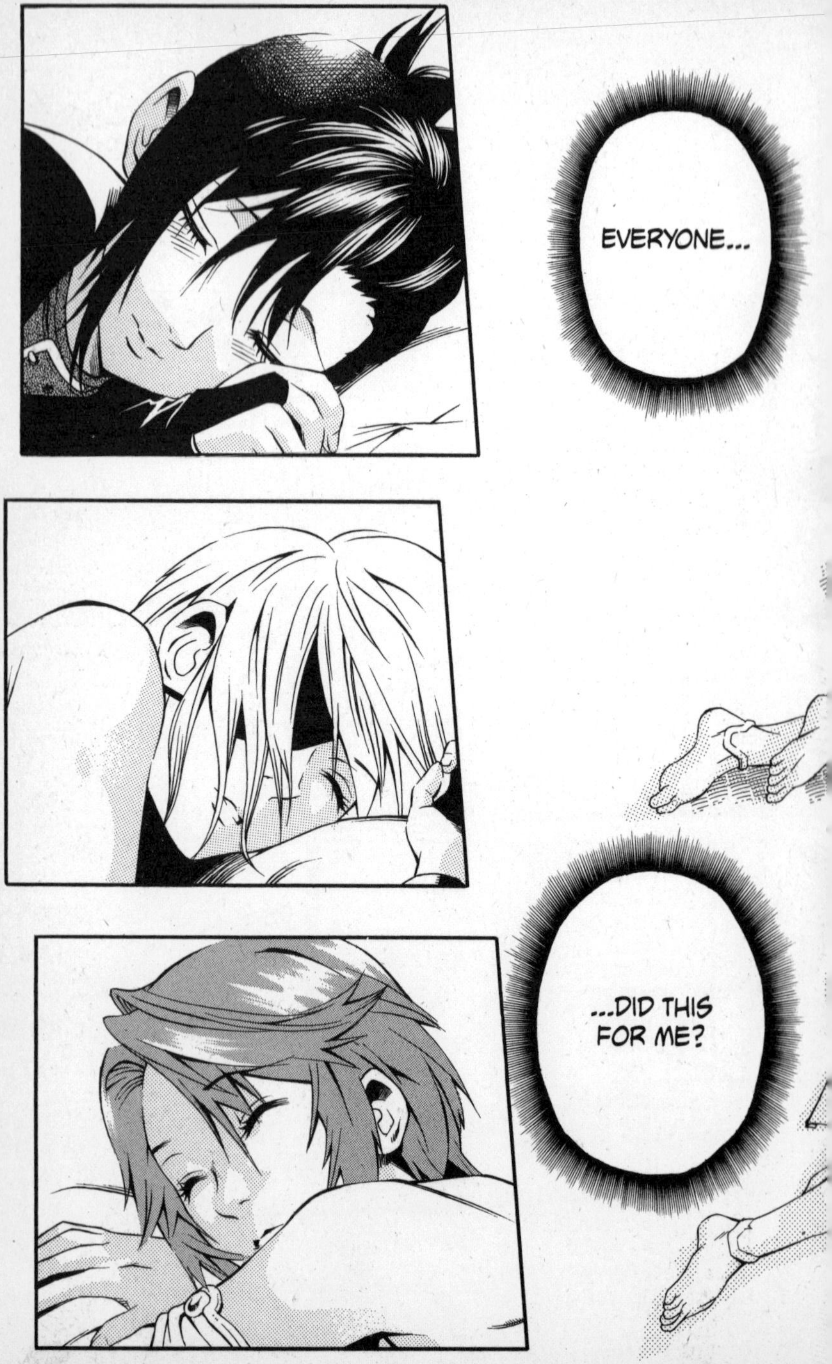
EVERYONE...
...DID THIS FOR ME?

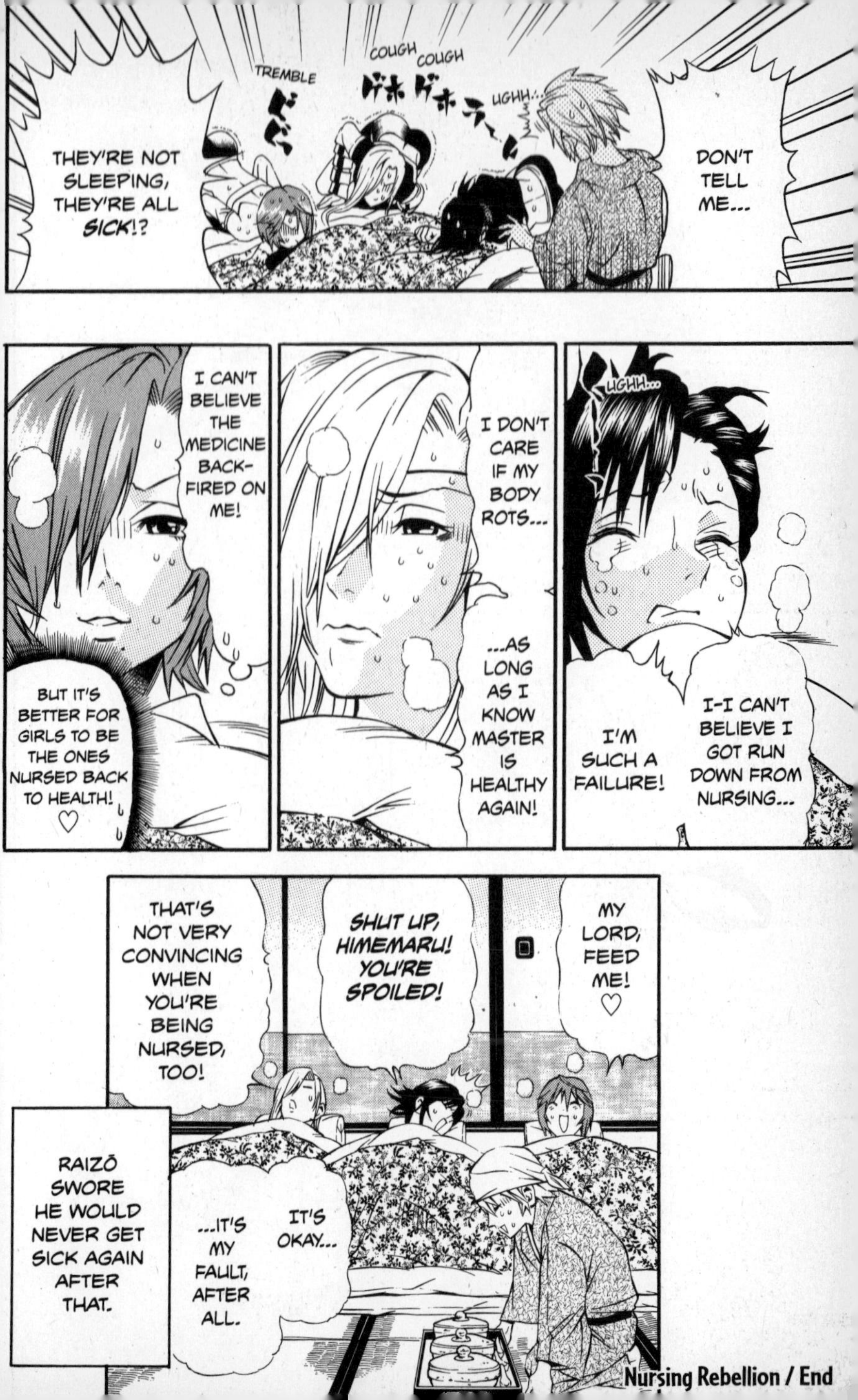
DON'T TELL ME...
UGHH...
COUGH COUGH
TREMBLE
THEY'RE NOT SLEEPING, THEY'RE ALL SICK!?
UGHH...
I-I CAN'T BELIEVE I GOT RUN DOWN FROM NURSING...
I'M SUCH A FAILURE!
I DON'T CARE IF MY BODY ROTS...
...AS LONG AS I KNOW MASTER IS HEALTHY AGAIN!
I CAN'T BELIEVE THE MEDICINE BACK-FIRED ON ME!
BUT IT'S BETTER FOR GIRLS TO BE THE ONES NURSED BACK TO HEALTH! ♡
MY LORD, FEED ME! ♡
SHUT UP, HIMEMARU! YOU'RE SPOILED!
THAT'S NOT VERY CONVINCING WHEN YOU'RE BEING NURSED, TOO!
IT'S OKAY...
...IT'S MY FAULT, AFTER ALL.
RAIZŌ SWORE HE WOULD NEVER GET SICK AGAIN AFTER THAT.
Nursing Rebellion / End

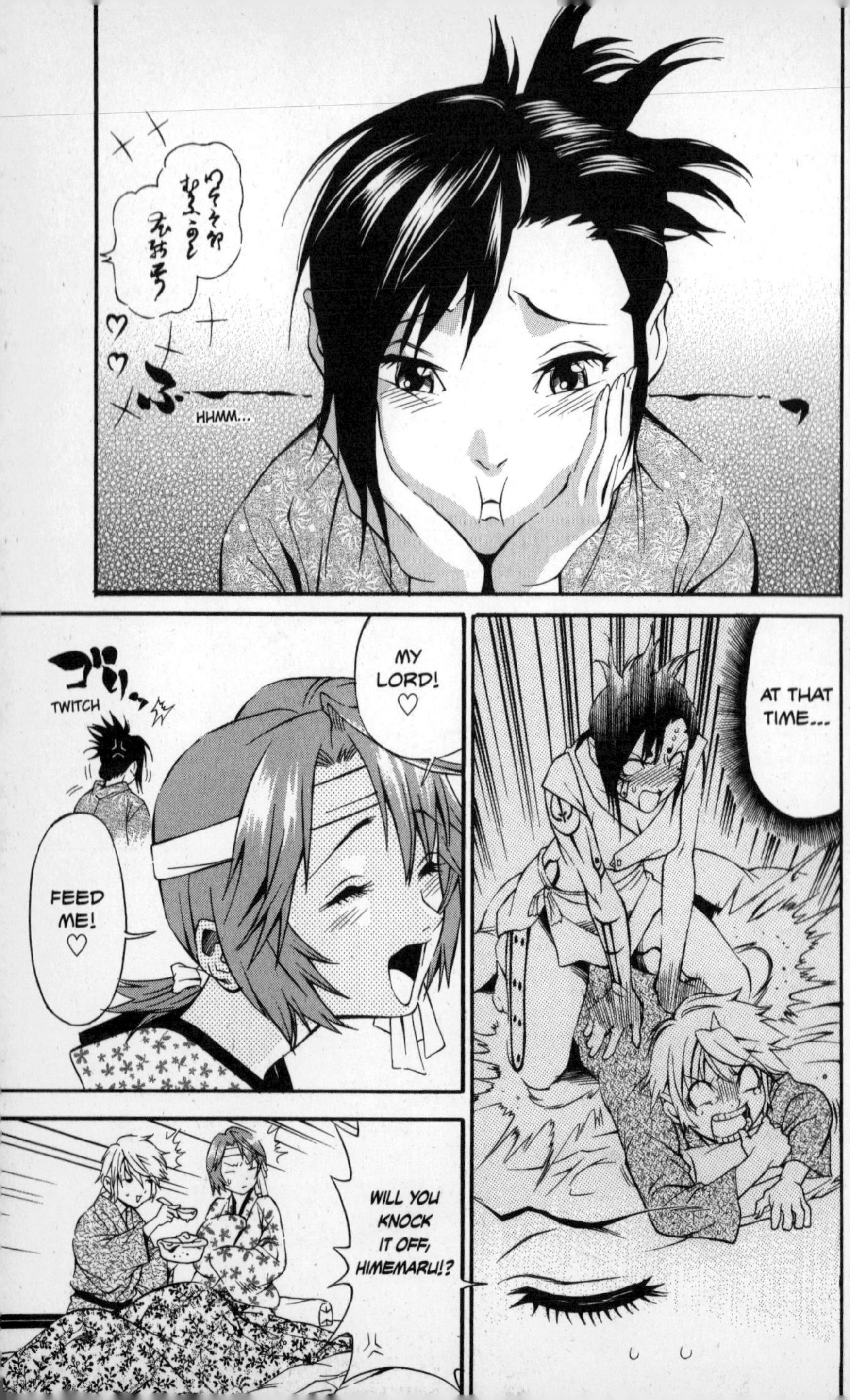
ふ
HHMM...
AT THAT TIME...
MY LORD! ♡
TWITCH
FEED ME! ♡
WILL YOU KNOCK IT OFF, HIMEMARU!?

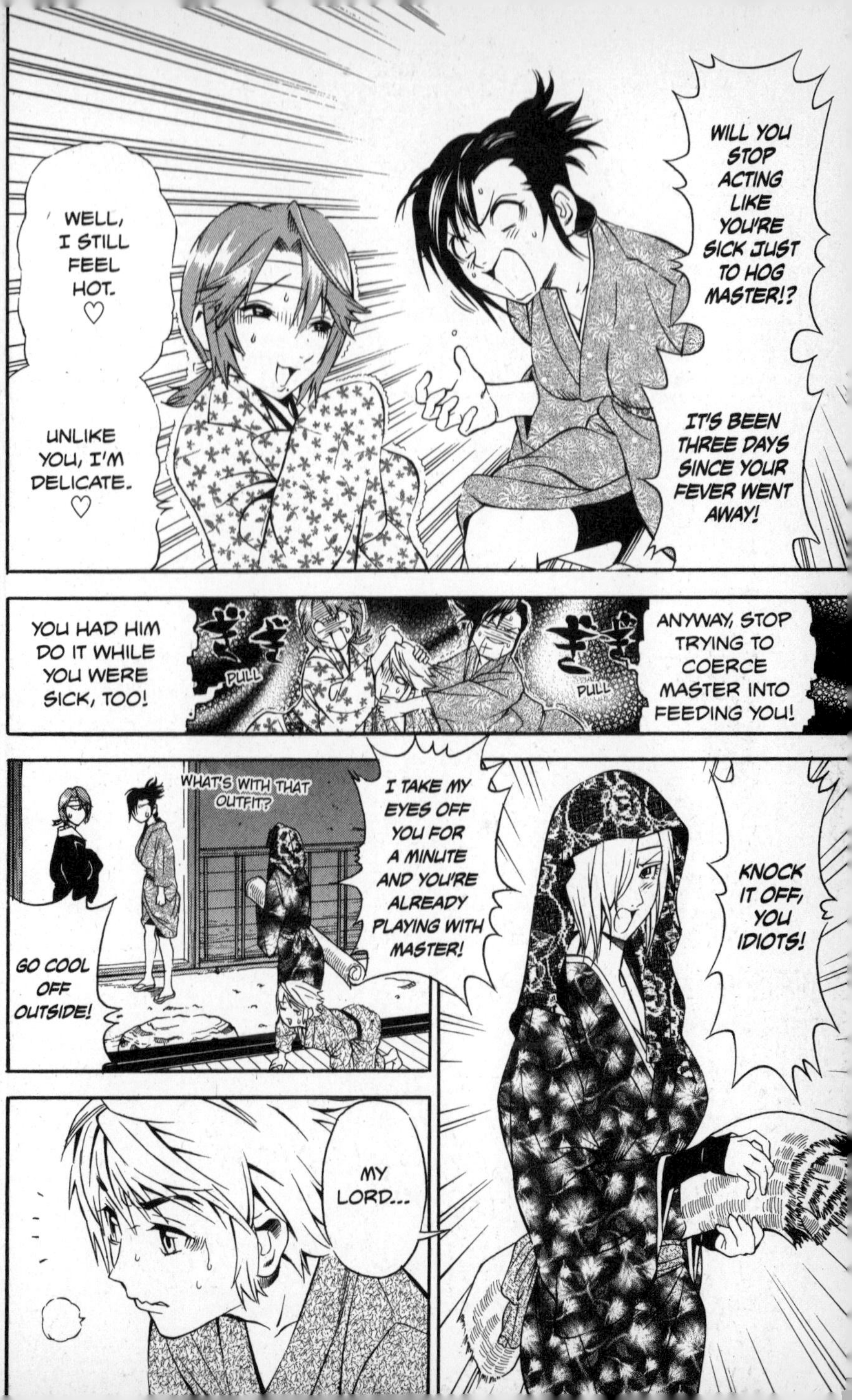
WILL YOU STOP ACTING LIKE YOU'RE SICK JUST TO HOG MASTER!?
IT'S BEEN THREE DAYS SINCE YOUR FEVER WENT AWAY!
WELL, I STILL FEEL HOT. ♡
UNLIKE YOU, I'M DELICATE. ♡
ANYWAY, STOP TRYING TO COERCE MASTER INTO FEEDING YOU!
PULL
PULL
YOU HAD HIM DO IT WHILE YOU WERE SICK, TOO!
KNOCK IT OFF, YOU IDIOTS!
I TAKE MY EYES OFF YOU FOR A MINUTE AND YOU'RE ALREADY PLAYING WITH MASTER!
WHAT'S WITH THAT OUTFIT?
GO COOL OFF OUTSIDE!
MY LORD...

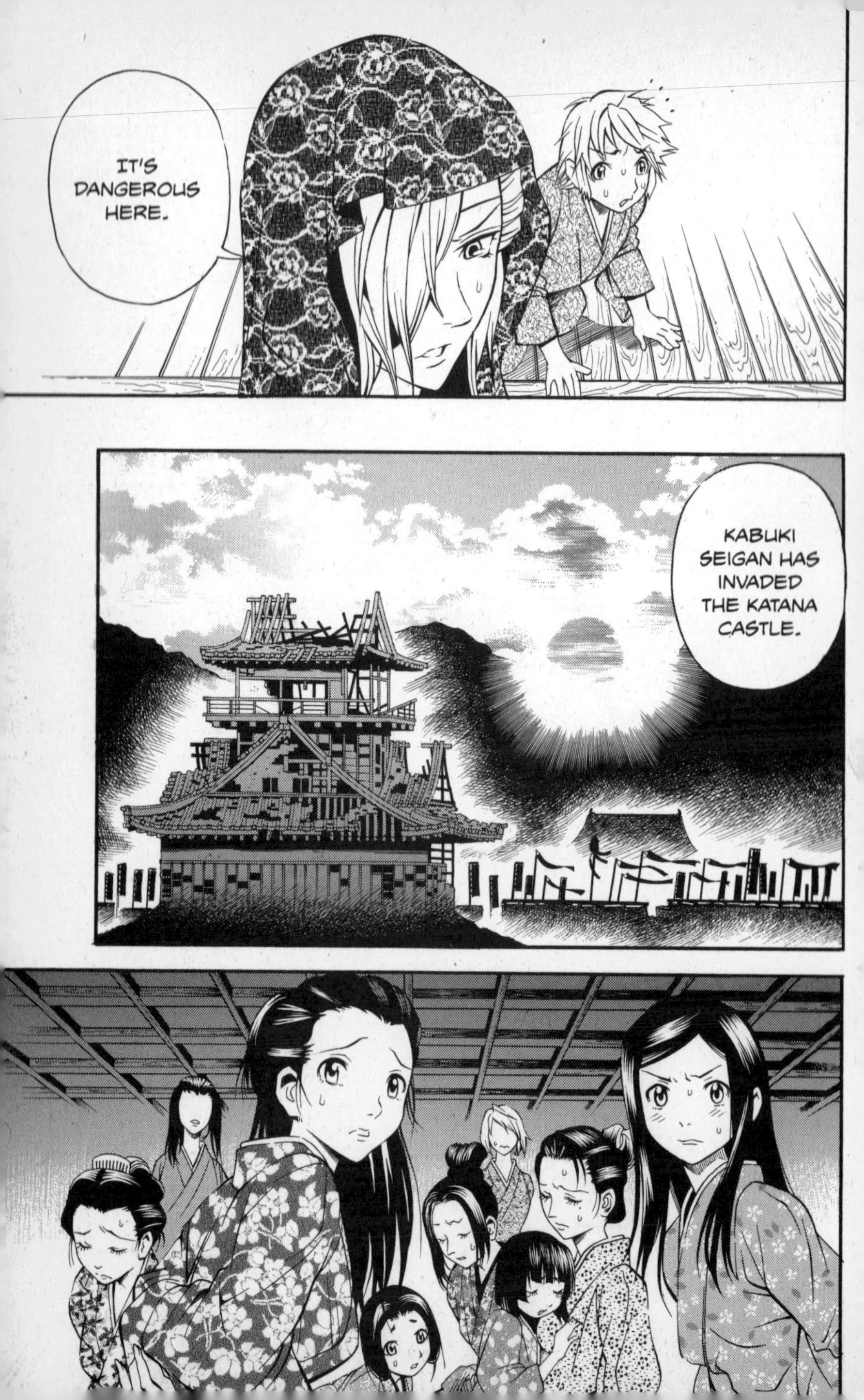
IT'S DANGEROUS HERE.
KABUKI SEIGAN HAS INVADED THE KATANA CASTLE.

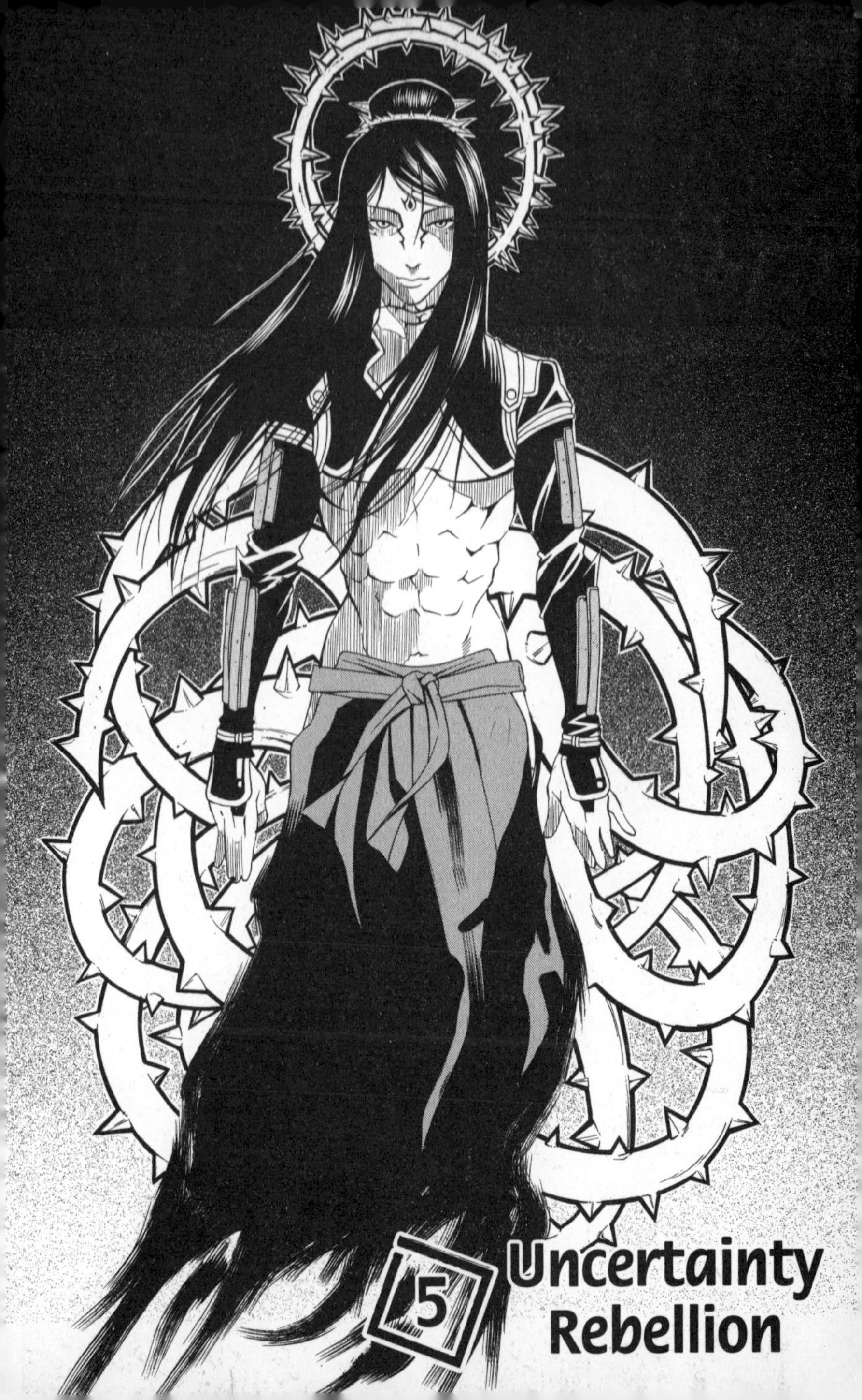
5
Uncertainty
Rebellion

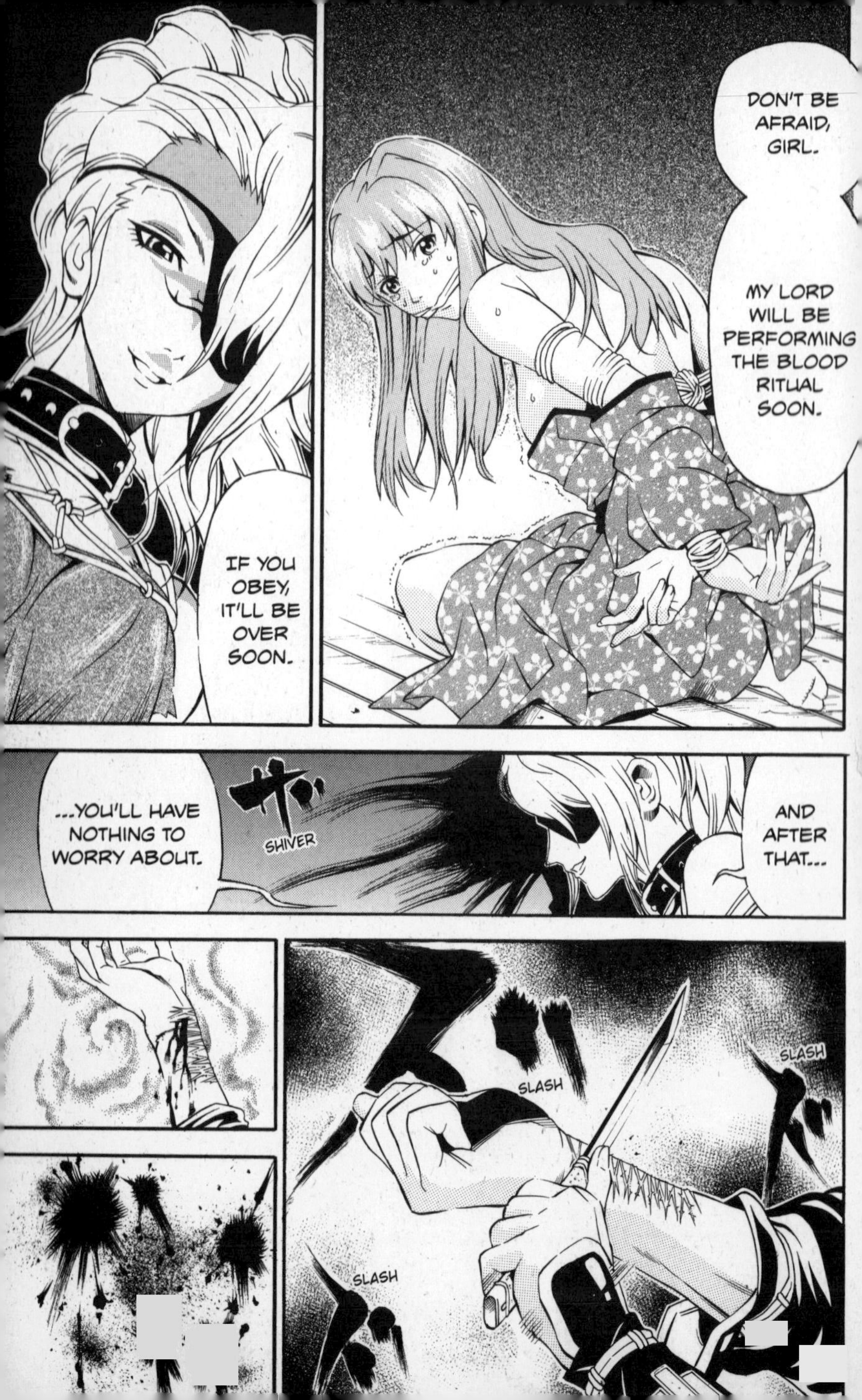
DON'T BE AFRAID, GIRL.
MY LORD WILL BE PERFORMING THE BLOOD RITUAL SOON.
IF YOU OBEY, IT'LL BE OVER SOON.
AND AFTER THAT...
SHIVER
...YOU'LL HAVE NOTHING TO WORRY ABOUT.
SLASH
SLASH
SLASH

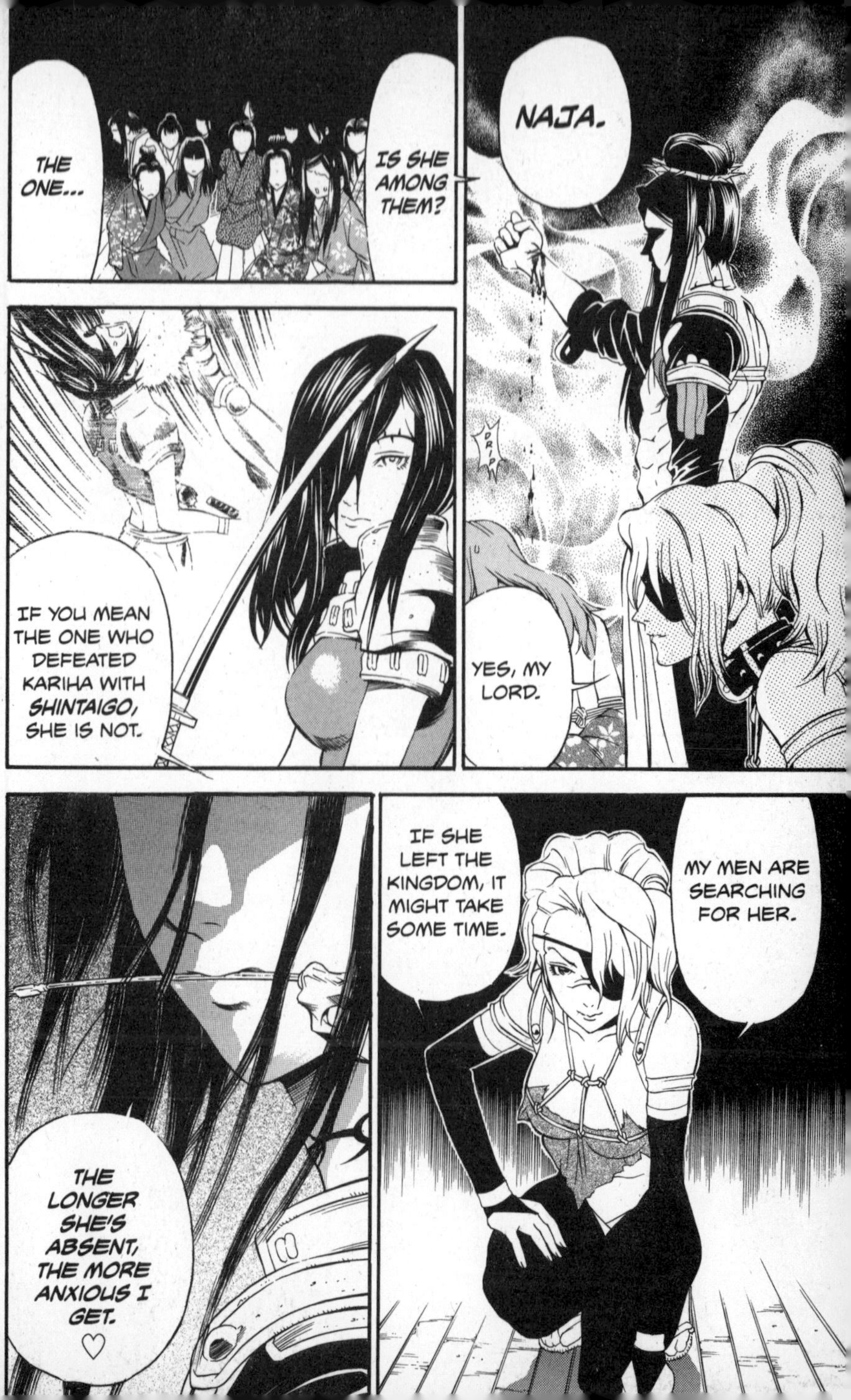
NAJA.
DRIP
YES, MY LORD.
IS SHE AMONG THEM?
THE ONE...
IF YOU MEAN THE ONE WHO DEFEATED KARIHA WITH SHINTAIGO, SHE IS NOT.
MY MEN ARE SEARCHING FOR HER.
IF SHE LEFT THE KINGDOM, IT MIGHT TAKE SOME TIME.
THE LONGER SHE'S ABSENT, THE MORE ANXIOUS I GET. ♡

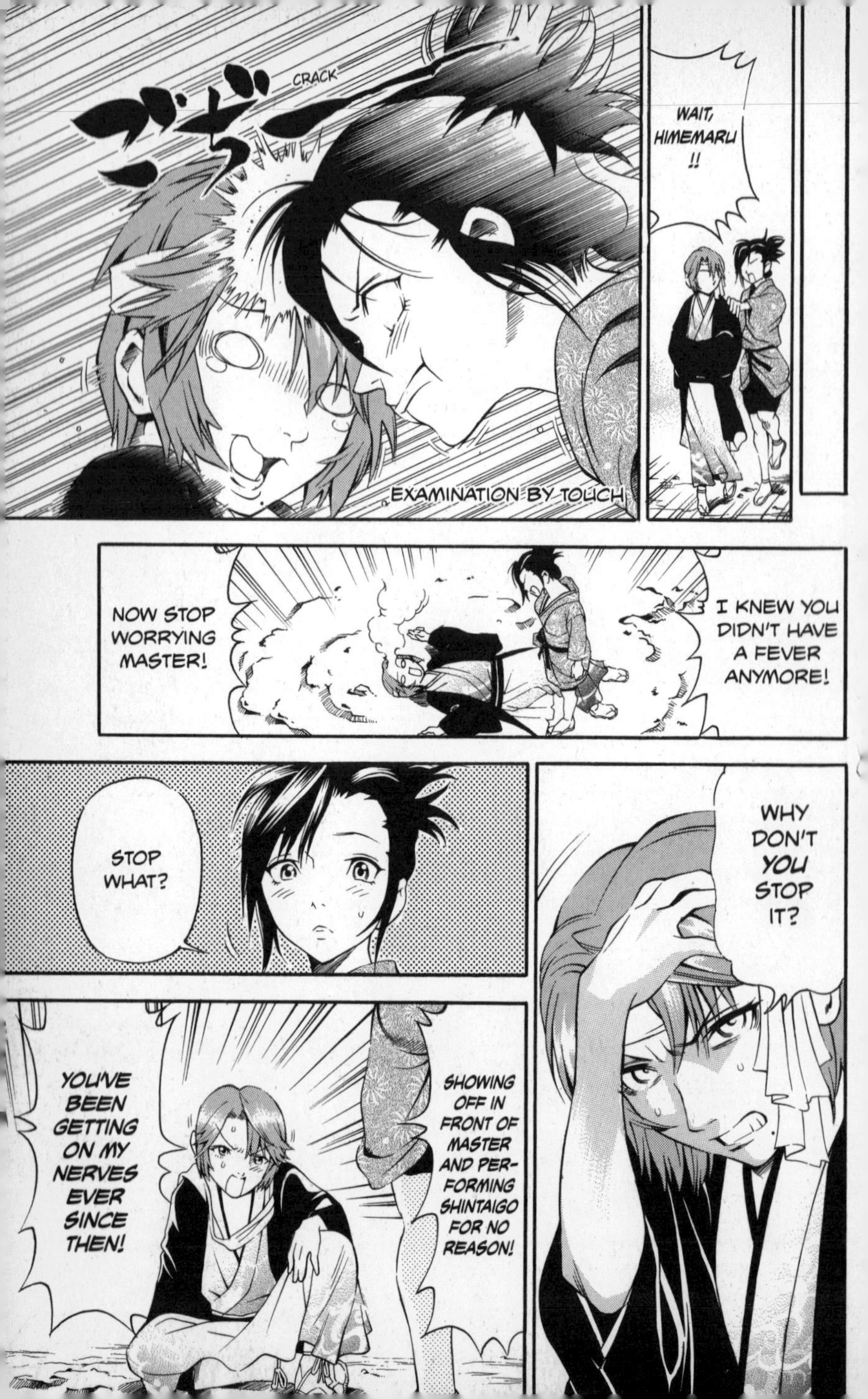
WAIT, HIMEMARU !!
CRACK
EXAMINATION BY TOUCH
I KNEW YOU DIDN'T HAVE A FEVER ANYMORE!
NOW STOP WORRYING MASTER!
WHY DON'T YOU STOP IT?
STOP WHAT?
SHOWING OFF IN FRONT OF MASTER AND PERFORMING SHINTAIGO FOR NO REASON!
YOU'VE BEEN GETTING ON MY NERVES EVER SINCE THEN!

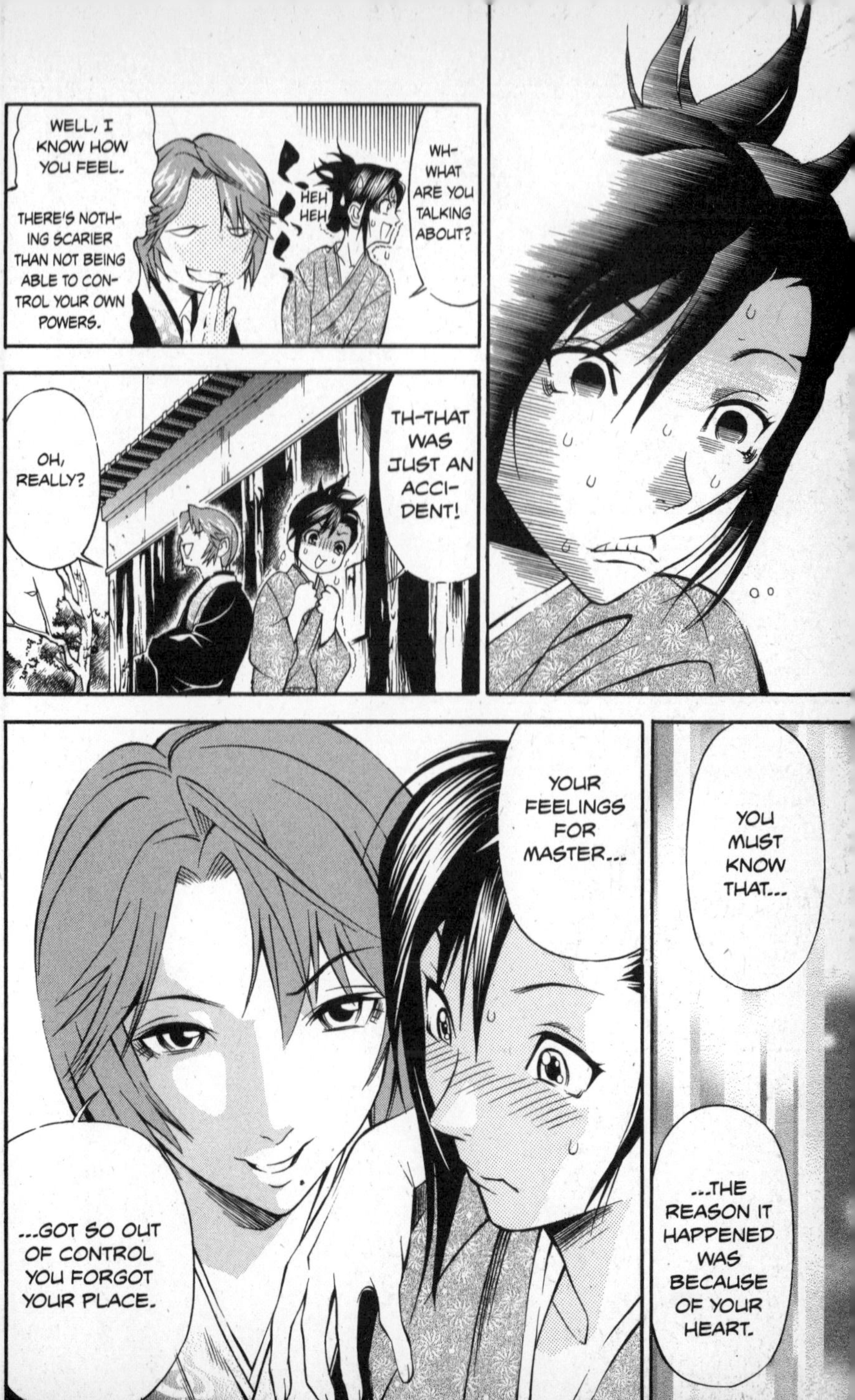
WH-WHAT ARE YOU TALKING ABOUT?
HEH HEH
WELL, I KNOW HOW YOU FEEL.
THERE'S NOTHING SCARIER THAN NOT BEING ABLE TO CONTROL YOUR OWN POWERS.
TH-THAT WAS JUST AN ACCIDENT!
OH, REALLY?
YOU MUST KNOW THAT...
...THE REASON IT HAPPENED WAS BECAUSE OF YOUR HEART.
YOUR FEELINGS FOR MASTER...
...GOT SO OUT OF CONTROL YOU FORGOT YOUR PLACE.

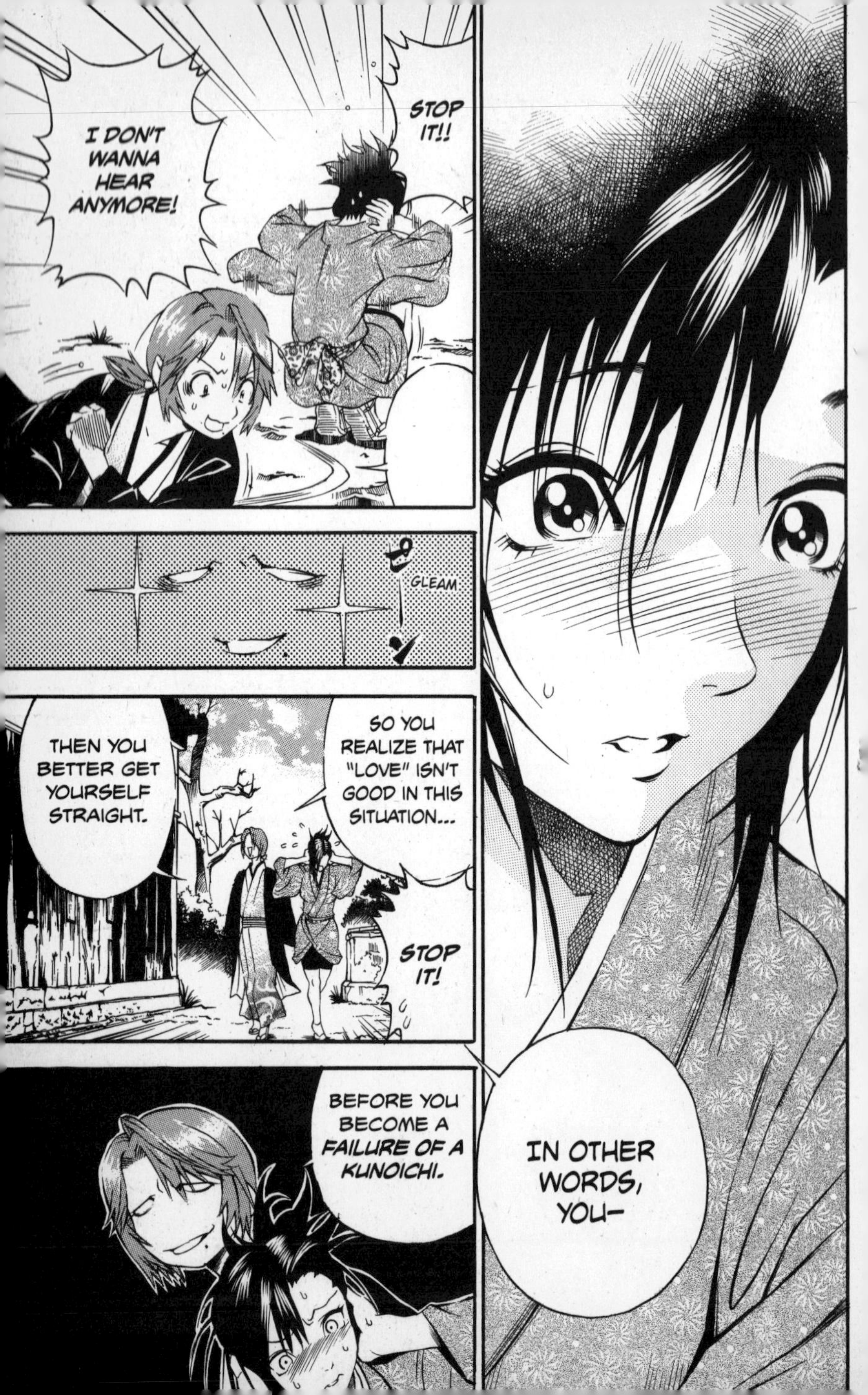
IN OTHER WORDS, YOU–
STOP IT!!
I DON'T WANNA HEAR ANYMORE!
GLEAM
SO YOU REALIZE THAT "LOVE" ISN'T GOOD IN THIS SITUATION...
THEN YOU BETTER GET YOURSELF STRAIGHT.
STOP IT!
BEFORE YOU BECOME A *FAILURE OF A KUNOICHI*.

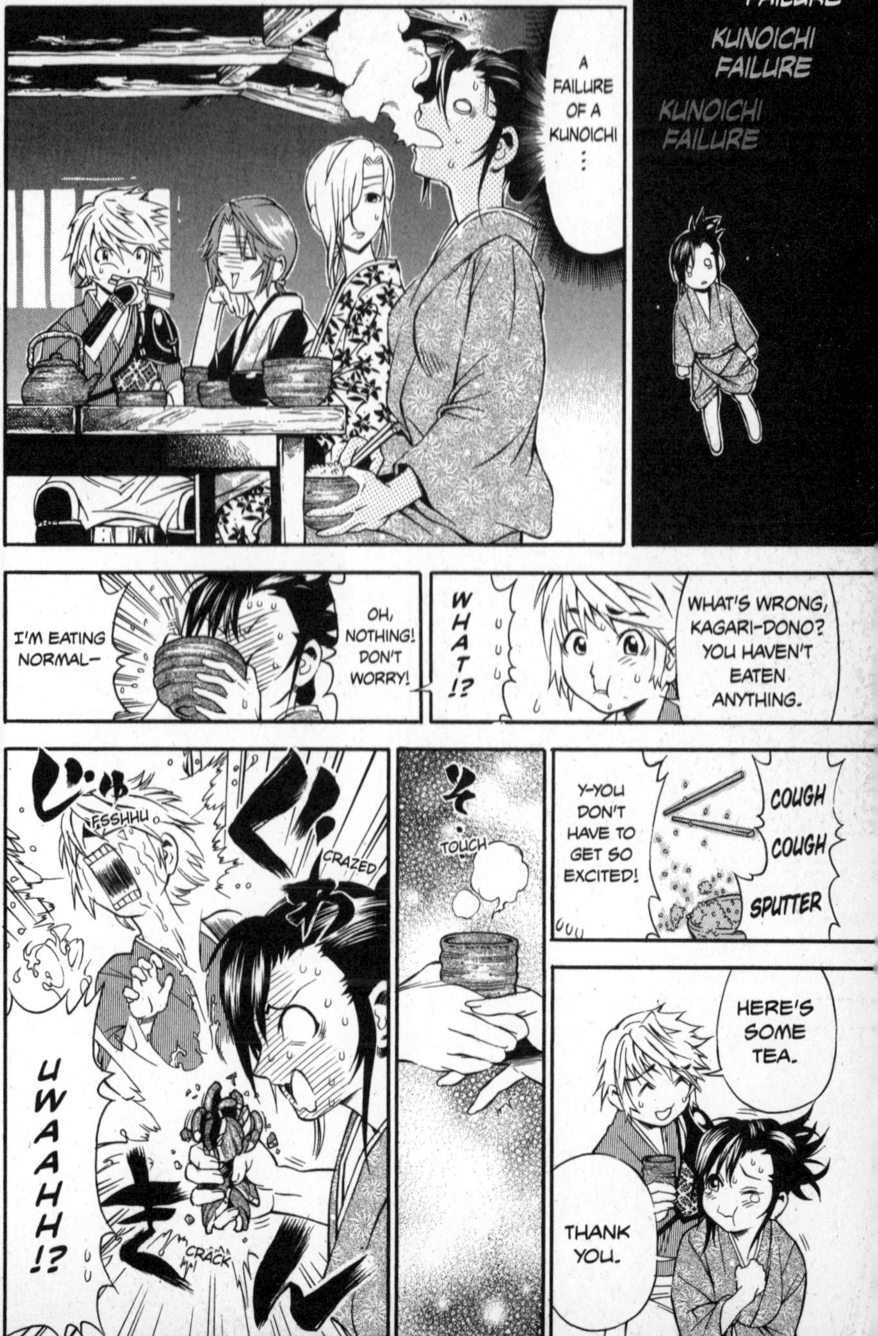
KUNOICHI FAILURE
KUNOICHI FAILURE
KUNOICHI FAILURE
A FAILURE OF A KUNOICHI...
WHAT'S WRONG, KAGARI-DONO? YOU HAVEN'T EATEN ANYTHING.
WHAT!?
OH, NOTHING! DON'T WORRY!
I'M EATING NORMAL—
COUGH
COUGH
SPUTTER
Y-YOU DON'T HAVE TO GET SO EXCITED!
HERE'S SOME TEA.
THANK YOU.
TOUCH
CRAZED
FSSHHU
UWAAAHH!?
CRACK

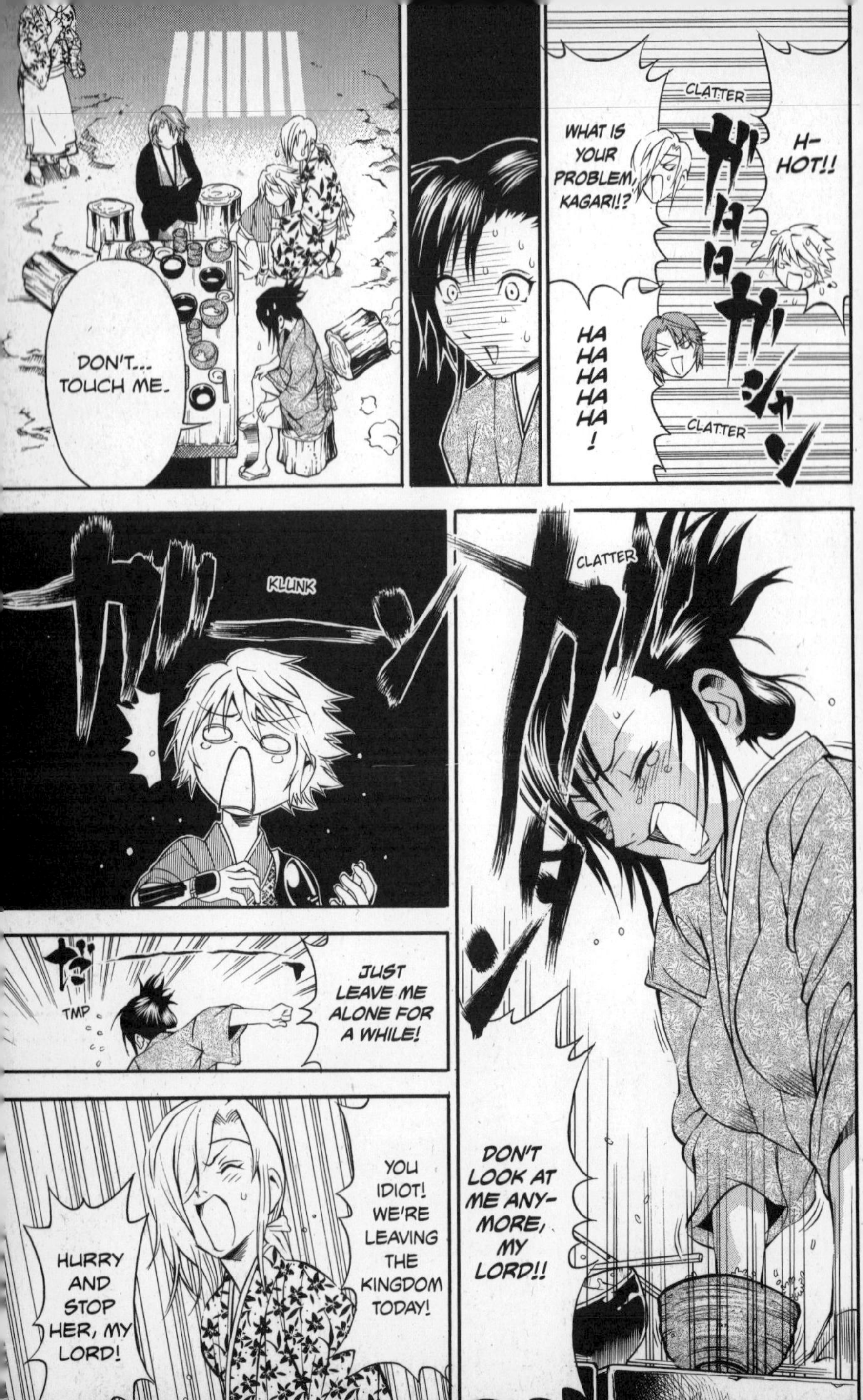
CLATTER
H-HOT!!
WHAT IS YOUR PROBLEM, KAGARI!?
HA HA HA HA HA!
CLATTER
DON'T... TOUCH ME.
CLATTER
DON'T LOOK AT ME ANY-MORE, MY LORD!!
KLUNK
JUST LEAVE ME ALONE FOR A WHILE!
TMP
YOU IDIOT! WE'RE LEAVING THE KINGDOM TODAY!
HURRY AND STOP HER, MY LORD!

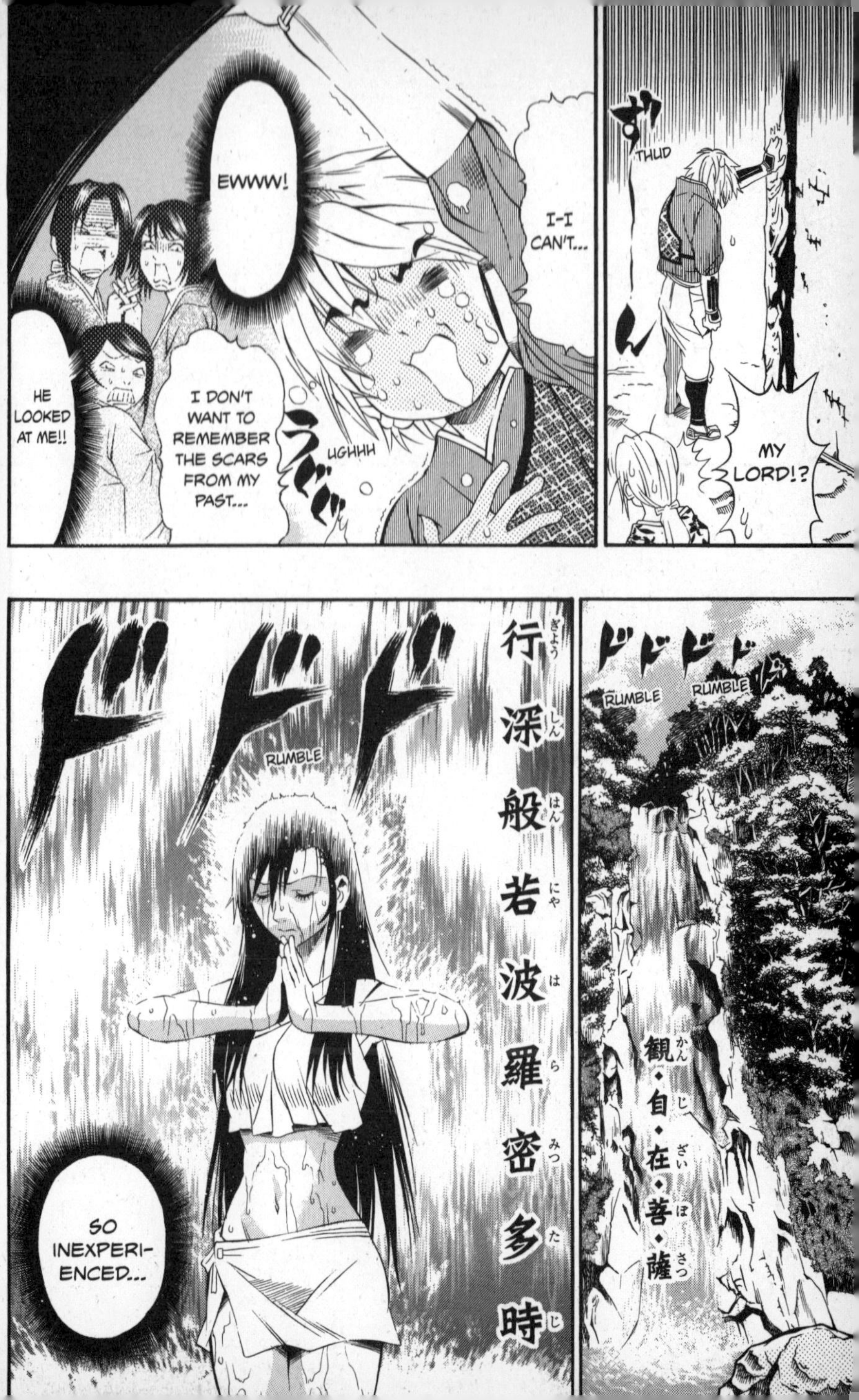
THUD
MY LORD!?
I-I CAN'T...
EWWW!
UGHHH
I DON'T WANT TO REMEMBER THE SCARS FROM MY PAST...
HE LOOKED AT ME!!
ドドドド
RUMBLE
RUMBLE
観・自・在・菩・薩
行深般若波羅蜜多時
RUMBLE
SO INEXPERIENCED...

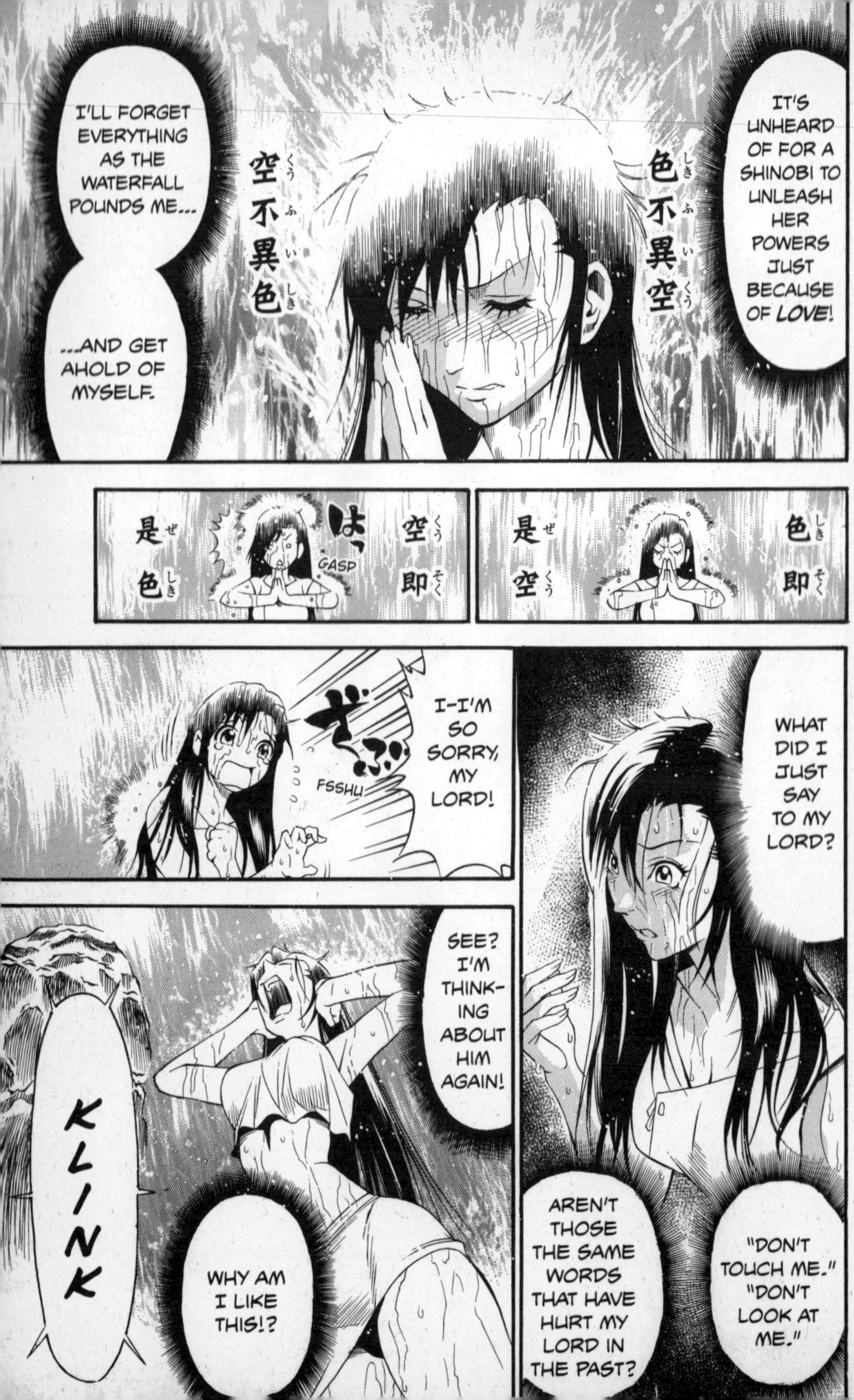

IT'S UNHEARD OF FOR A SHINOBI TO UNLEASH HER POWERS JUST BECAUSE OF *LOVE*!
色不異空
空不異色
I'LL FORGET EVERYTHING AS THE WATERFALL POUNDS ME...
...AND GET AHOLD OF MYSELF.
色即
是空
空即
はっ
GASP
是色
WHAT DID I JUST SAY TO MY LORD?
"DON'T TOUCH ME." "DON'T LOOK AT ME."
AREN'T THOSE THE SAME WORDS THAT HAVE HURT MY LORD IN THE PAST?
I-I'M SO SORRY, MY LORD!
ざぶっ
FSSHU
SEE? I'M THINKING ABOUT HIM AGAIN!
WHY AM I LIKE THIS!?
KLINK

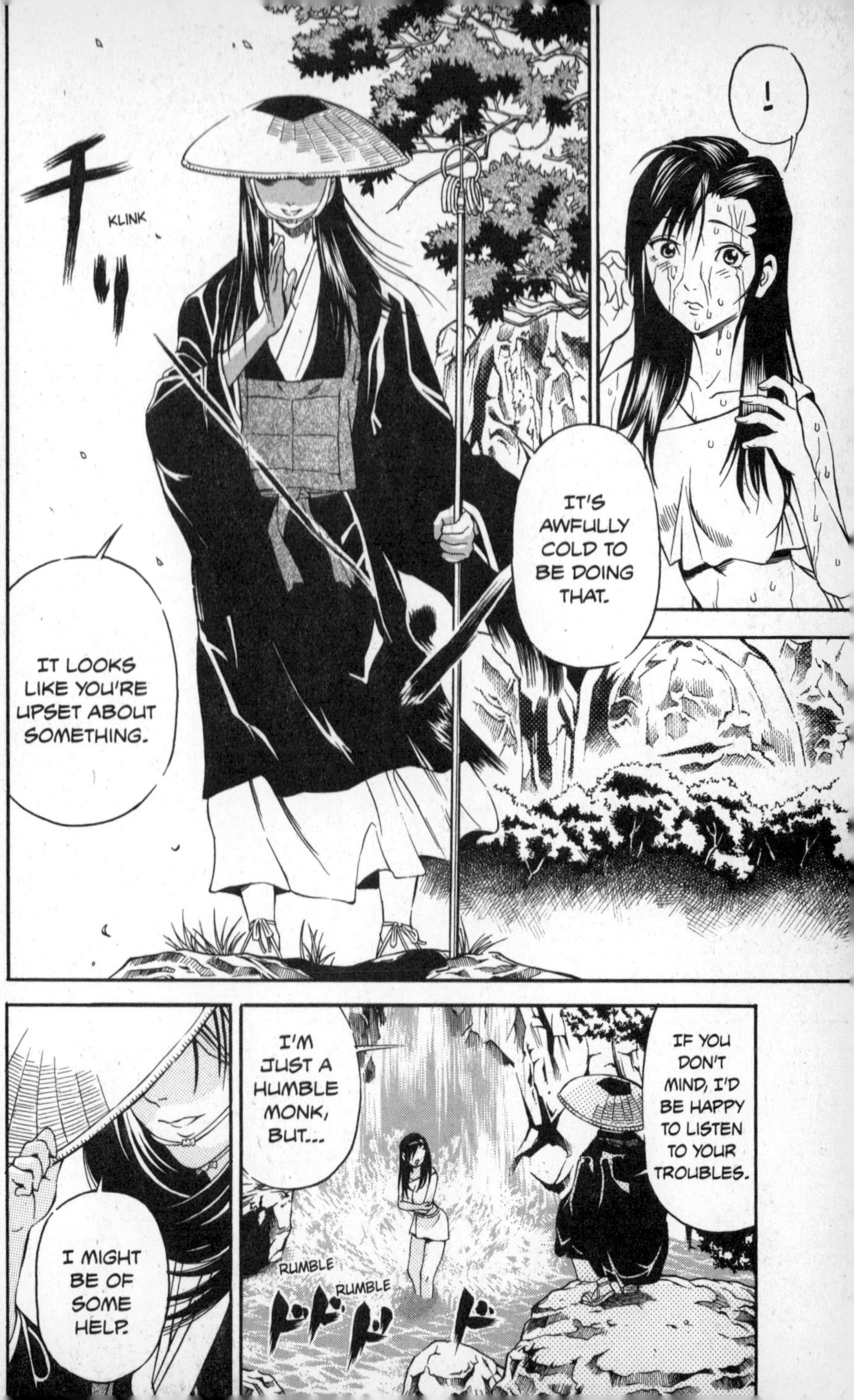
!
IT'S AWFULLY COLD TO BE DOING THAT.
チリ
KLINK
IT LOOKS LIKE YOU'RE UPSET ABOUT SOMETHING.
IF YOU DON'T MIND, I'D BE HAPPY TO LISTEN TO YOUR TROUBLES.
I'M JUST A HUMBLE MONK, BUT...
RUMBLE
RUMBLE
I MIGHT BE OF SOME HELP.

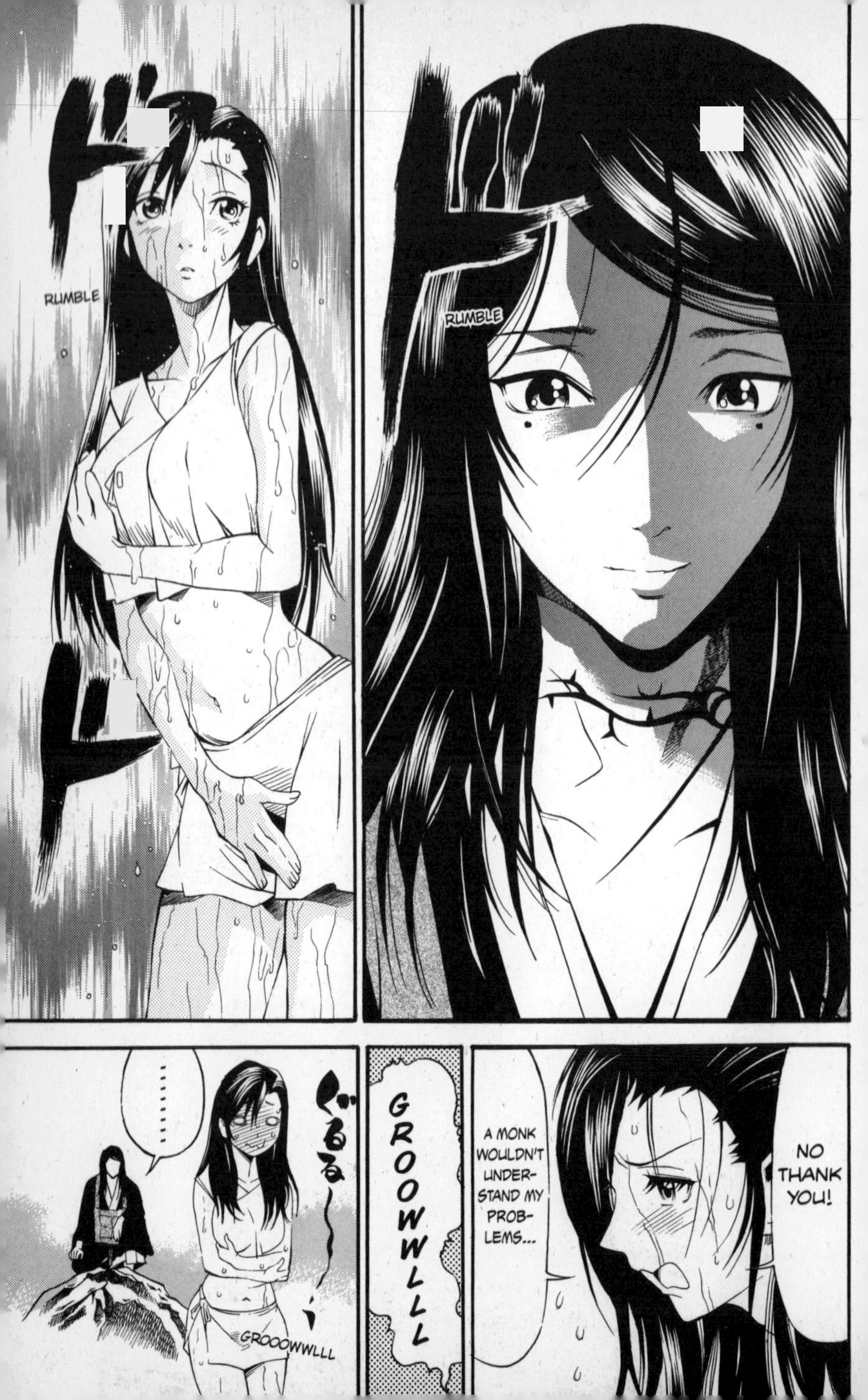
RUMBLE
RUMBLE
NO THANK YOU!
A MONK WOULDN'T UNDER-STAND MY PROB-LEMS...
GROOWWLLL
......
GROOOWWLLL

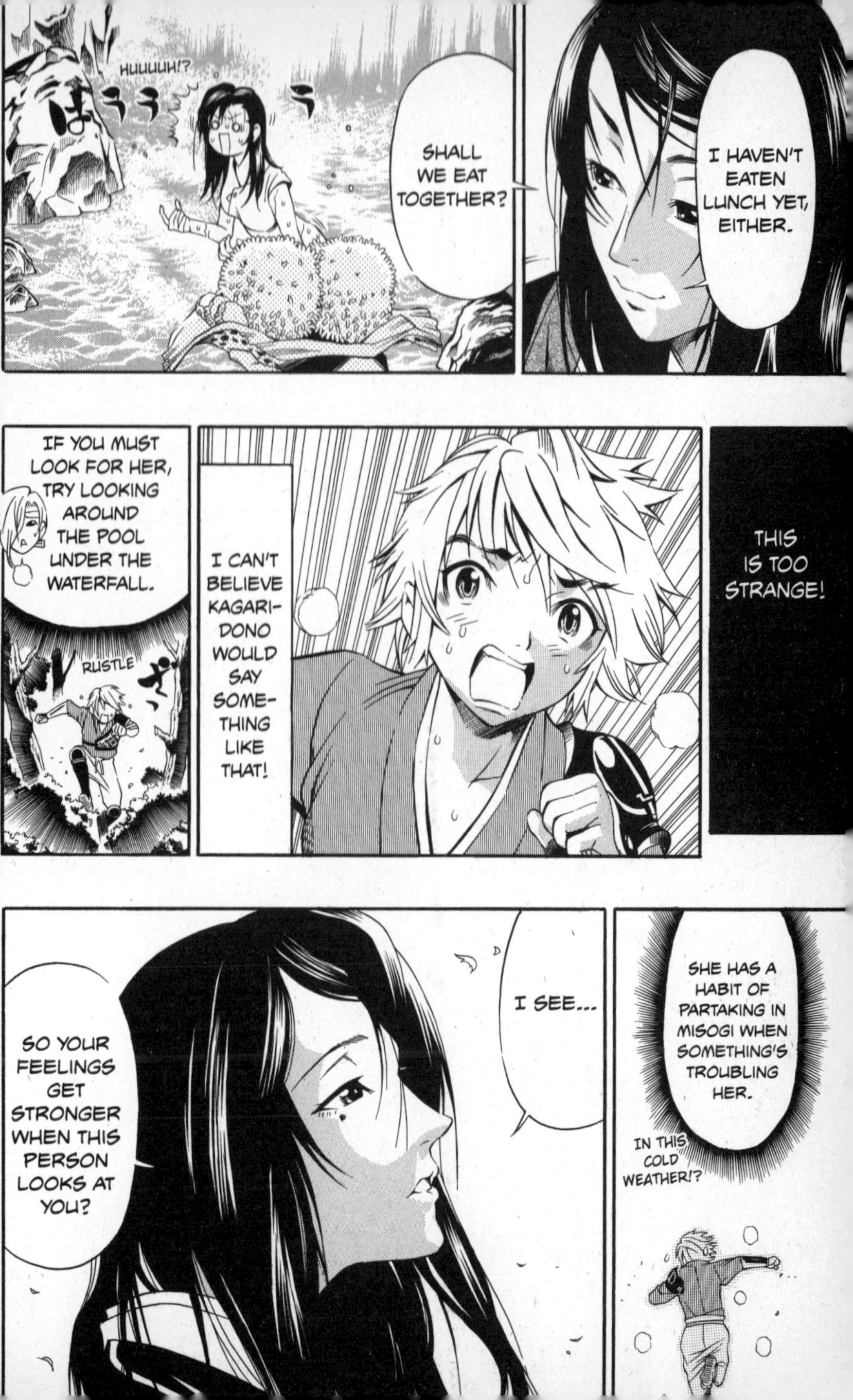
I HAVEN'T EATEN LUNCH YET, EITHER.
SHALL WE EAT TOGETHER?
HUUUUH!?
THIS IS TOO STRANGE!
I CAN'T BELIEVE KAGARI-DONO WOULD SAY SOME-THING LIKE THAT!
IF YOU MUST LOOK FOR HER, TRY LOOKING AROUND THE POOL UNDER THE WATERFALL.
RUSTLE
SHE HAS A HABIT OF PARTAKING IN MISOGI WHEN SOMETHING'S TROUBLING HER.
IN THIS COLD WEATHER!?
I SEE...
SO YOUR FEELINGS GET STRONGER WHEN THIS PERSON LOOKS AT YOU?

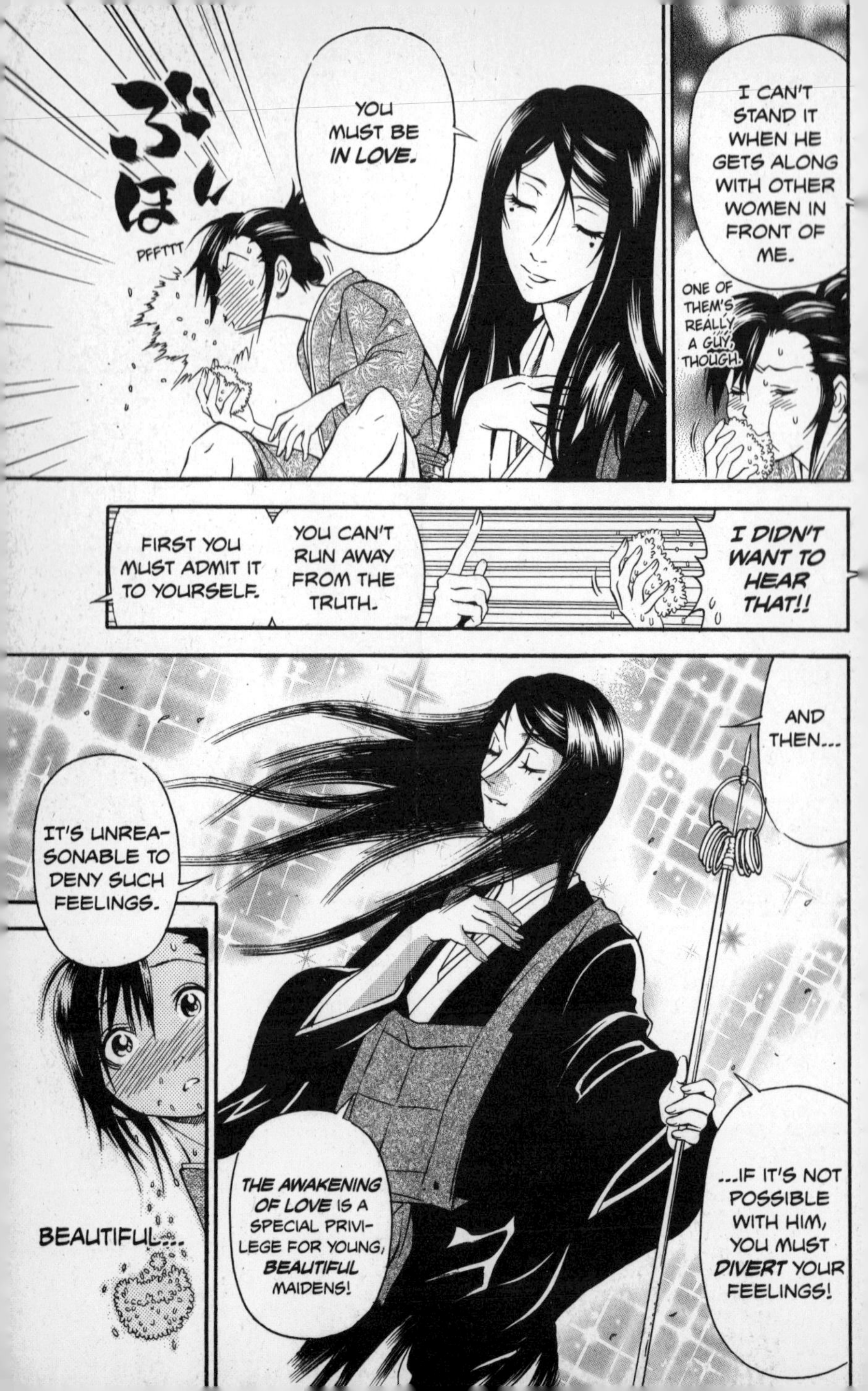
I CAN'T STAND IT WHEN HE GETS ALONG WITH OTHER WOMEN IN FRONT OF ME.
ONE OF THEM'S REALLY A GUY, THOUGH.
YOU MUST BE *IN LOVE.*
PFFTTT
I DIDN'T WANT TO HEAR THAT!!
YOU CAN'T RUN AWAY FROM THE TRUTH.
FIRST YOU MUST ADMIT IT TO YOURSELF.
AND THEN...
...IF IT'S NOT POSSIBLE WITH HIM, YOU MUST *DIVERT* YOUR FEELINGS!
THE AWAKENING OF LOVE IS A SPECIAL PRIVI-LEGE FOR YOUNG, *BEAUTIFUL* MAIDENS!
IT'S UNREA-SONABLE TO DENY SUCH FEELINGS.
BEAUTIFUL...

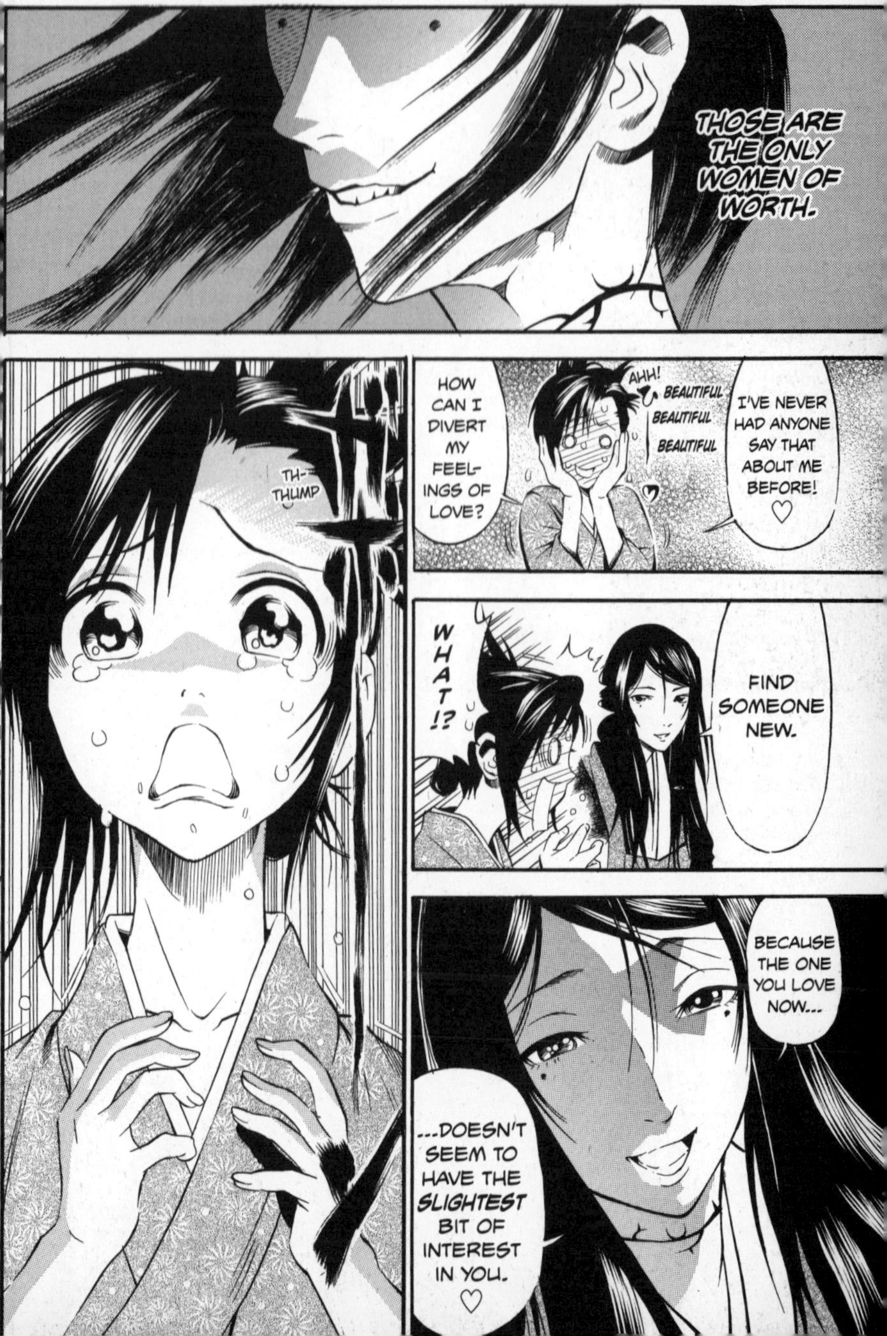
THOSE ARE THE ONLY WOMEN OF WORTH.
I'VE NEVER HAD ANYONE SAY THAT ABOUT ME BEFORE! ♡
BEAUTIFUL BEAUTIFUL BEAUTIFUL
AHH!
HOW CAN I DIVERT MY FEEL-INGS OF LOVE?
FIND SOMEONE NEW.
WHAT!?
BECAUSE THE ONE YOU LOVE NOW...
...DOESN'T SEEM TO HAVE THE SLIGHTEST BIT OF INTEREST IN YOU. ♡
TH-THUMP

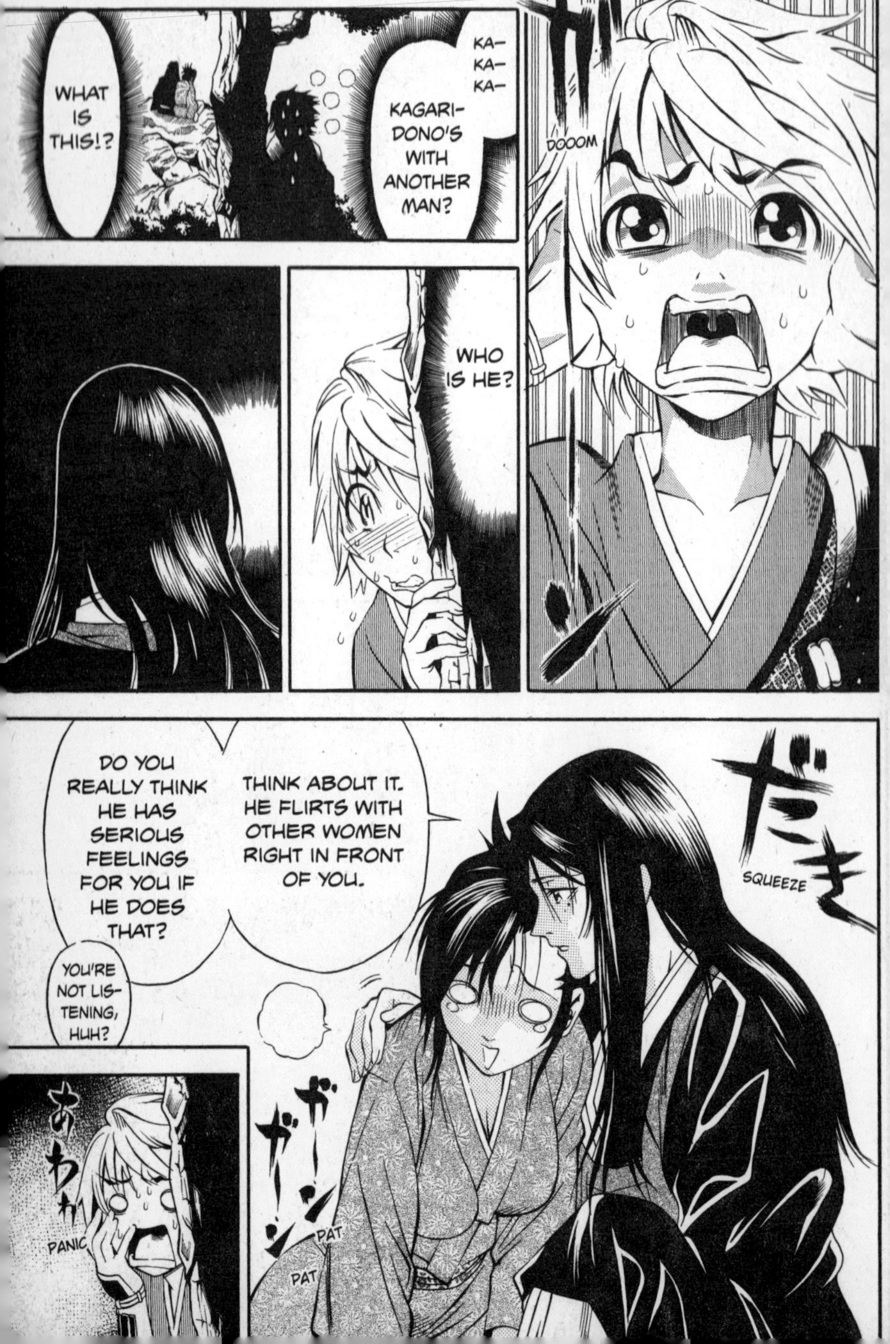
DOOOM
KA- KA- KA- KAGARI-DONO'S WITH ANOTHER MAN?
WHAT IS THIS!?
WHO IS HE?
SQUEEZE
THINK ABOUT IT. HE FLIRTS WITH OTHER WOMEN RIGHT IN FRONT OF YOU.
DO YOU REALLY THINK HE HAS SERIOUS FEELINGS FOR YOU IF HE DOES THAT?
YOU'RE NOT LIS-TENING, HUH?
PAT
PAT
PANIC

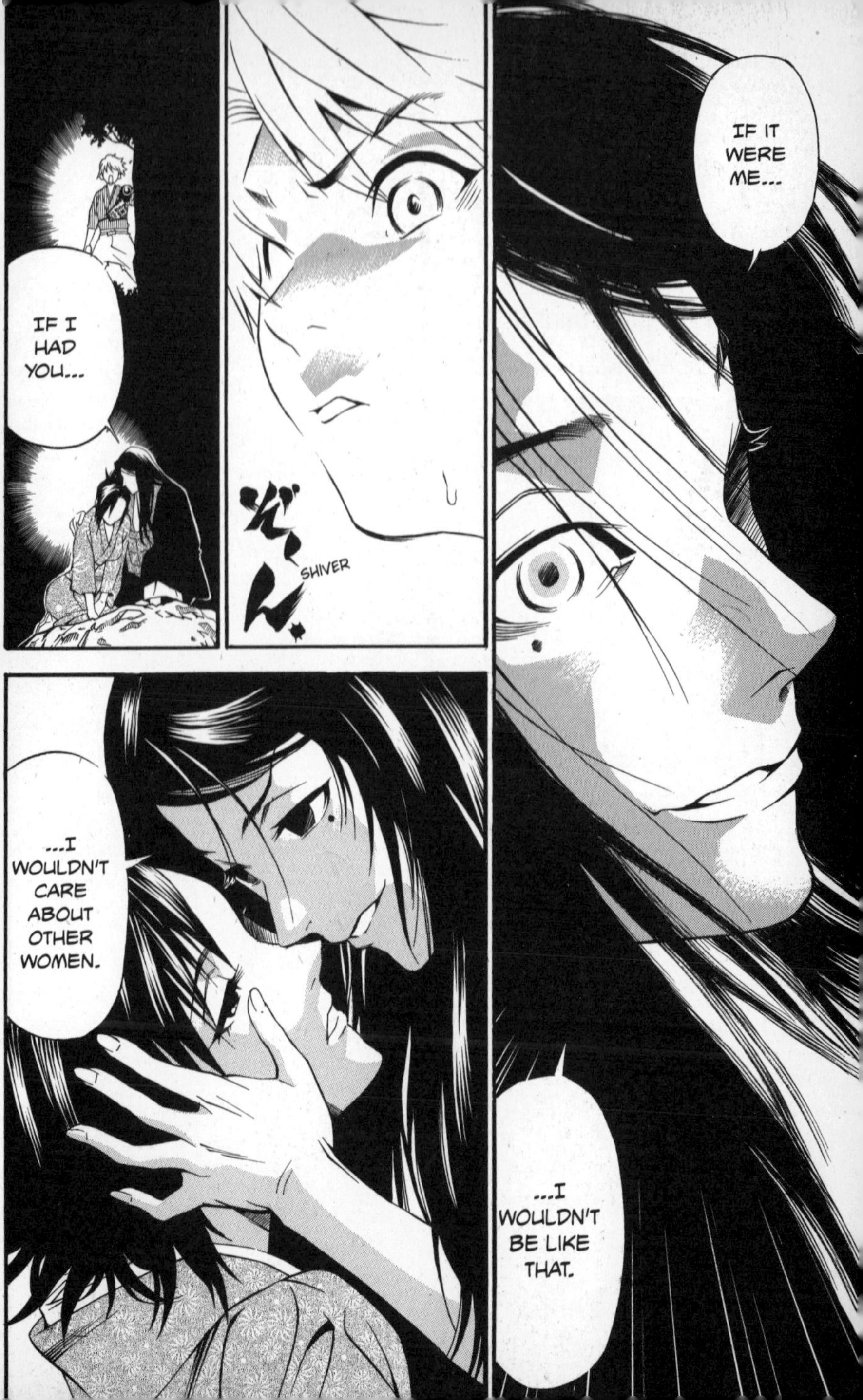
IF IT WERE ME...
...I WOULDN'T BE LIKE THAT.
SHIVER
IF I HAD YOU...
...I WOULDN'T CARE ABOUT OTHER WOMEN.

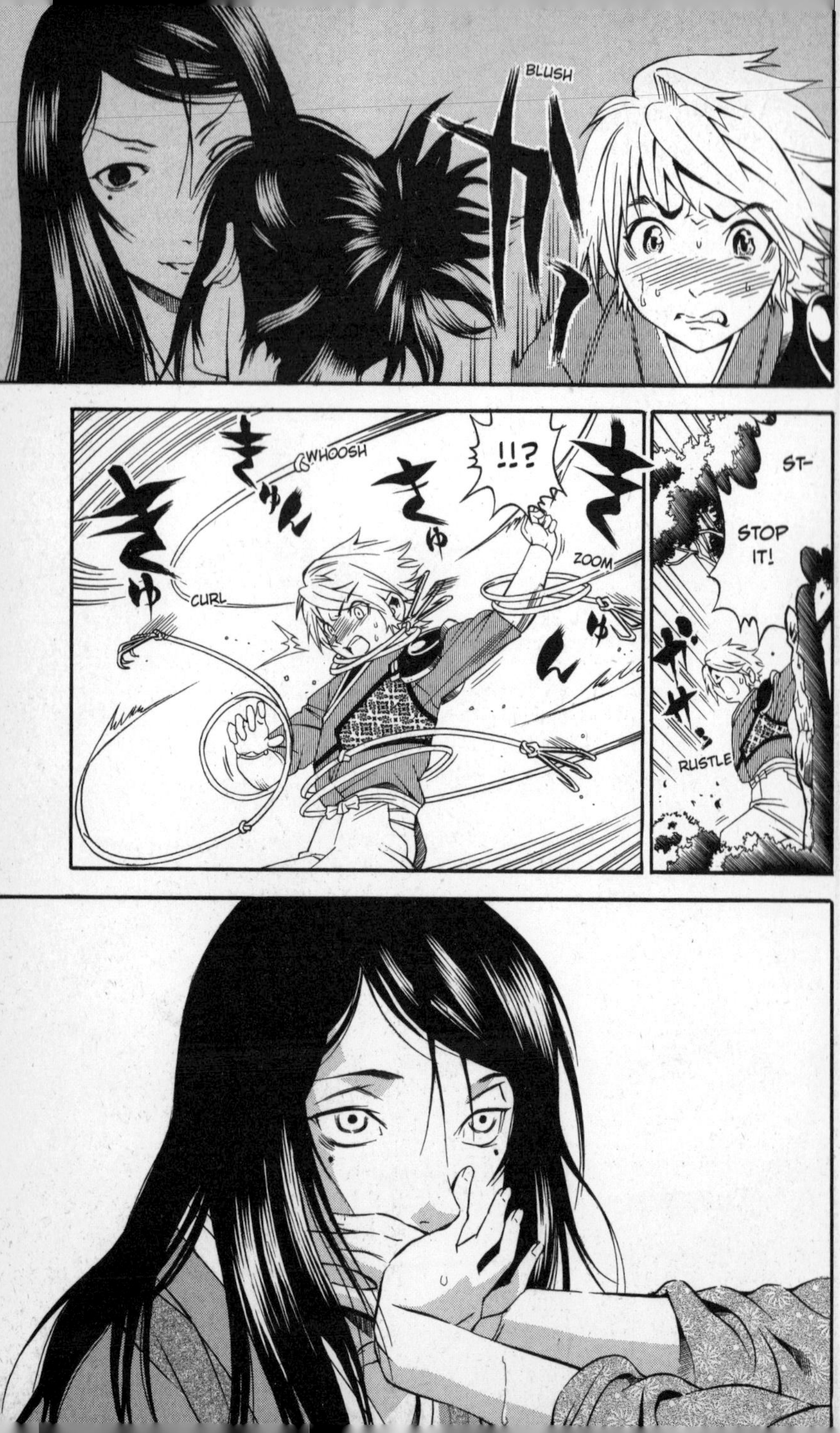
BLUSH
ST-
STOP IT!
RUSTLE
!!?
WHOOSH
ZOOM
CURL

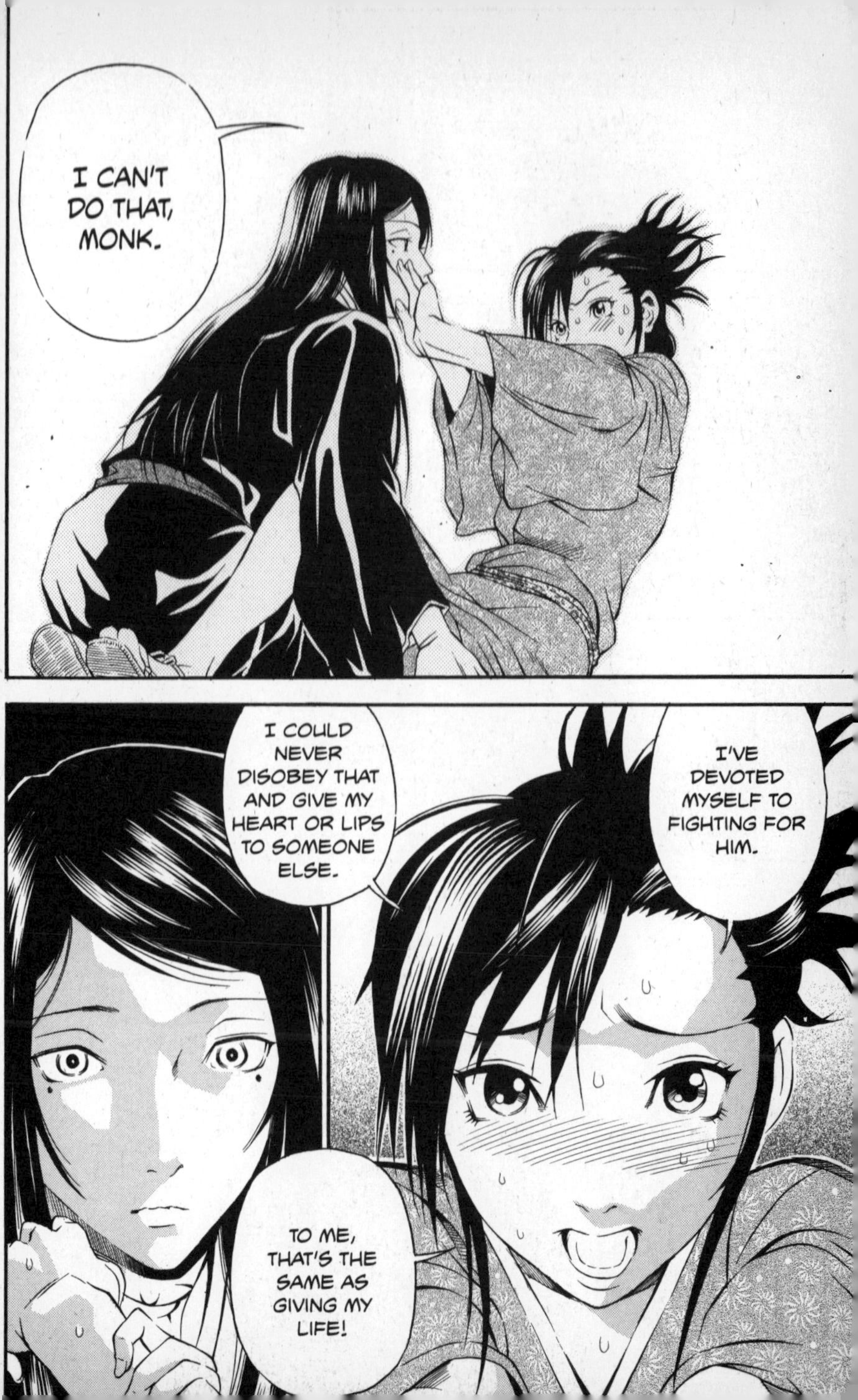
I CAN'T DO THAT, MONK.
I'VE DEVOTED MYSELF TO FIGHTING FOR HIM.
I COULD NEVER DISOBEY THAT AND GIVE MY HEART OR LIPS TO SOMEONE ELSE.
TO ME, THAT'S THE SAME AS GIVING MY LIFE!

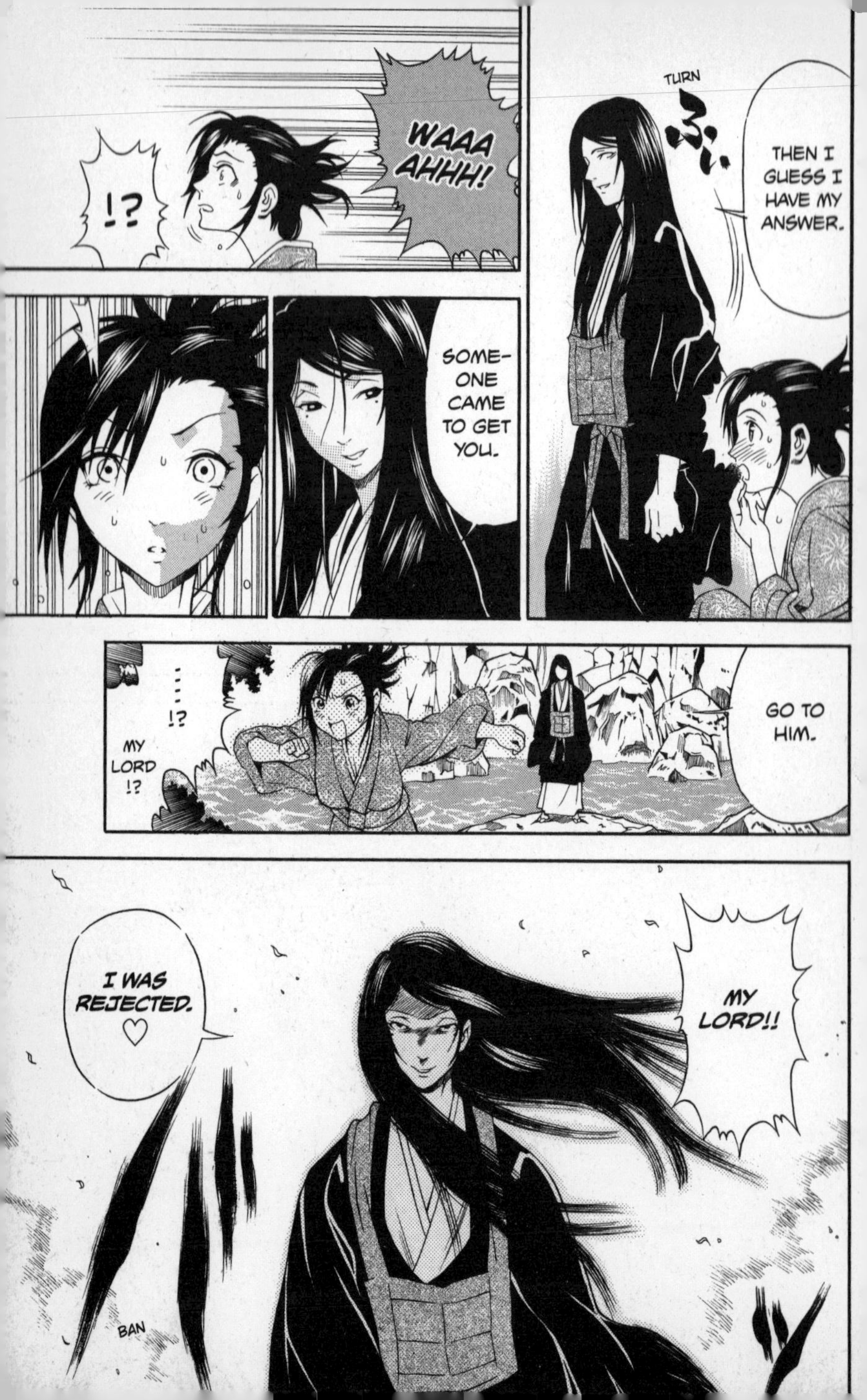
TURN
ふい
THEN I GUESS I HAVE MY ANSWER.
WAAA AHHH!
!?
SOME-ONE CAME TO GET YOU.
GO TO HIM.
......!?
MY LORD !?
MY LORD!!
I WAS REJECTED. ♡
BAN

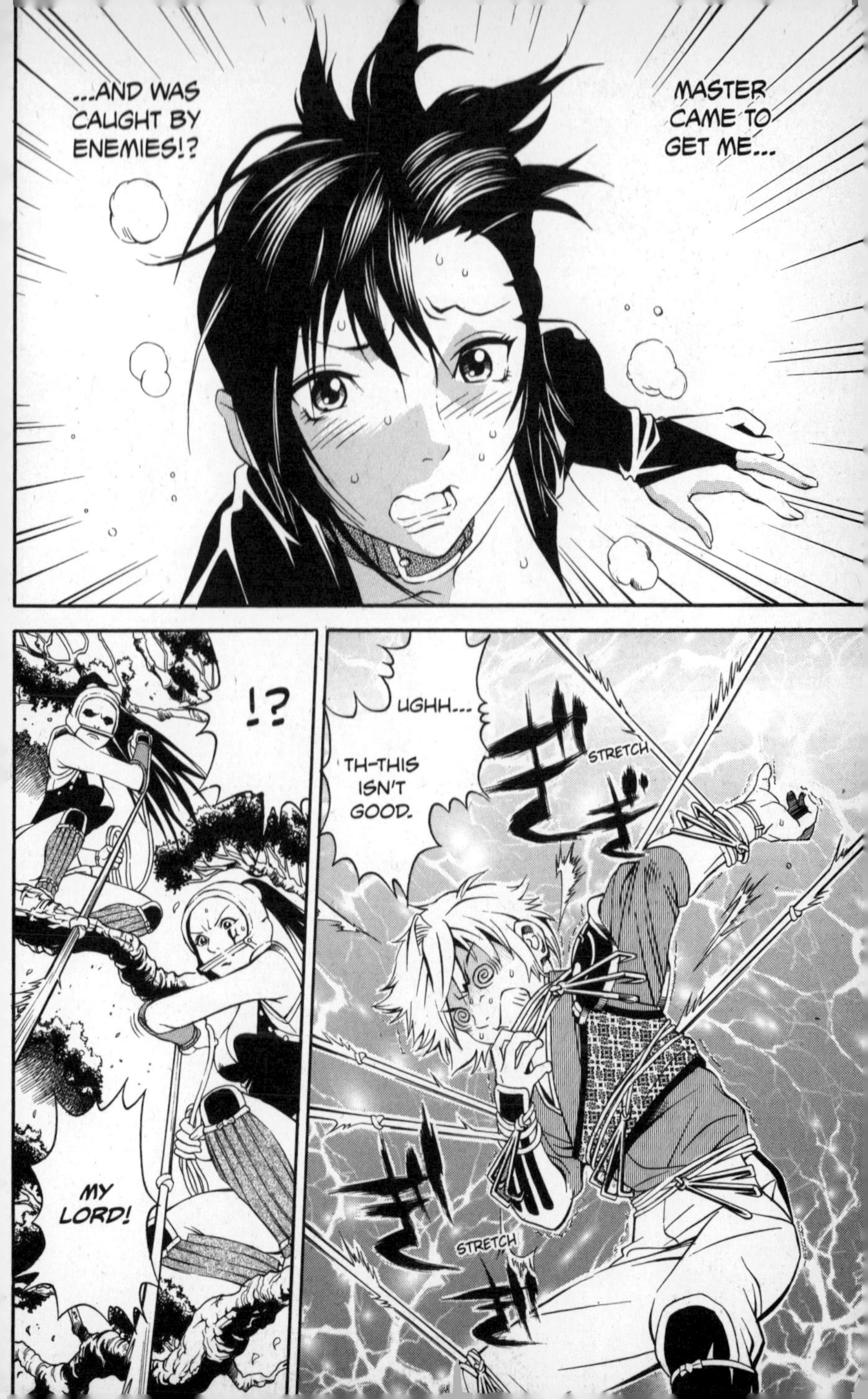
MASTER CAME TO GET ME...
...AND WAS CAUGHT BY ENEMIES!?
UGHH...
TH-THIS ISN'T GOOD.
STRETCH
STRETCH
!?
MY LORD!

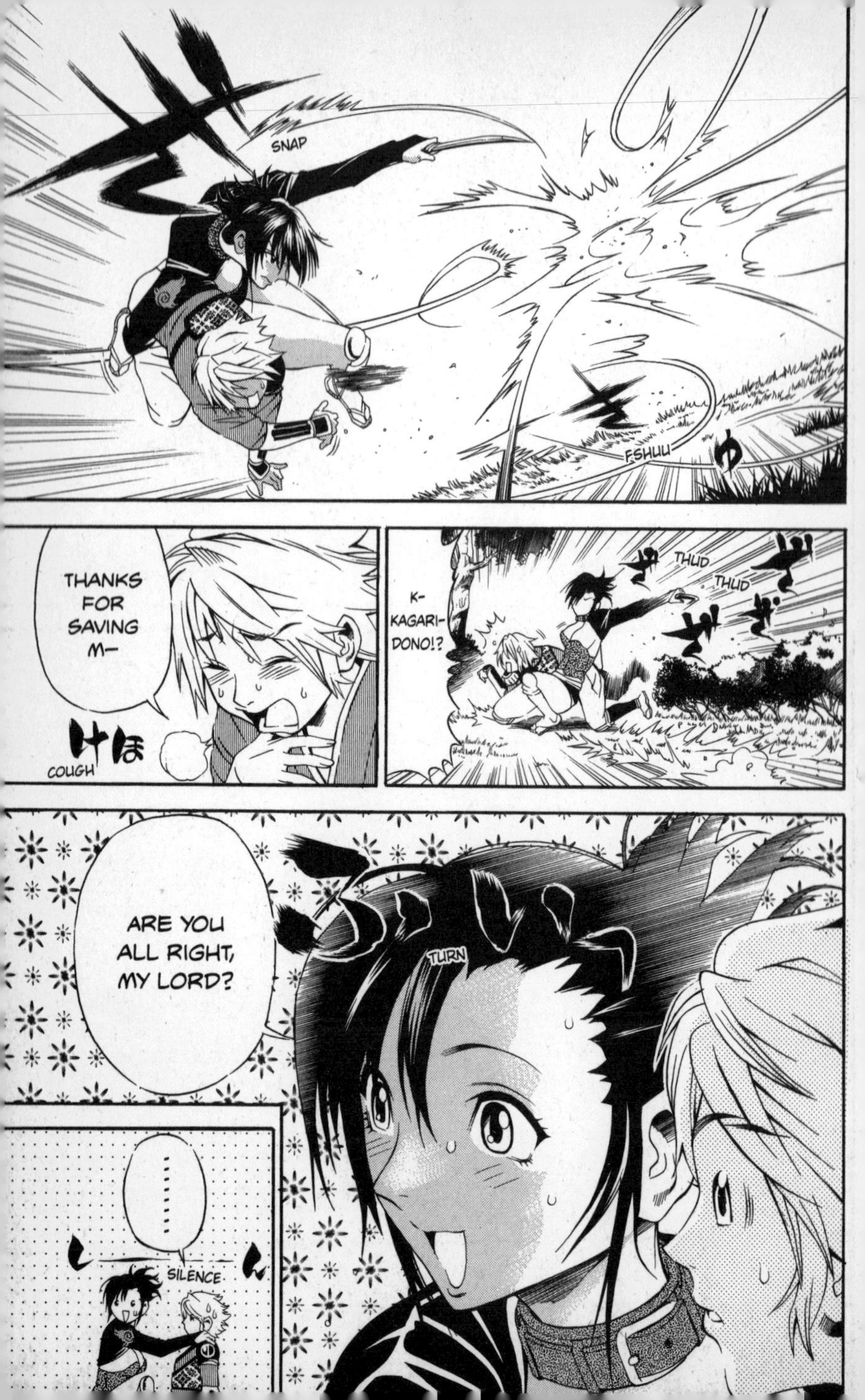
SNAP
FSHUU
THUD
THUD
K-KAGARI-DONO!?
THANKS FOR SAVING M—
COUGH
ARE YOU ALL RIGHT, MY LORD?
TURN
......
SILENCE

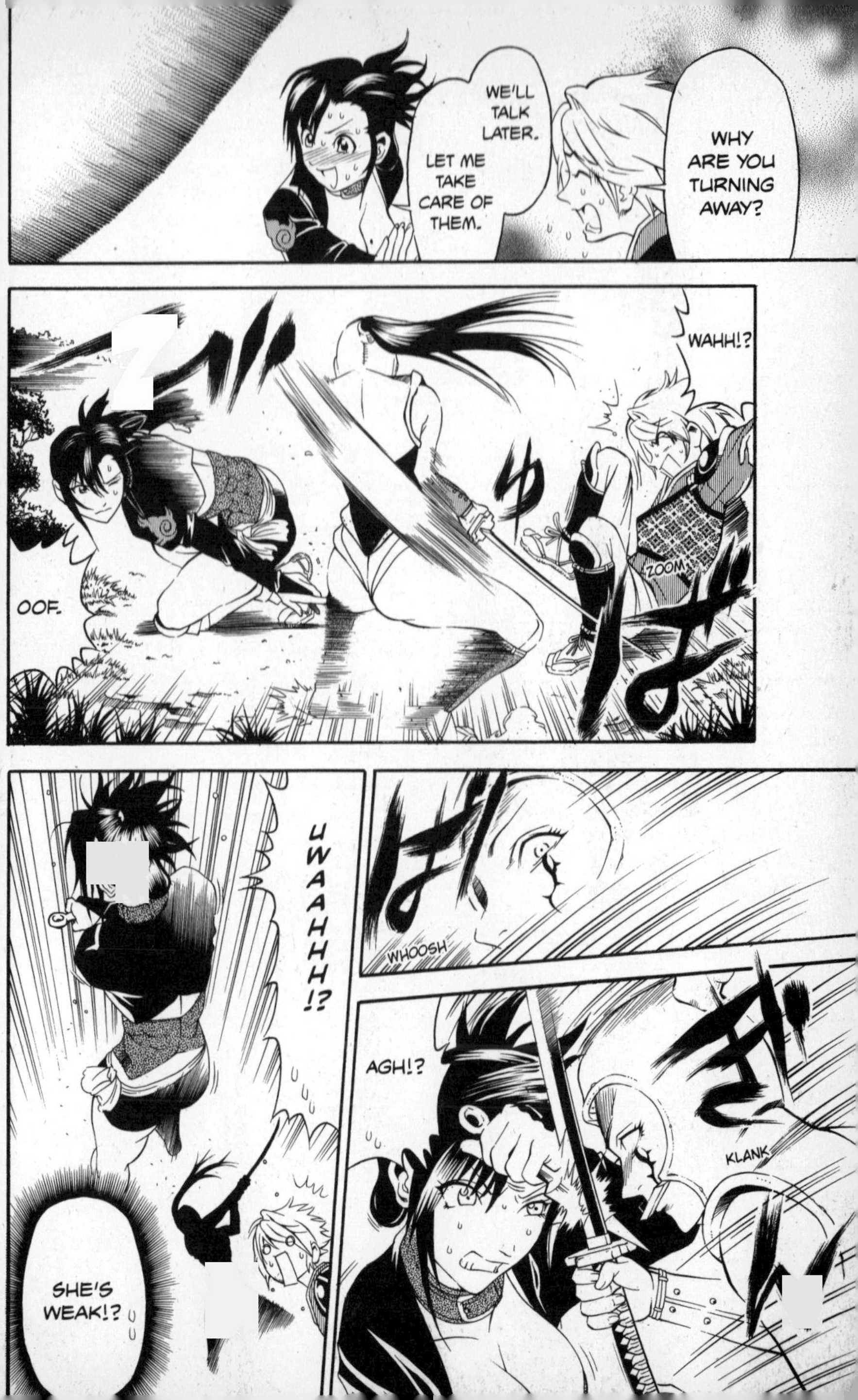
WHY ARE YOU TURNING AWAY?
WE'LL TALK LATER.
LET ME TAKE CARE OF THEM.
WAHH!?
ZOOM
OOF.
WHOOSH
KLANK
AGH!?
UWAAAHHH!?
SHE'S WEAK!?

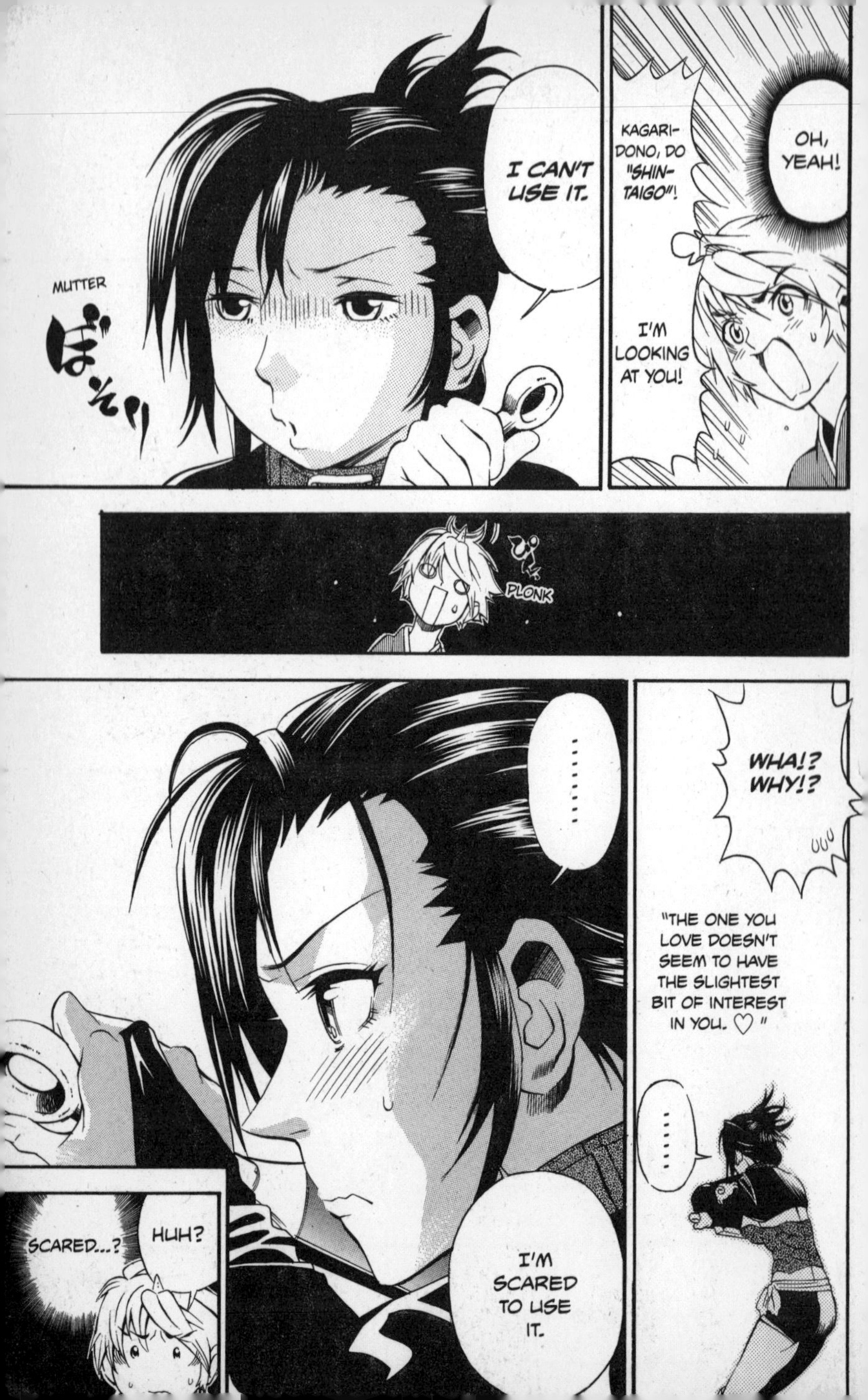
OH, YEAH!
KAGARI-DONO, DO "SHIN-TAIGO"!
I'M LOOKING AT YOU!
I CAN'T USE IT.
MUTTER
PLONK
WHA!? WHY!?
"THE ONE YOU LOVE DOESN'T SEEM TO HAVE THE SLIGHTEST BIT OF INTEREST IN YOU. ♡"
......
......
I'M SCARED TO USE IT.
HUH?
SCARED...?

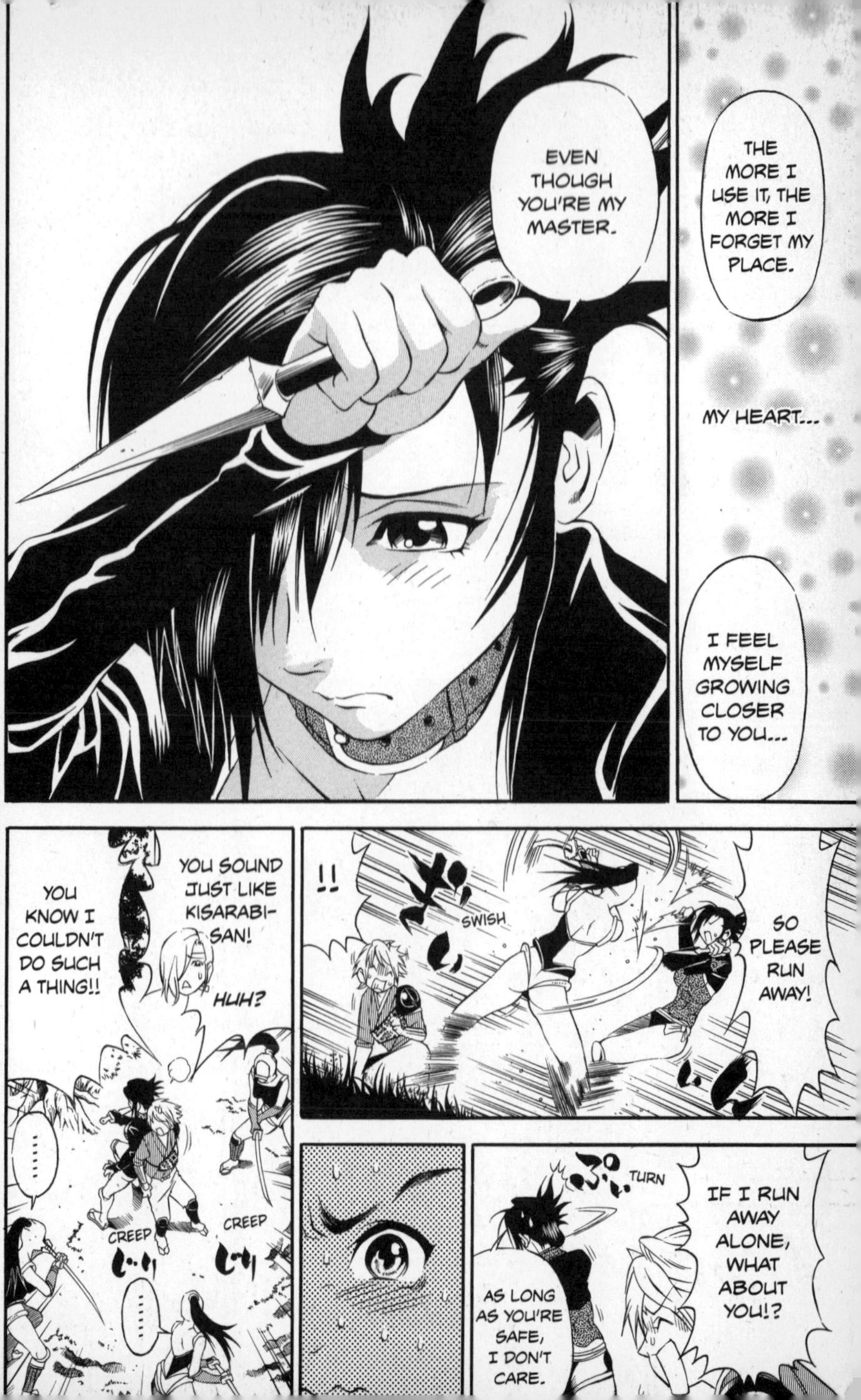
THE MORE I USE IT, THE MORE I FORGET MY PLACE.
MY HEART...
I FEEL MYSELF GROWING CLOSER TO YOU...
EVEN THOUGH YOU'RE MY MASTER.
SO PLEASE RUN AWAY!
!!
SWISH
IF I RUN AWAY ALONE, WHAT ABOUT YOU!?
TURN
AS LONG AS YOU'RE SAFE, I DON'T CARE.
YOU SOUND JUST LIKE KISARABI-SAN!
HUH?
YOU KNOW I COULDN'T DO SUCH A THING!!
......
CREEP
CREEP
......

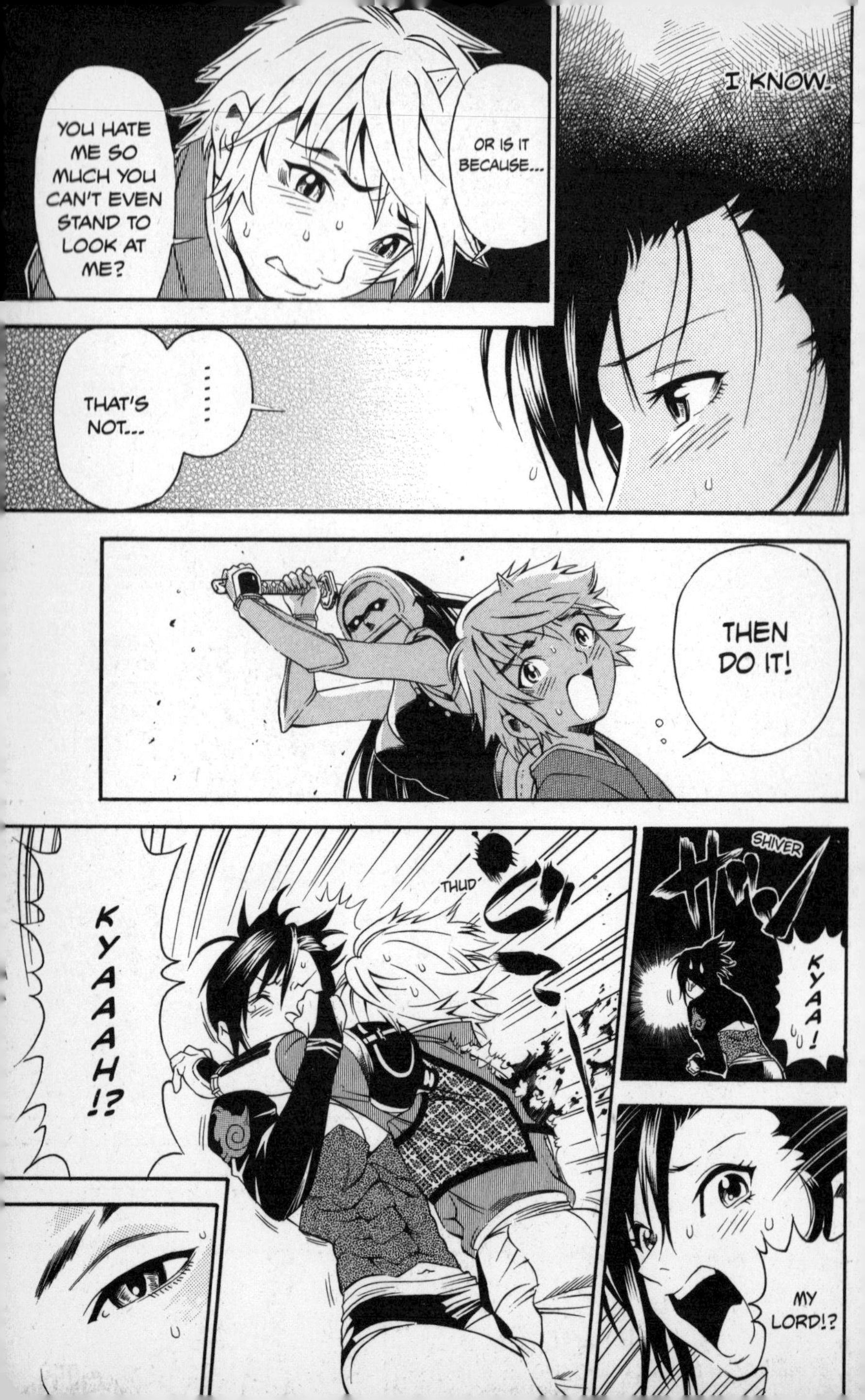
I KNOW.
OR IS IT BECAUSE...
YOU HATE ME SO MUCH YOU CAN'T EVEN STAND TO LOOK AT ME?
......
THAT'S NOT...
THEN DO IT!
SHIVER
KYAA!
MY LORD!?
THUD
KYAAAAH!?

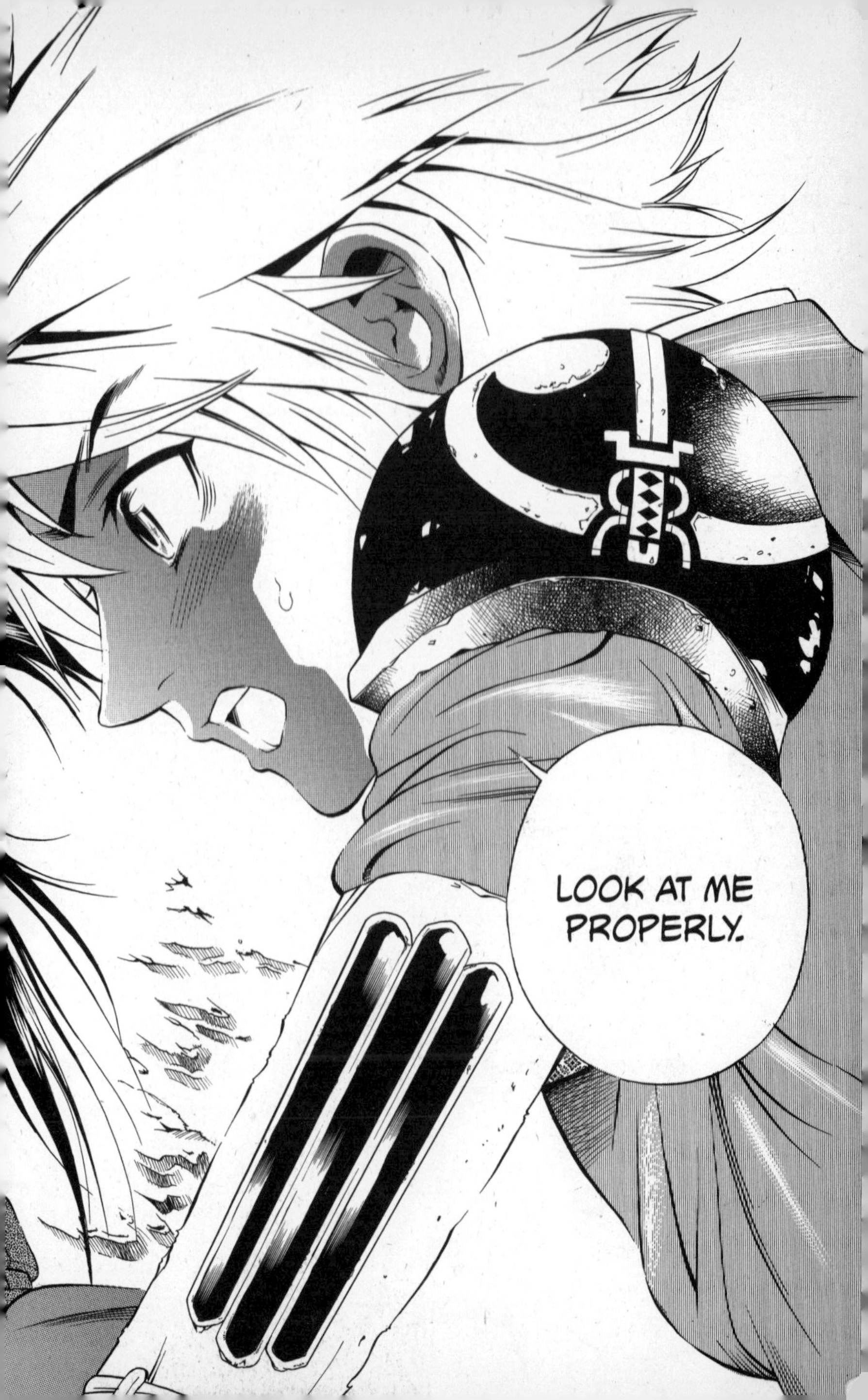
LOOK AT ME PROPERLY.

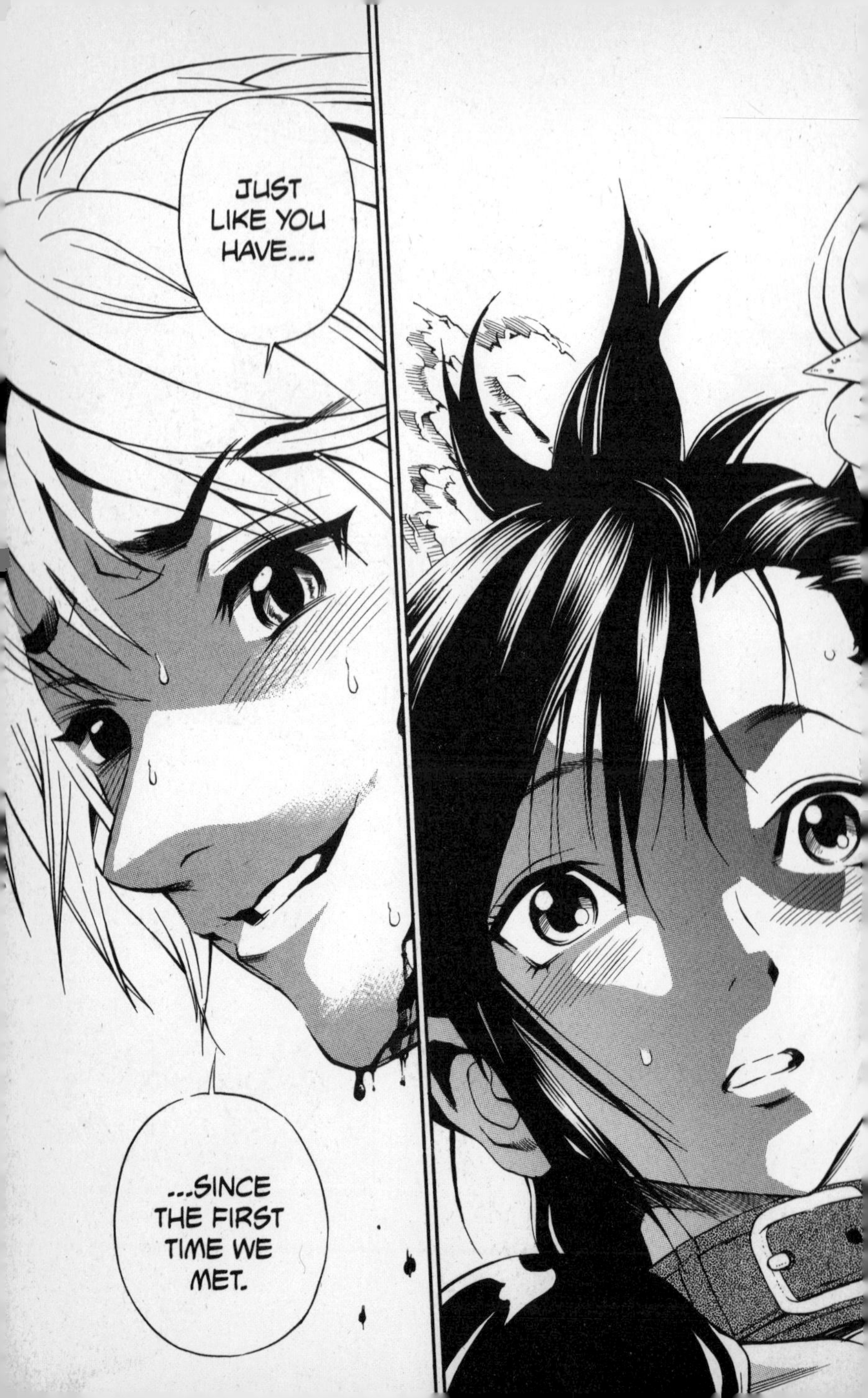
JUST LIKE YOU HAVE...
...SINCE THE FIRST TIME WE MET.

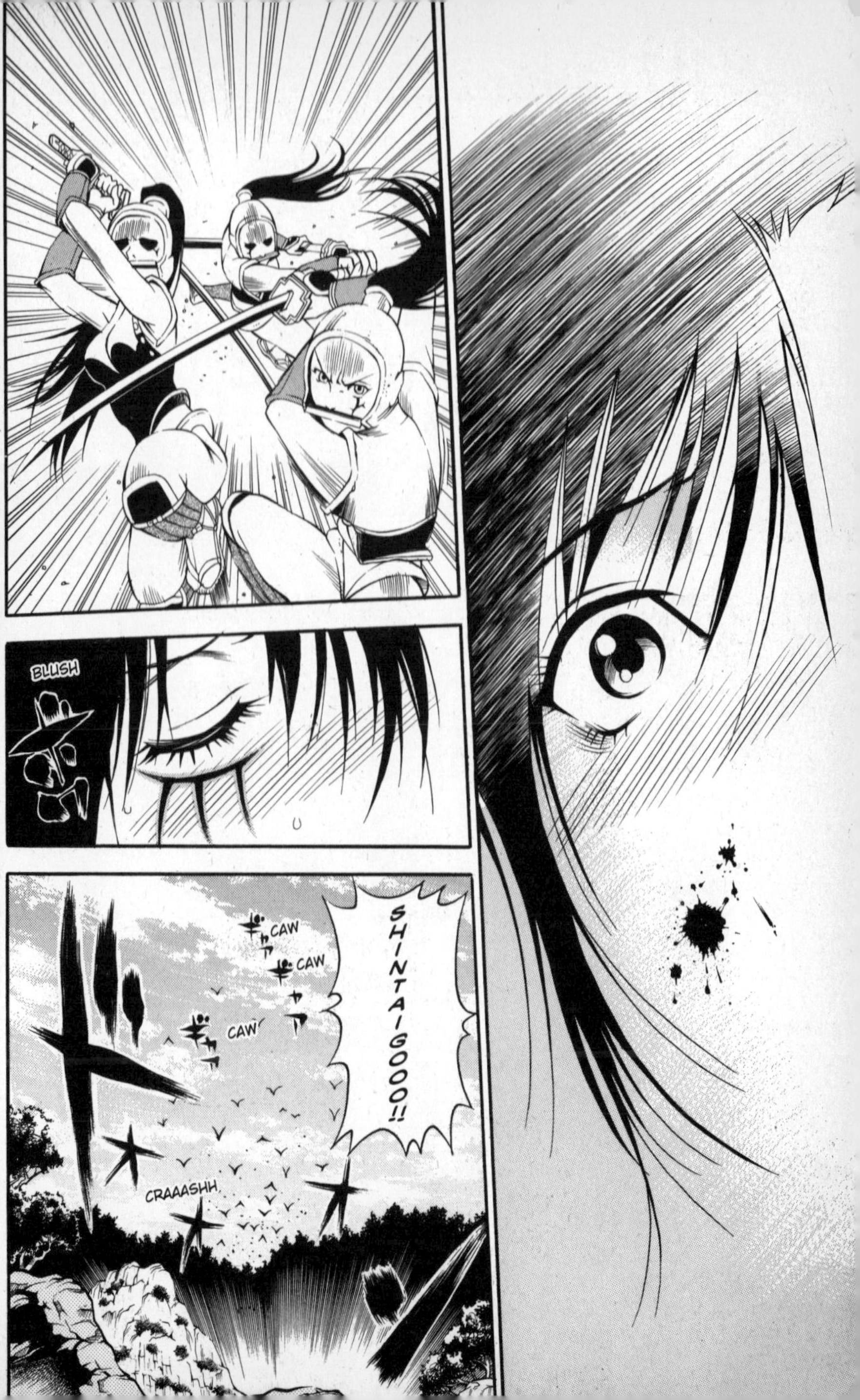
BLUSH
SHINTAIGOOOO!!
CAW
CAW
CAW
CRAAASHH

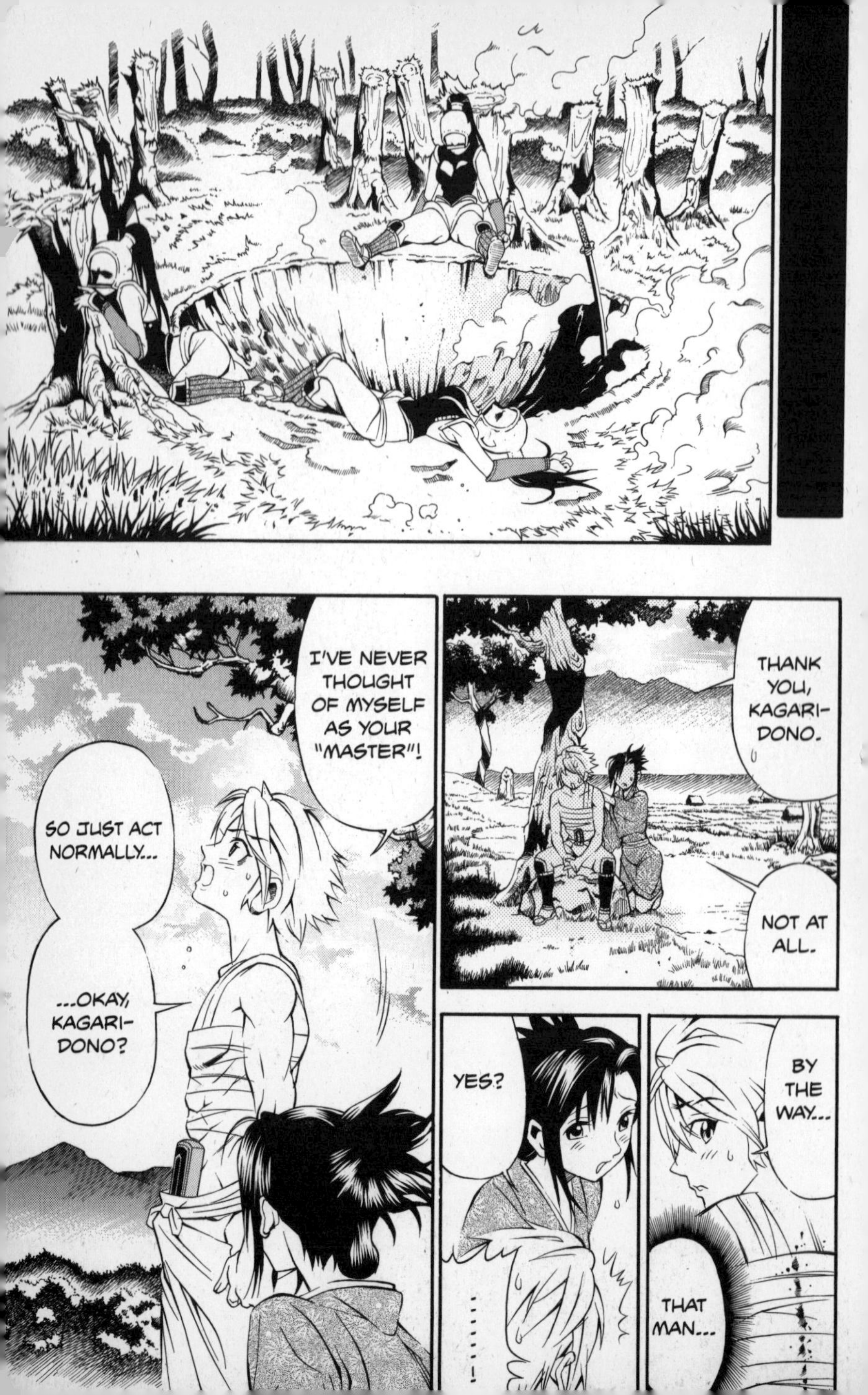
THANK YOU, KAGARI-DONO.
NOT AT ALL.
BY THE WAY...
THAT MAN...
YES?
......!
I'VE NEVER THOUGHT OF MYSELF AS YOUR "MASTER"!
SO JUST ACT NORMALLY...
...OKAY, KAGARI-DONO?

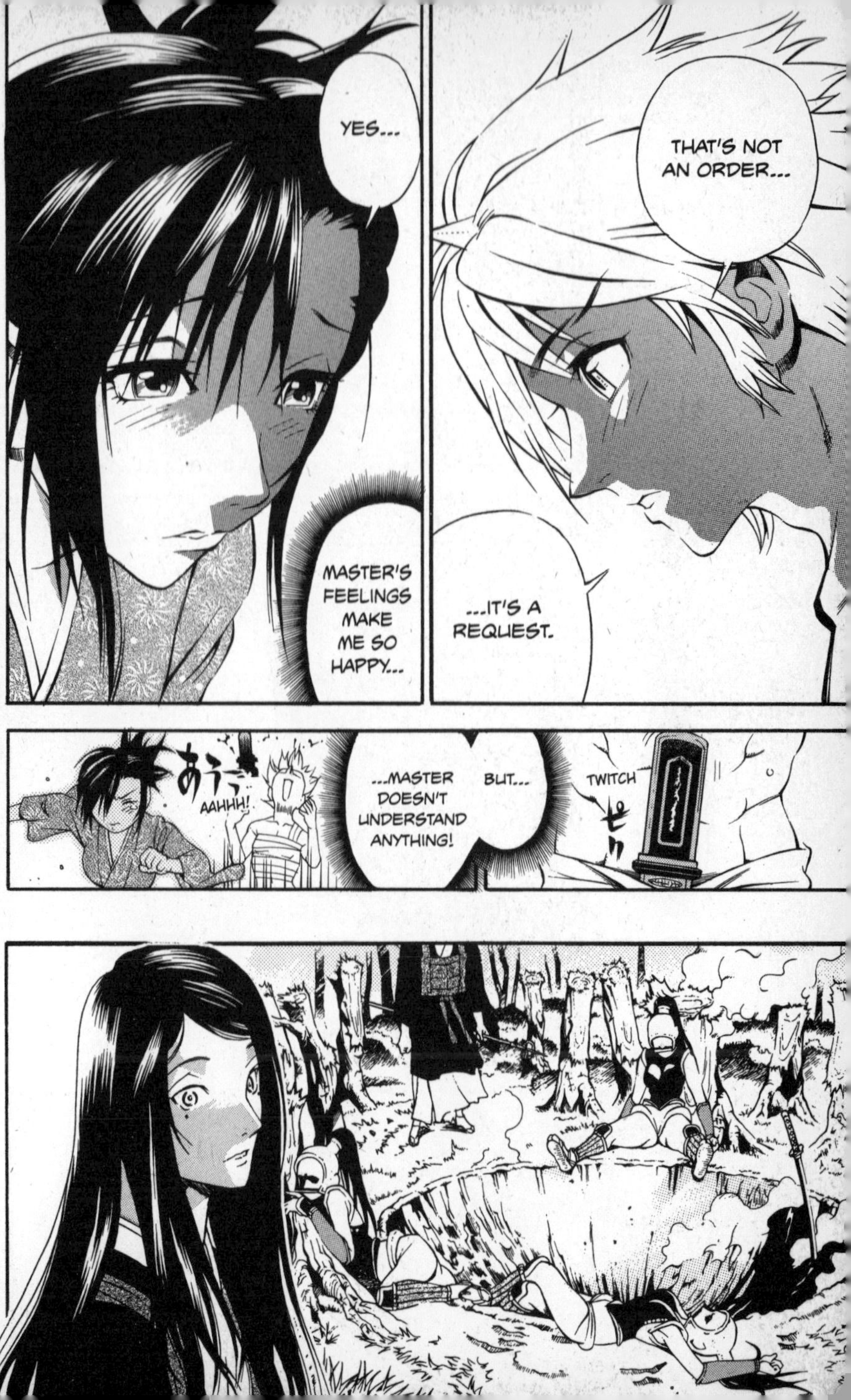
THAT'S NOT AN ORDER...
...IT'S A REQUEST.
YES...
MASTER'S FEELINGS MAKE ME SO HAPPY...
TWITCH
BUT...
...MASTER DOESN'T UNDERSTAND ANYTHING!
AAHHH!

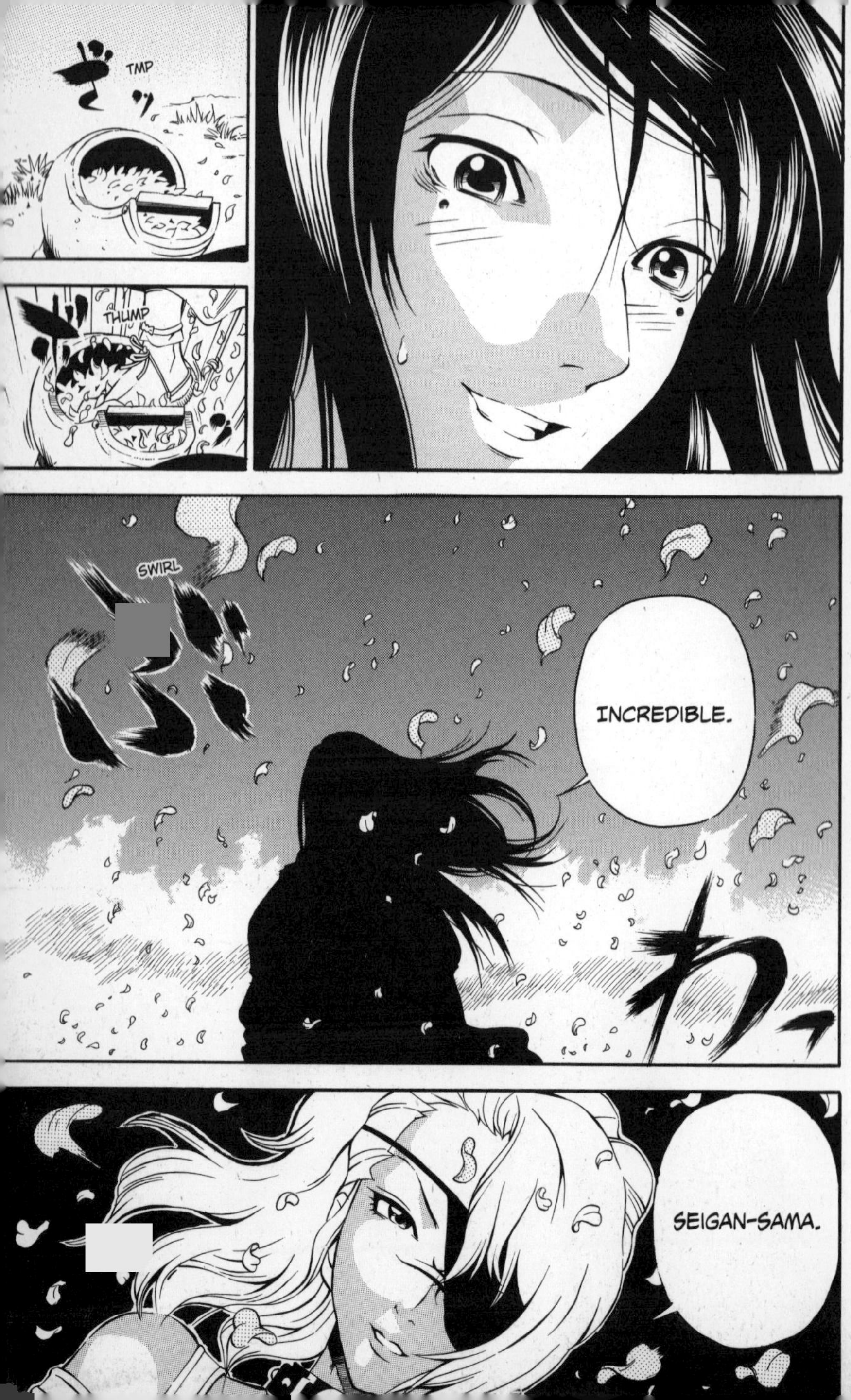
TMP
THUMP
SWIRL
INCREDIBLE.
SEIGAN-SAMA.

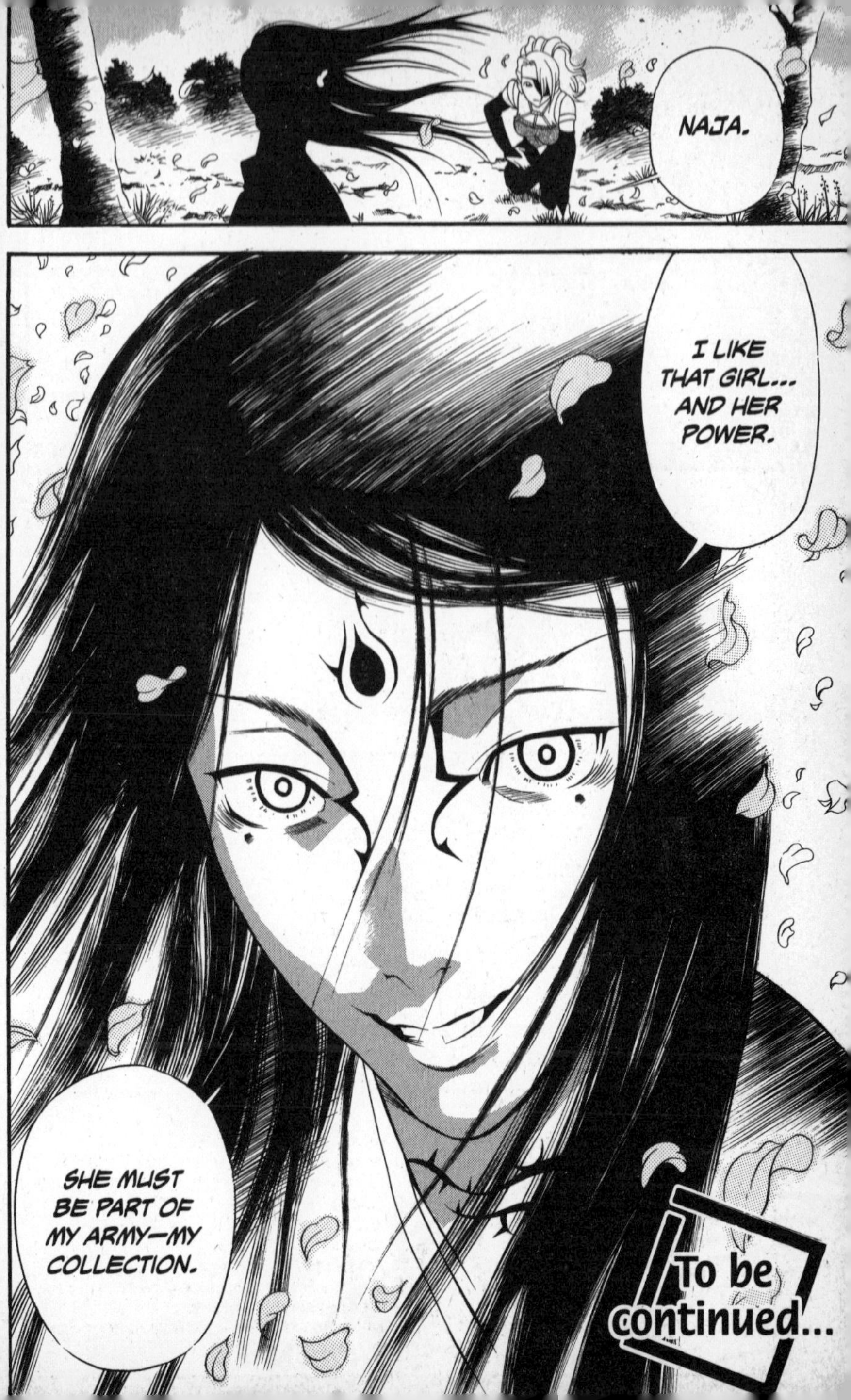
NAJA.
I LIKE THAT GIRL... AND HER POWER.
SHE MUST BE PART OF MY ARMY—MY COLLECTION.
To be continued...

Bonus manga *Ninja Girls*

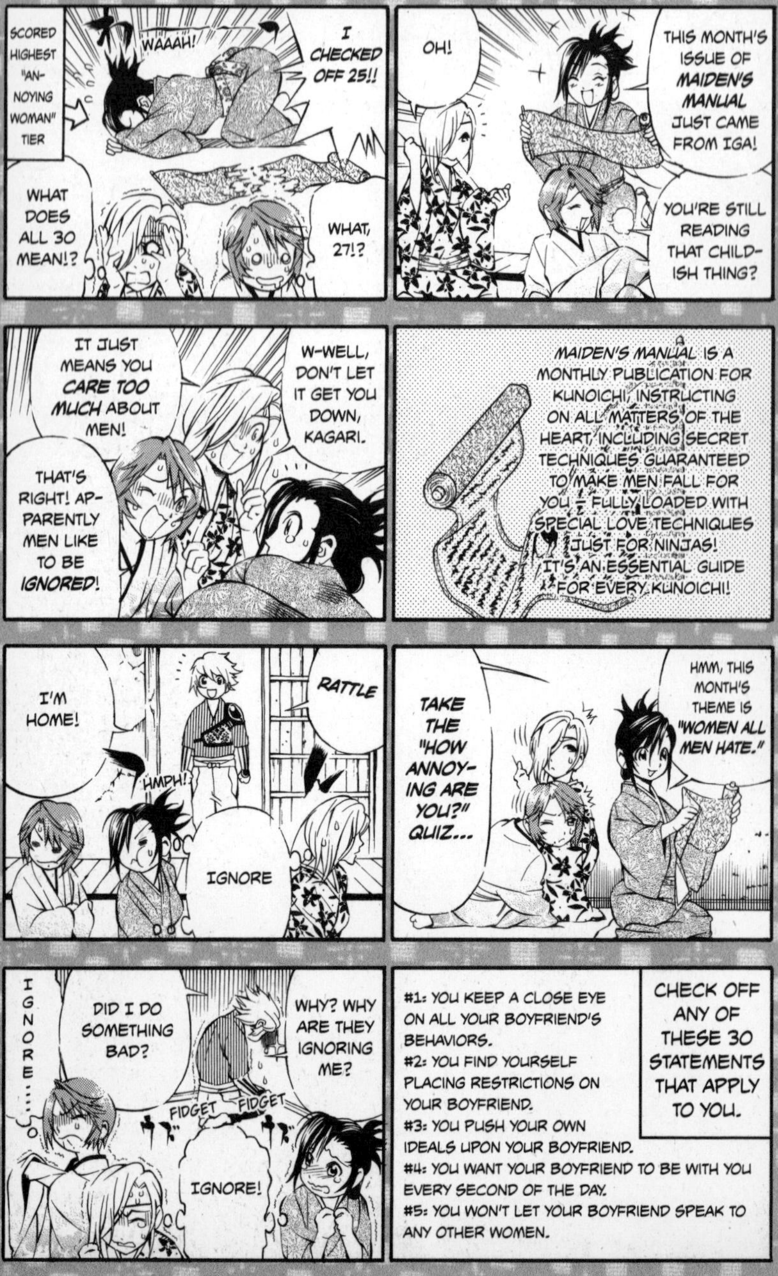
THIS MONTH'S ISSUE OF MAIDEN'S MANUAL JUST CAME FROM IGA!
OH!
YOU'RE STILL READING THAT CHILDISH THING?
MAIDEN'S MANUAL IS A MONTHLY PUBLICATION FOR KUNOICHI, INSTRUCTING ON ALL MATTERS OF THE HEART, INCLUDING SECRET TECHNIQUES GUARANTEED TO MAKE MEN FALL FOR YOU — FULLY LOADED WITH SPECIAL LOVE TECHNIQUES JUST FOR NINJAS! IT'S AN ESSENTIAL GUIDE FOR EVERY KUNOICHI!
HMM, THIS MONTH'S THEME IS "WOMEN ALL MEN HATE."
TAKE THE "HOW ANNOYING ARE YOU?" QUIZ...
CHECK OFF ANY OF THESE 30 STATEMENTS THAT APPLY TO YOU.
#1: YOU KEEP A CLOSE EYE ON ALL YOUR BOYFRIEND'S BEHAVIORS.
#2: YOU FIND YOURSELF PLACING RESTRICTIONS ON YOUR BOYFRIEND.
#3: YOU PUSH YOUR OWN IDEALS UPON YOUR BOYFRIEND.
#4: YOU WANT YOUR BOYFRIEND TO BE WITH YOU EVERY SECOND OF THE DAY.
#5: YOU WON'T LET YOUR BOYFRIEND SPEAK TO ANY OTHER WOMEN.
I CHECKED OFF 25!!
WAAAH!
SCORED HIGHEST "ANNOYING WOMAN" TIER
WHAT, 27!?
WHAT DOES ALL 30 MEAN!?
W-WELL, DON'T LET IT GET YOU DOWN, KAGARI.
IT JUST MEANS YOU CARE TOO MUCH ABOUT MEN!
THAT'S RIGHT! APPARENTLY MEN LIKE TO BE IGNORED!
RATTLE
I'M HOME!
HMPH!
IGNORE
WHY? WHY ARE THEY IGNORING ME?
DID I DO SOMETHING BAD?
IGNORE......
FIDGET FIDGET
IGNORE!

About the Creator

Hosana Tanaka

※ Debuted after winning the Shōgakukan Newcomer Award.

※ Received attention after first series Code Name: BF was serialized in 2004 in *Shūkan Shōnen Sunday*, a weekly manga magazine.

※ 2005 brought the serialization of Ninja Girls in *Gekkan Shōnen Sirius*, a monthly manga magazine.

※ Birthday: January 13. Zodiac Sign: Capricorn.

TRANSLATION NOTES

Japanese is a tricky language for most Westerners, and translation is often more art than science. For your edification and reading pleasure, here are notes on some of the places where we could have gone in a different direction in our translation of the work, or where a Japanese cultural reference is used.

Sengoku era

Sengoku jidai (Warring States Era) lasted from the mid–fifteenth century to the beginning of the seventeenth century. As its name suggests, it was a time of civil war in Japan, with regional lords (*daimyo*) taking control because of a weak central government. The most famous *daimyo* were Oda Nobunaga, known for his military prowess, and Tokugawa Ieyasu, who went on to become the first shogun of Japan's final shogunate.

THE IGA–
NINPO
SHINTAIGO...

SPURT

Iga, page 3

Iga is a city located in Mie prefecture, Japan. It's the origin of one of the most famous ninja schools in Japan, Iga-style ninjutsu. The *kunoichi* in *Ninja Girls* often talk about the town of Iga, where they most likely were trained as ninjas. Modern-day Iga still holds on to its roots via its famous Iga Ninja Museum.

Ninpo, page 3

Ninpo literally means "ninja arts" or "ninja technique."

THAT'S THE POWER OF THE IGA-NINPO SHINTAIGO!

IT'S HARD TO BELIEVE IT WHEN I LOOK LIKE THIS, BUT I'M THE MASTER OF A SPECIAL ART CALLED "SHINTAIGO"!

CLENCH

Shintaigo, page 3

Kagari's special *ninpo* attack. It's written with the characters "god," "body," and "conjunction."

SO IT'S THAT KUNOICHI AGAIN...

Kunoichi, page 34

A *kunoichi* is a female ninja. The kanji is written with strokes resembling the strokes in the kanji for "woman."

Ihai, page 50

An *ihai* is a mortuary tablet that's often placed on a Buddhist altar to honor a deceased loved one. It's usually a wood or stone tablet that's engraved with the deceased person's posthumous name, which is given to them by the Buddhist priest who performed their funerary rites.

WHY DIDN'T YOU EVER TELL ME ABOUT SUCH AN IMPORTANT THING!?

SHAKE SHAKE

IT'S NO USE TALKING TO THE IHAI, IT WON'T ANSWER.

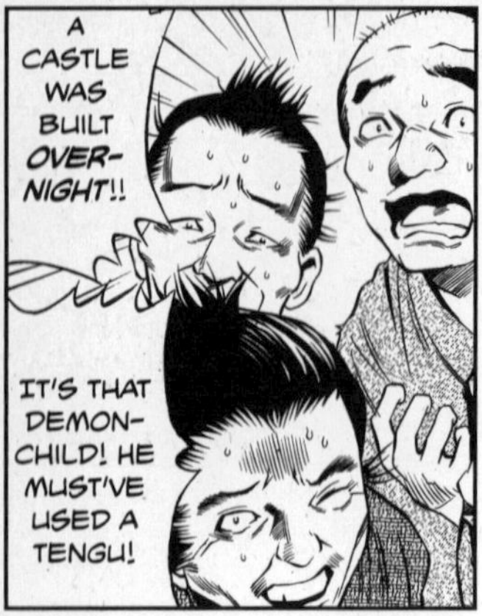
A CASTLE WAS BUILT OVER-NIGHT!!
IT'S THAT DEMON-CHILD! HE MUST'VE USED A TENGU!

***Tengu*, page 55**
A supernatural creature, often depicted as a demon with an extremely long nose.

***Shinobi*, page 70**
Another word for ninja. *Shinobi* was the more commonly used term for ninja until its usage declined in popularity after World War II.

***Rasengan*, page 78**
Kisarabi's special *ninpo* attack. It's written with the characters meaning "wizard" and "eye."

***Shamisen*, page 92**
A three-stringed musical instrument played with a plectrum.

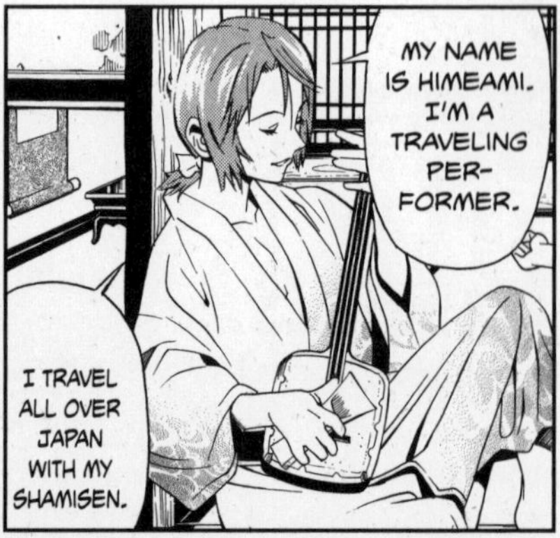
MY NAME IS HIMEAMI. I'M A TRAVELING PER-FORMER.
I TRAVEL ALL OVER JAPAN WITH MY SHAMISEN.

***Mugen*, page 93**
Himemaru's special *ninpo* attack. It's written with the characters meaning "dream" and "bow string."

Heart of Perfect Wisdom Sutra, page 166

Kagari is chanting excerpts of the Heart of Perfect Wisdom Sutra, a Buddhist mantra. In order to maintain authenticity, we have retained the Japanese. Here is the Japanese romanization followed by a literal translation:

kan ji zai bō satsu
gyō shin han nya ha ra mitsu ta ji
shiki fu i kuu
kuu fu i shiki
shiki soku ze kuu
kuu soku ze shiki

The all-compassionate bodhisattva Avalokitesvara
was practicing profound Prajna wisdom
form is emptiness
emptiness is form
form does not differ from emptiness
emptiness does not differ from form

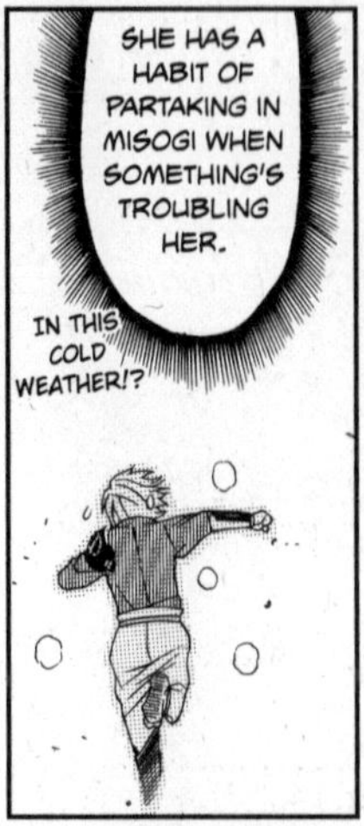
SHE HAS A HABIT OF PARTAKING IN MISOGI WHEN SOMETHING'S TROUBLING HER.
IN THIS COLD WEATHER!?

Misogi, 170

Misogi is a rite of purification that involves dousing one's body with cold water, usually under waterfalls.

Psycho Busters

MANGA BY AKINARI NAO
STORY BY YUYA AOKI

PSYCHIC TEENS ON THE RUN!

Out of the blue, a beautiful girl asks Kakeru to run away with her. This could be any boy's dream come true, but there's something strange afoot.

It turns out that this girl is on the run from a shadowy government organization intent on using her psychic abilities for its own nefarious ends. But why does she need Kakeru's help? Could it be that he has secret powers, too?

- Story by Yuya Aoki, creator of *Get Backers*

Special extras in each volume! Read them all!

SHIKI TSUKAI

STORY BY TO-RU ZEKUU
ART BY YUNA TAKANAGI

DEFENDING THE NATURAL ORDER OF THE UNIVERSE!

The *shiki tsukai* are "Keepers of the Seasons"—magical warriors pledged to defend the planet's natural order against those who would threaten it.

When 14-year-old Akira Kizuki joins the *shiki tsukai*, he knows that it'll be a difficult life. But with his new friends and mentors, he's up to the challenge!

Special extras in each volume! Read them all!

NEGIMA!™

BY KEN AKAMATSU

Negi Springfield is a ten-year-old wizard teaching English at an all-girls Japanese school. He dreams of becoming a master wizard like his legendary father, the Thousand Master. At first his biggest concern was concealing his magic powers, because if he's ever caught using them publicly, he thinks he'll be turned into an ermine! But in a world that gets stranger every day, it turns out that the strangest people of all are Negi's students! From a librarian with a magic book to a centuries-old vampire, from a robot to a ninja, Negi will risk his own life to protect the girls in his care!

Ages: 16+

Special extras in each volume! Read them all!

VISIT WWW.DELREYMANGA.COM TO:
- View release date calendars for upcoming volumes
- Sign up for Del Rey's free manga e-newsletter
- Find out the latest about new Del Rey Manga series

BY OH!GREAT

Itsuki Minami needs no introduction—everybody's heard of the "Babyface" of the Eastside. He's the strongest kid at Higashi Junior High School, easy on the eyes but dangerously tough when he needs to be. Plus, Itsuki lives with the mysterious and sexy Noyamano sisters. Life's never dull, but it becomes downright dangerous when Itsuki leads his school to victory over vindictive Westside punks with gangster connections. Now he stands to lose his school, his friends, and everything he cares about. But in his darkest hour, the Noyamano girls give him an amazing gift, one that just might help him save his school: a pair of Air Trecks. These high-tech skates are more than just supercool. They'll enable Itsuki to execute the wildest, most aggressive moves ever seen—and introduce him to a thrilling and terrifying new world.

Ages: 16 +

Special extras in each volume! Read them all!

VISIT WWW.DELREYMANGA.COM TO:
• Read sample pages
• View release date calendars for upcoming volumes
• Sign up for Del Rey's free manga e-newsletter
• Find out the latest about new Del Rey Manga series

TOMARE!

[STOP!]

You are going the wrong way!

Manga is a completely different type of reading experience.

To start at the *beginning*, go to the *end*!

read the traditional Japanese way—
osite of how American books are read.
other end of the book, and read each
right side to the left side, starting at
encing manga as it was meant to be.